Privatization and Public-Private Partnerships

E. S. SAVAS
Baruch College
City University of New York

New York, 2/7/2004

To Jesse —
With my best wishes for your continued success. It was great having you in our class

Steve Savas

CHATHAM HOUSE PUBLISHERS
SEVEN BRIDGES PRESS, LLC
NEW YORK • LONDON

PRIVATIZATION AND PUBLIC-PRIVATE PARTNERSHIPS

Seven Bridges Press, LLC
135 Fifth Avenue
New York, NY 10010-7101

Publisher: Robert J. Gormley
Managing Editor: Katherine Miller
Production Supervisor: Melissa A. Martin
Cover Design: Timothy Hsu
Composition: Linda Pawelchak/Lori Clinton
Printing and Binding: Versa Press, Inc.

LIBRARY OF CONGRESS CATALOGING-IN-PUBLICATION DATA

Savas, Emanuel S.
    Privatization and public-private partnerships / E.S. Savas
    p.   cm
    Includes bibliographical references and index.
    ISBN 1-56643-073-9 (pbk.)
    1. Government productivity—United States.   2.
Privatization—United States   3. Administrative agencies—United
States—Cost effectiveness.   I. Title
    JK468.P75 S278 2000
    352.3′75′0973—dc21   99-6053
                                                              CIP

Manufactured in the United States of America
10   9   8   7   6   5   4   3   2

*Lovingly dedicated
to my wonderful wife, Helen,
for her love, patience, support, and understanding,
and to my sons, Jonathan and Stephen,
and their wives, Anastasia and Lorrie,
who have brought me great happiness*

Contents

PART THREE

The Practice of Privatization

Tables

Figures

Preface

SCHOPENHAUER SAID, "All great ideas go through three stages: In the first stage, they are ridiculed. In the second stage, they are strongly opposed. And in the third stage, they are considered to be self-evident." Privatization has reached the third stage.

My journey in the world of privatization started thirty years ago, when a major snowstorm struck New York City on Sunday, 9 February 1969. The city was disastrously unprepared, handled the cleanup badly, and was snowbound for many days, precipitating a political firestorm. Mayor John V. Lindsay asked me, the first deputy city administrator, to examine what happened and determine what to do so it would not happen again. I discovered that during a snow emergency the city's Sanitation Department was actually out plowing streets only about half the time; the rest was spent on warm-up breaks, fueling breaks, coffee breaks, and wash-up breaks. That made me wonder how the agency performed when there was no emergency and it was doing its principal job, collecting garbage and trash. That summer, after developing a snow plan—which is in use to this day—I compared the performance of the department with that of the private sector and found that the former cost almost three times as much per ton of trash collected. Thereupon I recommended to the mayor that the city experiment by competitively hiring private contractors to service three of the city's sixty-three sanitation districts and comparing their work with that of the city agency in three matching districts.

This innocent heresy brought the ire of some city and union officials, the feeling that I was simply foolhardy, and a suggestion by the city's deputy budget director that I be fired, a suggestion supported by a prominent professor of public administration who wrote that my idea was absurd. A commission was formed to look into my recommendation, but it was dissolved after the mayor changed political parties and sought union backing during his brief campaign for president. Nothing happened in New York, but I went into academia, began my research—it was awfully lonely at first—and, based on that research and my experiences, became an advocate for prudent privatization. Along the way I served a second tour of duty in government, appointed by President Ronald Reagan as assistant secretary of the U.S. Department of Housing and Urban Development. In that capacity I supported research to improve the efficiency of local government services through privatization and promoted the privatization of housing assistance by replacing public housing with vouchers. This latter program, too, was greeted with outrage at the time, but now both liberals and conservatives are demolishing conventional public housing and issuing vouchers for private housing instead.

Early attacks on privatization were based on the mistaken assumption that it was antigovernment; it was not. My first published article, "Municipal Monopoly," in *Harper's Magazine* in 1971, stressed that the issue was not public versus private but monopoly versus competition and called for more competition in public services. Another fallacy was that privatization was anti-people and devoid of the compassion thought to be inherent in government programs. No, people are harmed by badly run government programs. The purpose of privatization is to improve government performance and thereby improve the lives of those most dependent on government, while saving money and improving services for all taxpayers and thereby improving their lives as well. Private nonprofit agencies run better homeless shelters at lower cost than does government. Finally, opponents argued against relying on the private sector, citing mismanagement and corruption in private firms. This once was hurled at me as a trump card in a city council hearing. Of course there are badly run private firms, but the same ills can be found in government agencies as well. Moreover, poorly performing private firms tend to go out of business, while poorly performing public agencies are often given more money to try to overcome their shortcomings—witness big-city school systems.

These arguments can still be heard from time to time but are weak and waning. Privatization is routinely accepted as a pragmatic tool to improve government. Throughout the world it has been adopted—sometimes improperly—as the key to a vibrant economy and, ultimately, a better society.

The intellectual predecessors of what came to be called privatization include Milton Friedman, Gordon Tullock, Anthony Downs, William Niskanen, and Peter Drucker (who coined the term *reprivatize,* the precursor to *privatization,* also in 1969). Frankly, as a managerial technocrat recruited by the mayor from IBM where I was manager of urban systems, I did not know about the base of ideas they had built. I simply saw contracting with the private sector as an obvious way to introduce much-needed competition into the delivery of public services, reinvigorate public agencies, and break up malfunctioning municipal monopolies that more often than not (at least in New York) were controlled by public-employee unions rather than by public officials.

My first comprehensive book on the topic, *Privatizing the Public Sector: How to Shrink Government*, written in 1980 and published two years later, was intended to draw attention to this still novel idea. My 1987 book, *Privatization: The Key to Better Government*, documented with many examples the brisk headway that privatization was making, and it was gratifying to see it published in thirteen foreign editions. This new book builds on the 1987 book and treats privatization as a routine, pragmatic strategy for improving government. It describes step-by-step how to implement the different forms of privatization and overcome obstacles along the way. It is intended to serve the needs of public officials, students of public management, management consultants, contractors, and businessmen and women who have a commercial interest in selling services to government. It summarizes much of what I have learned in thirty years of experience with numerous state and local governments, the federal government, and in forty-seven countries. The purpose of this book is to help develop better government "appropriately limited in size and functions, but fully capable of providing the legal, economic and [collective] goods infrastructure that will permit the private sector to reach its full potential."[1]

I am grateful to all who have contributed to my education in this area, particularly Elinor Ostrom; my early collaborators, Barbara Stevens and Eileen Brettler Berenyi; and John Diebold, who suggested and supported my first book on privatization, an edited volume published in 1977. The thoughtful reviews of this manuscript by my long-time friend and co-worker Peter Tropp and my colleague at Baruch College Arthur Levine improved the book immeasurably, as did the invaluable suggestions of Grover Starling. Katharine Miller did an excellent job of editing at Chatham House. I thank my doctoral student, Anthony Ioannides, and my graduate assistant, Merih Anil, for their help. Finally, through copious citations, I acknowledge my debt to the many others, notably Robert W. Poole Jr., who have toiled productively in this bountiful vineyard.

New York, 9 February 1999

[1]Ronald C. Moe, "Exploring the Limits of Privatization," *Public Administration Review*, vol. 47 (1987):453–60.

PART ONE

The Background of Privatization

CHAPTER ONE

Introduction

HUMAN SOCIETIES HAVE developed several kinds of institutions to satisfy their needs: (1) the family, clan, or tribe—the most basic unit of society—which is, after all, the original department of housing, health, education, welfare, and human services; (2) voluntary groups of all sorts, including religious, charitable, neighborhood, civic, business, union, recreational, ethnic, and interest-based affinity groups; (3) the market, and the varied array of organizations operating therein; and (4) government, an important agent for exercising collective action.

What is the role of government, and what is the role of the other—let us call them private—institutions of society? Who should do what and to whom? At any given time and place, what is the best allocation of societal responsibilities among these powerful but very different actors? What is it that the family can best do? What can safely be left to spontaneously self-organized, voluntary groups and to the marketplace? What should government do?

Tectonic shifts are underway throughout the world. Socialism has collapsed everywhere it was tried. The welfare state is tottering in Europe and America. Family values and religion are emerging as powerful forces in the United States, and, underscoring their importance, it has been noted that the traditional, family-centered societies of Asia by and large have avoided the social problems that bedevil Americans, particularly in inner cities.

The trend is unmistakably away from government and toward the other institutions—in a word, privatization. Privatization can be defined broadly as relying more on the private institutions of society and less on government to satisfy people's needs.[1] It is the act of reducing the role of government or increasing the role of the other institutions of society in producing goods and services and in owning property. In general, both the public and private sectors play important roles, and it is increasingly common to refer to "public-private partnerships," a less contentious term than "privatization." A public-private partnership is defined as any arrangement between a government and the private sector in which partially or traditionally public activities are performed by the private sector. Further discussion of these definitions appears in chapter 4.

Some opponents regard privatization as a simplistic call to cut back government and regress to a Darwinian state where only the fittest survive and the poor and sick are left to cope as best they can. This is a serious misunderstanding of the concept. Privatization can be at least as compassionate as the welfare state; properly implemented, it offers even more for the less fortunate among us.

Privatization appears in several forms. Contracting with private firms to collect garbage and trash, maintain public buildings, process claims, or repair military aircraft is a form of privatization, and so is contracting with a not-for-profit agency to deliver "meals on wheels" to elderly shut-ins or to operate a child-care center. Awarding franchises to companies to finance, build, own, and operate highways, tunnels, and waterworks is also privatization. Issuing food stamps and housing vouchers to the poor and providing education vouchers to the parents of school children are privatized approaches far different from—and better than—government-run farms and grocery stores, public housing projects, and failing inner-city public schools. Urban dwellers practice privatization when they form neighborhood security patrols, and so do suburbanites who join volunteer fire departments. It is also privatization when government retires from the business of insuring home mortgages or running buses and lets the marketplace provide those services. Finally, selling off a government-owned railroad, factory, or coal mine is privatization, a necessary element in the untidy transition to a market economy in the post-socialist countries.

The distinction between *public* and *private* is elusive. We speak of a park or a government office building as being publicly owned, but we use the same term to describe Microsoft because it has many stockholders and any member of the public may buy part of the company; it is a private firm that is publicly owned. In the same way, a public restaurant is one that caters to the public at large, although it may be owned by a sole proprietor. Confusingly, we use the same word, *public,* to describe three very different conditions: government ownership, widespread ownership, and open access. This semantic confusion is nevertheless instructive, for it implies that government ownership—and by extension, government action—is not necessary to achieve widespread (i.e., "public") benefits. Privatization capitalizes on this underappreciated truism and takes advantage of the full array of ownership and operating relations to satisfy people's wants and needs and thereby to serve the public interest.

Throughout this book the term *service* or *public service* refers not only to a narrow task such as maintaining street lights, delivering mail, running a bus service, or operating a telephone system, but to broad functions as well, such as assuring pensions for retirees, defending a nation against external threats, clothing the populace, supplying food, manufacturing goods, and protecting endangered species and the environment. The analysis in this book is applicable to all cultures and socioeconomic systems regardless of the institutional means by which such goods and services are currently supplied.

The Forces Influencing Privatization

Several major influences have propelled the privatization movement: pragmatic, economic, philosophical, commercial, and populist. The goal of the pragmatists is better government, in the sense of a more cost-effective one. Economic affluence reduces people's dependence on government and increases their acceptance of privatized approaches. The goal of those who approach the matter philosophically—some would say ideologically—is less government, one that plays a smaller role vis-à-vis private institutions; this is the Jeffersonian view—government which governs least governs best. The goal of commercial interests is to get more business by having more of government's spending directed toward them. And the goal of the populists is to achieve a better society by empowering people so they can satisfy their common needs, while diminishing the power of large public and private bureaucracies.

The characteristics of these five influences are summarized in table 1.1. (p. 6), and each is discussed in turn.

Pragmatic Forces

When the cost of government activities is rising but the public's resistance to higher taxes is also rising, public officials seek any medicine that promises to relieve this fiscal stress. Typically, the first resort is creative bookkeeping, which masks the magnitude of the disparity between revenues and expenditures. But the growing adoption of generally accepted accounting principles in government tends to foreclose this surreptitious option. The second resort is borrowing to close the gap. But lenders are unwilling to support wasteful government enterprises in developing coun-

TABLE 1.1—THE INFLUENCES PROMOTING PRIVATIZATION

Influence	Effect	Reasoning
Pragmatic	Better government	Prudent privatization leads to more cost-effective public services.
Economic	Less dependence on government	Growing affluence allows more people to provide for their own needs, making them more receptive to privatization.
Ideological	Less government	Government is too big, too powerful, too intrusive in people's lives and therefore is a danger to democracy. Government's political decisions are inherently less trustworthy than free-market decisions. Privatization reduces government's role.
Commercial	More business opportunities	Government spending is a large part of the economy; more of it can and should be directed toward private firms. State-owned enterprises and assets can be put to better use by the private sector.
Populist	Better society	People should have more choice in public services. They should be empowered to define and address common needs, and to establish a sense of community by relying less on distant bureaucratic structures and more on family, neighborhood, church, and ethnic and voluntary associations.

tries, and, in the United States, public antipathy to more government spending leads to voter rejection of bond referendums and the election of antispending candidates. If creative bookkeeping, higher taxes, and more borrowing are out, then the remaining choices for public officials are narrowed to two: cutting services or raising productivity.

Naturally, eliminating or cutting back government activities is unpopular among beneficiaries of the activity, and therefore increasing productivity is more attractive politically, even though this option often encounters opposition from public employees. Privatization is a fundamental strategy to improve the productivity of government agencies. It invokes the power of private property rights, market forces, and competition to give people more for their money. Market incentives can be brought into play in "managed competition," the process discussed in chapter 7, whereby public employees are forced to compete against private contractors. Government-owned enterprises (GOEs, also called government-sponsored enterprises, government corporations, public authorities, public-benefit corporations, state-owned enterprises (SOEs), or parastatals—the last two terms are commonly used outside the United States*) are thrust into market environments.

---

*For simplicity, GOE and SOE will generally be used throughout this book, the latter primarily in a foreign context.

Chapter 6 presents strong evidence that privatization, properly carried out, generally leads to large increases in efficiency while maintaining and even improving the level and quality of public services. That is why cost-conscious public officials, spurred by good-government groups and others who favor privatization, and acting on a nonpartisan basis, are turning to privatization for better public management and as the key to more cost-effective government.

In the former socialist countries, public despair at the ever-declining standard of living compared to other industrialized nations brought about a political and economic revolution that featured privatization and a return to market economics, although this was often done in a corrupt manner and failed to bring the expected benefits quickly enough. In the European Community, the need to reduce deficits in order to satisfy the Maastricht agreement and promote economic integration is accelerating the privatization of inefficient, state-owned enterprises.

The word *govern* comes from a Greek root, "kybern," which means "to steer." (The same root appears in *cybernetics,* the science of control.) The job of government is to steer, not to row.[2] Delivering services—whether repairing streets or operating an airline—is rowing, and government is not very good at rowing. Privatization is a pragmatic policy for restoring government to its fundamental role, steering, while relying on the private sector to do the rowing.

Economic Forces

The growing pressure on public funds noted previously has paradoxically been accompanied by growing personal affluence. This means that more people can afford to buy books instead of borrowing them from libraries, use their own automobiles instead of relying on public buses, and pay for their sport and recreation. Moreover, as Nathan Glazer writes, "This [affluence] leads many to believe they could manage the education of their children, or their own health, more effectively and with greater satisfaction—and perhaps with a better return for their expenditure—by allocating their own funds to a range of competing organizations, public and private, rather than by paying taxes."[3]

At the time the welfare state was born, only the rich could protect themselves from the accidents and disasters of industrial society; the vast multitudes needed social insurance from the state, that is, a basic minimum of protection provided by the state against life's misfortunes. Now, however, with their growing economic capacity, a substantial number of citizens can manage for themselves. The welfare state is withering away because it is being undermined by market forces, which are changing the conditions of supply and demand for education, health care, housing, pensions, and other components of "welfare." Consumers are increasingly able to pay for, and are therefore demanding, better education, health care, housing, pensions, and other goods and services than the state supplies. These are goods that private suppliers are increasingly able to provide through market alternatives.[4] In short, economic factors are making people less dependent on government goods and services and more accepting of privatized approaches to their needs.

Philosophical Forces

The role of government differs in different societies, and even within a single society it changes over time, waxing and waning over decades and centuries. One can visualize the situation conceptually as in figure 1.1. The goods and services (in the broad sense described previously) that a society enjoys are represented as points. Some of them are provided by the public sector and some by the private sector. (This is awfully simplistic because many activities involve both sectors, often in intricate public-private partnerships, as discussed in chapter 4; nonetheless, it is a useful dichotomy for the present purpose.) The location of the boundary line between the two sectors differs in different countries. Table 1.2 shows the extent of government involvement in the economies of various countries before the collapse of the socialist states; for example, in the Soviet Union the state produced 96 percent of gross domestic product (GDP), and the figure's boundary line would have been in the lower right-hand corner.

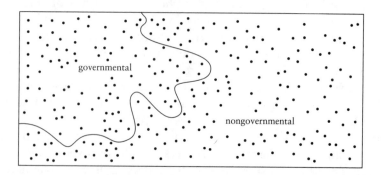

FIGURE 1.1—CONCEPTUAL REPRESENTATION OF SERVICES DESIRED BY SOCIETY

TABLE 1.2—THE ROLE OF STATE-OWNED ENTERPRISES (SOES) IN SOCIALIST AND MARKET ECONOMIES

Country	GDP produced by SOEs (in percentages)	Year
Socialist economies		
Czechoslovakia	97	1986
East Germany	97	1982
Soviet Union	96	1985
Yugoslavia	87	1985
Poland	82	1985
China	74	1984
Hungary	65	1984
Unweighted average for socialist economies	85	
Market economies		
France	17	1982
Austria	15	1978–79
Italy	14	1982
New Zealand	12	1987
Turkey	11	1985
United Kingdom	11	1983
West Germany	11	1982
Portugal	10	1976
Australia	9	1978–79
Denmark	6	1974
Greece	6	1979
Spain	4	1979
Netherlands	4	1971–73
United States	1	1983
Unweighted average for market economies	9	

Source: Derived from B. Milanovic, *Liberalization and Entrepreneurship: Dynamics of Reform in Socialism and Capitalism* (Armonk, N.Y.: M. E. Sharpe, 1989), 15, 20.

Note: Percent GDP produced by SOEs excludes government services.

The boundary also changes its shape and shifts position over time. For example, in the United States more and more mail is being delivered by the private sector, and the role of the government mail service is shrinking in relative terms. In contrast, government's role in medical care (namely, paying for it) has expanded enormously in recent decades. In other words, different sections of the boundary can be moving in opposite directions at the same time and may even pulsate over long periods.

Despite these contrary shifts, in the United States overall there has been much waxing and little waning of government. Chapter 2 summarizes the facts about the size and growth of government and discusses why it grows. Many view this trend with alarm and see it as a danger to democracy. The rallying cry of the Reagan Revolution was "Get government off our backs and out of our pockets," while in Thatcherite Britain it was "Rolling back the frontiers of the state."

The reasoning of those who subscribe to this view is based on political and economic philosophy. As more of people's earnings are taken by government, as decisions about the disposition of these moneys are made by increasingly distant and unresponsive organs of government, and as government's presence pervades more areas of human activity, freedom and liberty are being lost. In drawing up the Constitution and the Bill of Rights, America's Founding Fathers took great pains to protect citizens from their government. History taught them that government could be a serious threat to the individual rights they cherished. Government institutions could become instruments of tyranny even in a democratic society: those who mobilize majority support could use government coercion to deprive those in the minority. Therefore the framers of the Constitution designed a system that imposed the minimal level of collective coercion necessary to secure the blessings of liberty. At each turn, the power of government was circumscribed by checks and balances and the political and civil rights of the citizenry.

Individual freedom is not the only value endangered by a powerful government. Justice is also highly prized, and equality is an important component of justice. Reasonable and humane people will differ on the degree of inequality or, conversely, the extent of redistribution that is acceptable and can still be considered just, but government greatly affects the level of equality, for better and for worse, by taking from some and giving to others.

In a world of finite resources, efficiency is also an important societal goal. One should extract the maximum from each ton of raw material and from each hour of work. Efficiency is good because it produces a higher standard of living. Just as freedom and justice are menaced by an overly powerful government, so is efficiency. But, on the other hand, governmental efficiency can be a threat to liberty—we've all heard about dictatorships whose excuse for being is their alleged efficiency.

Freedom, justice, and efficiency are all essential, and each is alloyed with the other. They represent different and sometimes conflicting goals, and a balance must be struck among them, for example, trading some individual freedom or some economic efficiency for more justice. Government is a tool that society employs to help attain these goals and to strike the balance, but in excess it threatens all three goals.

Another dimension to the philosophical concern about big government is the harm that comes if a society distrusts its government. Modern civilization requires individuals to cede substantial control over vital aspects of their lives to impersonal institutions. Personal autonomy has been reduced, and responsibility for the well-being of the individual has been assumed by collective institutions—principally government. But if government is not sufficiently responsive or accountable, and if it acquires a life of its own, then people feel that it is not living up to its end of an implied agreement: to do those things that only government can do, and to do them well. They lose faith in government.

In many countries, people accurately view government as an evil to be endured, a horde of self-aggrandizing officials and civil servants. In the United States, antigovernment sentiment grew more rapidly than antibusiness sentiment between 1958 and 1980,[5] although this feeling abated somewhat after 1980, when a new administration began to reduce the role of the federal government. Nevertheless, public confidence in the federal government has never been lower. A 1995 poll showed that only a quarter of Americans trust the federal government to do the right thing most of the time, down from three-quarters in 1964, and only 11 percent had "a great deal" of confidence in the federal government, the lowest figure in thirty years.[6] A 1999 survey of 18- to 24-year olds found that they see little connection between government's problem-solving role and their daily concerns.[7] The average American believes it wastes 48 cents of every tax dollar; five people of every six want fundamental change in Washington.[8]

When it comes to ability to get things done, the U.S. public has rated the private sector higher than political institutions.[9] As for quality of service, local governments and public transportation were rated at the very bottom, on par with real-estate firms and even lower than auto-repair shops.[10] Clearly the much-needed social and business reforms adopted earlier in this century were themselves in need of reform, as mistakes, excesses, and waste proliferated, and as institutional arteriosclerosis inevitably set in.

The election of President Jimmy Carter, the non-Washington candidate, and the three elections of President Ronald Reagan (counting then Vice-President Bush as an expected Reagan surrogate), the avowed anti-Washington and anti-big-government candidate, reflected popular reaction against the growing role that government had assumed. Bill Clinton ran as a different Democrat and announced the end of the era of big government. His Administration, too, endorsed and enacted a privatization strategy, citing pragmatic reasons.[11]

We have briefly reviewed the arguments against big government from the perspective of political philosophy. Another line of reasoning is based on economic philosophy. The long-term well-being of society will be maximized if economic decisions are left mostly to the marketplace, with government assuring that no one is left without the basic necessities of life. But government has a strong effect on the economy, and this inevitably means that decisions affecting the economy, such as regulation, will often be made on political grounds instead of economic grounds. Therefore, big government, in contrast to small government, will gradually make a society poorer than it would otherwise be. "It's a good thing we don't get all the government we pay for!" said Milton Friedman.[12]

Based on political and economic philosophy, therefore, advocates of these viewpoints want to shift the boundary line in figure 1.1 so as to reduce the role of government and expand the role of the private sector. This is privatization, and hence the movement originally drew its strongest support from this sector. (The politician, on the other hand, who implicitly sees the market as his rival because it diminishes the area subject to his control, wants to shift the boundary in the other direction.) Paradoxically, the ideologues who do not want government made more efficient (because this would support the case for continuing government's current role) find themselves allied with the pragmatists who support privatization on the very grounds of greater efficiency. The philosophical proponents of privatization want *less* government, in the sense of power; the pragmatic proponents merely want *smaller* government, in the sense of a more efficient one.

Commercial Forces

Further support for privatization comes from commercial interests. The thinking is straightforward. Government spends a lot of money, much of it on salaries for its employees. Much of the work performed by government employees consists of routine commercial activities that are in no way unique to government, such as maintenance of buildings, grounds, vehicles, ships, and airplanes; typing and data processing; handling insurance claims and sending out bills; and collecting trash and repairing streets. Business groups advocate more privatization of such in-house government activities and support legislation that would prohibit using government employees to perform work that private, taxpaying businesses can perform.

Another segment of the private sector sees substantial business opportunities in large capital projects for government, such as roads, bridges, airports, and waste-to-energy plants. Private firms can finance, build, or operate any of these kinds of facilities. The novel element here is financing the facility; in many circumstances this can be an appealing option for a government hard-pressed to raise capital funds in a timely manner in order to build a prison facility to relieve overcrowding or a wastewater-treatment plant to clean up a river.

In countries with nationalized industries or assets (and no country is entirely without them), commercial pressures come from business leaders who see mismanagement, underutilized assets, and slothful practices in an environment sheltered from competition. They encourage denationalization, a particular form of privatization, because they foresee excellent prospects for those enterprises or assets if they were sold and brought into the private sector. They see the potential for innovation, whereas continuing stagnation, growing inefficiency, and a continued drag on the private sector seem likely if the enterprise is left unperturbed in the public sector. This reasoning applies to the entire array of state-owned enterprises, including manufacturing plants, mines, oil fields, transportation lines, communication systems, banks, bakeries, breweries, timber forests, and open land.

For these reasons, commercial forces are expected to be active supporters of privatization, although their interests are very different from the concerns of the pragmatists and of those who endorse privatization on the basis of political or economic philosophy. As is shown in chapter 11, however, business interests that are prospering under the status quo oppose privatization.

Populist Forces

The fifth source of support for privatization is populists, who are *against* both big government and big business and *for* other, more local institutions and the empowerment of people. They find allies among advocates of family values[13] and "communitarians."[14] Their point of view has been articulated as follows:

> This country's "public" systems, governmental and private, have
> become too institutionalized, too bureaucratized, too professional-
> ized, too protective of their own interests. . . . These major systems
> must be made instead to work for people. . . . It is possible to
> redesign the institutional arrangements . . . to make the life-support
> systems of a community both competitive and equitable. . . . Choices

should be expanded. . . . No private or public buyer should rely on a sole source of supply.[15]

The two elements of the populist position are that people should have greater choice in public services and they should be empowered to define their common needs and address them without undue reliance on cumbersome bureaucracies. They can rely instead, to a much greater degree, on neighborhood, civic, church, ethnic, and other voluntary associations. The process of formulating common needs, and working through traditional local institutions to satisfy those needs, will reinforce a much-needed sense of community.[16]

Such institutions are imperiled, however. A large and powerful government can displace and swamp them, draining the life blood out of the community. Voluntary groups are supplanted by issue-oriented lobbies that seek to use the power of government to impose their values and spending preferences on others. The minister is replaced by a community mental health agency. The family gives way to Departments of Health, Education, Welfare, Housing, and Human Services.

These traditional, nongovernment institutions provide safety to society by their very redundancy—their interests overlap—and help to arrive at an adaptive equilibrium among the conflicting goals of freedom, justice, and efficiency. To the extent that one institution, such as government, gains great strength at the expense of the others, it limits their contribution to these goals, eliminates the diversity they afford, and thereby increases society's dependence on government alone to choose and impose particular allotments of freedom, justice, and efficiency.

Adherents of this world view understand that *collective* action does not necessarily mean *government* action. They endorse privatization because it enhances choice and affords opportunities to strengthen traditional institutions and reinforce a local sense of community; it means free markets, localism, voluntarism, and deregulation. Seeking a better society, populists also press for privatization, and they join forces with those philosophically committed to less government, pragmatists who want better government, and commercial interests that seek to do more of government's work.

The History of Privatization

Utilizing the private sector to satisfy people's needs is as old as the family. What is new, however, is the deliberate use of privatization as a tool to improve the functioning of government—and even of entire societies, as in post-socialist Eastern Europe and China. The intellectual foundation for privatization was laid by Milton Friedman.[17] Privatization was first suggested in 1969 (and the word, in the form *reprivatize,* was first used) by the Austrian-born American management professor Peter F. Drucker.[18] In the same year, independently, as a frustrated New York City official trying to improve the city government's performance, I began recommending contracting with private firms as a pragmatic policy to break up municipal monopolies and thereby to improve the cost-effectiveness of municipal services.[19] Research and writing in the 1970s by Savas,[20] followed by Poole,[21] Spann,[22] Rothbard,[23] and Fisk *et al.,*[24] among others, and a monthly privatization newsletter that Poole started in 1976, which continues to this day,[25] strengthened the case for privatization. Strong opposition from public-employee unions was already expressed as early as 1977.[26] As a result of all this attention, privatization of municipal services by contracting became widespread in the United States by 1980[27] and mushroomed after that.[28] Meanwhile, in Britain, policy advocates at the Adam Smith Institute, with whom I collaborated, began promoting privatization in the mid-1970s.

The elections of Margaret Thatcher as prime minister of Britain and Ronald Reagan as president of the United States, in 1979 and 1980 respectively, gave high visibility and a pronounced ideological impetus to what became the privatization movement. A dramatic series of denationalizations—privatization by sale of state-owned companies—took place in Britain starting in 1979: British Petroleum (1979), British Aerospace (1981), Britoil (1982), National Freight Corporation (1982), Cable & Wireless (1983), Jaguar (1984), British Telecom (1984), British Aerospace (1985, final portion of holdings), British Gas (1986), British Airways (1987), Rolls Royce (1987), and British Airports Authority in 1987.[29] Water utilities followed in 1989 and electric utilities in 1990. Compulsory tendering (required competitive bidding) of local government services in Britain was mandated in 1988.

Despite an ambitious array of privatization proposals unveiled by the Reagan Administration (in which I served as an assistant secretary) in 1985, relatively little privatization by sale took place at the federal government level, in part because the United States has relatively few government-owned enterprises. Conrail, the government-owned freight railroad, was sold but President Reagan's effort to sell the United States Enrichment Corporation, which prepares enriched uranium for nuclear reactors—was blocked by a Democratic Congress. (President Clinton, supported by a Republican Congress, accomplished this a decade later.) Considerable contracting out of support services (for example, data processing, food service, building maintenance, and guard services) was carried out by federal government agencies, and privatization by contracting continued to grow in local governments both for support services and for direct services to the public (waste collection, street cleaning, ambulance service, and park maintenance, for example).

In the 1980s many industrialized Western nations, stimulated by the British example, embarked on privatization programs[30] and so did many developing nations,[31] the latter pushed in part by Western donor nations and by international agencies that had grown impatient with the poor performance of state-owned enterprises that they had previously financed. The exceptionally strong economic performance of the newly industrializing countries of East Asia, which relied extensively on private enterprise and a market orientation, also provided a stimulus and served as a model emulated by the developing countries that had mistakenly relied on state enterprises and were falling behind at an alarming rate. In Latin America, by the end of the 1980s, Mexico, Brazil, Chile, and Argentina had all elected presidents who adopted strong privatization policies.

Among the socialist countries, China was the first to embrace privatization, beginning with agriculture in 1978. Eliminating state-owned and collective farms and allowing what was, in effect, private farming, resulted in greatly increased food production and an end to the famines that had characterized the prior period. Private sector industrial and retail operations were allowed in the 1980s as part of China's economic reform program but were usually presented as involving multiple ownership, that is, town and village cooperatives, joint ventures, partnerships, and, later, stockholder-owned enterprises. The collapse in 1989 of the socialist bloc in Eastern Europe promptly led to privatization in Hungary, Poland, and Czechoslovakia. The Soviet Union changed its legal framework in 1990 to allow private ownership of the means of production, opening the door to privatization there even before its spectacular collapse in 1991. Widespread privatization in Russia took place by 1994, although the process there was a poor one characterized by wholesale looting of state enterprises and theft ("self privatization") of state property. Bulgaria, Romania, Slovenia, the Baltic states, and the other states of the former Soviet Union also privatized, although at widely varying speeds. Estonia and Kyrgyzstan were perhaps the most successful. Vietnam, in desperate economic straits, allowed private enterprises to emerge, and Cuba began selling public housing to the tenants, something Britain did a decade earlier.

By the mid-1990s privatization of state and local services in the United States was universal, having penetrated even large cities with strong public-employee unions, and it had become a policy of the federal government.[32] Moreover, it was not a partisan or factional issue: it was being adopted by Democrats and Republicans, liberals and conservatives, and blacks and whites.

Overview of the Book

The book is divided into three parts: the background, theory, and practice of privatization. Chapter 2 completes the background discussion by examining the growth of government, the reasons for that growth, and its harmful consequences.

Part 2 presents the theoretical basis for privatization. Beginning with chapter 3, it examines the basic goods and services that people want and need and discusses the intrinsic characteristics that permit them to be categorized usefully as private, toll, common-pool, or collective goods. Going further, it clarifies the role of collective action in supplying each of these kinds of goods. Chapter 4 distinguishes between providing, producing, and arranging services and describes ten different institutional arrangements or structures for delivering services. The chapter goes on to show that each category of goods can be delivered by any of several delivery arrangements, although certain kinds of goods cannot be supplied by certain arrangements. The chapter compares the different service arrangements, pointing out the advantages and disadvantages of each and shedding light on the question of which arrangement to use when there is a choice.

The remainder of the book, part 3, examines privatization in practice. Chapter 5 explains why privatization is carried out, identifies the different forms of privatization, that is, how to make the transition from a more governmental to a more privatized arrangement, and presents privatization guidelines. Chapter 6 summarizes the results of privatization based on studies from around the world. The next two chapters describe in detail the process of privatization by contracting (chapter 7) and by divesting assets and enterprises (chapter 8). Chapter 9 examines the privatization of infrastructure through public-private partnerships, and chapter 10 looks broadly at the privatization of education and of the welfare state. Chapter 11 addresses the problems of implementing privatization, identifying the various barriers and reviewing opposition arguments. Finally, chapter 12 reviews the worldwide success of privatization and looks ahead at emerging trends in public governance and public management.

CHAPTER TWO

The Growth of Government

THE FIVE FORCES propelling privatization have an inviting target—governments that are large and growing throughout the world. This chapter examines the size and growth of governments in the United States. After a brief look at other industrialized nations, the remainder of the chapter explores the reasons why governments grow.

The Size of Government

Three different measures are used here to define the size of government: the number of government units, their expenditures, and the number of people they employ. Each is discussed in turn.

Number of Governments

People sometimes think of government as one giant organization, but in fact there are many governments in the United States—87,454 of them in 1997 to be exact. Table 2.1 shows the number of different government

TABLE 2.1—NUMBER OF GOVERNMENT UNITS IN THE UNITED STATES

Kind of government	1942	1957	1967	1977	1987	1997
Federal	1	1	1	1	1	1
State	48	50	50	50	50	50
County	3,050	3,050	3,049	3,042	3,042	3,043
Town and township	18,919	17,198	17,105	16,822	16,691	16,629
Municipal	16,220	17,215	18,048	18,862	19,200	19,372
School district	108,579	50,454	21,782	15,174	14,721	13,726
Special district	8,299	14,424	21,264	25,962	29,532	34,683
Total	155,116	102,392	81,299	79,913	83,237	87,454

Source: Bureau of the Census, U.S. Department of Commerce, *1997 Census of Governments,* Volume I (Washington, D.C.: Government Printing Office, 1998).

units and the changes over time. The number of townships has been shrinking while the number of municipalities has been growing, an indication of increasing urbanization and the incorporation of previously unincorporated areas. The number of special districts shows rapid growth, a reflection of the continuous creation of intergovernmental arrangements to perform various functions in metropolitan areas. As a result, and reversing a prolonged decline that resulted from the consolidation of school districts, the total number of government units is growing again.

Government Expenditures

While the total number of governments has been growing slowly in recent decades, their expenditures have been growing rapidly. Total spending by all levels of government in the United States in 1996 was $2.993 trillion,[1] as shown in table 2.2. This does not include "off-budget spending," that is, outstanding federal loans, guaranteed loans, and borrowing by federally sponsored enterprises. (As loan defaults occur, honest bookkeeping requires that the losses appear somewhere as expenditures.) In less than 40 years, measured in constant dollars, expenditures have more than quadrupled, almost tripled on a per capita basis, and grown by more than half as a fraction of gross domestic product (GDP), to 32.2 percent.

Taking a longer perspective, real federal debt went from $2,600 for a family of four in 1900 to $40,950 in 1950 and to $62,000 in 1992 (all in constant 1990 dollars).[2] In terms of spending, the U.S. government is now primarily in the business of writing checks to its citizens, who receive about a trillion dollars a year in transfer payments, more than half the federal budget.[3] In addition to direct government spending, governments require businesses to spend money to comply with regulatory edicts, money that also

TABLE 2.2—FEDERAL, STATE, AND LOCAL GOVERNMENT EXPENDITURES

Year	Total ($ billions)	In constant 1992 dollars ($ billions)	In per capita constant 1992 dollars	As percentage of GDP
1960	151.3	649.4	3,622	23.1
1970	333.0	1,088.2	5,353	28.3
1980	958.7	1,587.3	7,008	30.2
1990	2,218.8	2,370.5	9,532	31.4
1996	2,993.3	2,728.6	10,375	32.2

Source: Derived from *Facts & Figures on Government Finance*, 31st ed. (Washington, D.C.: Tax Foundation, 1997), tables A4, B1, B25.

comes ultimately from the pockets of the public. These statistics offer a measure of the rapidly expanding size and role of government.

International comparisons of government outlays as a fraction of GDP appear in table 2.3. The United States is at the low end of the range of industrialized nations, near Japan. Most Western European nations have significantly higher fractions of their economies in the hands of government, and most show growth in this measure from 1980 to 1996, but the fraction is beginning to decline as countries adopt the productive economic policies practiced in the United States and reduce the extreme measures of the welfare state.[4] For example, public-sector expenditures in the Netherlands, which had soared to 67 percent of GDP in 1983, dropped to 50 percent by 1996.[5]

Government Employment

Another measure of the size and growth of government in the United States is the number of employees, shown in table 2.4. In 1995, the number of

TABLE 2.3—GENERAL GOVERNMENT OUTLAYS AS A PERCENTAGE OF GDP

Country	1980	1996
Sweden	60.1	65.4
Denmark	56.2	61.6
Finland	38.1	57.2
Belgium	58.3	54.5
France	46.1	54.1
Italy	42.1	53.4
Austria	48.1	52.2
Netherlands	55.8	50.0
Germany	47.9	49.6
Greece	30.4	46.2
Canada	38.8	45.6
Norway	43.3	44.8
Portugal	23.8	43.5
Spain	32.2	43.1
United Kingdom	43.0	41.6
Ireland	49.2	39.7
Iceland	32.5	38.0
Australia	31.4	36.4
Japan	32.0	36.2
United States	31.4	33.3
Average	42.0	47.3

General outlays refers to usual government functions and excludes expenditures for government business enterprises.

Source: *Facts & Figures on Government Finance*, 31st ed. (Washington, D.C.: Tax Foundation, 1997), table G8.

TABLE 2.4—GOVERNMENT EMPLOYMENT

Year	Number of employees[a] (in millions)	As percentage of population[b]	As percentage of all employees[c]
1970	13,028	9.36	17.3
1980	16,213	9.58	16.9
1990	18,389	9.72	14.6
1995	19,521	9.83	14.8

[a]Full-time and part-time, nonmilitary employees of federal, state, and local governments.

[b]Noninstitutional population 16 years old and older.

[c]Includes only nonagricultural civilian workers 16 years old and older.

Source: *Statistical Abstract of the United States,* 1990 and 1997 (Washington, D.C.: U.S. Department of Commerce); derived from tables 487 and 624 in 1990 edition, tables 507 and 619 in 1997 edition.

full-time-equivalent government employees, not counting the military, was 19.5 million, about 1 out of every 7 nonagricultural civilian workers. In the forty-five years between 1950 and 1995, the government workforce grew at a compounded annual rate of 2.8 percent, more than four times that of the population as a whole (0.6 percent) and more than that of private-sector employment (2.1 percent). By 1992, more people were working in government than in manufacturing.

Salamon explains the curious fact that the number of federal employees increased by 50 percent while federal expenditures rose by 400 percent between 1950 and 1978: the period saw a large increase in "third-party government," that is, indirect spending of federal money by states and other entities receiving grants and loans, for example.[6]

Remarkably, 30,000 of the 82,000 governments in the United States in 1982 had no employees! These "zero-employee governments," generally serving very small communities, used dedicated volunteers to negotiate and supervise contracts for services by larger communities nearby.[7]

Why Government Grows

It is evident that government and government spending have grown, but why? It is often asserted that government spending is as large as it is because people favor this level of spending. But this tautology is too facile; closer examination of the issue is warranted.

Three major factors have contributed to the growth of government: (1) increased demand for government services, by current and would-be service recipients; (2) increased supply of government services, by service producers; and (3) increased inefficiency, which results in more government staffing and spending to provide the same services.

Increased Demand for Services

The demand for government services has increased for several reasons: demographic changes in the population; income growth; income-redistribution policies; the desire to rectify societal ills, avoid risk, and promote culture; fiscal illusion; and preservation of existing programs.

Demographic changes.   Inflation, population growth, and an increase in defense-related expenditures account for much of the absolute growth of government, but the real growth was large even after allowing for these effects. Part of the explanation has to do with a change in the composition of the population to one that demands more government services. For example, if the number of retirees increases and if inflation-adjusted pension payments are made to them out of general government funds rather than from an actuarially sound retirement fund, government expenditures will increase even if all else remains unchanged.

The same phenomenon can be observed at the local government level when the population of a city changes so that a larger fraction of its residents are dependent on government-provided social and welfare services, even if population size remains unchanged. Faced with this increased demand, welfare-related expenditures will rise. Yet this explains only part of the observed increase. Of the $3.9 billion increase in the human services budget in New York City over a ten-year period, only 40 percent was the result of inflation and a larger workload; 60 percent was caused by other factors, mostly growing inefficiency.[8]

Urbanization also creates a demand for services. As urbanization increases, people get in one another's way. More police officers are needed. New kinds of government action are called for to regulate and ameliorate harmful and potentially harmful side effects of individual actions—for instance, to control pollution, to reduce noise, to test foods and drugs, to inspect restaurants, and to separate certain activities by zoning. All these require more government spending.

Income growth.   The growth in real per capita income contributes to the growth in government spending, as people demand, and can afford, disproportionately more government services. This may be seen in the demand for more spending on education (e.g., more specialized courses, more costly equipment, more luxurious school facilities and furnishings), larger budgets for libraries and cultural events, a higher level of services such as street repair and recreation programs, and a willingness to spend more for environmental protection.

The opposite phenomenon can also be observed, however. With more money, people rely less on government services. Instead of patronizing public swimming pools, they build their own. They use private automobiles and taxis instead of buses, and arrange for their own recreation by joining tennis and golf clubs instead of patronizing public facilities. They buy books instead of borrowing them from libraries, and increase their personal security by installing alarms and locks and hiring guards. If they suspect the quality of their drinking water, they switch to bottled water. Examining these contradictory factors, Borcherding estimates that only about a fourth of the real increase in public spending in this century can be attributed to increased affluence.[9]

Income redistribution.   One theory attributes much of the growth of government to the fact that the median income is less than the average income; by definition, this means that a majority of voters have lower-than-average incomes. Hence, "those with the lowest income use the political process to increase their income. Politicians . . . attract voters with incomes near the median by offering benefits . . . that impose a net cost on those with incomes above the median."[10] This is especially feasible when taxation is progressive. The analysis concludes that government grows wherever the majority is free to express its will, despite the fact that large government is a threat to freedom.

This bleak forecast is wrong, however. Although government has grown, the income redistribution predicted by this theory has not occurred: the proportions of total income going to the highest and lowest quintiles in the United States were fairly constant for many decades and recently the gap has been growing, not shrinking.

The fact remains, however, that redistribution programs have been the principal areas of large and rapid government growth, by societal consensus: income security, health, housing, education, and welfare (broadly defined). But there is little agreement about particular programs. The federal government pays for babysitting (day care), but should it also pay for midnight basketball? Humane, new social programs are initiated but scandals plague many of them. Displaced workers get unemployment insurance, but so do school employees and forest rangers during scheduled seasonal vacations. There are health clinics for infants but also questionable assembly-line medical tests. There are classes for the handicapped but also remedial reading courses in public universities devoted to higher education. "There's a lot of money in poverty," but some of it goes not to the deserving poor but to shady opportunists who operate "nonprofit" neighborhood programs with unknown goals and unreported achievements.

Satisfying special interests.   Special interest groups—accurately called distributional coalitions by Mancur Olson—use their lobbying power to influence government policies and thereby gain a greater share of society's wealth. Such lobbying has a bigger payoff than merely producing goods and services and does more harm to society:

> Lobbying increases the complexity of regulation and the [size and] scope of government. . . . A lobby that wins tax reduction for income of a certain source or type makes the tax code longer and more complicated; a lobby that gets a tariff increase for the producers of a particular commodity makes trade regulation more complex than if there were a uniform tariff [or] no tariff at all. . . . Someone has to administer the increasingly complex regulations. . . . This increases the scale of bureaucracy and government [and] also . . . leads to government expenditures and programs to serve special-interest groups.[11]

Rectifying societal ills.   There are strong demands for government action to correct or at least ameliorate a wide variety of perceived shortcomings in society. This approach rests on the assumption that (1) there is a broad consensus as to what constitutes a desirable improvement; (2) we know how to bring about the improvement; and (3) government can do it—the presumption of governmental efficacy.[12]

Rewards accrue in the political arena for publicizing problems and initiating programs that purport to solve them, however intractable the causes.[13] Costly, symbolic gestures are common, such as the well-intentioned attempts to eradicate poverty, to provide high-paying jobs for the unskilled, and to give college degrees to the unqualified.[14] Unfortunately, not every deplorable condition succumbs to government programs.

Risk aversion.   Government programs have been initiated to absorb societal risks. For example, governments make large, risky investments in basic research, such as nuclear fission and space exploration. This is all well and good, but they have also been drawn into financing the production of ethanol fuel from corn and from garbage, where the role of government can be questioned: once outside the laboratory, a product should stand on its own in the marketplace.

Risks that are inherently individual, however, have also been thrust on government. Examples are guaranteed markets for producers of unwanted, surplus products, guarantees for bank accounts in mismanaged institutions, and mortgage insurance for people who want to buy houses they cannot afford. These reflect the understandable yearning to reduce risks, but a riskless society is found only in the cemetery. Life is risky, and an imprudent attempt to collectivize risk is doomed to costly failure,[15] as in the savings and loan fiasco that cost taxpayers hundreds of billions of dollars.

Cultural uplift. In some countries more than others, government growth is spurred in part by demands for government involvement in theater, television, and the arts in order to promote high cultural standards. Left to private patrons, the standards presumably would be too plebeian and insufficiently uplifting. The problem with this ennobling vision, of course, is the lack of evidence that the aesthetic tastes of politically appointed cultural commissions are markedly superior to those of private philanthropists.

Fiscal illusion. Fueling the increase in government spending is the illusion that government services are a bargain because government does not make a profit. Studies of municipal services (reviewed in chapter 6), disprove this common assertion, however, by demonstrating that the prices charged by profit-making contractors are substantially lower, on average, than the cost of nonprofit municipal work.[16]

Even government officials are generally unaware of the cost of their services. A large-scale study found that the true costs of a particular municipal service were 30 percent greater on average than the amounts reported in the cities' budgets.[17]

Ordinary citizens are often misled as to the cost of government. Surveys show that they consistently underestimate the amount of taxes they pay because of ingenious "fiscal extraction devices" used by governments to raise revenues unobtrusively, without drawing the taxpayer's attention.[18] Utility bills are favorite sources of relatively invisible taxes. Property taxes are concealed in rents and mortgage payments. Sales taxes are collected by every retailer. Policies that obscure costs are particularly effective in gaining votes without having to raise taxes. Farmers gain from a crop-restriction program, for example, but the costs are invisible because they are spread among all buyers of that product, and the public reaction is muted compared to taxes and visible payments.

The newest fiscal extraction device is the government lawsuit aimed at extorting payoffs from vulnerable industries. The $206 billion paid by the tobacco industry to a group of states in 1998 is a case in point. The excuse is that smokers who ignored decades of warnings and got sick received medical treatment via government programs, and therefore it is only fitting that the industry should pay the states. The sale of a legal product has thus been criminalized. (No one dares suggest that people who wantonly engage in risky behavior should shoulder more of their medical expenses.) With higher taxes politically unpopular, government has found a way to extract money from anybody who buys anything made by a conglomerate that includes tobacco among its products. The firearms industry is the next target on the hit list, probably to be followed by the liquor industry and perhaps the food industry, the former no doubt to be held responsible for drunken drivers and the latter for selling foods that have fat and cholesterol. Instead of policy being made by democratically elected legislatures, it was made by the threat of mass litigation in the courts.

The ultimate fiscal illusion was to be found in the former Soviet Union, where sophisticated individuals would tell a foreign friend in all sincerity that they paid little in the way of taxes and that only a trivial amount was withheld from their pay. Only a moment's reflection is needed to realize that when everyone works for the state, and there is no labor market, all an employee knows is his take-home pay—he knows neither his true wages nor the amount withheld.

Indeed, the Soviet Union offered many excellent examples of this fallacy. For example, I once found myself in a friendly confrontation in Moscow after listening to smug assertions about their "free medical care," in pointed contrast to the medical care system in the United States. I noted, however, that doctors and nurses are paid in the Soviet Union, and so are the construction workers who build hospitals and the workers who produce medical supplies. Obviously, the Soviet people paid all these costs. The service was not free; the people were merely ignorant of the cost, which is a different matter altogether.

The end result of fiscal illusion is pressure for government services in the belief that they are free, or at least a bargain.

Program preservation. As times and needs change, new programs should emerge and old ones should disappear. The former occurs readily, but the latter occurs slowly, at best. Political leaders learned long ago that depriving someone of an existing benefit is like snatching a lion cub from its mother. Madsen Pirie recounts the amusing story of public bathhouses that survive in England. When their closure is periodically attempted, on grounds of economy and because they are no longer needed, the few users chain themselves to the railings and cause such a fuss that the budget-cutters' will is sapped and they retire in defeat. In contrast, the loudest advocates of lower taxes and smaller government would be deemed mad if *they* were to chain themselves to bathhouse doors and demand their closure in order to achieve such piddling savings.[19] A similar public outcry forced the mayor of New York to drop his plan to remove neighborhood fire-alarm boxes that were obsolete, superfluous, and a hazard because they were a source of false alarms that delayed firefighters' responses to real fires.

Increased Supply of Services

Whereas increased demand provides the "pull" for more government services, the desire by producers to supply more services provides a "push."

Gaining votes.   Elected officials gain considerable political income when government grows; therefore, it is more advantageous for them to levy taxes and distribute them as subsidies to all than not to collect them, even though each individual citizen may be no better or worse off. That is, from a political viewpoint, an ideal program is one that extracts taxes as invisibly and painlessly as fiscal illusion can permit, and results in an individual check, signed by the elected official, mailed to each citizen shortly before Election Day.

The raising of revenues to be distributed is often hidden and diffuse, shared by all, while the spending is visible and concentrated, targeted at particular beneficiaries. James Q. Wilson analyzed the distribution of costs and benefits of public-sector programs. In most tax-paid programs, either costs and benefits are both spread over a large number of individuals, or the costs are widespread but the benefits are targeted on a small group. Both kinds of programs are attractive to office seekers.[20]

Legislators who want to curry favor with interest groups point to the benefits but ignore the costs. Ogden Nash expressed the point well in a delightful bit of doggerel entitled "The Politician:"

> He gains votes ever and anew
> By taking money from everybody and giving it to a few,
> While explaining that every penny
> Was extracted from the few to be given to the many![21]

Representative government facilitates this outcome. Individuals elect representatives to take care of government business on their behalf. Most people then pay no attention to the details of government except for those few actions that affect them greatly. Consider a bill to spend $100 million for highways. It would mean substantial contracts for construction companies and suppliers of construction materials, jobs for a few thousand construction workers, and benefits to local highway users. The cost of the program would be only a dollar for the average taxpayer, and so there is no reason for him to bother for even a moment about the program. He knows little about it and is oblivious to the bill because it will not affect him. The direct beneficiaries, however, will know a great deal about the bill and its intricacies (they probably helped draft it) and will strive to assure its passage. Legislators know that this is how people behave and that by supporting the bill they are likely to get the votes of the beneficiaries at the next election, but their action will have no effect on the votes of citizens who have no interest in the bill.[22] In short, politicians use public money to buy votes.

Only in the aggregate are costs recognized as counterbalancing benefits, and it takes an exceptional political leader to identify, aggregate, and mobilize a concerned constituency around this issue. President Reagan, for example, was able to assemble such a movement against taxes and big government. Good government groups, chambers of commerce, and civic associations can be enlisted in such efforts.

Congressmen earn electoral credits not only by creating various federal programs but also by interpreting them:

> The legislation is drafted in very general terms, so some agency
> must translate a vague policy mandate into a functioning program,
> a process that necessitates the promulgation of rules and regula-
> tions. . . . At the next stage, aggrieved and/or hopeful constituents
> petition their Congressmen to intervene in the complex process of
> the bureaucracy. The cycle closes when the Congressman lends a
> sympathetic ear, piously denounces the evils of bureaucracy, inter-
> venes in the latter's decisions and rides a grateful electorate to ever
> more impressive electoral showings. Congressmen take credit
> coming and going.[23]

Budgetary imperialism.   Nobel Laureate James Buchanan points to other incentives for growth that influence those within government. More government work and more government expenditures mean more opportunities for larger salaries, higher status, more perquisites, and bigger bribes.[24] The larger the organization to be managed and the greater the total resources under one's responsibility, the greater the salary. Along with a more imperial scope come suitably larger and nicer offices, more assistants, car and chauffeur, plaques and photographs of important personages on office walls, invitations to governors' mansions and the White House, and assorted other status symbols.

The effect of larger public agencies can be seen in education. The consolidation of small school districts into larger ones results in more administrators per pupil, contrary to expectations, and higher salaries. In the absence of any proven relationship between educational inputs and outputs, the effect of court decisions equalizing per-pupil expenditures is to transfer income to teachers and administrators when total education expenditures rise.[25]

Further support for budgetary imperialism is found in income data: the highest median income in the country is in the suburbs of Washington, D.C., and the inflation of job titles and federal salaries has resulted in much higher pay in government than for corresponding work in the private sector.[26]

Budget maximization is a powerful driving force in government agencies, as William Niskanen noted insightfully, and much of the observed growth can be attributed to this principle.[27] Bureaucrats take actions that maximize their budgets not only for the pecuniary motives ascribed by Buchanan but also for nobler purposes that are congruent with the public interest. If a public official wants to increase his agency's effectiveness, it is easier, quicker, and less painful if the agency is expanding. Creating a new unit, hiring fresh people, getting more money, and setting off with enthusiasm in a promising new direction, is a lot easier than firing incompetents, changing inherited attitudes, turning around a misguided unit, or galvanizing a tired one into action. In short, even the most selfless public servant can honestly say that he is better able to serve the public interest if he has a bigger budget, but the end result is a budget-maximizing bureaucracy.

A final point in this category: It's *fun* spending other people's money! Those who have served in government and made expenditure decisions may admit to the satisfying thrill, the power, and the regal sense of self importance—to say nothing of the flattery from grateful beneficiaries—that comes with dispensing tax moneys, all at no cost to one's own pocket!

Enlarging campaign staffs.   Larger government brings other political benefits as well. The officeholder can utilize his staff in election campaigns, a time-honored tradition. The larger the agency, the larger the campaign staff. If done crassly, it is illegal, but "constituent service and citizen feedback" have wide latitude.

The problem-finding elite.   Our society has been producing a large number of educated people, many of whom do relatively better in government than in the private sector, according to this view.[28] Many are particularly adept at detecting societal ills, from rare occupational hazards to obscure but endangered fish species. They constitute a problem-finding elite whose numbers multiply as they seek ever more problems and selflessly offer their services to search for solutions.[29] These problem-enhancing, publicity-seeking entrepreneurs ("policy entrepreneurs"[30]) may be frustrated professionals in the relevant field, bureaucrats breathing new life into tired agencies, legislators trying to carve a niche, scientists after research funds, or journalists looking for topics that will sell. Whether government is the appropriate instrument for treating the newly uncovered problem is another story.[31]

The therapeutic state.   As government grew, its legitimacy was increasingly questioned. Therefore a new mission gradually emerged: government was to be compassionate, feeling your pain. Thus the therapeutic state was born.[32] The new, therapeutic mission both fuels and legitimizes government's expansion into new spheres of society's and individuals' lives. The sensitivity industry is booming, the caring professions swarm to the government honeypot, and, no doubt, grief counselors will soon be found at two-alarm fires. Criminals are suffering from pathologies, victims of their childhood. Welfare policy is concerned not only about behavior but also about the inner workings of people. In education, the therapeutic state requires an approved frame of mind, self-esteem: "A compassionate government's work is never done. That work, and the government that undertakes it, is unlimited."[33]

Command-and-control policies.   In many developing countries, particularly those with colonial pasts, the problem of nation building was thought to demand strong, centralized planning and control. The few educated people were brought into government to run the economy. Western lenders provided money—but only to the government, both for convenience and for what proved to be illusory security. Government growth was forced, as government tried to run practically everything: farms, factories, mines, hotels, utilities, transportation systems, and all kinds of businesses. Only in this way, it was thought, could rapid, purposeful progress be made.

Market alternatives seemed too untidy, uncoordinated, slow, and, above all, insufficiently responsive to the nation's commanders; certainly markets were not to be entrusted with the country's meager capital resources. Command and control of an economy dominated by government agencies was to be the shortcut to development. Unfortunately, time has judged most of these efforts harshly. It was good for the commanders but bad for most others. State-owned enterprises and commanders multiplied but the standard of living stagnated or declined.

Government monopolies.   Many government agencies operate as monopolies, in effect, because of several contributing factors.[34] First, a common activity of government has been to provide services that by their nature are monopolies. Second, in the name of administrative efficiency and rational management, bureaus with partially overlapping functions have generally been combined, leaving the surviving agency with monopoly status. Third, at the local government level, consolidation, school mergers, annexation, formation of a regional government or authority, and city expansion to encompass unincorporated areas result in an area-wide monopoly.[35]

Lacking competitors, a monopoly agency can exploit its position in a variety of ways.[36] For one thing, its budget is particularly resistant to reduction. When asked to cut back on expenditures, the agency may present a budget with the cuts focused on the most visible and popular programs. This is known as the Washington Monument strategy, whereby the National Parks Service helpfully offers to trim its budget by closing the city's most popular tourist attraction.

An iniquitous practice of private monopolies is "tie-in sales," forcing consumers to purchase unwanted goods and services. If they do not buy these goods, they cannot buy the monopolized good they really want. Government monopolies may behave no differently. Consider a city police department that says, in effect, "If you want uniformed police to do patrol work, you have to have uniformed police to answer the telephones and enforce parking regulations, too." Such a department resists creation of a separate, specialized, low-cost, civilian unit whose function is solely to enforce parking regulations. Its reasons for resistance include a desire to maximize both the number of police officers and the departmental budget, but also, it is alleged, to retain the power to extend courtesies to grateful offenders and police-fund contributors.

Should this illustration of governmental "tie-in sales" tactics seem farfetched, note that the city of Plaquemine, Louisiana, tried to force its water customers to purchase city power as well. The U.S. Supreme Court ruled, however, that the city is not automatically exempt from antitrust laws that prohibit such actions.[37] The net effect of government's monopoly status is pressure for more government growth.

Purposeful inertia.   Supply-side pressures for government growth need not be active; inertia alone can suffice. Edward Gramlich cites Richard Rose and Terence Karran to the effect that when it comes to taxation, "politicians prefer non-decision making to decision making, automatic revenue growth to discretionary revenue growth, incrementalism to fundamental reform, and all other aspects of . . . inertial behavior. This in turn means that the revenue system . . . in most times and places is on automatic pilot. Economic growth or inflation brings in revenues, these are spent, and only a few . . . raise questions about fundamental tax reform, truth in taxation through indexing for inflation, and other such unpleasantries."[38]

Employee voting.   It is in the self-interest of public employees to have government grow. More than the average voter, therefore, they are motivated to vote, and to vote for candidates whose programs will enlarge government expenditures. After all, they are the most direct beneficiaries of government spending, except for citizens and firms who receive direct payments from government. Furthermore, they are numerically strong enough to affect the outcome of elections.

Government employees are more likely to vote and their voting strength is significant. It is estimated that public employees representing a sixth of the workforce cast more than a quarter of the votes.[39] The conventional wisdom in New York City is that municipal employees, each one influencing the votes of three relatives or friends, control a million votes, a number that greatly exceeds the margin of victory in any mayoral election.

The political power of public employees and their unions goes beyond their voting strength. Political campaign contributors and campaign workers are a potent influence on officeseekers. The situation lends itself to collusion whereby officeholders can award substantial pay raises to employees with the unspoken understanding that some of the bread cast upon those particular waters will float back as contributions; moreover, a sudden increase in worker absenteeism during the campaign season might be conveniently overlooked by the city official who understands that the workers are temporarily engaged in a higher calling.

In recognition of this danger, the Hatch Act prohibited direct political activity by federal employees. There is no counterpart legislation at state or local levels, however, and the effectiveness of the Hatch Act itself has been diluted by court decisions. Similar considerations were no doubt responsible, at least in part, for the fact that until 1961, residents of the District of Columbia were denied the right to vote in federal elections; they were presumed to be direct or indirect employees of the federal government.

Demand for government jobs. Another contribution to the growth of government is the simple demand for a government job. In 1990 there were 101,000 applicants for 1,000 openings in the New York City Department of Sanitation. Asked why so many people wanted to collect garbage and sweep streets in all kinds of weather, one applicant replied, "Money, benefits, hours, security." In five years, the salary with overtime is close to $50,000 for a job that requires only a high school diploma and a commercial driver's license.[40]

The boldest expression of this demand also occurred in New York City, during my tenure as First Deputy City Administrator. In response to an announcement of several hundred job openings for police officers, more than 100,000 people applied for the civil service examination. Tens of thousands passed the test, but, of course, relatively few were hired because of the city's limited need; the names of the others were put on the list of eligibles from which additional appointments might someday be made. What happened next was straight from the theater of the absurd: the people on the list formed an association, conducted demonstrations, and lobbied vigorously among city and state officials, demanding the enlargement of the police department and the appointment of more police officers.

Many developing countries succumbed to similar demands and allotted much of their foreign aid to create government jobs, with little or no work expected from many of the patronage-blessed jobholders. This did not prove to be a promising path to economic development. In one such country where I worked, the most numerous and visible class of employees was "office aide," whose principal duties were to keep the offices clean, make coffee, and hand-deliver messages to other offices, despite the existence of a well functioning telephone and fax system.

Overproduction. Yet another factor on the supply side favoring government growth is the overproduction of services, that is, supplying more or better services than the public would willingly select if it had a direct choice and knew the true cost. This was studied by examining the frequency of residential refuse collection in cities where residents had both a greater choice of service level (number of pickups per week) and more information about the cost of different service levels than in other cities. Where government paid for the service through taxes, collection was more frequent than in cities where service was mandatory but each household made its own arrangement with a private firm and paid the latter directly for the service. Evidently the close connection between costs and benefits in the latter cities led to thriftier citizen choices.[41]

Increased Inefficiency

A third major factor that accounts for the growth of government is growing inefficiency: spending more money and employing more people to do the same work. Of course, this happens in private firms, too, but a harsh correction tends to occur quickly in this sector. William Baumol points out that in some occupations productivity cannot be raised, for instance, a violinist cannot fiddle more rapidly or give more performances in a day, yet his remuneration will rise along with general wage levels. Therefore, the unit cost of his work, the cost of an identical performance, will rise with time.[42] Some extrapolate Baumol's reasoning and argue that many government activities are like this, that productivity cannot be increased, so government spending rises for the same work. But this explanation is not generally true for tangible services in public works, policing, and fire fighting, for example; all of these benefit from technological changes that improve productivity. Even one-on-one services such as counseling have become more productive thanks to telephones and to computerized record-keeping and information retrieval. This excuse, extended to government from the performing arts, does not ring true.

Overstaffing.   Public-service agencies and government-owned enterprises consistently show overstaffing, sometimes by as much as several hundred percent, as shown in chapter 6. A particularly striking example can be found in New York City, not because it is worse than other governments, but, on the contrary, because it is relatively open to scrutiny. Over a twenty-five-year period, the number of police officers rose from 16,000 to 24,000, but the total annual hours worked by the entire force actually declined. The entire 50 percent increase in personnel was devoted to shortening the workweek, lengthening the lunch hour and vacation period, and providing more holidays and paid sick leave. Moreover, inefficient staffing was legitimized by a state law that called for an equal number of police officers on duty on each shift, despite the fact that crime statistics showed few criminals working in the small hours of the morning. Because of this legislated inefficiency, if more police were needed for assignment to evening duty, when most street crimes occur, more would also have to be hired and assigned when there was little for them to do. (The legislation was not inadvertent; it was strongly desired by the police union.)[43]

In the New York City school system, during a period of constant pupil enrollment, a 50 percent increase in the number of teachers and the addition of one paraprofessional for every two teachers produced only a slight decrease in class size. Instead, classroom time was reduced for teachers, and some teacher duties were delegated to the paraprofessionals. It is by no means obvious that the result was better teacher preparation and better pupil education.

Moreover, bureaucrats beget bureaucrats. Administrative growth occurs because of the interactive nature of managerial work. More managers means more meetings; therefore, there is a multiplier effect: adding a 40-hour-a-week manager can actually *increase* the net demand for time by up to 37.9 hours a week! That is, adding one manager may require adding another, ad infinitum.[44]

Overpaying.   Several studies show that, on average, public employees are paid significantly more than workers in the private sector, up to 41 percent more.[45] These studies have been criticized, however, because they did not take into consideration any differences in activities. To remedy this shortcoming, another study compared workers performing essentially the same jobs in the public and private sectors; it concluded that at lower levels public employees are paid more than their private-sector counterparts, while at higher levels the private sector pays more.[46] But this finding is suspect because it fails to look at total compensation per hour worked. This is the only accurate way to measure and compare pay levels. The key here lies in the terms "total compensation" (which includes generous fringe benefits) and "per hour worked" (which adjusts for the liberal vacation, holiday, and sick-leave policies in the public sector). A study by the Bureau of Labor Statistics confirms that fringe benefits in the public sector are relatively high; the benefits of federal employees were 27 percent greater than those of private-sector, nonagricultural employees.[47] "Public sector trade unions have been extremely successful in gaining advantages for themselves in the pay hierarchy by exploiting their monopoly bargaining positions."[48] "Union effects on total compensation of municipal employees are greater than those on wages."[49] To illustrate this "wage illusion"—the supply-side analog of the demand-side "fiscal illusion" discussed previously—an apparent public-employee wage rate of $265 per day was really 48 percent higher, $392, when it was correctly calculated as total compensation per day actually worked.[50]

Inefficiency caused by overpayment to employees is evident in publicly operated mass transit. Because most passenger trips occur during rush hours, few bus drivers are needed between those two periods, so using part-time drivers makes obvious sense. This is fought tenaciously, however—and successfully—by the transit unions. As a result, some drivers for the New York City Transit Authority drove four hours in the morning, took a four-hour Mediterranean-style break at midday at full pay, and drove four hours in the afternoon on overtime; in total, they drove for eight hours but were paid for fourteen.[51] Subsequently the pattern was changed: they were paid for only twelve hours—but drove only six! This was an even worse ratio from the taxpayers' viewpoint, but in a meeting with the senior vice-president for surface transit this was presented to me, proudly, as an improvement.

Labor-to-output ratios for several public services in New York City revealed that average productivity was either unchanged or had declined for state and local government employees.[52]

A careful study of the growth of expenditures for health, education, and welfare concluded that enormous additional sums were spent on higher real salaries and more jobs without evidence of increased outputs or higher quality of services.[53]

Overbuilding.   Another contribution to inefficiency is the government bias toward capital spending and against routine maintenance. This bias can best be understood by considering the high visibility of the former and the near invisibility of the latter. A ground breaking or a ribbon cutting presents an excellent opportunity for crowds, speeches, photographs, television coverage, durable mementos, and wine-and-cheese receptions for potential campaign contributors. Thus, capital budgets create political capital and cement political ties. In contrast, what kind of ceremony can one organize to celebrate the prompt repair of a leaking sewer? Simple cost-benefit analysis also reveals the virtues of capital projects: the sponsoring politician gets 100 percent of the credit but incurs only 3 percent of the cost, assuming thirty-year bonds.[54]

Thus, while inefficiency is not restricted to government activity, declining productivity and increasing inefficiency contribute to the growth in the size and cost of government.

Discussion

The three factors discussed here—recipient demands, producer pressures, and inefficiency—are closely linked. These characteristics result in spending coalitions that cause these programs to grow.[55] The coalition that forms to create, nurture, and expand a program consists of four groups: beneficiaries and near-beneficiaries (the latter expect to become beneficiaries as the program expands); service providers (e.g., construction firms and construction workers engaged in road-building programs); government administrators; and political activists (e.g., officeholders, officeseekers, and problem-finding elites). The partners in the coalition interact to gain gradual expansion of their program. Inefficiency comes into play and the number of beneficiaries, providers, and administrators swells as more adherents are amassed into the spending coalition.

Spending coalitions also tend to promote big, inefficient programs over small, efficient ones. The latter are "[doomed] in the world of competing bureaucracies as large contractors, high-priced lobbyists, and government agencies promote and protect the big programs at the expense of the smaller ones."[56]

Evidence indicates that excessive government growth results in stunted economic growth: "As the size of government has expanded in the United States, growth of real GDP has steadily fallen. ... [T]he growth of real GDP in the 1990s is only about half what it was during the 1960s and well below even that of the turbulent 1970s."[57]

The same effect has been noted by the Organization for Economic Cooperation and Development (OECD) among its members. As government expenditures of OECD's 23 countries rose from an average of 27 percent of GDP in 1960 to 48 percent in 1996, average annual economic growth fell from 5.5 to 1.9 percent. Moreover, the greater the government's share of GDP, the greater the decline in growth, and vice versa. This was also the pattern in Hong Kong, Singapore, South Korea, Taiwan, and Thailand when they were the world's fastest growing economies: government expenditures consumed only 20 percent of GDP on average, a figure essentially unchanged for twenty years.[58]

An international review by the World Bank concluded that the large and growing role of governments in the last fifty years has been counterproductive to a significant degree. "Market failures" were thought to be the problem impeding economic development and prosperity, and government was to correct them. The vast size and reach of government influence proved, however, to be ineffective. The report calls for a profound change in the role of government, namely, to be a facilitator and regulator and to rely more on citizens, communities, and markets.[59]

Governments grow in response to public demands, in response to the desires of service producers to supply more services, and as a consequence of inefficiency. If unchecked, these factors would lead to an unstable and uncontrollable spiral of continued growth: the bigger the government, the greater the force for even bigger government. Budgets would expand, resulting in the appointment of more officials and the hiring of more workers. These would go to work at once to enlarge their budgets, do less work, hire still more workers, obtain better-than-average raises, and vote for more spending programs, while encouraging their constituents and beneficiaries to do the same. The forecast would appear ominous: sooner or later, everyone will be working for government and government will absorb and spend all of the nation's gross domestic product.

But simple extrapolations of this sort cannot be correct. Government growth is not a one-way street. A backlash is occurring as countervailing, homeostatic forces come into play: taxpayer revolts such as California's revolutionary Proposition 13 in 1978 (which capped property tax increases), state-mandated caps on local expenditures, term limits, and proposals for spending restrictions and a balanced-budget amendment. The public, apparently despairing of the ability or will of its elected representatives to reduce expenditures, took the matter directly into its hands through Proposition 13 and reduced government revenues, like a parent rebuking a spendthrift child by cutting his allowance. Political leaders can sometimes gain more support by cutting back on spending programs than by initiating new ones. In cities with severe financial problems municipal agencies have been reduced in size. Revenue cuts, revenue limitations, reinvented government, and privatization are politically popular. Voters reject spending proposals, elect more frugal officials, and flee from high-tax jurisdictions. Ronald Reagan was elected governor and president because of his antigovernment stance: Get government off the backs of the people. He gave effective voice to the public mood and, marshaling bipartisan support, drastically slashed personal income taxes and put an end to "bracket creep" whereby tax collections rose more rapidly than inflation (hitherto a main staple of purposeful inertia). Whether or not he meant it, President Clinton announced the end of big government, and the growth of government does indeed seem to be slowing, as table 2.2 (p. 19) reveals.

Moreover, public employees are not united in a headless conspiracy; they feel just as victimized as other taxpayers when they receive poor and costly services in return for their tax dollars: Proposition 13 was supported by 44 percent of families that included public employees.[60] Under budgetary stringency, the objectives of one government bureau are at odds with those of another, and instead of making common cause to enlarge their total budget, they fight each other to obtain a larger share of a shrinking pie.

A more educated, critical, and sophisticated citizenry no longer regards government action as synonymous with the public interest. It has learned to expect unintended, adverse consequences of attempts at social engineering, and it recognizes limits in the state's ability to define—let alone attain—the public good. The extent to which these forces can counterbalance or overcome the propensity of government to grow remains to be seen.

PART TWO

The Theory of Privatization

CHAPTER THREE

Basic Characteristics of Goods and Services

HUMAN BEINGS REQUIRE many different kinds of goods and services. Air, water, food, clothing, and shelter are the basic necessities of life, but unless one is a hermit, additional goods and services are desired: fire protection and banking services, education and old-age security, transportation and communication, recreation, health care and waste removal, theaters and cemeteries, museums and beauty parlors, landscaping and tailoring, books and locks, money and satellites. Advanced societies, no less than primitive tribes, seek protection from human enemies and assistance from divine beings, and therefore they support warriors and weapon makers to provide the former and priests and shamans to provide the latter services.

This vast jumble of goods and services can be sorted and classified according to two characteristics: exclusion and consumption. The resulting classification determines the roles of government and of the nongovernmental (private) institutions of society in supplying the goods and services.[1]

Exclusion

Goods and services—henceforth these terms will be used synonymously— are subject to exclusion if the potential user of the goods can be denied the goods or excluded from using them unless he meets the conditions set by the potential supplier. In other words, the goods can change hands only if both the buyer and seller agree on the terms of sale.

This is a perfectly ordinary condition. All the commonplace goods that we buy in the marketplace clearly have this exclusion property. I may walk off with my bag of groceries or my haircut only after my grocer or barber agrees. (We ignore the case of theft.) But there are vast numbers of other goods that do not possess this simple property. A consumer can simply help himself to such goods as long as Mother Nature or another supplier makes them available. As one example of such a good, consider fish in the sea. Their consumption cannot conveniently be prevented or excluded; fishermen can take them without paying.

Exclusion is more a matter of cost than of logic, however; it is feasible or infeasible to the extent that the cost of enforcement is relatively low or high. Hence, exclusion admits of degrees. Exclusion from fishing in the open ocean is difficult; commercial fishing boats can be inspected and controlled at their docks but significant effort is required, and pleasure craft would require even more effort. On the other hand, exclusion in the purchase of goods from a store is easily feasible.

Some goods cannot be classified so neatly. For example, it is feasible to charge admission (and therefore to practice exclusion) for a grandstand seat to a fireworks display, but many others outside the grounds will also see the show, although not as well as those in the seats. It is simply not feasible to enclose a large enough area so that no one can witness the show free of charge—unless the show is a poor one with no high-altitude bursts. One can think of these as two different goods: a good seat from which one can be excluded if he doesn't pay, and a bad seat from which one cannot be excluded.

A lighthouse presents an interesting case. Built at considerable expense on a rocky coast and consuming large amounts of costly energy, the lighthouse shines its beacon to help seamen navigate the treacherous waters nearby. This is a valuable service for the seafarer, but he does not pay the lighthouse keeper for it; he can avail himself of it freely and cannot be excluded from doing so. After all, what is the keeper to do? Turn off the beacon when he knows that a particular nonpaying user is in the area? In fact, this *is* an excludable good, and in England lighthouses were privately owned and operated until 1842: ships using the nearby port were charged a fee.[2] To be precise, the use of the lighthouse's service without paying cannot be excluded; the use of the port can be. Companies that insure ships could perform a similar function, incorporating fees into their insurance premiums to support lighthouse operations, although this would not be as direct a user charge.

Changing technology can render exclusion more or less difficult. For example, the combination of electronic toll collection, computers, and sophisticated cameras that photograph automobile license plates now makes it possible to charge (practice exclusion) for the use of urban roadways. Cable systems, satellites, and videotapes make it possible to charge for television programs.

Consumption

The other relevant characteristic of goods and services has to do with consumption. Some goods may be used or consumed jointly and simultaneously by many customers without being diminished in quality or quantity, while other goods are available only for individual (rather than joint) consumption; that is, if they are used by one consumer, they are not available for consumption by another. A fish and a haircut are examples of a good and a service subject to individual consumption; the fish is no longer available to another diner, and neither are the services of the barber while he is cutting someone's hair. Other, comparable barbers may be available to others in need of tonsorial attention—just as similar fish are available to other diners—and the very same chair and barber will be available in a few minutes, but the fact remains that the services of that particular barber at that particular time are devoted to and consumed entirely by the one user.

Contrast these cases with a television broadcast. My family's "consumption" of a program, by enjoying it on our television set, in no way limits its "consumption" by anyone else, or even by millions of other viewers who may turn on their sets. The program remains equally available for joint consumption by many users and is in no way diminished or made less useful by our act of consumption.

We should not be confused by the fact that a large fish may be fed to several people at a dinner party; that act does not confer upon the fish the property of joint consumption, in the sense used here. Similarly, my solitary viewing of a television show does not transform that telecast into an individually consumed good.

Another illustration of a joint-consumption good is national defense. The protection I receive from the armed forces in no way subtracts from the protection available to my neighbor; his consumption of that particular good is undiminished by my own.

Other examples of goods that are subject to joint consumption are parks and streets. One person's use of Grand Canyon National Park does not preclude another's use of it; it is a jointly consumed good, as is a city street. In both cases, however, if the total number of joint users is large relative to the capacity of the park or street, then the quantity and quality of the available good is severely diminished. That is, parks and streets are not pure joint-consumption goods like the television broadcast. They are subject to congestion, i.e., "congestible." To a degree, they are like a haircut, an individually consumed good. In fact, few goods are pure joint-consumption goods; most fall along a continuum between pure individual and pure joint consumption, just as they fall along a continuum between feasible and infeasible exclusion.

Classifying Goods and Services

What has been said so far is displayed in figure 3.1 for several transportation services; figure 3.2 shows water supply represented in a similar diagram. The two properties, exclusion and consumption, constitute the two dimensions of the diagram and are shown as continuous variables; their extreme values are at the ends of the scales. As shown in the transportation diagram, exclusion becomes more feasible as one goes from a city street to a highway to a turnpike (limited access roadway). Consumption becomes progressively more joint in going from private automobile to taxi to bus—all three of which are readily subject to exclusion.

Figure 3.3 (p. 46) employs the same basic diagram and further illustrates the concept by displaying additional goods and services, located in accordance with their respective degrees of exclusion and joint consumption. Obviously, subjective judgment is involved in the precise placement of services in this diagram; the reader is invited to sketch his or her own version.

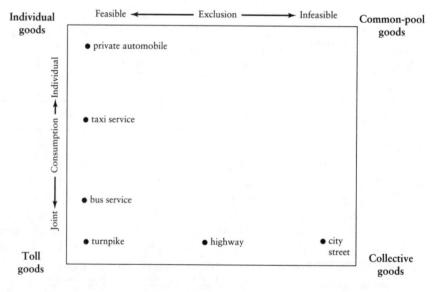

FIGURE 3.1—EXCLUSION AND CONSUMPTION PROPERTIES OF TRANSPORTATION
SERVICES AND FACILITIES

The four corners of the basic diagram correspond to pure forms: (1) pure individually consumed goods for which exclusion is completely feasible; (2) pure jointly consumed goods for which exclusion is completely feasible; (3) pure individually consumed goods for which exclusion is completely infeasible; and (4) pure jointly consumed goods for which exclusion is completely infeasible. These four idealized types of goods and services are important enough and will be referred to often enough to justify naming them, as is done in the diagram, where they are termed (1) individual goods (often called private goods), (2) toll goods, (3) common-pool goods, and (4) collective goods (often called public goods). The common terms, "private goods" and "public goods," are studiously avoided here, both because those terms are weighted with too much confusing baggage and because "public" has many meanings, as noted in chapter 1. Indeed, Aaron Wildavsky and Jesse Malkin recommend abandoning the traditional distinction between public and private goods.[3] The reason for classifying goods this way is fundamental: the nature of the good determines the conditions needed to supply it.

The goods that appear in figure 3.3 near the corners can be considered individual goods, toll goods, common-pool goods, or collective goods, although none is a pure or ideal type. In the upper left of the diagram

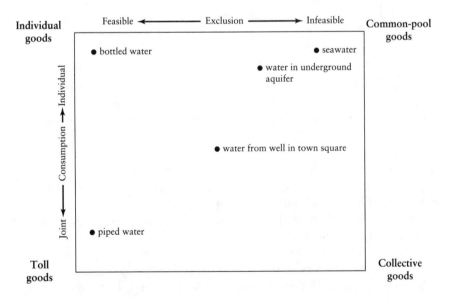

FIGURE 3.2—EXCLUSION AND CONSUMPTION PROPERTIES OF WATER-SUPPLY SERVICES

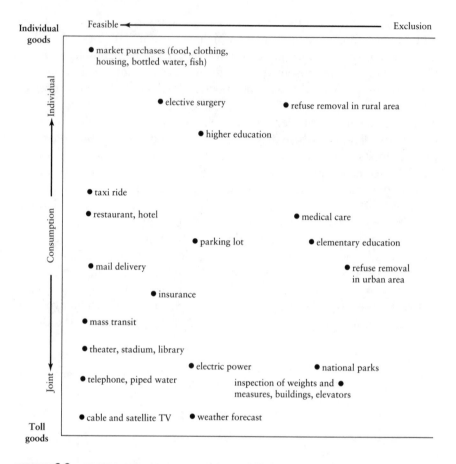

FIGURE 3.3—EXCLUSION AND CONSUMPTION PROPERTIES OF VARIOUS GOODS AND

appear the ordinary goods and services that one buys in the marketplace: shoes, bread, automobiles, housing, haircuts, dry cleaning, watch repair, and so on. They are all pure or nearly pure individual goods.

In the lower right of the diagram are collective goods. Air-pollution control is as pure a collective good as one can find. National defense is a collective good, but even this is impure, or congestible: an army busy defending one part of a country may be unavailable to protect another part. Police protection is almost as pure a collective good, but any finite force on patrol can be "consumed" by individual calls for service, making the good temporarily unavailable to others. For this reason, it is shown above and to the left of national defense. On the other hand, fire protection used

Exclusion ————————————————————→ Infeasible   Common-pool goods

● fish in a stocked lake   minerals in the ocean ●   ●   ●
                                                        fish in   air
                                                        the sea

open range for grazing ●

river, lake ●

street parking ●   religious observance ●

watching marathon ●

Central Park ●   fire protection ●

police patrol ●

immunization ●
                                    lighthouse ●
imprisonment of criminals ●

national defense, broadcast TV ●   Collective goods

SERVICES ("PURE" GOODS ARE SHOWN AT THE FOUR CORNERS)

to be a toll good or even a somewhat individual good, for it was common in the nineteenth century to have private fire companies protect only their paying subscribers, whose homes were marked with identifying placards. Today we recognize that when a house is on fire, many people besides the homeowner benefit by having the blaze extinguished before it spreads. Furthermore, it is no longer technically feasible to exclude service in densely packed, high-rise, multiple dwellings. Changing conditions have caused fire protection in urban areas to migrate into the class of collective goods.

Central Park in New York City was also a toll good when it was first created. It has a wall around it, interrupted by many gates that were once tended by gatekeepers who charged admission. The wall and gates are still there, but the gatekeepers have long since gone, exclusion is no longer practiced, and the park is used—and abused—as a collective good. National parks have limited access points and are therefore toll goods, but a determined backpacker can hike into one through the wilderness and, realistically, cannot be excluded. Because the quality of a park depends on the number of users and the uses they make of it, parks are shown as being more individually consumed than some other toll and collective goods.

Air is a common-pool good. It can be taken freely and compressed, or polluted, but then it is changed into a purely individual good that is unavailable to others in its original condition. A fish in a stocked lake is somewhere between a common-pool good and an individual good (the lake could be patrolled and only those who purchase a license could be granted access to the fish), but once a fish is caught and in the creel, it is an individual good.

Water in an underground aquifer is a common-pool good, free to be tapped by any well digger who owns a tiny parcel of land above it, but once it is brought into a water distribution system, it becomes a toll good. Rivers, lakes, and other waterways are common-pool goods of sorts, whether they are used for transportation, as sources of water, or to dispose of waste material. As figure 3.3 shows, they are decidedly impure common-pool goods because exclusion is not impossible.

Sewer service and electric power are toll goods, as are bridges, turnpikes, stadiums, theaters, and libraries, although none of these is as pure a toll good as cable TV because they are subject to excessive demand and congestion, which result in inferior products.

Radio and TV broadcasts satisfy the criteria for collective goods, yet they are supplied at no charge to listeners and viewers; they are given away by advertisers and ultimately paid for by purchasers of the advertised products.

Some readers may be confused upon seeing, in figure 3.3, weather forecasts identified as toll goods, inasmuch as people in the United States are used to getting weather forecasts free on radio, TV, and in newspapers. This happens because the U.S. Weather Bureau gives away this toll good, which is produced at public expense. The bureau could conceivably charge for the information and the media could buy it, just as they purchase information from international wire services. Alternatively, private firms could provide weather forecasts to the media, either by sale or free as a way to advertise their specialized and localized forecasting services. Like weather forecasts, the U.S. Navy is provided at taxpayers' expense, but it is a collective good because, unlike weather forecasts, its service is not subject to exclusion: there is no way the navy can charge for its protective services or a citizen can reject its protection.

Mass transit is a toll good, taxi service is more of an individual good, and a private automobile is a more purely individual good. In general, on-street parking is a collective good, although where there are parking meters it has been made into a toll good that is impure insofar as the street has limited capacity. Streets are a collective good, for it is difficult to exclude the use of a street for passage; that is, it is costly to construct and staff barriers.

With respect to elementary education, joint consumption occurs to some degree and, although a child can be excluded from a school, he or she could be schooled at home, and therefore exclusion from education is only partial. With respect to graduate school, however, accepting one applicant may mean rejecting another, consumption is more individual, and higher education is more of an individual good. The relative positions of elementary and higher education are displayed in figure 3.3.

Health care presents an interesting case that cannot be analyzed without considering separate kinds of treatment. Medical care for illnesses and accidents, elective and cosmetic surgery, and treatment for vitamin deficiencies and metabolic disorders are individual goods. On the other hand, public health measures such as mosquito abatement, rat control, and immigration control to prevent the entry of contagious diseases are obviously collective goods.

Immunization and treatment for communicable diseases, whether sore throats or diphtheria, at first glance seem to satisfy all the criteria of individual goods. A person with such an illness can certainly be denied treatment, and, if admitted to a hospital, the bed the patient occupies and the nursing and medical care he or she receives are no longer available to others. It is evident, however, that treating such illnesses provides important side benefits, "positive externalities," in that others are protected from the disease. Therefore, strangers are not excluded and they receive benefits jointly with the patient without reducing the latter's benefits. Like fire protection, this is a collective good.

This lengthy exercise in classifying goods and services should make it evident that the nature of the good—individual, toll, common-pool, or collective—determines the willingness of consumers to pay for it and, inevitably, the willingness of producers to supply it. Hence the nature of the good determines whether or not collective intervention is needed to procure the good in satisfactory quantity and quality. The next four sections explore this issue for each type of good.

Individual Goods

Individual goods pose no conceptual problem of supply; the marketplace provides them. Property rights, enforceable contracts, and free markets are all that is needed. Consumers demand the goods; entrepreneurs recognize the demand, produce the goods, and sell them voluntarily to willing buyers at a mutually acceptable price. Collective action with respect to individual goods for the most part is confined to addressing market failures: assuring product safety (e.g., of food, drugs, airplanes, and buildings) and honest reporting (of weights and measures, interest rates, labels on clothing), enforcement of contracts and antimonopoly laws, and dealing with negative externalities. Of course, no one can buy all the individual goods he may desire, and some may be too poor to afford even the rudimentary necessities without assistance. (Any mention of market failure should be paired with corresponding mention of nonmarket failure, that is, the failure of nonmarket approaches, including government failure.)[4]

Individual goods are sometimes supplied by governments even though the market can supply them. This was true of virtually all individual goods in the Soviet Union, for example, but it is also true of some individual goods in the United States, such as pensions (the Social Security system). The permanent shortage of consumer goods and services in the Soviet Union was a growing popular source of dissatisfaction and a major contributor to the collapse of the USSR.

Toll Goods

Like individual goods, toll goods can be supplied by the marketplace. Because exclusion is readily possible, users have to pay and therefore suppliers will supply the goods. Individuals and organizations, for-profit or not-for-profit, can purchase and give away toll goods, such as recreational facilities and libraries.

Nevertheless, some toll goods present problems that require collective action. These are the toll goods said to be natural monopolies, where the cost per user decreases as the number of users increases. The result is that it is most economical to have a single supplier, as in cable television, communication networks, electric power, gas distribution, water supply, and sewer service. Collective action is often taken to create and award these monopolies and then to regulate them so that the owners do not exploit their monopoly privileges.

A growing number of economists disagree with this rationale for regulation.[5] They cite the fact that many toll goods that were once monopolies no longer are. Railroads face competition from airplanes, trucks, buses, barges, and boats. Telephone communication is challenged by microwave transmission, and cable TV by satellites and videotapes. Indeed, it is argued, if a monopoly is "natural," surely there is no need to protect it by legislation. Moreover, even a natural monopoly may be contestable:[6] it could be awarded by competitive bidding for a limited period. Collective action is required to carry out this competitive process among would-be suppliers operating in the marketplace.

In any event, toll goods, like individual goods, can be supplied in the marketplace, but in many countries toll goods are supplied by government (usually with a user charge). An alternative to government provision of such goods is explored in chapter 9.

Common-Pool Goods

Unlike individual and toll goods, common-pool goods pose a supply problem. With no need to pay for such goods, and with no means to prevent their consumption, such goods will be consumed—even squandered—to the point of exhaustion, as long as the cost of collecting, harvesting, extracting, appropriating, or otherwise taking direct possession of the free goods does not exceed the value of the goods to the consumer. No rational supplier will produce such goods, and they would exist only through the beneficence of man or nature. Whales, tigers, and elephants are living—or rather dying—proof of the problem of managing common-pool goods that belong to whoever takes them. They are being consumed to the point of extinction, even though they are naturally renewable.

Market mechanisms cannot supply common-pool goods. One way to conserve the natural supply, however, is through collective action. In the case of endangered species of animals, this takes the form of international efforts to achieve voluntary agreement among the consumers to limit their consumption. (This is also true of Antarctica, currently a common-pool good.) Alas, such voluntary action has proven too thin a reed to support such a burden, as enforcement is very difficult. Another approach is to ban the sale of common-pool goods after they have been appropriated from their natural state. (Not all common-pool goods lend themselves to this approach.) Following this tactic, in the United States the sale of products made of alligator hides, tiger skins, ostrich feathers, and other endangered species is prohibited; in Kenya the government tries to prohibit the sale of elephant tusks and rhinoceros horns. The commissions, agencies, regulatory bodies, and enforcement units created to deal with the problem of common-pool goods are providing a service that is, in effect, a collective good.

Just as whales and tigers have been appropriated from the common pool and consumed as individual goods, some rivers and lakes are common-pool goods that have been used freely as dumps for toxic and noxious wastes and therefore have been debased into lower-quality, less available, partly consumed, individual goods. This destruction of common-pool goods, the pollution of waterways, has also brought forth collective action. Controls have been established over pollution sources such as industrial plants and waste-water-treatment facilities. In effect, a new service is provided—water-pollution control (a collective good)—in order to assure a continued supply of the desired common-pool good—unpolluted waterways.

The moon is a far-out example of a common-pool good. It could be used as a source of raw materials or as a communication or military base, but it is at least temporarily protected from overconsumption because of the high cost of using it. Nevertheless, space is already being degraded as a common-pool good as more and more waste products (thousands of objects) from space explorations orbit the Earth.

These examples illustrate the problems inherent in common-pool goods: the danger of depletion, the conventional approach to the problem by creating collective goods (services usually performed by government agencies) to safeguard the common-pool goods, and the limited effectiveness of such efforts because exclusion is difficult.

Because of the inadequacy of this approach, a diametrically different alternative is receiving growing attention: free-market environmentalism. It is an approach based on the concept of property rights and market mechanisms.[7] Simply put, when a common-pool good is transformed into an individual good that has an owner, conservation and successful management become possible. A private owner (of elephants, wilderness land, or water) wants to maximize the long-term value of his property and will follow prudent practices in husbanding the erstwhile common-pool goods that he owns. For the same reason, an underground oil deposit whose drilling rights belong to a single producer can be managed more effectively than one that can be tapped from dozens of overlying parcels of land. Conversely, land that is owned by "the public" tends to be treated as a common-pool good, and may be overgrazed and destroyed—"the tragedy of the commons."[8] Aristotle put it concisely more than 2,000 years ago: "that which is owned in common by the greatest number has the least care devoted to it."[9]

An interesting extension of these ideas can be applied to ocean fishing. In the United States, the price of fish has risen rapidly, even along the ocean shore. Paradoxically, fish is an expensive food because fish are free. That is, as a quintessential common-pool good, they are free for the taking, and, as a result, the ocean is overfished, the supply is depleted (just like the overgrazed commons), each fishing boat catches fewer fish, and thus the process is inefficient and the cost per fish is high. It has been suggested that off-shore fish be treated the same as off-shore oil, as the property of all U.S. citizens; scientific quotas would be set on the annual catch permitted, and rights to catch fish within that quota would be sold at auction. Transforming the common-pool good into an individual good, by creating transferable property rights—the privatization of ocean fisheries—is likely to solve the problem of overfishing.[10] (See chapter 12 for an application of this concept to the conservation of ocean salmon.)

Collective Goods

It is collective goods that pose a serious problem in the organization of a society. The marketplace is unable to supply such goods because, by their nature, they are used simultaneously by many people and no one can be excluded from enjoying them. Therefore every individual has an economic incentive to be a "free rider," that is, to use such goods without paying for them and without sharing in the effort required to supply them. How then can a society provide such goods? Answer: through voluntary or coerced contributions.

Collective goods can be supplied by voluntary action. In small groups that share similar values, such as the voluntary associations identified in chapter 1, social pressures are usually sufficient to assure that each person contributes his or her fair share to secure commonly desired collective goods. Volunteers provide fire protection and emergency ambulance service, collecting contributions from their neighbors to cover the cost of supplies and equipment. Philanthropists provide parks, and local merchant groups provide street lighting, street cleaning, and protective patrols, just as national advertisers provide broadcast television.

But if voluntary action fails to provide an adequate supply of collective goods, for example, where the social unit is large and diverse, contributions must be obtained by legally sanctioned coercion, such as tax collection and compulsory military service. This transforms free riders into forced riders. This is where government is needed, a government, one hopes, that is democratically created and which, therefore, can itself be considered the result of voluntary action. It is of paramount importance, however, to recognize that collective goods do not necessarily require government action and that is why the term *collective goods* is used here instead of the more common, but misleading, *public goods*.

The Problems Posed by Collective Goods

Collective goods have troublesome properties. They are generally hard to measure and they offer little choice to the consumer. Moreover, they raise a basic question about the size and composition of the collective entity that should make decisions about collective goods.

Measuring and Choosing Collective Goods

Unlike individual goods, which are relatively easy to count, account for, and package for unit sales, collective goods generally do not allow such ease of handling. How many units of national defense should be purchased? How much police protection? One can count the number of firefighters in a fire department, but that is not a reliable measure of the amount of protection they provide. One can report the area of a park, but that says little about it; appearance and ambiance are inherent aspects of that particular good. Street mileage can be measured and traffic and potholes can be counted, but these hard facts hardly begin to capture the important features of that particular collective good. The product of an air-pollution control department can be measured only indirectly, in terms of air quality, and even that is subject to extraneous factors, such as a strong breeze. For these reasons, it is often difficult—but not impossible—to define and measure the performance of an organization charged with providing a collective good. And this difficulty means that it is difficult to specify the amount of the good to be provided and to estimate what it should cost.

The very nature of a collective good means that an individual has little choice with respect to consuming the good, and he must generally accept it in the quantity and quality available. The ordinary citizen can demand that a policeman be stationed in front of his home, that his street be swept daily, and that his neighborhood park look like a royal garden, but his voice is diluted, and although his taxes may rise, the collective goods he receives are not likely to change much. Neither the individual who feels that the country is in danger and needs more military might nor the individual who feels that the nation's security is threatened by too much military power in the hands of fallible mortals will be satisfied, for he has no individual choice in the matter. He may write to his representative in Congress but must settle for what he can get.

A further consequence of these characteristics is that because it is impossible to charge directly for the use of collective goods, payment for them is unrelated to demand or consumption. Therefore, instead of relying on a market mechanism, one must rely on a political process to decide how much of the goods to produce and how much each user must pay in taxes. Furthermore, to the extent that most collective goods are impure and permit individual consumption to some degree, the decision as to who gets them—how the goods are allocated—is also relegated to the political process. These profound differences between individual and collective goods are reviewed and summarized in table 3.1.

How Large Is the Collective?

What exactly is the collective that should decide about collective goods? How big should it be? Who or what should it encompass? These questions place us squarely in the midst of the unending debate on federalism and the proper allocation of responsibilities among the different levels of government. There may be agreement that a collective assessment (e.g., a tax) is required to assure supply of a collective good, but what is the scale of the community that should be assessed? The entire nation? A region, state, county, or city? A neighborhood? The residents on a city block, or in a large condominium building on that block?

A basic principle of public finance is that the beneficiaries of a collective good should pay, but they may not be so easy to identify. While it is easy to see that national defense benefits the entire nation, and so everyone should pay for it, consider the other end of the scale, the lowly

TABLE 3.1—PROPERTIES OF INDIVIDUAL AND COLLECTIVE GOODS

Characteristic	Individual good	Collective good
Consumption	Entirely by individual	Joint and simultaneous by many
Payment for goods	Related to consumption; paid for by consumer	Unrelated to consumption; paid for by collective assessment
Exclusion of those who will not pay	Easy	Difficult
Measurement of quantity and quality of goods	Easy	Difficult
Measurement of performance of goods producer	Easy	Difficult
Individual choice to consume or not	Yes	No
Individual choice as to quantity and quality of goods consumed	Yes	No
Allocation decision	Made by market process	Made by political process

pothole. Lying silently in wait for the unwary motorist, the pothole jars teeth, destroys front-end alignments, bends wheel rims, and snaps axles. Surely its elimination (pothole repair) would benefit many and is a collective good. But who should pay? One line of reasoning is that potholes are found all over the country and are a *nationwide* problem, therefore, they are a *national* problem and should be the responsibility of the *national* government; ergo they should be repaired using funds from the national government, collected from taxpayers nationally. This beguiling syllogism is badly awry, however. By this reasoning, every widespread need, including street sweeping, can be dropped in the lap of the largest available collective agent, the national government, if not yet the United Nations.

A more careful analysis of the pothole can be carried out. The basic principle is that the smallest collective unit that embraces most of the beneficiaries should provide the collective good. In the case of potholes on city streets that are public thoroughfares, the city is the appropriate unit in size. City taxpayers should pay. Note how this policy affects out-of-town visitors: they benefit from well-paved streets, but to the extent that they purchase gas, go shopping, stay in hotels, and eat in restaurants, they contribute both directly and indirectly to the city's coffers and thereby pay a share of the street-maintenance costs. Similarly, distant purchasers of goods manufactured in the city benefit from well-paved streets in that city, because their goods are not damaged when trucked from the factory through the city's streets. They pay for the benefit, however, because the price they pay includes the cost of local taxes paid by the manufacturer and trucker to maintain their city's streets. In other words, we see that even with a small and local collective unit, beneficiaries pay for the collective good regardless of where they are located; the basic principle remains valid. It is the nature of each collective good and the identity of its beneficiaries that determines the appropriate level of responsibility for supplying the good.

The Growth of Collective Goods

The problem of providing collective goods is compounded further by the fact that the number of such goods has grown in recent decades. This has occurred for three reasons. First, the basic nature of some goods has changed, either because of changing technology that affects their exclusion and consumption characteristics or because of changed conditions. The migration of fire protection from individual good to collective good, due to urbanization, exemplifies this shift. The same is true of refuse removal:

in a rural setting it is an individual good but in a city it is a collective good, because both my neighbor and I will benefit if he has his refuse collected regularly, and we will both suffer if he does not.

A second reason for the growth of collective goods is that some have been created by the need to conserve common-pool goods. Air- and water-pollution control, and the negotiation and enforcement of agreements concerning common-pool goods such as whales, tigers, and Antarctica, are examples of such newly created collective goods.

The third reason is that people can and do create collective goods by transforming their individual goods, thereby shifting the burden of payment onto collective shoulders. For example, the small-town resident who throws his garbage on the side of the road instead of subscribing to a refuse-collection service eschews the individual good called waste collection and creates a need for the collective good called highway cleaning.

The reverse is also occurring, however. Some collective goods can be replaced, in part at least, by individual goods. Locks, karate lessons, alarm systems, and home fire-extinguishers are individual goods being used increasingly as partial substitutes for the collective goods of police and fire protection. Furthermore, a wealthy person can transform collective goods into individual goods by having private guards, swimming pool, and gardens. Technological advances make it possible to transform other collective goods into toll or individual goods; for example, autos can now be charged for the use of particular thoroughfares during congested periods, as had long been advocated by William Vickrey.[11]

Worthy Goods

The largest cause of government growth in the United States and Europe, as was noted previously, is the societal decision that certain individual and toll goods, such as food, education, and mass transit—and then all the benefits of the welfare state—are so worthy that their consumption should be encouraged regardless of the consumer's ability to pay. As a result, these *worthy goods* have either been subsidized by government or produced directly by government and supplied to all or to a broad class of eligibles. If no use is made of the exclusion property of individual and toll goods, that is, if there is little or no charge for their use, then in effect the good is being treated as a common-pool or collective good.

There are two different ways to view this transformation. One is to adhere to the basic definitions. Individual and toll goods, because of their innate exclusion and consumption characteristics (as long as the techno-logical means of delivery remain unchanged), cannot be redefined and they do not migrate. Society, acting through government, simply decided to pro-vide certain individual and toll goods—worthy goods—completely or partly at collective expense.

The other way to view the transformation is to consider those indi-vidual and toll goods as having migrated into the class of common-pool and collective goods; that is, on figures 3.1 to 3.3 (pp. 44–47) these goods drifted to the right edge. The explanation of this migration is that (1) everyone benefits to some degree when worthy goods are consumed (i.e., there are positive externalities) and so their consumption can be con-sidered partly joint, which causes a drop downward on the diagram; (2) exclusion has been abandoned because these are goods that all should have, and so they have been shifted to the right on the diagram; the result is more common-pool and collective goods. These two views are comple-mentary and lead to the same result.

The political decision to supply and encourage the consumption of worthy goods regardless of the consumer's ability or willingness to pay results in direct subsidies to private individuals and enterprises or in pro-duction of services by government units. Examples abound: sports arenas, stadiums, cultural centers, museums, and exhibition halls are often built with taxpayer funds and operated with subsidies from taxpayers. Agribusi-nesses and other businesses get government grants and subsidies. Individ-uals receive welfare payments and social services of various kinds, as well as public housing, health care, job training, and day-care services.

The straightforward toll goods of electric, gas, and telephone service may be in the early stages of being similarly treated. For example, a demand that they be provided without charge under certain circumstances, hence rendering them indistinguishable in practice from collective goods, arose following a particularly tragic incident in New England one winter when an elderly couple, incapable of caring for themselves yet living alone, froze to death when their utilities were unwittingly turned off for non-payment of bills.

Not long ago education was regarded as an individual good. Exclusion and individual consumption were clearly identifiable attributes of this good. An education bestowed great and obvious benefits on the recipient, and this much-prized good was sought and sold in the marketplace. In time, however, a new understanding gained ground: the entire society benefited significantly if everyone was educated, much like vaccination. Education was considered to have major, positive side effects associated with it, and therefore it was not only made freely available to all, but its consumption was made mandatory up to a certain age.

An even better example of changing social values, and the designation of an individual good as a worthy one to be supplied at no cost to the beneficiary, is the most basic good: food. Does there exist a purer individual good? Nevertheless, the inevitable consequence of treating food as a purely individual good is that some would starve. Therefore, food is distributed to the poor at collective expense. Whether this action should be taken by government or by other societal institutions can be debated. Another individual good, housing, was similarly defined as a worthy good, and public housing was built for eligible consumers. Unfortunately, public housing has had a mixed record, and support for it is waning. A better approach, a voucher system, for this worthy individual good is described in a later chapter.

At the extreme, one can detect or ascribe joint-consumption characteristics to every individual good and assert that a citizen who lacks one will become disaffected from the larger society; this will lead to social instability, which threatens everyone. By this reasoning, all individual goods have side benefits and positive externalities that benefit everyone and hence should be provided at collective expense. Even cosmetic surgery would qualify, as we would all prefer to face attractive people instead of unattractive ones.

Such tortured interpretations have unfortunate consequences, however. As has been said, all goods are somewhat subject to individual consumption. When they are subsidized, underpriced, or given away without charge, the demand for them increases and public expenditures increase to supply more of them: free goods can become very expensive. But what often happens is that such goods become indistinguishable from common-pool goods and are subject to all the inherent problems of such goods: rampant waste, thoughtless consumption, and possible exhaustion. Anyone associated with free-lunch programs in schools is keenly aware of the prodigious waste that occurs, and scandals associated with free summer-lunch programs in large U.S. cities revealed the same thing: large amounts of food treated as a worthless good and discarded, much like underpriced bread in the Soviet Union that was fed to hogs because it was cheaper than conventional feed. To the extent that the handling of "junk mail" is underpriced, postal service is an impure toll good that has tended to become a casually consumed, exhaustible, common-pool good, like unmetered municipal water.

Medical care in the United States also illustrates this process. Most medical care could be characterized as an individually consumed good readily subject to exclusion, that is, an individual good. However, a gradual change in societal values led to the belief that individual medical care has joint-consumption properties: a lot of people feel better when a sick person is cured. Thus, medical care was proclaimed a right and subsidized or provided "free," and demand exploded. Thus, to a significant degree, medical care became a common-pool good, there for the taking like the fish in the sea. The end to this trend is yet to be seen. Some people want to make medical care a pure collective good, "free" for all, a cure possibly worse than the disease. Others, sobered by the history of government-created, collective goods in the welfare state, re-emphasize the individual-good nature of medical care and advocate strengthening market incentives to contain costs and preserve quality. The outcome remains to be seen.

One can postulate the general rule that individual goods and impure toll goods subsidized to a significant degree or provided without a user charge—that is, goods whose exclusion property is abandoned—will be treated as common-pool goods, subject to all the problems of such goods. The only restraints to infinite consumption of such goods are their exhaustion and the cost of taking the goods. In the case of medical care, it is the nurses, doctors, and hospital beds that can be exhausted, and it is the fuss and bother of making appointments, waiting in lines, and filling out reimbursement claims that constitute the cost of taking the toll-free goods.

Nevertheless, there is general agreement that a humane society should assure the provision of certain individual goods—food, shelter, medical care, and a subsistence income—to the deserving poor (however defined). The unending welfare debate centers on who should be eligible, the amount of assistance, the means of providing it, and the conditions society should impose on the recipient.

The growth of government-supplied individual and toll goods is evidenced by the changing pattern of government expenditures. As illustrated in table 3.2, spending for agricultural subsidies, training and employment, social services, health care, Medicare, income maintenance programs, Social Security, and transportation—all of which are predominantly individual and toll goods—constitutes an estimated 57 percent of all federal government expenditures in the year 2000, up from 27 percent in 1962. (Moreover, the individual and toll goods were identified very narrowly here, so this is a low estimate of the fraction of total spending.) Providing collective goods, one of the most fundamental purposes of government and a reason for its existence, is now a relatively minor activity. This is a source of profound unease for libertarians and conservatives, and highlights the important question of the proper role of government in today's society.

TABLE 3.2—FEDERAL GOVERNMENT SPENDING FOR INDIVIDUAL AND TOLL GOODS (IN BILLIONS OF 1998 DOLLARS)

Function	1962	2000 (est.)
Farm income subsidies	3.222	7.541
Training and employment	0.189	8.005
Social services	0.110	17.841
Health-care services	0.528	132.659
Medicare	0	216.868
Unemployment compensation	3.809	28.230
Housing assistance	0.165	29.174
Food and nutrition maintenance	0.275	39.833
Other income security	2.338	81.230
Social Security	14.365	412.640
Transportation	4.290	43.131
Total	29.291	1,017.156
Total Outlays	106.821	1,785.046
Above functions as percent of total outlays	27	57

Source: *U.S. Budget for Fiscal Year 1999* (Washington, D.C.: U.S. Government Printing Office, 1998), table 3.2, 50–64.

Summary

The starting point for determining the proper roles of government and the private sector is an examination of the goods and services needed in a modern society. Two important properties are useful for classifying goods and services: exclusion and consumption. A good has the property of exclusion if its acquisition or use can readily be denied by the supplier. A suit of clothes has this property; a fish in the sea does not. A good is characterized as a joint-consumption good or an individual-consumption good depending on whether it can or cannot be consumed jointly and simultaneously by many users. A television broadcast is a joint-consumption good; a loaf of bread is not.

Goods can be classified according to the degree to which they possess these two properties. The result is four idealized kinds of goods: individual goods (characterized by exclusion and individual consumption), toll goods (exclusion and joint consumption), common-pool goods (nonexclusion and individual consumption), and collective goods (nonexclusion and joint consumption). Figure 3.4 summarizes these relationships.

Individual goods and toll goods can be supplied by the marketplace, and collective action plays a relatively minor role with respect to such goods, primarily overcoming market failures, establishing ground rules for market transactions, ensuring the safety of individual goods, and regulating

	Easy to exclude	Difficult to exclude
Individual consumption	individual goods (e.g., food, clothing, shelter)	common-pool goods (e.g., fish in the sea)
Joint consumption	toll goods (e.g., cable TV, telephone, electric power)	collective goods (e.g., national defense, felons)

FIGURE 3.4—THE FOUR KINDS OF GOODS IN TERMS OF INTRINSIC CHARACTERISTICS

the means of supplying those toll goods that are natural monopolies. Collective action is indispensable, however, for assuring the supply of collective goods and for providing those individual and toll goods that society decides are to be subsidized and supplied as though they were collective goods. Coercion may be needed to overcome the "free rider" problem. Collective action is often used to protect natural common-pool goods, although in many cases private property rights can do the same even more effectively. Collective action can be taken by private, voluntary organizations, not only by government.

More and more individual and toll goods have been deemed "worthy" and are being treated as collective or common-pool goods. Indeed, the big growth in government has taken place in expenditures for individual and toll goods. Such goods now account for at least 57 percent of all federal government spending, compared to only 27 percent in 1962. In other words, providing goods and services that are intrinsically collective by nature, which is one of the fundamental reasons for the creation and existence of governments, is no longer the dominant activity of the federal government in the United States.

CHAPTER FOUR

Alternative Arrangements for Providing Goods and Services

IN THE PRECEDING chapter we saw the role of collective action in supplying the four kinds of goods. For individual, toll, and common-pool goods, collective action is needed primarily for regulation. In effect, such regulation is a collective good that assures satisfactory supplies of those goods.

With respect to collective goods, collective action is necessary to pay for the goods and thereby to make sure that they are produced. With respect to worthy goods, collective action is needed to decide (1) which individual and toll goods are to be deemed worthy goods, (2) how much of them to supply, and (3) how to pay for them. The essence of collective action, therefore, consists of making decisions and raising money.

Collective action does not mean government action. Groups of people can and do agree voluntarily on collective decisions and collective fund raising even without the formal methods and sanctions available to governments. For example, carpools represent informal collective activity. Swimming pools, golf courses, tennis courts, and cultural institutions are often provided by voluntary membership associations: interested people agree to form a club and pay for the facility through membership dues, entrance fees, and other collective fund-raising actions.

These examples of voluntary collective action are toll goods, where exclusion is possible. Can voluntary associations provide collective goods where exclusion is infeasible? Yes. Some cities have enclaves of private streets for which maintenance is financed by homeowner or neighborhood associations. Collective action in such circumstances may be legally enforceable by a requirement or covenant in the property deed stipulating that anyone buying property in the area is required to belong to the association and pay a portion of its expenses. Housing cooperatives and condominiums also have such features.

But collective action can be entirely voluntary and still be effective in providing collective goods. When the collective organization is relatively small and its members have similar values and interests, informal social pressures can be adequate to assure that everyone contributes his or her fair share and no one is a "free rider." A volunteer fire department is a common example. Tenant patrols and block patrols in crime-ridden areas of large cities are additional examples of voluntary collective action used to provide public safety, a collective good. Payment can be in the form of contributed services, rather than money.

When the number of affected individuals is large and interests are diverse, purely voluntary action is no longer adequate to provide collective goods. Organizations such as governments have to be created with the authority to use force if necessary to take the money or property needed to supply collective goods. People become "forced riders." In short, government is an instrument for making and enforcing decisions about collective goods: which ones to provide, which ones (of those that are intrinsically individual or toll goods) to finance at least partly by involuntary collective contributions, how to allocate the costs or contributions, and how to allocate the goods themselves if they are not pure collective goods and are subject to congestion.

Collective goods may be produced directly by public employees working for public agencies, but other institutional arrangements can also deliver collective goods. For example, governments can purchase collective goods such as fire protection and street cleaning from private firms. Even an "inherently governmental" function, one that is a basic function of government, can be supplied in various ways, as this chapter shows, not only by government employees. Certain functions, however, are reserved for government: making and enforcing laws; spending governments funds; and deciding to deprive individuals of life, liberty, or property.

Providing, Arranging, and Producing Services

It is useful to distinguish the three basic participants in the delivery of a service: the service consumer, the service producer, and the service arranger or provider. The consumer obtains or receives the service directly and may be an individual, everyone residing in a defined geographic area, a government agency, a private organization, a class of individuals with common characteristics (e.g., poor people, students, exporters, auto workers, or farmers), or a government agency obtaining support services.

The service producer directly performs the work or delivers the service to the consumer. A producer can be a government unit, a special district, a voluntary association of citizens, a private firm, a nonprofit agency, or, in certain instances, the consumer himself. The Department of Defense produces national defense services, as does Boeing. A county government may produce public health services. A tenant association produces a service when it patrols its building. A private firm under contract to the municipality produces tree-pruning and grass-mowing services in a public park. An individual who brings his empty bottles to the recycling center is acting as both producer and consumer of that service.

The service arranger (also called the service provider) assigns the producer to the consumer, or vice versa, or selects the producer who will serve the consumer. Frequently, but not always, the arranger is a government unit. The service arranger may be the municipality in which the consumer is located, the federal government, a voluntary association, or the service consumer himself. For collective goods, the arranger can usefully be viewed as the collective-decision unit, the unit that articulates the demand for such goods. As discussed later, it is possible to have joint arrangers.

The distinction between providing or arranging a service and producing it is profound.[1] It is at the heart of the entire concept of privatization and puts the role of government in perspective. With respect to many collective goods, government is essentially an arranger or provider—an instrument of society for deciding what shall be done collectively, for whom, to what degree or at what level of supply, and how to pay for it. For example, government may levy taxes to pay for cleaning the sidewalks, or it may require property owners to clean them at their own expense or effort.

When a city government hires a paving contractor to resurface a street, the city is the arranger, the firm is the producer, and the people who use the street are the consumers of this particular collective good—street repaving. A county government is the service arranger when it contracts with a church group, the producer, to operate a day-care center for working mothers, the consumers. A National Merit Scholarship winner is a consumer of educational services but also acts as service arranger by choosing a college to produce the educational service, as does the federal government when it hires a contractor to manage and operate a national laboratory.

A government that decides to provide a service at collective expense does not have to produce the service using government employees and equipment. Opposition to privatization often comes from those who do not appreciate the difference between providing and producing and mistakenly assume that if government divests itself of the producer function, it must automatically abandon its role of provider as well. Thus, false alarms are raised about privatizing services that are said to be "inherently governmental"; the responsibility for providing the service can be retained by government, and government can pay for it, but government does not have to continue producing it directly.

The arranger has significant responsibilities with respect to collective goods such as: to levy and collect assessments, and to decide which services are to be provided, the level of service, and the level of expenditures to be made, all in the absence of unanimous agreement among members of the collective unit.

When the arranger and the producer are one and the same, a *bureaucratic* cost is incurred, the cost of maintaining and operating a hierarchical system. When the arranger is different from the producer, there is a *transaction* cost, the cost of hiring and dealing with an independent producer. The relative magnitude of these two costs determines whether it is worth separating the arranging and producing functions.[2]

Institutional Arrangements

Given the difference between providing and producing services, we can identify distinct institutional arrangements for delivering services, while bearing in mind that unambiguous definitions are not always possible. Different arrangements arise because government can serve as arranger or producer, and so can the private sector. This leads to four classes of arrangements, which can be further divided into ten particular arrangements according to the specific ways that the arranger, producer, and consumer interact. Figure 4.1 depicts the conceptual relationship among the

Producer	Arranger	
	Public	Private
Public	• Government service • Intergovernmental agreements	• Government vending
Private	• Contracts • Franchises • Grants	• Free market • Voluntary service • Self-service • Vouchers

FIGURE 4.1—ARRANGEMENTS FOR PROVIDING "PUBLIC" SERVICES
Note: See Table 4.10 (p. 107) for greater detail.

ten arrangements. Special attention should be drawn to the seven arrangements in which the private sector is the producer. Privatization generally involves the use of one or more of these arrangements, which are examined in turn in the remainder of this chapter: (1) government service, (2) government vending, (3) intergovernmental agreements, (4) contracts, (5) franchises, (6) grants, (7) vouchers, (8) free market, (9) voluntary service, and (10) self service.[3]

One might point to an eleventh arrangement, a mandate, where government requires a private entity to provide a service but leaves it up to the "mandatee" to arrange it. Government-mandated medical insurance provided by employers is an example. This is not treated as a separate arrangement here, however, inasmuch as it is actually implemented through one of the other institutional arrangements.

Government Service

The term *government service* denotes the delivery of a service by a government unit using its own employees; government acts as both the service arranger and the service producer. The unit may be a government department or bureau, or a government corporation such as the Tennessee Valley Authority or AMTRAK. Examples of conventional municipal, county, state, and federal government services are legion.

Nationalized or state-owned enterprises are also referred to here as "government services" even though they do not operate as government departments. For example, Renault, the French automobile manufacturer, was nationalized shortly after World War II, and so the French government, in effect, makes automobiles. In Greece and Mexico some private firms that had received government loans, which they were unable (or unwilling, in the corrupt case of the Philippines under President Marcos) to repay, ultimately fell into the hands of the government. In this way, many governments found themselves running hotels, mines, factories, merchant ships, and miscellaneous other commercial businesses far from their traditional roles. Elsewhere ideology prevailed and led to similar outcomes. Socialist governments in developing countries were led by foreign advisers to believe that state-owned enterprises were the fast track to economic development. City governments in the Soviet Union operated hotels, bakeries, breweries, retail shops, and factories that made household goods.[4] In Egypt nationalization under President Nasser led to a remarkable situation in which the government was making beer (in a Moslem country, no less) and Coca-Cola. Part 3 of this book discusses the privatization of such enterprises.

Government Vending

One can purchase goods and services from a government agency, for example, buying rights for water, minerals, and timber, and for grazing livestock on government-owned land, and one can lease such government assets as buildings and land. The New York City Police Department "rents out" its officers for private events at stadiums and theaters, for $27 per hour.[5] A private sponsor of a parade on public streets or a rock concert may pay to have a public agency clean up afterward. In Michigan, private bus companies could buy workers' compensation insurance from the state's Accident Fund[6] (which has since been privatized by selling it to an insurance company). In these cases, government is competing with private firms. Government is the producer and the private individual or organization is the arranger.

Government vending, as defined here, is not the same as imposing a user fee for government services. When government charges for supplying water, power, or bus rides, or forces private firms to purchase government services, for example, unemployment insurance from a state agency, it is merely charging the consumer directly for the government service, for which the government is the arranger. In government vending, the consumer is the arranger.

Intergovernmental Agreements

One government can hire or pay another one to supply a service. A local school district does that when, lacking a high school of its own, it arranges to send its pupils to the high school in a neighboring district and pays that district. It is also commonplace for small communities to purchase library, recreation, and fire-protection services from specialized government units that are organized by and sell their services to several general-purpose governments in the region. Counties often contract with cities and pay them to maintain county roads within city limits. States contract with cities and counties to provide social services. Reassignment of service responsibilities between jurisdictions is occurring to a significant degree in an attempt to handle regional problems better and to cope with rising costs. Such institutional arrangements are *intergovernmental agreements*. One government is the producer, but another is the service arranger.

Intergovernmental agreements are common. A 1992 study with responses from 1,504 municipalities and counties in the United States found that intergovernmental agreements were widely used for sixty-four common local government services. Table 4.1 lists selected services provided through

**TABLE 4.1—CITY AND COUNTY SERVICES SUPPLIED
BY INTERGOVERNMENTAL AGREEMENTS**

Service	Percentages of cities and counties using intergovernmental agreements
Mental-health programs	67
Child-welfare programs	63
Public-health programs	57
Prisons/jails	53
Drug/alcohol-treatment programs	52
Tax assessment	51
Bus transportation	49
Sanitary inspection	48
Homeless shelters	40
Libraries	39
Hospital operation/management	39
Delinquent tax collection	38
Airport operation	35
Programs for the elderly	34
Sewage collection and treatment	33
Animal shelters	29
Solid-waste disposal	27
Water treatment	26
Museums	26

Note: Based on 1,504 responses to a survey of 4,935 governments.

Source: Derived from Rowan Miranda and Karlyn Andersen, "Alternative Service Delivery in Local Government, 1982–1992," *Municipal Year Book 1994* (Washington, D.C.: International City Management Association, 1994), 26–35, table 3/6.

this arrangement by more than 25 percent of the responding localities. Intergovernmental agreements were most frequently used for social services.[7]

The Lakewood Plan makes extensive use of this institutional arrangement for service delivery. Lakewood, a city in Los Angeles County, was purchasing forty-one different services from the county in 1981; seventy-six other cities also purchased one or more services from the county. The cities formed an organization to tend to their common concerns, the California Contract Cities Association. All these cities purchased election services; other county services being marketed included animal regulation; emergency ambulance service; enforcement of health ordinances; engineering services; fire and police protection; library services; sewer maintenance; park maintenance; recreation services; tax assessment and collection; hospitalization of city prisoners; personnel services such as recruitment, examination, and certification; prosecution; building inspection; weed abatement;

school fire-safety officers; mobile-home and trailer-park inspection; milk inspection; rodent control; mental health services; tree trimming; bridge maintenance; preparation and installation of street signs; street sweeping; traffic-signal maintenance; traffic striping and marking; traffic-law enforcement; business-license issuing and enforcement; and crossing guards.

Contracts

Governments contract not only with other governments but also with private firms and nonprofit organizations for goods and services. In this arrangement the private organization is the producer and government is the arranger, which pays the producer. Such "contracting out" is the arrangement most commonly referred to when talking about privatizing conventional public services (as distinguished from privatizing government-owned enterprises and assets). In a contract arrangement, government ideally is (1) an articulator of democratically expressed demands for public goods and services, (2) a skillful purchasing agent, (3) a sophisticated inspector of the goods and services that it purchases from the private sector, (4) an efficient collector of fair taxes, and (5) a parsimonious disburser of proper and timely payments to the contractor.

Government contracting is commonplace. Most of the tangible goods—supplies, equipment, and facilities—used by governments in the United States are purchased from contractors, as little manufacturing, construction, or food production is actually done by government employees. This is true even of sensitive military equipment, for although some munitions are manufactured in federal arsenals, most are obtained from private producers. At the local level, roads, schools, and government offices are generally constructed for governments by private builders under contractual arrangements, and pencils, desks, fire hoses, uniforms, food (for pupils, patients, and prisoners), automobiles, guns, garbage trucks, and computers are bought from private vendors.

In addition to contracting for material goods, municipal governments contract with private organizations for "output" services delivered directly to the public, such as refuse collection, ambulance service, street-light maintenance, street paving, and a wide variety of social services—the last mostly through not-for-profit organizations. Governments also contract for a wide variety of "input" services, i.e., support services such as grounds maintenance, custodial functions, secretarial and clerical work, laundry service, computer center operation, vehicle repair, microfilming, photography, printing, claims processing, and transportation.

More unusual examples also abound. In 1998 New York City contracted out the management and maintenance of its world-famous Central Park to a nonprofit organization that had proved its capability over twenty years.[8] The U.S. Mint contracts out part of its coin-production work. During the Cold War a private contractor manned and operated the Distant Early Warning line, to detect airplanes and missiles coming toward North America over the Arctic Ocean. The U.S. government hired a private firm to carry out monitoring and surveillance of the cease-fire line in Sinai between Egyptian and Israeli forces, a task that traditionally would have been performed by a military unit. Mercenary troops have been used since ancient times and private air forces came into being in recent times to conduct wars under contract.

In Britain the Local Government Act of 1988 mandated competitive tendering (contracting) for six common municipal services: residential refuse collection, street cleaning, cleaning of public buildings, vehicle maintenance, grounds maintenance, and catering services.[9] In Denmark most cities contract with a private firm, the Falck Company, for fire and ambulance service; the majority of the population receives protection by this arrangement. In Sweden about two-thirds of the people receive fire protection from private contractors.[10]

Services generally can be separated into their component subservices, which may be provided through various arrangements. Thus, police service can be disaggregated into police communication, preventive patrol, traffic control, parking enforcement, towing away illegally parked cars, detention facilities, training courses, police-car maintenance, and so forth.[11] Different components of this array of services can be provided through different institutional structures in the same local government: government service, intergovernmental contracts, contracts with private firms, and voluntary service, for example. This issue is pursued later in this chapter.

An important variant of contracting for service arises when government retains ownership of a facility or asset but contracts with a private firm to operate it. Examples are water-supply systems, wastewater (i.e., sewage) treatment plants, resource recovery plants, sanitary landfills, maintenance garages, parking garages, airports, hospitals, arenas, and convention centers. This differs from leasing in that the private firm does not use the asset in its own business but manages it on behalf of the government and is paid by the government.

It is interesting to note that a contract can have a negative price; that is, the private producer could pay the government for the right to perform the service. For example, abandoned automobiles in some cities are picked up by private firms under contract to the city, and, depending on scrap prices, their bids call for payment either to or from the city. This may also be true for the collection of recyclables.

Extent of contracting.   Virtually all governments contract for services. A 1987 survey of all cities with populations over 5,000 and counties over 25,000 revealed that 99 percent contracted out services.[12] (The survey response rate was only 19 percent, however.) All told, at least 200 services are provided by contractors to governments in the United States; they are identified in table 4.2.

TABLE 4.2—CITY AND COUNTY SERVICES CONTRACTED OUT TO PRIVATE FIRMS

Addiction treatment, adoption, air-pollution abatement, airport operation, airport fire and crash response, airport services, alarm-system maintenance, alcohol treatment, ambulance, animal control, architectural, auditorium management, auditing

Beach management, billing and collection, bridge (construction, inspection, and maintenance), building demolition, building rehabilitation, buildings and grounds (janitorial, maintenance, security), building and mechanical inspection, burial of indigents, bus-system management and operation, bus-shelter maintenance

Cafeteria and restaurant operation, catch-basin cleaning, cemetery administration, child protection, collection of child-support payments, civil defense communication, clerical, communication maintenance, community-center operation, composting, computer operations, consultant services, convention-center management, crime laboratory, crime prevention and patrol, custodial services

Data entry, data processing, day care, debt collection, document preparation, drug and alcohol treatment programs

Economic development, election administration, electrical inspection, electric power, elevator inspection, emergency maintenance, emergency medical services, environmental services

Family counseling, financial services, fire alarm services, fire-hydrant maintenance, fire prevention and suppression, flood-control planning, foster-home care

Golf-course management and operation, graphic arts, guard service

Health inspection, health services, home-care service, homeless-shelter operation, hospital management, hospital services, housing inspection and code enforcement, housing management

Industrial development, insect and rodent control, institutional care, insurance administration, irrigation

Jail and detention, janitorial services, juvenile delinquency programs

Labor relations, laboratory, landscaping, laundry, lawn maintenance, leaf collection, legal, legal aid, library operation, licensing, lottery operation

Management consulting, mapping, marina services, median-strip maintenance, mosquito control, moving and storage, museum and cultural facilities

Noise abatement, nursing, nutrition

Office-machine maintenance, opinion polling

Paratransit system operation, park management and maintenance, parking enforcement, parking lot and garage operation, parking meter servicing, parking ticket processing, patrolling, payroll processing, personal services, photographic services, physician

TABLE 4.2—(CONTINUED)

services, planning, plumbing inspection, police communication, port and harbor management, printing, prisoner transportation, probation, property acquisition, public administrator services, public health services, public relations and information, public works

Records maintenance, recreation services, recycling, rehabilitation, resource recovery, risk management

School buses, secretarial services, security services, sewage treatment, sewer maintenance, sidewalk repair, snow (plowing, removal, sanding), social services, soil conservation, solid waste (collection, transfer, disposal), street services (construction, maintenance, resurfacing, sweeping), street lighting (construction and maintenance), surveying

Tax collection (assessing, bill processing, receipt), tennis-court maintenance, test scoring, towing, traffic control (markings, sign and signal installation and maintenance), training of government employees, transit management, transportation of elderly and disabled, treasury functions, tree services (planting, pruning, removal)

Utility billing, utility meter reading

Vehicle fleet management, vehicle maintenance, vehicle towing and storage, voter registration

Wastewater treatment, water-meter reading and maintenance, water pollution abatement, water supply and distribution, weed abatement, welfare administration, worker compensation claims

Zoning and subdivision control, zoo management

Table 4.3 shows the percentage of cities and counties, out of a total survey response of 1,504 governments (31 percent of those queried), that contracted in 1992 with private for-profit and nonprofit organizations for each of sixty-four services.[13] This survey parallels earlier ones conducted in 1982[14] and 1988.[15] The table also shows the percentage of respondents that use in-house work forces exclusively or in part. (Some cities use their own employees for part of the work and contract out the remainder; for example, private buses may operate under contract on some bus routes while other routes are operated by a county agency.) On average, each service is contracted out by 21 percent of local governments. The thirteen services listed in the health and human services category are most frequently obtained by contract, primarily from not-for-profit agencies, although competitive contracting for social services from for-profit firms is growing;[16] on average each service in that category is contracted out by 28 percent of the communities. The thirty-five services listed in the public works, transportation, and support categories are also commonly contracted out, mostly to for-profit firms; on average each service is contracted out by 24 percent of the communities.

State agencies also contract out, although the available data from 1997, shown in table 4.4, are presented in a different format than that in table 4.3. Transportation, administrative and general services, corrections, and social

TABLE 4.3—CITY AND COUNTY SERVICES SUPPLIED IN-HOUSE AND BY CONTRACT

| | Percentage of cities and counties | | | |
| | using their own employees | | contracting with | |
Service area	entirely	in part	for-profit companies	nonprofit agencies
Public works and transportation	57	22	22	2
Public utilities	45	6	31	3
Public safety	60	11	15	3
Health and human resources	28	17	11	17
Parks and recreation	72	19	7	3
Culture and arts	32	19	3	23
Support functions	65	19	14	1
Weighted average	55	18	16	5

Note: Row totals do not equal 100% because other arrangements (e.g., franchise, voluntary, and grants) are also used.

Source: Derived from Rowan Miranda and Karlyn Andersen, "Alternative Service Delivery in Local Government, 1982–1992," *Municipal Year Book 1994* (Washington, D.C.: International City Management Association, 1994), 26–35, appendix.

services were the most commonly privatized program areas. A total of 416 state agencies, representing all fifty states, privatized an average of 7.5 services per agency. The data refer to privatization by all methods, not only contracting, but the latter accounts for 80 percent of state privatizations.[17]

An estimated $42 billion was spent in 1976 by all governments in the United States on purchased services, including both private and intergovernmental contracts,[18] but by 1992 the federal government alone was contracting out $44.4 billion in services (as distinguished from the purchase of physical goods).[19] (As long ago as 1977, of the activities classified as commercial and industrial in the Defense Department—functions such as food service, laundry, airplane and vehicle maintenance, and construction—about a quarter of the total effort as measured in man-years was being purchased from the private sector.[20]) These are all rough figures, as it is difficult to identify and tabulate the relevant activities on a uniform basis. As for the amount of money spent by state and local governments on contracts for services, reliable data are lacking.

Growth of contracting. A total of 596 cities responded to both the 1982 and 1992 surveys, which were very similar, and fifty-nine municipal services were included in both surveys. This provided an unparalleled opportunity

TABLE 4.4—PRIVATIZED STATE PROGRAMS

Service area	Number of state programs
Transportation	453
Administration and general services	310
Corrections	295
Social services	287
Natural resources and environmental protection	277
Mental health and retardation	219
Juvenile rehabilitation	215
Health	207
Higher education	190
Parks and recreation	137
Education	101
Labor	95
Public safety and state police	77
Treasury	63

Source: Keon S. Chi and Cindy Jasper, *Private Practices: A Review of Privatization in State Government* (Lexington, Ky.: Council of State Governments, 1998), 22–49.

to measure a very elusive parameter: the degree of privatization. By comparing the same services in the same cities after ten years, it was found that the average privatization level increased from 12.6 to 27.8 percent, that is, the number of privatized services in those cities more than doubled, increasing by 121 percent.[21] This study was not restricted to contracting, however; it also included franchising, vouchers, volunteers, and self-service in its measure of privatization, although these other arrangements were used by fewer than 5 percent of the cities. The breadth of privatization arrangements used for these fifty-nine services also increased: the number of *arrangements* used to deliver these services in those cities rose by 40 percent as cities took advantage of a larger array of alternatives to deliver the services. Among medium-sized cities, the degree of privatization was greatest in wealthy, fiscally healthy, suburban cities.[22]

Characteristics of contracting.   Contracting is feasible and works well under the following set of conditions: (I) the work to be done is specified unambiguously; (2) several potential producers are available, and a competitive climate either exists or can be created and sustained; (3) the government is able to monitor the contractor's performance; and (4) appropriate terms are included in the contract document and enforced. Details on how to contract for services are presented in chapter 7.

Of all the privatization options, contracting has engendered the most discussion and heated debate. The battle lends itself readily to ideological posturing and unsubstantiated assertions by both sides. The arguments cited in favor of contracting can be summarized as follows:

1. Contracting is more efficient because (a) it harnesses competitive forces and brings the pressure of the marketplace to bear on inefficient producers; (b) it permits better management, free of most of the distracting influences that are characteristic of overtly political organizations; (c) the costs and benefits of managerial decisions are felt more directly by the decision maker, whose own rewards are often directly at stake.

2. Contracting makes it possible for government to take advantage of specialized skills that are lacking in its own workforce; it overcomes obsolete salary limitations and antiquated civil service restrictions.

3. Contracting permits a quicker response to new needs and facilitates experimentation with new programs.

4. Contracting allows flexibility in adjusting the size of a program up or down in response to changing demand and changing availability of funds.

5. Contracting avoids large capital outlays; it spreads costs over time at a relatively constant and predictable level.

6. Contracting permits economies of scale regardless of the size of the government entity.

7. Contracting a portion of the work offers a yardstick for comparing costs.

8. Contracting fosters good management because the cost of service is highly visible in the price of the contract, whereas the cost of government service is usually obscured.

9. Contracting can reduce dependence on a single supplier (a government monopoly) and so lessens the vulnerability of the service to strikes, slowdowns, and inept leadership.

10. Contracting creates opportunities for entrepreneurs from minority groups.

11. Contracting limits the size of government in terms of the number of employees.

12. Contracting spurs private-sector research on innovative ways to satisfy society's needs.

There is substantial opposition to privatization, as is discussed in chapter 11, and opponents of contracting out—usually leaders of government-employee unions and often middle managers in government—counter these arguments in favor of privatization and raise the following warnings:

1. Contracting is ultimately more expensive because of
   - corrupt practices in awarding contracts;[23]
   - "outrageous and pernicious work practices" among private-sector unions;[24]
   - high profits, whereas government is nonprofit;
   - the cost of layoffs and unemployment for government workers;
   - the shortage of qualified suppliers and therefore the lack of competition;
   - the cost of managing the contract and monitoring contractor performance;
   - the low marginal cost of expanding government service;
   - cost-plus-fixed-fee contracts, which provide no incentive for efficiency;
   - the absence of effective competition after government gets out of the business, leaving government at the mercy of the contractor in subsequent contracts.
2. Contracting nullifies the basic principle of merit employment and subverts laws regarding veterans' preference in government employment; it is demoralizing to employees, deprives government of the skills it needs in-house, and therefore is fundamentally debilitating of government capability.
3. Contracting limits the flexibility of government in responding to emergencies.
4. Contracting results in undesirable dependence on contractors and leaves the public vulnerable to strikes and slowdowns by the contractor's personnel and to bankruptcy of the firm.
5. Contracting depends on adequately written contracts, which are difficult to draw up, and results in a loss of government accountability and control.

6. Contracting limits the opportunity to realize economies of scale.

7. Entrusting services to private organizations increases the political power of the latter and creates a lobby for more government spending.

8. Contracting results in disproportionate job losses among members of minority communities, many of whom are government employees.

9. Contracting causes a loss of autonomy for the contractor, for example, co-opting a private, nonprofit social service agency and thereby decreasing the agency's effectiveness in the long run by muting its role as critic and social conscience.

Many of these claims and counterclaims are obviously in direct conflict. The contractor is said to lose autonomy to government and yet is held to be neither accountable to nor under sufficient control of the government. It is claimed that contracting both reaps and dissipates economies of scale. It surmounts civil service obstacles and subverts the merit system. It increases and reduces government flexibility. It makes scarce talents available to the government and deprives government of those same talents. It is efficient and inefficient.

Some of the arguments against contracting can be turned around. As for vulnerability to service disruption, strikes by government employees have the same effect as strikes by private employees. Those who fear a loss of accountability and control under contract service ignore the problem of holding someone accountable in government and ignore the complaint, often voiced by elected officials, that they cannot adequately control government agencies.

Considerable academic attention has been devoted to the theoretical differences in motivation and performance of public and private organizations. William Niskanen Jr., Graham Allison, Thomas Borcherding, Charles Wolf Jr., Lawrence Bailis, Anthony Downs, Hal Rainey, Marshall Meyer, Lyle Fitch, Peter Drucker, James Bennett, and Manuel Johnson are among the many who have considered the matter.[25] One can summarize this literature as follows:

1. In the public sector there is little incentive to perform efficiently, and management lacks effective control over human and capital resources; in the private sector generally there are

both carrots, in the form of raises and promotions, and sticks, in the form of demotions and firings.

2. Because capital budgets and operating budgets are generally arrived at through separate processes in the public sector, the opportunity to make tradeoffs between the two is limited. For example, it is more difficult to coordinate an investment in labor-saving equipment with a reduction in the size of the labor force.

3. Whereas a private firm generally prospers by satisfying paying customers, a monopolistic public agency can prosper even if the customers remain unsatisfied. When a private company performs poorly, it tends to go out of business; when a public agency performs poorly, it often gets a bigger budget. Paradoxically, the budget can grow even as customer dissatisfaction grows; in this respect a rising crime rate is good for a police department, a housing shortage is good for a housing agency, and an epidemic is good for a health department.

For all these reasons, one would expect the private sector to be a more efficient producer of services, and therefore "contracting out" would be superior to "in-house" work. It must be stressed, however, that the difference does not arise because the people in the public sector are somehow inferior to those in the private sector; they are not. The issue is not public vs. private but monopoly vs. competition.

Nevertheless, opponents of contract work raise these legitimate points, and no matter how persuasive the theoretical analysis or how deep the convictions of interested individuals, the issue must be resolved by empirical evidence. Such evidence is presented in chapter 6.

Franchises

Franchising is another institutional arrangement used for providing services. An exclusive franchise is an award of monopoly privileges to a private firm to supply a particular service in a specified area, usually with price regulation by a government agency. (*Concession* is another term for this arrangement.) Nonexclusive or multiple franchises can also be awarded, as in the case of taxis. Leasing of government facilities, buildings, or land to private firms for business use could be considered a form of franchising. Franchises are not the same as simple licenses for selling food and liquor, practicing medicine, and the like, which involve no comparable arrangement between government and the licensee. "Public-private partnership" is in vogue as a substitute for "franchise"—and, for that matter, for practically any agreement between government and the private sector.

With franchises, as with contracts, government is the arranger and a private organization is the producer; however, the two are differentiated by the means of payment to the producer. Government (the arranger) pays the producer for contract service, but the consumer pays the producer for franchise service.

Franchises are particularly suitable for providing toll goods, such as electric power, gas and water distribution, wastewater treatment, waste-to-energy incinerators, telecommunications service, ports and airports, roads and bridges, and bus transportation. Intercity toll roads in France are financed, built, owned, operated, and maintained by private firms for a fixed number of years and then turned over to the government. The "chunnel" under the English Channel is a franchise from the British and French governments. Private toll roads are reappearing in the United States.[26] Concessions for food and other services on limited-access highways and in publicly owned parks, stadiums, airports, and so on, are also franchises. Table 4.5 shows the use of franchises for selected local government services.

TABLE 4.5—CITY AND COUNTY SERVICES SUPPLIED BY PRIVATE FIRMS UNDER FRANCHISE ARRANGEMENTS

Service	Percentage using franchises
Gas utility operation and management	20
Electric utility operation and management	15
Commercial solid-waste collection	14
Residential solid-waste collection	13
Solid-waste disposal	7
Airport operation	6
Vehicle towing and storage	5
Utility meter reading	4
Ambulance service	2

Note: Based on 1,504 responses to a survey of 4,935 local governments.

Source: Derived from Rowan Miranda and Karlyn Andersen, "Alternative Service Delivery in Local Government, 1982–1992," *Municipal Year Book 1994* (Washington, D.C.: International City Management Association, 1994), 26–35, table 3/7.

Grants

Toll goods and individual goods can be subsidized if their consumption is to be encouraged. They can be provided through two different arrangements: grants and vouchers. A *grant* is a subsidy given by government to the producer. The grant may be in the form of money, tax exemption or other tax benefits, low-cost loans, or loan guarantees. The effect of such grants is to reduce the price of the particular good for eligible consumers, who can then go to the subsidized producers in the marketplace and buy more than they would otherwise be able to.

Under a grant arrangement the producer is a private firm (either profit-making or not), both the government and the consumer are involved as coarrangers (the government selects certain producers to receive grants, and the consumer chooses the specific producer), and usually both the government and the consumer make payments to the producer.

There are numerous examples of grants. It seems as though every industry has had some special grant or tax-abatement program tailored for it; subsidies for farm products are obvious examples. Health facilities have also been receiving large grants over a prolonged period to make medical care available and accessible to more people. Other grants have gone to the private housing–construction industry to build low-cost housing, and to privately owned bus lines. Cultural institutions, performing arts groups, and artists receive government grants, reflecting a judgment that their services benefit the public at large and should therefore be subsidized.

Vouchers

Like grants, *vouchers* are designed to subsidize the consumption of particular goods by a particular category of consumers. Unlike grants, however, which subsidize the producer and paternalistically restrict the consumer's choice to subsidized producers (if the consumer wishes to use the subsidy), vouchers subsidize the consumer and permit him or her to choose freely among the specified goods in the marketplace. With vouchers as with grants, the producer is a private firm, but with grants both government and the consumer select the producer, whereas with vouchers the consumer alone makes the choice.

Vouchers may be direct or indirect. Food stamps go directly to an individual to be spent at the grocer's, whereas for housing the individual selects the housing unit and the government agency sends the monthly payment to the owner. Vouchers can be capped or uncapped; that is, they may have a definite dollar value, as do food stamps or housing vouchers, or they can be open ended, as in Medicare, which pays all but a stated portion of medical expenses, or the GI Bill, which paid college tuition expenses for veterans. Other issues in the design of voucher programs include eligibility of recipients; regulations on using the vouchers; the relation between the value of the voucher and the cost of service; requirements for co-payments or deductibles; whether or not the individual can add a supplementary payment to the voucher; and the nature of the payment—an expenditure, a tax credit, or a tax subsidy.[27]

To provide food for low-income people, one could have a system of government-run farms, canneries, and food markets as in the former Soviet Union, or a system like Mexico's CONASUPO, a government agency that buys food at market prices and sells it at a loss through stores located in low-income areas. Alternatively one could give to eligible recipients vouchers (food stamps) to be used in ordinary, existing food stores and thereby take advantage of market systems for growing, processing, and distributing food. Not only are vouchers far more cost-effective, but they afford greater dignity to the recipient, who buys food at the same store everyone else uses instead of at a special store labeled, in effect, "This store is for poor people only." CONASUPO by contrast, is not targeted and can subsidize anybody. (My friend, a well-paid United Nations employee stationed in Mexico City, used to do his shopping at the agency's stores, and stories abound of maids going in chauffeured autos to do the household shopping for their masters.) Urban bus systems have the same shortcoming if they are subsidized and fares do not cover the full costs: all riders receive fare subsidies instead of only a targeted population. Vouchers for low-income passengers would be more cost-effective.

With a voucher the consumer is strongly motivated to shop wisely and look for bargains because the money will go farther and can buy more; the behavior of a subsidized consumer should be indistinguishable from that of an unsubsidized one. The advantages of vouchers are recognized, and their use by state and local governments has been growing. They are used for food, housing, medical services, transportation, child care, education, programs for the elderly, home care, ambulance service, recreation and cultural services, and drug and alcohol treatment. They are also being used for job training for experienced but displaced workers.[28] Less common uses are in criminal justice (as rewards for turning in guns and for good behavior on parole), and in environmental protection (for turning in gas-powered lawn mowers and for installing low-flush toilets).[29]

As with all arrangements, there are limitations as to how and when to use vouchers. The ideal conditions under which a voucher system will work well can be summarized as follows:[30]

1. There are widespread differences in people's preferences for the service, and these differences are accepted by the public as legitimate.

2. There are many competing suppliers of the service, or start-up costs are low and additional suppliers can readily enter the market if the demand is there.

3. Individuals are well informed about market conditions, including the cost and quality of the service and where it may be obtained.

4. The quality of the service is easily determined by the user, or else the producer is licensed and inspected by the state.

5. Individuals have incentives to shop aggressively for the service.

6. The service is relatively inexpensive and purchased frequently, so the user learns by experience.

Food stamps satisfy all these conditions. Medicare and Medicaid satisfy only the first condition: Competition by service providers is conspicuously absent because of regulation by state agencies and medical societies; consumers are not well informed about service cost and quality; the quality of service is difficult for consumers to gauge; consumers have little incentive to shop; and the service is purchased infrequently. A different approach to medical care for the indigent would be to replace Medicaid "vouchers" with health-insurance vouchers; the latter satisfy the above conditions better than the former. Vouchers that would enable poor people to purchase health insurance offer the prospect of ending the inflationary pressure on health-care costs and bringing them under control.

To the extent that enhanced citizen choice is valued, vouchers (subsidies to consumers) are better than grants (subsidies to producers), although in both cases beneficiaries are restricted to the particular good. Cash grants without this restriction would allow even greater choice, but they have a serious defect: people have a limited capacity to consume food and shelter but an unlimited capacity to consume money. Taxpayers may be willing to pay for life's necessities for the poor but less willing to trust welfare recipients with cash allowances. Moreover, people who are ineligible are more likely to try to obtain cash assistance than to obtain food stamps and public housing; these programs are relatively unattractive to the nonpoor

and therefore can be better targeted to help the truly needy.[31] Nevertheless, cash is used in one successful voucher program: day care for children.
Mothers required to work or undergo training in exchange for assistance
can get cash to pay for informal child care.

Note that vouchers as defined here are entirely different than vouchers
in Russia and other post-socialist countries, where they are used to give citizens shares of former state-owned enterprises as a means of establishing
private ownership. The use of such vouchers is discussed in chapter 8.

Free Market

The *market system* is the most common of all service arrangements. It is used
to provide most ordinary individual and toll goods. The consumer arranges
for service and selects the producer, which is a private firm. Government is
not involved in the transaction in any significant way, although it may establish service, safety, and labeling standards. For example, a common arrangement for refuse collection in small American cities is private collection. For
reasons of public health the local government may require that all households have their refuse collected at least once a week but may leave it up to
each household to select and pay a private firm for the service. Similarly, government can require an industrial plant to clean its effluent stream, but the
work can be performed through the marketplace.

Market arrangements are widely used to supply such necessary goods
and services as food, clothing, water, electricity, housing, health care, education, transportation, manufactured goods, and income for retirees.

Voluntary Service

Charitable organizations, through their voluntary efforts, provide many
human services to people in need. Other voluntary associations perform
community services such as recreation programs run by sports enthusiasts,
protective patrol by neighborhood associations, and fire protection by volunteer fire departments. These services might otherwise be provided
directly by government agencies. In this arrangement, the voluntary
mutual-aid association acts as service arranger and either produces the service directly, using its members or employees, or hires and pays a private
firm to do the work.

The organization may be an existing one or may be specifically created
for a particular purpose. For individuals to coalesce and form such an
organization, certain conditions must prevail: (1) the need or demand for

the activity is clear and enduring; (2) enough individuals are motivated to volunteer their time and money to satisfy the need; (3) the service is within the technical and material means of the group; and (4) the results are evident to the group and provide psychic rewards and reinforcement. The community of interest may be geographic, as exemplified by a homeowner or neighborhood association formed to deal with local needs for greater safety, cleaner streets, more recreation, and so forth. Voluntary groups can also come together to provide worthy individual goods that deserve to be handled on a collective basis, although the goods may not be localized in a geographic sense. For example, individuals who share similar concerns form charitable associations that focus on particular illnesses (e.g., heart, lung, Lou Gehrig's disease, cystic fibrosis) and on specific social problems (e.g., family planning, unwed mothers, adoption, drug abuse). This is privatization by philanthropy.[32]

Although formal volunteer efforts are widespread, there is little information available as to their extent, except for volunteer fire departments, which constitute more than ninety percent of all fire departments in the United States[33] but account for only a small fraction of all firefighters because big-city fire departments are large and have few volunteers. Existing organizations with a broad purpose may undertake specific services when the need arises. For instance, many religious organizations responded to the plea of New York's mayor for help in providing food and lodging for some of the city's "street people." A 1999 survey showed that volunteerism among young people is on the rise.[34] Voluntary efforts by the private sector can handle even major national undertakings, such as the 1984 Olympic Games in Los Angeles and the $265 million restoration of the Statue of Liberty.

One of the greatest virtues of voluntary organizations is innovation, the ability to identify and address local needs creatively and promptly. The Children's Scholarship Fund, for example, was established by prominent business leaders alarmed by the shortcomings of public schools. It is spending $140 million for 35,000 poor children to attend private or parochial schools.[35] Philanthropic giving overall is substantial: in 1997 Americans donated $143 billion to officially registered nonprofit organizations, of which $109 billion was given by individuals.[36] Immense amounts of time and a great deal of money are also donated to informal, unincorporated voluntary organizations, but these go unrecorded.

Here is an amusing illustration of innovative voluntary action in the public interest. Under a 1980 law eagerly sought by the city, New York could no longer be sued for injuries or damages caused by a pothole or broken sidewalk unless the city had been informed previously about the existence of that particular defect. Negligence lawyers, seeing their liveli-hood threatened, banded together and formed the Big Apple Pothole and Sidewalk Protection Corporation. This new, civic-minded, voluntary insti-tution hires workers who patrol the streets and mark the defects they find on maps, which they then formally turn over to the city! The document runs to 6,000 pages, which suggests that the lawyers will not soon starve for lack of work.[37]

While one can laugh at the transparency of it all, the lawyers' self interest serves a public purpose. The city government, although responsi-ble for maintaining public thoroughfares, wanted to avoid the conse-quences of neglecting that responsibility. The private pothole patrol forces the city to weigh the cost of doing its job against the cost of negligence claims, which amounted to $42 million in 1997—of which the lawyers got a third.[38] The lawyers, in pursuit of private gain, achieve a public ben-efit, just as Adam Smith foretold.

Self-Service

The most basic delivery mode of all is self-help, or *self-service*. Protection against fire and theft is obtained primarily by rudimentary self-service mea-sures, such as installing smoke alarms and locking doors. The person who brings newspapers to a recycling center, bandages a cut, or saves money for retirement is practicing self-service.

The family as a self-service unit is the original and most efficient department of housing, health, education, welfare, and human services, providing a wide range of vital services to its members. Families dissatis-fied with conventional schools are braving formidable bureaucratic forces by teaching children at home; about two percent of K-to-12 children are home schooled. About one of every eight workers in the United States pro-vides direct care for aged parents, a figure expected to more than triple by 2002.[39] In Japan 70 percent of people over sixty years old live with younger relatives; only 6.3 percent of Americans over sixty do so.[40] The Japanese therefore have less need for government-supported nursing homes and senior-citizen housing.

The terms *coproduction* and *coprovision* are sometimes used to refer to voluntary and self-service arrangements and to voluntary citizen contri-butions of time or money to public agencies[41] (e.g., a volunteer in a county hospital or a donation to a school to buy a computer). Because they attempt to cover too disparate a set of actions, and because the prefix "co" is plainly inappropriate for the self-service arrangement, the words are avoided here in favor of the simpler and more descriptive terms we have used.

Arrangements for Common Services

Some services may be provided under many of the ten arrangements described here. Table 4.6 (see pp. 88–89) shows how these arrangements are actually utilized in the United States to provide major local government services.[42] For example, transportation is provided through all ten of the arrangements, refuse collection and education through nine of the ten, and even fire protection, the least versatile (in this respect) of the principal local government services (although not shown in the table), is provided through five different arrangements: government service, intergovernmental agreement, contract, voluntary service, and self-service.

Mixed Arrangements

The ten organizational arrangements we have discussed here at length can be thought of as pure structures that can be employed either alone or in combination to provide a service. Specifically, it is possible to make effective use in service delivery of multiple, hybrid, and partial arrangements.

Multiple Arrangements

Multiple arrangements can be employed by a jurisdiction for a single service. For example, in Indianapolis, five different arrangements were utilized in different districts for the collection of residential refuse: municipal service, contract service, voluntary service, free market, and self-service.[43] There is nothing wrong with using multiple structures simultaneously for the same service. On the contrary, by fostering comparison and competition among the different service producers, the result is likely to be superior performance; redundancy is good.[44] This point is pursued further in chapter 7.

Hybrid Arrangements

In addition to *multiple* arrangements—the use of more than one arrangement to provide the same service in the same area—there are *hybrid* arrangements. For example, a franchised bus line that receives an operating subsidy (i.e., a grant) from the government represents a hybrid arrangement. The grant arrangement is the most common partner in hybrid arrangements, and it may be used to subsidize franchise, self-service, market, or voluntary arrangements. As noted previously, a grant may be in the form of a direct payment, a low-interest loan, or favorable tax treatment. In another hybrid arrangement, a local government may have contracts with two or more

TABLE 4.6—INSTITUTIONAL ARRANGEMENTS USED TO SUPPLY COMMON MUNICIPAL SERVICES

Institutional arrangement	Education	Police protection	Streets and highways	Parks and recreation
Government service	Conventional public school system	Traditional police department	Municipal highway department	Municipal parks department
Government vending	Local public school accepts out-of-district pupil and is paid by parents	Sponsor pays city for crowd control by police at concert	Circus pays town to clean streets after parade	Sponsor pays town to clean park after company picnic
Inter-governmental agreements	Pupils go to school in the next town; sending town pays receiving town	Town buys patrol services from county sheriff	County pays town to clean county roads located in town	City joins special recreation district in the region
Contracts	City hires private firm to conduct vocational training program	City hires private guard service for government buildings	City hires private contractor to clean and plow city streets	City hires private firm to prune trees and mow grass
Franchises				Firm is authorized to operate city-owned golf course and charge fees
Grants	Private colleges get government grant for every enrolled student			
Vouchers	Tuition voucher for elementary school, GI Bill for college			
Free market	Private schools	Banks hire private guards	Local merchant association hires street cleaners	Commercial tennis courts and golf driving range
Voluntary service	Parochial schools	Block association forms citizens' crime-watch unit	Homeowners' association hires firm to clean local streets	Private tennis club and fitness center
Self-service	Home schooling	Install locks and alarm system, buy gun	Merchant sweeps sidewalk in front of his shop	Swimming pool at home

Hospitals	Housing	Refuse collection	Transportation
County hospital	Public housing authority	Municipal sanitation department	Public transit authority that runs bus service
		Stores pay town to collect their solid waste	Company hires city bus and driver for a special event
City arranges for residents to be treated at regional hospital	Town contracts with county housing authority	City joins regional solid-waste authority	City is part of a regional transportation district
County hospital hires firm for cafeteriaservice	Housing authority hires contractor for repairs and painting	City hires and pays contractor to collect garbage	School board hires bus company for pupil transport
		City franchises private firm to collect garbage and charge residents	Government gives company exclusive right to operate bus service
Government grant to expand nonprofit hospital	Grant to private firm to build and operate low-income housing	City charges user fee but subsidizes elderly and low-income households	Government subsidizes bus purchases for private bus firm
Medicaid card permits holder to get medical care anywhere	Voucher enables low-income tenant to rent any acceptable, affordable unit		Transportation voucher for elderly and handicapped to use for taxis, etc.
Proprietary (for-profit) hospitals	Ordinary private housing	Household hires private firm to provide service	Free market for jitneys, private cars for hire
Community-based nonprofit hospital	Housing cooperative	Homeowners' association hires firm to provide service	Carpools organized by groups of suburban neighbors
Self medication, chicken soup, other traditional cures	Do-it-yourself home construction	Household brings refuse to town disposal site	Driving one's own car, cycling, walking

private day-care providers but allow an eligible mother to choose the one for her child; this is a hybrid of a contract and a voucher.

Partial Arrangements

Partial arrangements are also widely employed. Services are usually comprised of a bundle of separate but coordinated activities, each of which could be supplied separately through different arrangements. As a result, a comprehensive service may be part governmental, part contract, part voucher, and part self-service, for example.

Complex services can be divided along either operational or functional lines. Operationally, for instance, prison activities include food service, medical service, inmate counseling, education and vocational training, recreation, facility maintenance, security, and industrial work programs. All these services have been contracted out, while the main activity of housing and guarding the prisoners is usually carried out by a state corrections agency. The service in this case is part contract and part governmental. Increasingly, however, private contractors build and own prisons, charging the state government on a daily basis for each prisoner.

In bus transportation, the following operations can be separated and handled by private contractors, even if the basic service is performed mostly by a public agency: plowing snow from bus routes, towing disabled buses, maintaining buildings, and performing custodial work, body work, brake repairs, transmission repairs, engine repairs, painting, and so on. Again, the result is a combination of arrangements which together comprise the overall service.

A service can also be separated along functional lines, and partial contracting can again be employed. For example, a government agency can own the capital facilities required for a service but contract out the service itself. (For example, Minneapolis owns vehicle-impoundment lots but contracts out vehicle towing to firms that supply their own tow trucks and labor.) Conversely, an agency can produce the service but rent the privately owned buildings and equipment it needs. Another approach is to have the principal function run by a government agency but contract for support services such as accounting, printing, legal work, and transportation. Still another approach is to contract only the management of an otherwise governmental service; this has been done for public bus systems and public hospitals. A variant of this is to contract for managing only the support services of a hospital or school, or for managing a physical facility; in effect, the resident manager is a contract department head for the hospital or school administrator.

For capital-intensive facilities such as water-treatment plants, bridges, and airports, arrangements can get complicated because the simple trio of arranger, producer, and consumer does not begin to account for all the participants. These include the organizations responsible for planning, owning, financing, designing, building, managing, regulating, and bearing risk for the facility. These complex arrangements for infrastructure projects—identified broadly as joint ventures or public-private partnerships—are reviewed in chapter 9.

The Relationship between Arrangements and Kinds of Goods

Of the ten institutional arrangements for providing services, which can be used for what kinds of services? This question can be answered by referring to the intrinsic nature of the service in question. It is clear that individual goods can be provided by any arrangement, including voluntary service (i.e., simple charity). In the United States, except for worthy goods, individual goods are not generally supplied by government, intergovernmental agreement, contract, or franchise arrangements, although in principle they could be. Indeed, in some countries individual goods were routinely supplied by government. For example, in the Soviet Union most retail shops were operated by a municipal agency, and most food was grown on state farms (which explains the poor food supply). In some corrupt regimes exclusive franchises are (unnecessarily) created by governments to supply individual goods that are near-necessities; the result is equivalent to government-sanctioned extortion. This was the case with the colonial British monopoly on salt in India, which led to Mahatma Gandhi's first major nonviolent protest.

Toll goods, which, like individual goods, are subject to exclusion, can be provided through any of the ten arrangements except self-service (because toll goods involve joint consumption).

Collective goods can be supplied by government service, by intergovernmental agreement, by contract, or by a voluntary arrangement. They cannot be provided through franchises, grants, vouchers, vending, or the marketplace, as these structures all require exclusion to be effective, and collective goods, by definition, do not permit this.

Goods that are intrinsically common-pool goods are provided by nature, but we saw in chapter 3 that government action can, in effect, create such goods and give them away, in which case government service, intergovernmental agreements, contracts, grants, or vouchers can be used to supply them; free-lunch programs and medical care have been identified previously as falling into this class of government-created common-pool goods. Voluntary arrangements can also create and supply such goods, as exemplified by a charitable organization that offers food and shelter to the needy.

The situation is summarized in table 4.7, which shows the different arrangements that can be used to supply each of the different kinds of goods. The table makes it clear that each kind can be provided through more than one arrangement. Voluntary service, government service, intergovernmental agreements, and contracts are the only arrangements that can supply all four kinds of goods. Self-service is the most limited arrangement, for it can supply only individual goods.

Comparing the Arrangements

What are the relative advantages and disadvantages of each arrangement? If more than one arrangement can be used to deliver a particular service, which is best? In what way? Several important attributes must be considered in attempting to answer these questions.

Specificity of Service

Some services can be specified with little ambiguity and little chance of misunderstanding. Others cannot, and they therefore allow different interpretations of what the service entails. This is particularly true of services whose quality is difficult to measure, such as day care and other social services. These services present an added level of complexity in contracting, although not an insuperable one.

Services that can be specified in detail can readily be provided by any of the arrangements, but those that can be defined only in broad terms

TABLE 4.7—KINDS OF GOODS AND THEIR DELIVERY ARRANGEMENTS

Service arrangement	Individual goods	Toll goods	Collective goods	Common-pool goods
Government service	x	x	x	x
Government vending	x	x		
Intergovernmental agreements	x	x	x	x
Contracts	x	x	x	x
Franchises	x	x		
Grants	x	x		x
Vouchers	x	x		x
Free market	x	x		
Voluntary service	x	x	x	x
Self-service	x			

cannot easily be provided by intergovernmental agreement, by contract, by franchise, or by grant, unless the service is already being performed, in which case a service arranger says, in effect, "I can't describe it but I like what you're doing and I'd like to buy some of it too." This is what happens when a school district sends its students to a school in a neighboring district, for instance, or engages a firm that is carrying out a totally different program of education, such as the Edison Project.[45]

If a service cannot be clearly specified, how can anyone or any arrangement supply it satisfactorily? In particular, how can a government agency or anyone else perform that service satisfactorily if it is not at all clear what the service calls for, and what "satisfactory" means? Only with close supervision, extensive monitoring, frequent feedback from the consumer to the producer, close coordination between upper and lower echelons of the producing organization, frequent adjustments and corrections, and, in effect, constant negotiation between the consumer and the producer to balance expectations, capabilities, and achievements. These conditions can best be achieved where no third party stands between the consumer and producer, a situation realized when the consumer is the arranger (e.g., food stamps) and also when the producer is the arranger (e.g., block patrol). Table 4.10 (see p. 107) shows that the former circumstance obtains under market and voucher arrangements and the latter under government, voluntary, and self-service arrangements.

Availability of Producers

For some services, many producers are already in existence or can readily be encouraged to enter the field; in other cases, there are few producers and it is difficult to attract more, either because a large capital investment may be needed or because of other barriers to entry. This factor, too, affects the choice of service arrangement, as contract, market, and voucher arrangements will work satisfactorily only if there are relatively many producers from which to choose. Chapter 7 discusses how to increase the number of potential producers.

Efficiency and Effectiveness

The three fundamental criteria of service performance are efficiency, effectiveness, and equity. Equity is discussed later in this chapter; efficiency and effectiveness are examined here.

One of the most fundamental determinants of the efficiency and effectiveness of any arrangement is competition; that is, the degree of competition that an arrangement permits will, to a major extent, determine how efficiently that arrangement will supply a service. Competition means that the consumer has a choice, and citizen choice is a revered principle in democratic societies. Provided that there are enough producers to select from, market, contract, and voucher systems are most conducive to fostering competition and thereby achieving economic efficiency.

Franchising, grants, intergovernmental contracting, government vending, and voluntary arrangements permit some degree of competition, although not as great as the aforementioned three. Government services, in contrast, generally operate as unrivaled, unregulated monopolies—even though relatively few such services are natural monopolies—and government bureaus in this situation are inherently subject to inefficiencies and inadequacies. They can take advantage of their monopolistic position to maximize their budgets or the total remuneration—monetary and nonmonetary—of their managers and workers per unit of work.

Scale of Service

The scale of a service will generally affect its efficiency. The optimal scale of different services will differ, depending entirely on the technical characteristics of the production process. A one-room schoolhouse with a single teacher handling twelve different grades will not be as effective in providing a desired standard of education as a larger school with more specialized teachers, a library, audiovisual equipment, and the like. Similarly, it is extremely inefficient for a small town with a one-man police force to have a full-time police dispatcher, a spare police car to use when the other is undergoing repair, and a full-time mechanic. At the other end of the scale, a very large police department may require so many coordinators, so many layers of supervisors, and so many reports and file clerks that it, too, is very inefficient. Some intermediate-size department is likely to be most efficient.

Government service is likely to be inefficient because the production unit must, by definition, be the same size as the consumer unit, without regard to the optimal size. Therefore, if the most efficient size for a school system is one that serves 50,000 people, then cities with populations of 1,000, 10,000, 100,000, or 1 million will all be inefficient if each has its own school system.

All of the arrangements except government service, and self-service government vending, can achieve economies of scale by allowing the size of the producer to be independent of the size of the arranger, thereby permitting the producer to be of optimal size. Intergovernmental agreements are more flexible than government service in this regard, but they are not as flexible as contract or voucher arrangements, for the producer is limited to the size of either an existing jurisdiction or a new jurisdiction that could be created by aggregating existing ones. Contracting and franchising are most flexible in their ability to take advantage of scale economies. If the most efficient size of a producer is smaller than the size of the jurisdiction that arranges for the service, then the jurisdiction can divide its territory into two or more separate areas, each of optimal size. If the jurisdiction is too small, then the franchisee or contractor can nevertheless achieve optimal size by selling its services to other nearby jurisdictions as well. (This is a feasible option even in the case of a franchise service that requires a large capital investment in a geographically circumscribed area, such as water supply or sewage treatment.)

For example, consider a small town that collects residential garbage using a two-truck municipal unit. Assume that the optimal size of a provider for this service is eight to ten trucks, because of economies of scale. This town, and other nearby small towns, would save money by contracting with a private firm of the right size that sells its services to several towns in the area.

Relating Benefits and Costs

Efficiency is more likely to be realized when there is a direct link between paying for the service and realizing its benefits, and the consumer has an economic incentive to shop wisely. Such a link exists only for private and toll goods. The consumer pays the producer directly in market, voucher, grant (in some cases), and franchise arrangements; these do not involve any third party as an intermediary. For example, the consumer pays the grocer directly with food stamps (a voucher), and the telephone subscriber pays the local telephone company (a franchise). Voluntary service may have this characteristic, as in a housing cooperative or a country club, for example.

One might say that government service does not interpose an intermediary between the consumer and the producer either, for the taxpayer-consumer pays the producer (government); however, unless a user charge is levied, the link between the act of paying taxes for government service and the act of consuming a particular service is far more attenuated than it is for market, voucher, grant, or franchise arrangements.

Responsiveness to Consumers

Direct contact between consumer and producer should result in more responsive service as well, particularly when the consumer can exercise some choice. This relation prevails when the consumer is the arranger, as in market and voucher systems, in voluntary service when no contract is involved, and in arrangements that involve multiple grantees and franchisees. This is obviously true for self-service.

Susceptibility to Fraud

At first glance, it appears that several of the arrangements are particularly vulnerable to corruption, which, in addition to its moral impact, increases the cost of service. The award of government contracts, franchises, and grants is obviously susceptible to bribery, collusion, and extortion. Vouchers are vulnerable to a variety of fraudulent schemes, as evidenced by the counterfeiting, theft, sale, and illegal redemption of food stamps. Opponents of these arrangements cite these weaknesses and point to the apparent superiority of government services (and by implication, intergovernmental agreements) in this respect. This matter is discussed in detail in chapter 11, which concludes that the situation is symmetrical and that neither the public nor the private sector is exempt from this problem.

Economic Equity

Do the arrangements differ in their ability to provide services to consumers in a fair and equitable manner? Two separate issues can be distinguished here: equity with respect to financial means; and equity with respect to race, religion, or other such characteristics. This section deals with the former and the next section with the latter.

Many consider the market mechanism to be inherently equitable in that all people are treated equally and (in principle) everyone pays the same amount of money for the same thing. Others consider the market mechanism to be inherently inequitable because incomes are distributed unequally and therefore rich people and poor people cannot both buy the same things. Those who make this latter argument equate equity with equality. They view market, voluntary, and franchise arrangements as similarly inequitable, insofar as the ability to obtain service is dependent on income, as in paying for water, electric power, transportation, or recreation. The other organized arrangements (excluding self-service), however, are alike with respect to this issue. Grants, contracts, intergovernmental agreements, and government service can all be used to dispense services in whatever manner is deemed equitable by the appropriate government body, as can vouchers, which are deliberately designed to equalize access to services.

This is an important point. Many who oppose privatization on the grounds that it is unfair to the poor assume mistakenly that privatization requires a pure market arrangement, and they conjure up the vision of every family, rich and poor alike, paying individually to send their toddler off to school, for example. This is not the case at all, as we have seen. Collective goods can be provided by contract and financed by taxes; private goods and toll goods for the needy can be supplied by vouchers; both approaches allow whatever degree of redistribution is desired by society. The arrangements differ in the extent to which they facilitate redistribution of goods and services.

Racial Equity

There is another important dimension to equity besides economic redistribution: equality of treatment without discrimination on grounds of race, color, or creed. Does privatization make any difference to members of minority groups? This question can be divided into two, more focused questions: What is the effect of different arrangements on jobs for minorities, and what is their effect on services for minorities?

Effect on employment. The federal government and many state and local governments were among the first organizations in the United States to eliminate discriminatory hiring practices. As a result, they tend to have relatively more minority employees, and more of them in higher-paid positions by virtue of promotions and seniority. (In 1980, 27.1 percent of all employed blacks worked for government, compared to 15.9 percent of whites.[46]) At first glance, therefore, it might appear that privatization will cause proportionately more job losses and fewer job opportunities for minority workers.

There is little justification for this fear. In the first place, privatization creates jobs in the private sector, and private firms no less than governments are subject to laws prohibiting discrimination in hiring and can be made to conform to the letter and spirit of the law as closely as state and local governments can. In fact, private firms may be better in this respect than the federal government: Congress exempted itself from the laws on equal employment opportunity and did not have to practice "affirmative action" in hiring congressional staff members. In any event, the major study of this issue found that minority workers displaced from municipal jobs by privatization were hired by private contractors in about the same proportion as they had been employed by city departments.[47]

In the second place, nondiscriminatory hiring is not always the practice in governments. Many government agencies throughout the world are dominated by particular ethnic, linguistic, religious, or tribal groups; indeed, an individual agency is often considered the private preserve of one group. In the United States this practice is contrary to official policy and is fading, but it can still be observed in older eastern cities. In other countries the practice is often a matter of policy that is understood but is not made explicit. (In Southeast Asia, for example, privatization is viewed as tantamount to "Sinofication" because many private entrepreneurs are ethnically Chinese.)

I observed a case in the United States wherein a change from municipal to contract service resulted in a fairer distribution of jobs for minorities. The contractor's newly hired workforce closely reflected the city's current demographic composition, whereas the agency's own workforce reflected the city's earlier composition because an older immigrant group still dominated the civil service.

The third and final point with respect to the job issue has to do with entrepreneurial opportunities. Privatization affords ambitious members of minority groups the opportunity to start their own businesses and to prosper. Minority communities in urban areas are particularly well situated in this regard. Many municipal services require only modest amounts of capital and are technologically simple, requiring no professional training. These characteristics are attractive to many potential businessmen and businesswomen in minority communities. These individuals can start firms that would supply municipal services by contract or franchise. In New York City, black immigrants from the Caribbean started van services to improve transportation in minority communities but the city's bus agency fights them tooth and nail to restrict their operations and put them out of business. Legitimizing those operations and incorporating them into the city's transit network would be good public policy and has long been advocated[48]— unsuccessfully so far, due to the power exercised by the transit employee union over the City Council.[49]

Governmental encouragement of minority entrepreneurship has usually been expressed in the requirement that a certain portion of contracts be set aside and reserved for minority firms or that prime contractors subcontract a certain fraction of their work to minority-owned firms. Despite the laudable intent of such restrictions, namely, to improve the economic condition of minority groups, such "set asides" have been marred by the creation of dummy corporations, paper exchanges of assets, fictitious billing, influence peddling, and other evasions of the spirit if not the letter of such laws. These quota-based methods have been attacked in courts and legislatures as discriminatory, and their survival is questionable.

The opportunity for market-based (instead of quota-based) minority entrepreneurism via privatization was recognized by the Bedford-Stuyvesant Restoration Corporation, an economic development unit in a minority community in Brooklyn, New York. The corporation created an indigenous, neighborhood-based, locally owned company to bid for municipal work, but opposition to any contracting from public employee unions aborted the plan. Basically, the political power of the latter was greater than that mustered in the minority community.

Despite this local setback, numerous minority entrepreneurs in the United States have started in business through privatization. The trucking industry provides a useful lesson about the business opportunities available to minority entrepreneurs through the marketplace. For many years it was necessary for a would-be trucker to prove beforehand that his entry into the business was a "public necessity and convenience." (Surely the best way to demonstrate this is to allow someone to enter the business and see if he survives!) The effect of such regulation was to keep blacks out of the trucking business, even though the minimal capital and training requirements made this an eminently suitable activity for black entrepreneurs. The situation changed in the early 1980s after trucking deregulation. Modest as it was, deregulation tended to transform this activity from a restricted franchise to a market arrangement, enabling blacks, no longer subject to de facto exclusion, to triple their participation in the industry.[50]

In summary, job opportunities for members of minority groups appear to be pretty similar regardless of arrangement. In particular, government service seems no better or worse than any other arrangement on this score. Moreover, as explained in chapter 11, no job losses need occur when public services are privatized by contracting.

Effect on services.   Turning to the other part of the main question, do the arrangements differ with respect to level and quality of services to minorities? This is not merely a hypothetical concern. A court found that the town of Shaw, Mississippi, which had racially segregated neighborhoods, supplied its tax-paid municipal services—street lights, sewers, and paved streets—in a highly discriminatory manner. Whereas the town's population was 60 percent black, (1) all the modern street lamps were in white neighborhoods; (2) 98 percent of all the homes fronting on unpaved streets were occupied by blacks; and (3) 19 percent of black-owned homes were without sewer service, compared to only 1 percent of white-owned homes.[51] All three inequitably distributed services were supplied directly by the local government.

Obviously, a government that discriminates against some of its citizens as a matter of unspoken policy can do so using contracts, grants, vouchers, or any other arrangement in which it has a hand. Sometimes, however, contracting can eliminate bias. For instance, a study I made uncovered the following practice in a city that once had municipal collection of residential waste. When the city agency could not complete its daily collections on time, it generally coped by skipping the black neighborhoods, which had relatively little political influence. When the city changed to a contractor, this no longer happened. The contractor methodically completed his assigned daily work, paying overtime if necessary, and was oblivious to the political strength or weakness of different neighborhoods.

Like all taxpayers, minority groups have a stake in more efficient use of public funds. Nevertheless, to the extent that minority groups have lower than median incomes on average, they are more dependent on government-provided services than wealthier groups and they rely more on private goods that have been collectivized. Therefore, any arrangement that results in better quality of service, or in more cost-effective service (which makes more money available to government) is likely to benefit minority groups more.

In summary, vouchers are particularly advantageous for low-income, minority-group members because it gives them greater choice. Housing vouchers and day-care vouchers are widely used by low-income groups, and blacks strongly favor vouchers for educating their children.[52] Minority groups seem to be served equally well or poorly by any of the different arrangements when it comes to equity in jobs, but when it comes to equity in services they are better off with vouchers or with any particularly efficient arrangement such as contracting.

Responsiveness to Government Direction

Public services can be used as a vehicle to advance other governmental purposes, such as regional economic development. The location of military bases in certain favored areas of the country exemplifies this traditional, pork-barrel approach. Government, grant, and contract arrangements are equally responsive to such guidance.

Contrary to what one may think, however, direct government service does not assure effective control or direction by elected officials. Executives from the private sector who are appointed to head government agencies are astonished at how little actual control they have over their agencies. The combination of ossified civil service rules, powerful public-employee unions, and inflexible traditions accounts for this effect. It explains much of the frustration encountered by would-be agents of change who enter office on platforms that promise reforms.

It is generally easier for a public agency to influence the behavior of a private organization than the behavior of another public agency.[53] Several examples illustrate this. City housing inspectors are better able to persuade private landlords than public housing authorities to correct deficiencies. A judge placed the Boston Housing Authority (BHA) in receivership and castigated it, accusing it of "gross mismanagement, nonfeasance, incompetence and irresponsibility." He concluded, "If the BHA were a private landlord, it surely would have been driven out of business long ago or its board jailed or most likely both."[54] Similarly, the director of the U.S. Office of Management and Budget remarked that if the Securities and Exchange Commission had jurisdiction over federal budget documents, members of Congress and the administration "would be in jail."[55]

The Tennessee Valley Authority also illustrates this point. It has been notably recalcitrant in reducing its air-polluting emissions despite pressure from environmental control agencies,[56] and it was accused of filing a misleading report to the Nuclear Regulatory Commission about an accident at one of its nuclear generating plants.[57] Perhaps the ultimate example of government agency immunity to the law is provided by two frustrated congressmen. Exasperated by evidence that the Postal Service practiced deceptive advertising with respect to its airmail and special delivery services, and calling it fraud, they asked for an investigation. The Federal Trade Commission declined on the grounds that it cannot investigate another government agency.[58]

No firm conclusion can be drawn from these anecdotal illustrations, but not even government service stands out as being more responsive to government direction or control than any other (with the obvious exception of voluntary and self-service arrangements).

Size of Government

Measured by the number of employees, government is largest under government service, of course, and least under market, franchise, voluntary, and self-service arrangements. Contracts, grants, and vouchers require government expenditures but relatively few government employees because the latter are needed only to administer services and not to produce them. In addition, if these last three arrangements are more efficient than government service, they tend to limit government spending, although not as much as franchise, market, voluntary, or self-service arrangements limit spending.

Vouchers and grants can lead to large government expenditures even though the number of government employees is small. Food stamps (vouchers) have cost about $30 billion per year, and housing grants have created a $250 billion debt.

Conclusion

The arrangements clearly differ with respect to the characteristics already discussed. These differences are summarized in table 4.8. When the discussion concluded that the arrangements are essentially equivalent with respect to a characteristic, that characteristic is omitted from the table, so that the listing shows only significant differences between arrangements. In the table, a double plus (++) sign (or a blank) appears when the arrangement possesses (or lacks) the indicated characteristic to a significant degree. If the characteristic is present to some degree, or to a minor extent, this fact is denoted by a single plus (+) sign. Obviously, these are subjective ratings.

Having said this, it is nevertheless possible to inspect the table and form some initial impressions. If one merely tabulates the number of pluses—an embarrassingly simplistic approach—the voucher system and the market system stand out with almost unbroken strings of positive attributes; government service, government vending, and intergovernmental agreements have the fewest positive attributes. This is a result of the values implicit in the table; all attributes are weighted equally, and so a different emphasis on redistribution, on efficiency, and on limiting the size of government would produce different outcomes. One can generate other versions of this table by adding other attributes and by assigning different weights to the listed attributes, for instance. This is left as an exercise for the reader.

However one tinkers with table 4.8, one can view it in the light of table 4.7 to determine the best arrangement for each of the different types of goods. Market and voucher arrangements are best for individual and toll goods, voucher and voluntary arrangements are best for what are now treated as common-pool goods, and contract and voluntary arrangements are best for collective goods.

The relatively high ranking of voluntary arrangements for delivering collective and common-pool goods should come as no surprise. Voluntary arrangements are, after all, a form of self-government and generally offer maximum citizen participation. Democratic government has its roots in a voluntary social contract among citizens.

TABLE 4.8—OPERATIONAL CHARACTERISTICS OF DIFFERENT ARRANGEMENTS

Characteristic	Government service	Government vending	Intergovernmental agreements	Contracts	Franchises	Grants	Vouchers	Free market	Voluntary service	Self-service
Handles poorly specified service	++						++	++	++	++
Requires multiple producers				++			++	++		
Promotes efficiency and effectiveness		+	+	++	+	+	++	++	+	
Achieves economies of scale			+	++	++	++	++	++	++	
Relates costs to benefits		+	+	++	+	++	++	++	++	++
Is responsive to consumer		++			++	+	++	++	++	++
Is relatively invulnerable to fraud			++				++		++	++
Facilitates income redistribution	++		++	++		++	++		+	
Is responsive to government direction	++		+	+	+	+				
Limits number of government employees				++	++	++	++	++	++	++

Privatization

In seven of the ten arrangements the private sector is the producer: contracts, grants, vouchers, franchises, free market, voluntary service, and self-service. In the other three arrangements government is the producer: government service, intergovernmental agreements, and government vending. Arrangements are a static concept. Privatization is a dynamic concept that in the simplest sense means changing from an arrangement with a government producer to one with a private producer. To move in the opposite direction is to nationalize, "governmentalize," or "deprivatize."

Privatization can also be viewed in a more complex way. Table 4.9 ranks the arrangements in descending order, with the most privatized arrangements at the top. Free market, voluntary service, and self-service arrangements, which are equivalent on this scale, are the ultimate in privatization because they have the least government involvement. A franchise is next in this progression because, although in its pure form it involves no direct expenditures, government is the arranger. Vouchers, grants, and contracts are ranked in descending order in the table because they involve a decreasing degree of citizen choice and increasing government expenditures. (Government generally pays only part of the cost under a grant or voucher arrangement but the entire cost of a contract.) Government vending is next because it relies on market incentives although government is the producer. Finally, an intergovernmental agreement is ranked higher than the government-service arrangement because it involves specifying and purchasing a service and is therefore more market oriented.

This hierarchy is useful because it allows finer distinctions. A move from a lower arrangement in table 4.9 to a higher one is a form of privatization

TABLE 4.9—HIERARCHY OF ARRANGEMENTS BY DEGREE OF PRIVATIZATION AND RELIANCE ON MARKET FORCES

Arrangement

Private-sector producer
 Free market; voluntary service; self-service
 Franchises
 Vouchers
 Grants
 Contracts

Government producer
 Government vending
 Intergovernmental agreements
 Government service

in that it means relying more on the private institutions of society—notably markets—and less on government; this is the definition of privatization offered in chapter 1.

Changing from government service to an intergovernmental agreement or government vending cannot logically be called privatization, but it does mean relying more on private-sector (market) mechanisms. Changing from a market to a grant arrangement (i.e., introducing a government subsidy) is the opposite of privatization because it makes less use of market forces, although the private sector delivers the service in both cases. Similarly, President Clinton's program to give students college scholarships (vouchers) after they have worked in community service is the opposite of privatization and a form of nationalization for it means greater government involvement. That is, instead of working at jobs that are completely of their own choosing to save enough for college, young people in this work program are denied freedom of choice in the labor market and are restricted to government-approved jobs if they want the vouchers.

The principal privatization transitions are

- changing from government to contract, grant, voucher, franchise, voluntary, or market arrangements
- eliminating grants (producer subsidies) in favor of voucher, voluntary, or market arrangements
- deregulating franchises where possible and eliminating price controls and entry barriers to permit market arrangements to respond to people's needs

One could add a fourth transition, one not usually considered a form of privatization: imposing a user charge for government-supplied toll and individual goods; if the user is also given a choice between government and a private supplier, this is a change from service government to a government-vending arrangement, which is more market driven. The remaining chapters address in detail the first transition listed here, because it is the most significant one in practice.

Public-Private Partnerships

The term *public-private partnership* is commonly used in three different ways. First, it is used loosely, and somewhat pretentiously, to refer to any arrangement in which the public and private sectors join together to produce and deliver goods and services. Contracts, franchises, and grants, for example, satisfy this definition, but this book generally employs the more precise names of the arrangements. Second, it is used here and elsewhere for complex, multipartner, privatized, infrastructure projects. Third, it refers to a formal collaboration between business and civic leaders and local government officials to improve the urban condition.[59] In this third case, corporations go beyond their usual role in the marketplace and become involved in schools, job training, downtown revitalization, urban redevelopment, and much more. Government becomes more than a tax collector and provider of conventional municipal services and becomes a real-estate developer, business lender, and so on. Religious and nonprofit leaders add their moral authority and community outreach to the joint effort. Important as this large topic is, it is beyond the scope of this book.

Summary

Collective action to supply goods and services requires a government or voluntary group to make decisions about the service to be provided, the level of service, and how to pay for it. One must distinguish between arranging (providing) for a service and producing (delivering) it. Ten different institutional arrangements are available for supplying goods and services: government service, intergovernmental agreements, government vending, contracts, grants, vouchers, franchises, markets, voluntary service, and self-service. They differ in the roles played by government, the private sector, and the consumer. Table 4.10 shows how the arrangements differ and how each arrangement is unique. The ten basic arrangements can be combined in multiple, hybrid, and partial arrangements, resulting in a rich variety of alternatives for delivering the services that people want.

The arrangements differ in their suitability for providing each of the four classes of goods. Generally speaking, several arrangements are available for supplying each class of goods; collective goods offer the fewest alternatives—only government service, intergovernmental agreements, contracts, and voluntary arrangements. Individual goods can be supplied by any arrangement.

Several important criteria can be used to evaluate the different arrangements: (1) specificity of the service, (2) availability of producers, (3) efficiency and effectiveness, (4) scale of service, (5) relationship of costs and benefits, (6) responsiveness to consumers, (7) susceptibility to fraud, (8) economic equity, (9) equity for minorities, (10) responsiveness to government direction, and (11) size of government.

The arrangements differ greatly with respect to these attributes, and no arrangement is ideal. Each has many positive features and lacks others;

TABLE 4.10—INSTITUTIONAL ARRANGEMENTS FOR PROVIDING PUBLIC SERVICES

Service arrangement	Arranger	Producer	Who pays?
Government service	Government	Government	Government
Government vending	Consumer	Government	Consumer
Intergovernmental agreements	Government (1)	Government (2)	Government (1)
Contracts	Government	Private sector	Government
Franchises (exclusive)	Government	Private sector	Consumer
Franchises (multiple)	Government and consumer	Private sector	Consumer
Grants	Government and consumer	Private sector	Government and consumer
Vouchers	Consumer	Private sector	Government and consumer
Free market	Consumer	Private sector	Consumer
Voluntary service	Voluntary association	Voluntary association	N.A.
Voluntary service with contract	Voluntary association	Private sector	Voluntary association
Self-service	Consumer	Consumer	N.A.

Note: Government (1) and Government (2) are two different governments.

N.A. = not applicable

each has advantages or disadvantages, depending on the application. There is generally more than one good way to provide a service, and this should be recognized when planning new services or rethinking old ones. Delivery arrangements should be selected by reason rather than by reflex.

Given these criteria and the subjective value judgments presented previously, one can rank the different arrangements. For both individual and toll goods, free-market and voucher arrangements are best. For common-pool goods, voucher and voluntary arrangements are best. For collective goods, contract and voluntary arrangements are best.

Privatization means changing from an arrangement with high government involvement to one with less. The most important privatized arrangements from a policy perspective are the free market, franchise, contract, voucher, and voluntary arrangements. Government can privatize individual and toll goods that it produces by divesting or withdrawing from the activity and allowing the market to supply them. It can privatize worthy goods by issuing vouchers, and collective goods by contracting and by encouraging voluntary action.

Part 3 goes on to discuss in detail how to privatize government services and enterprises.

The Practice
of Privatization

CHAPTER FIVE

Why and How to Privatize

HAVING EXAMINED THE theoretical basis for privatization, we now turn to pragmatic questions: Why privatize, that is, what problems call for privatization as a potential remedy? What are the objectives of privatization? What is the crucial ingredient of a privatization program? What is the ideal policy environment for successful privatization? What are the different forms of privatization? How does one manage the privatization process?

Why Privatize?

Dissatisfaction and recurrent problems with government activities invite privatization as a possible remedy for the problems. Of course, complaints about poor government performance are commonplace throughout the world, and much of this may be conventional and culturally obligatory grumbling and ridicule, but there is ample evidence that much of the dissatisfaction is justified.

The Need for Privatization: Symptoms and Diagnosis

Indicators of poor performance are much the same for both government services and government-owned enterprises (GOEs), and it is these symptoms that lead to the demand for privatization or other far-reaching structural reforms. Agencies, activities, enterprises, and assets that exhibit any of the following characteristics are potential candidates for privatization:

- inefficiency, overstaffing, and low productivity
- poor quality of goods and services
- continuing losses and rising debts of for-profit government enterprises
- lack of managerial skills or sufficient managerial authority

- unresponsiveness to the public
- undermaintenance of facilities and equipment
- insufficient funds for needed capital investments
- excessive vertical integration
- obsolete practices or products, and little marketing capability
- multiple and conflicting goals
- misguided and irrelevant agency missions
- underutilized and underperforming assets
- illegal practices
- theft and corruption

Frequently underlying all these symptoms is the fact that many government activities are performed by monopolies, which have little incentive to use resources efficiently or to use labor-saving practices and suffer no penalty for poor performance. Of course, some government agencies do very well, but these problems—many of them interrelated—abound in many government activities. To be sure, they can be found in the private sector as well, but private firms that perform poorly are taken over or go out of business, whereas government agencies that do poorly are immune to takeovers and may be given bigger budgets in an attempt, often in vain, to improve their performance. Each of these shortcomings is illustrated.

Inefficiency.   Evidence of poor government performance in terms of inefficiency, overstaffing, and low productivity is presented systematically in the next chapter, where the public and private sectors are compared and performance is contrasted before and after privatization. An example of an inefficient GOE with low productivity was Deutsche Telecom, the German telecommunications monopoly, which had twice as many employees per customer as American telephone companies. Poor performance of conventional municipal services is most readily apparent in solid-waste collection, where numerous studies show that the cost of monopolistic municipal collection is 30 to 40 percent greater than the price of collection by private contractors.[1]

Poor quality.   Poor water quality in public water systems is regrettably commonplace in developing countries, but in Washington, D.C., too, the water was found to be a potential health hazard in 1996. The Boston Housing Authority, a city agency that houses the poor, was placed in receivership by a judge who cited "indescribable conditions" that had caused "incalculable human suffering" and accused the directors of "gross mismanagement, nonfeasance, incompetence, and irresponsibility."

The projects operated by the Housing Authority had "leaky ceilings, frequent cessation of such basic services as heat, hot water, and electricity, of windows that do not open in hot weather and cannot be closed in cold weather, of infestations of rodents and insects, of mounds of rubbish and trash, of packs of wild dogs and of much more."[2]

Losses and debts.   Some state enterprises are not expected to break even or make money, but many are. Nevertheless, loss-making and debt-ridden government enterprises tend to be the rule rather than the exception even among the for-profit group, and this is the principal impetus behind the worldwide movement to privatize such entities. The underlying reason for this state of affairs is the lack of true financial accountability. That is, government agencies and GOEs are rarely subject to binding budget constraints; they can usually muster enough political pressure to extract more subsidies.[3]

Among the thousands of examples that could be cited are the Argentine state-owned airline and railroad systems, which were losing $1 million and $5 million per day respectively before they were privatized.[4] In the United States, after pouring almost $7 billion into Conrail, a group of bankrupt freight railroads that was consolidated in 1976, the Federal government was able to get only $1.65 billion when it sold the railroad by a public sale of shares in 1987. Under private ownership the railroad thrived and was sold for almost $10 billion just ten years later. Municipal stadiums and convention centers typically lose money and fail to bring the economic benefits proclaimed to support their costly construction. New York City's Off-Track Betting Corporation is a municipally owned bookmaker created to generate funds for the public schools, but after paying its standard fee to the city coffers it merely broke even—reportedly the only bookie in the world not making money hand over fist. The principal reason for this remarkable situation? Too many overpaid, underworked patronage employees and too many sweetheart leases for betting parlors on sites belonging to politically connected property owners.[5]

Lack of managerial skills and authority.   The common lack of managerial skills in government results both from the appointment of people whose only qualifications are political and from the persistence of relatively low salaries for upper management compared to the private sector.[6] But even good managers are hampered by restrictions such as civil service rules and one-sided, politically arranged labor agreements that effectively eliminate a manager's authority to reward good performance and to punish poor performance. (A whimsical note: Genghis Khan conquered Asia with an army less than half the size of New York City's civil service, but he had far greater managerial discretion to reward and punish than today's more circumscribed chief executives: he could award Persia to a successful general and lop off someone's head for poor performance.)

Unresponsiveness. A stunning illustration of unresponsive public services could be found in Argentina, where, before the national telephone company was privatized, one had to wait an average of 17 *years* to have a telephone installed![7]

Undermaintenance and insufficient capital investment. Because vehicle maintenance is paid for out of the operating budget but new vehicles are often paid for from the capital budget, it is often easier to buy a new truck than to maintain an old one; it is not surprising therefore that in some city agencies 40 percent of the agency's trucks are "down," that is, not in functioning order. This means that many more trucks are purchased than are necessary to carry out the work. On the other hand, the problem of insufficient funds to purchase needed capital equipment on a timely basis is vividly illustrated by the plaintive plea for new garbage trucks by a public worker director I met who was told by his city council that only police cars were to be bought that year, and only fire trucks the next, because both services were more important than public works.

Excessive vertical integration. This ponderous phrase describes the usual practice under communism whereby state enterprises provided housing, medical clinics, and vacation sites for their employees, as well as schools and recreation programs for employees' children, and sometimes even grew food, collected honey, and made sausages (as did an electronics plant I visited in Ukraine). But as First Deputy City Administrator in New York, I discovered that our Parks Department was manufacturing picnic tables and playground equipment at a cost many times the price at which they could be bought—also an example of excessive vertical integration. These examples from the Second and First Worlds respectively can be supplemented with a Third World case: Pakistan International Airlines has a poultry farm that supplies food for its in-flight meals. One wonders about the transferability of management skills between raising chickens and flying airplanes.

Obsolete products and little marketing capability.   The sausages and honey at the electronics plant were tasty, but unfortunately its electronic tape recorders were obsolete, and no one would buy them after entrepreneurs started bringing in modern products from East Asia following the collapse of the communist state. As for the lack of sales capability, this was not necessary under communism, where shortages were standard, factories produced whatever they were told to by the central state planning agency, and consumer needs did not count.

Multiple and conflicting goals.   Pity the hapless manager of the state-owned agriculture enterprise in Hungary who was charged with satisfying multiple, conflicting, and mutually exclusive goals: (1) starting a new hog farm in the eastern part of the country to promote regional economic development, even though hog feed could not be grown locally but had to be imported at considerable expense from the western part of the country— to which the pork was exported because that was also where the major markets were; (2) hiring many workers in order to reduce local unemployment; and (3) operating at a profit. Similarly, a huge smelter was built in Kyrgyzstan thousands of miles from the source of aluminum ore and from product markets.[8] These absurd situations are not unknown in the United States, where government laboratories sometimes are sited in accordance with similarly conflicting goals, for example, to provide a local economic boost and produce high-quality scientific results despite the fact that it is difficult to recruit and retain first-class scientists in that locale. For a very different example, consider the homeless shelters in New York, where complaints about poor conditions led to privatization of the city-run temporary shelters, by contracting with nonprofit agencies, but then the conditions became so good that new arrivals did not want to leave! Was the goal to attract clients who obviously had been living elsewhere or to provide the truly homeless with modest, temporary shelter?[9]

Misguided and irrelevant agency missions.   Agencies and state enterprises may be created to address particular needs, but that action may have been misguided, that need may have disappeared or been satisfied over time, and the agency may no longer be relevant, yet it survives due to a combination of inertia and the power of entrenched bureaucrats and other beneficiaries. The Rural Electrification Administration survives despite the essentially complete availability of electricity throughout the United States. Agricultural marketing boards, conceived ostensibly to stabilize agricultural prices and ameliorate gluts and shortages in food production, also fit this description.

A classical example of agencies that have long since outlived their usefulness, marketing boards in the United States attract public attention only when they issue orders to destroy thousands of tons of fruit in order to keep prices up. In Canada in 1996, a farmer was jailed for five months for not selling his barley to the Canadian Wheat Board but instead driving two miles across the border and selling some of it in the United States.[10]

In Africa, marketing boards have had a truly malevolent effect, contributing to famines by the following perverse mechanism: The boards were created and given the exclusive authority to buy and sell selected agricultural products, while other government agencies monopolized the sale of agricultural inputs such as seed and fertilizer to farmers. In order to curry favor and political support from urban dwellers, however, the price of food was kept artificially low by paying low prices to the farmers for their crops and selling them inputs at high prices. (Concentrated city residents are more potent politically than dispersed rural farmers.) The predictable result: farmers, losing money, were driven to subsistence agriculture, producing food for themselves but little food for markets, leading to famines in the cities.

Underutilized and underperforming assets.   Government agencies tend to hold onto vacant land and unoccupied buildings in the hope of encouraging expansion of their programs. ("We can do that; we have just the site!") Mental health facilities in the United States are examples, where much prime property that was vacated after deinstitutionalization remains underutilized.

To be fair, one must recognize that the problems are sometimes dropped into the laps of public-sector managers by political leaders. This happens when governments take over failing private enterprises "in order to save jobs," a pernicious practice that usually results in more widespread and prolonged suffering. On services subject to user charges, governments may impose price controls or eliminate the charges altogether "to keep prices affordable," thereby starving the service of resources and leading directly to shortages and poor performance; public bus services in American cities often exemplify this particular perversion. (Vouchers achieve the same goal, affordability, more effectively.) Governments may quite properly undertake large and risky capital projects that have uncertain outcomes and very long payback periods, such as space exploration, but because every project spawns numerous beneficiaries, government tends to continue the project long after it has become a white elephant and has no hope of success. The Synthetic Fuels Corporation in the United States was an example, established in the mistaken belief that the country was facing a fuel shortage.

Illegal practices. Government agencies sometimes engage in practices that are illegal or would be illegal for any other entity. For example, the New York State Power Authority routinely violated safety standards at its nuclear power plants and was fined more than half a million dollars by the Nuclear Regulatory Commission (a federal agency) in 1992 alone.[11] The Tennessee Valley Authority, a federal agency that also operates nuclear power plants, was accused of filing a misleading report about the severity of an accident.[12]

Theft and corruption. These ills are found in both the public and private sectors, of course, but can provide the impetus for privatization when egregious conduct is discovered in public agencies. The overthrow of Philippine President Ferdinand Marcos was triggered in part by his flagrant use of state enterprises to line his pockets and those of his cronies, and the new government initiated an extensive privatization program.

Another example of corrupt behavior was found in an unusual government activity: rounding up wild horses on federal lands in the western United States. Employees and officials of the Bureau of Land Management were accused of receiving money for illegally shipping the horses to slaughterhouses.[13] The horses could have been sold at auction with the proceeds going to the public purse instead of being appropriated by the employees.

A similar instance, and the fundamental lesson to be learned from it, is reported by Terry Anderson and Jane Shaw, who tell the sad tale of a major urban park, Ravenna Park in Seattle, that was destroyed by public ownership. Late in the nineteenth century, the park was assembled privately as a preserve of giant fir trees. It was opened to the public and attracted 8,000 to 10,000 visitors a day, at a fee that would be the equivalent of $3 today. After twenty-five years, the city condemned the property and took it over as a public park. Within fourteen years, all the giant firs were gone, apparently cut down and sold illicitly by park employees. Today it is a high-crime area with a concrete tennis court where once stood the largest tree, one with a twenty-foot diameter. Whereas the private owners recognized the latent public demand for a park preserve and found it profitable to create the park and treat it well, once the public owned it, public employees—who had no true ownership rights and therefore no long-term stake in it—found it profitable in the short-term to convert the trees into firewood.[14] The moral of the story is that private ownership (with attendant property rights) achieved a public purpose, while public ownership did not. Aristotle explained it well more than 2,000 years ago: "That which is owned in common by the greatest number has the least care devoted to it."[15]

Why Governments Privatize: Survey Results

Survey information sheds light on why governments privatize. A 1992 survey asked local officials in the United States why they consider privatizing. The questionnaire was directed to the chief administrative officer of every municipality with a population of more than 10,000 and every county with a population of more than 25,000, a total of 4,935 governments; 1,504 answers were received, a response rate of 31 percent.[16] Table 5.1 shows that an internal effort to reduce costs is the principal reason (about 90 percent of the respondents) that governments privatize and external fiscal pressures are the second strongest reason (about 53 percent). In other words, they privatize to save money. An earlier survey identified infrastructure decay as another important reason; that is, new or rehabilitated infrastructure is needed and municipalities see privatization as a means to satisfy the need despite their current budget problems.[17] (This was not offered as a choice in the 1992 survey.)

A 1992 survey of state government officials in the United States explored their reasons for considering privatization. Responses were received from 158 agencies in 29 states. All the responding agencies had used contracting and

TABLE 5.1—WHY LOCAL GOVERNMENTS ARE INTERESTED IN PRIVATIZATION

Reason	Percent of officials reporting this reason for considering privatization
Internal attempts to cut costs	90
External fiscal pressures	53
Unsolicited proposals (from private sector)	23
Political climate	23
State/federal mandates tied to intergovernmental financing	20
Concerns about liability	18
Citizen group	8
Other	7

Source: Adapted from Rowan Miranda and Karlyn Andersen, "Alternative Service Delivery in Local Government, 1982–1992," in *Municipal Year Book 1994* (Washington, D.C.: International City-County Management Association), 26–35, fig. 3/1.

almost all had privatized facilities and sold assets. Like local officials, state officials identified cost savings as the principal reason for privatization. Other dominant reasons for all three forms of privatization, differing only slightly in the rankings, are higher-quality services, rapid implementation, and provision of services that are otherwise not available. Another stated reason for contracting out is that it solves labor problems.[18]

A somewhat different survey of state officials in 1997 asked why privatization activity was increasing. The answers, ranked in descending order, were (1) cost savings, (2) greater political support for privatization, (3) more flexibility and less red tape, (4) faster implementation, (5) lack of state personnel and expertise, (6) increased innovation, and (7) higher quality service.[19]

Objectives of Privatization Programs

Governments should have specific objectives for privatization. Overcoming the problems listed at the beginning of this chapter are common objectives but there are others as well, some of them related or overlapping; several of the following objectives are most appropriate for developing countries:

- Reduce the cost of government
- Generate revenues, both by selling assets and then by collecting taxes from them
- Reduce government debt, for instance, through debt-equity swaps
- Supply infrastructure or other facilities that government cannot otherwise provide
- Bring in specialized skills needed for technologically advanced activities
- Initiate or expand a service quickly
- Lessen government interference and direct presence in the economy
- Reduce the role of government in society (build or strengthen civil society)
- Accelerate economic development
- Decentralize the economy and broaden the ownership of economic assets

- Show commitment to economic liberalization and increase business confidence
- Promote the development of capital markets (by creating and selling shares)[20]
- Attract new foreign and domestic investment and encourage return of flight capital
- Satisfy foreign lenders (including international bodies such as the World Bank)
- Improve living standards
- Gain popular support (by getting rid of malfunctioning bureaucracies)
- Reward political allies
- Weaken political opponents (for example, labor unions)

While all of these objectives may be desirable, some are mutually incompatible; moreover, the objective and the nature of the entity or activity to be privatized affect the method one chooses for privatizing, For instance, selling a monopoly GOE intact, with few post-sale conditions, to a single buyer in a competitive process will maximize the sale revenue but will not lead to broader ownership or to greater efficiency from the public's point of view, and it may not attract subsequent investment. In Panama I argued against the government's plan to sell the national telecommunications company in a way that would provide an immediate cash infusion for the current government, because the process was sure to lead to higher prices for the public. In Brazil, on the other hand, the government wisely broke up the state-owned telecommunications monopoly, which was worth about $30 billion, into twelve parts: three regional companies, eight cellular concessions, and a long-distance carrier, which together were worth only about $20 billion. The sale of competitive businesses would bring in much less than the sale of the intact monopoly, but the public would undoubtedly benefit through lower prices even though the government revenue from the sale would not be maximized. Ironically, the leftist political party opposed the sale on the grounds that the price was too low.[21]

Prime Minister Margaret Thatcher's long-term goal in undertaking her privatization program was nothing less than to change the attitude of the British people toward a free-market economy and away from creeping socialism. Her principal short-term objective was to enlarge the fraction of the British populace that had a stake in the economy. This was accomplished by carrying out a public sale of shares rather than a private sale by competitive bidding among prequalified companies; mounting an extensive and expensive advertising program to encourage ordinary citizens to invest in shares; selling shares to the enterprise's employees at a discount; limiting the number of shares sold to any single buyer; and setting the price of shares somewhat below their market value. (This all meant that the cost of administering the program was relatively high and the proceeds relatively low, thereby deliberately foregoing another objective of privatization, namely, maximizing immediate revenue from the sale.) She succeeded spectacularly in reaching *her* objective, however, increasing the fraction of UK adults who directly owned shares from 9 percent to 25 percent in only thirteen years.[22] Her intermediate goals were to make privatization irreversible, that is, to prevent the Labour Party from simply undoing her work when it next gained power, and to weaken the labor unions, which she considered a root cause of Britain's decline. In these goals, too, she was successful. More than 98 percent of employees bought the (discounted) shares in their company, defying their unions and the Labour Party, which urged them to boycott the sales. Later, when the Labour Party vowed to renationalize the newly privatized companies, it had to back down and promise *not* to do so because it encountered strong opposition from the unionized, share-owning workers.

In Bolivia the goal of privatization was to promote economic development, even at the cost of foregoing revenue from the sale of GOEs. The money (for half the shares) stayed instead in the newly privatized company, but the public benefited both from the new investments that were required of the buyer and from the creation of a retirement system financed by the subsequent sale of the government's shares.[23]

As an illustration of privatization used to reward political allies, privatization in Russia was carried out in a way that benefited the banks, which were strong supporters of embattled President Boris Yeltsin. An ironic and perverse instance of privatizing in order to reward political allies occurred in Nicaragua after the Sandinista government lost the first free election ever held in a communist country. Having nationalized not only enterprises when they seized power, but also land, houses, and automobiles belonging to their political opponents, the Sandinistas privatized these state-owned assets by giving them gratis to their supporters before ceding control to the newly elected democratic government!

From the perspective of a company being privatized, such as Conrail, privatization presents an opportunity to revolutionize the culture, strategy, and organization; emphasize cost efficiency in all aspects of operations; adopt consistent policies in allocating and exploiting company resources, including disinvesting; become more market oriented and adopt market pricing; give up subsidies; gain access to capital markets; and perhaps expand internationally.[24]

Competition: The Key Ingredient for Successful Privatization

The primary goal of any privatization effort is, or should be, to introduce competition and market forces in the delivery of public services, in the operation of public enterprises, and in the use of public assets. We vigorously oppose private monopolies in the private sector and break up monopolies that would restrain competition. The Sherman Antitrust Act of 1890, the Clayton Antitrust Act of 1914, antimonopoly units in the Department of Justice, and public utility commissions in every state protect the public against monopolies—private monopolies. (Critics of current regulations assert that now they are more likely to protect monopolies from competition.) We know that the public interest suffers without the goad of competition and in the absence of alternatives and choices. But in the public sector, perversely, we have relied heavily on monopolies to deliver public services and to operate the most important public enterprises, those that supply collective goods. We have unwittingly created and maintained such monopolies under the naive assumption that if the monopoly is a public one, it will somehow automatically operate in the public interest. Moreover, we often prohibit competition in the mistaken belief that competition constitutes wasteful duplication. We labor under the delusion that total reliance on a single supplier is the best way to assure satisfactory delivery of vital public services if the supplier is the government itself. But public monopolies can be expected to behave just like private ones, not because the people working in them are greedy or venal, but because the underlying incentives are the same and human beings inevitably respond to them in the same way. Thus, monopolies tend to become inefficient, ineffective, and unresponsive.

Because the basic assumption has gone unexamined, to improve government service the emphasis has been on better public administration, preservice education, in-service training, civil service reform, performance budgeting, planning-programming-budgeting systems (PPBS), zero-based budgeting (ZBB), computers, quantitative methods, reorganization, organizational development, sensitivity training, incentive systems, management by objectives, productivity programs, joint labor-management committees, total quality management, re-engineering, and the like. All of these were or may be desirable, but they fail to identify, let alone address, the underlying, structural problem of government monopoly, which is the dominant factor responsible for malperformance of government services. When this underlying problem is understood, it is clear that poor performance of government agencies and GOEs will not yield to managerial fads, preaching, indignation, or finger-pointing at villains; market forces must be brought to bear to overcome the monopoly mechanisms we have wittingly or unwittingly established in the public sector.

Introducing competition requires a conscious strategy of creating alternatives and fostering a receptive climate and attitude in favor of providing options for public goods and services.[25] Service-delivery options are essential. Total dependence on a single supplier, whether a government agency or a private firm, is dangerous. Without choice and flexibility, the ultimate consumer of public services, the citizen, is subject to endless exploitation and victimization. Government should have a chance to shop around, for when choice is replaced by compulsion, the fundamental relationship between citizens and public employees is altered; the latter are no longer public servants.

Public-service options provide a form of insurance: if several organizations are delivering the same service and one fails or is subject to too many work stoppages, or is inefficient or ineffective or unresponsive or unsatisfactory or too expensive, the public can turn to another supplier. Furthermore, separating the decision about supplying a service—what kind, what quality, how much—from the actual production process gives the citizen-consumer greater leverage and liberates him from the control of a single bureaucracy that determines what service he will get, how much of it he will consume, how it will be produced, and how much he will pay for it.

Such monopoly power has important consequences. When a service is financed by taxes without pricing and without citizen choice, there is no effective way to determine the level of popular support for the service except in the very long term. Ordinarily, customers who have a choice will seek out producers who will tailor their services to satisfy their customers' different needs. Citizens denied the right to choose one alternative over another cannot indicate their preferences to shape the service, and the ballot box is a poor substitute for communicating program preferences. In the absence of citizen choice, so-called public servants have a captive market and little incentive to heed their putative customers. Control of the service depends instead on the relative political power of the interested parties.

Competition can be fostered between different producers within the same or different institutional arrangements. For example, a civilian advisory board in the United States called for competitive analysis of intelligence information to reduce the monopolistic role of the Central Intelligence Agency. The French government, unwilling to end the state monopoly of television, nevertheless responded to complaints about its "incompetent, flippant, disjointed, and criminally wasteful" Office of French Radio and Television by establishing each of the three channels as a completely independent, competing, government institution.[26] Subsequently, two private franchises were awarded as well, and plans were made to privatize one of the three state stations.[27]

A refreshing and thought-provoking example of a deliberate effort to stimulate intergovernmental competition came from Yugoslavia before the breakup. The city fathers of Ljubljana, the capital of Slovenia, desired the services of city planners and solicited formal bids not only from their own city planning agency but also from the city planning agency of Zagreb, the capital of neighboring Croatia. An American observer reported that he had never seen city employees anywhere work as hard as Ljubljana's city planners, who wanted desperately to avoid the humiliation of having their city's work contracted out to their professional and ethnic rivals.[28]

Competition is at work in the United States in intergovernmental agreements where a county sheriff who provides police services to a local community recognizes that the community could form its own police department and thus tries harder to provide cost-effective services. The sale of government assets and enterprises, for example, the Student Loan Marketing Association (Sally Mae), restores or consigns such entities to the marketplace where, ideally, they occupy contestable niches and are subject to competition.

The Ideal Policy Environment for Privatization

Privatization of enterprises and assets is not enough. It is a means, not an end in itself. An appropriate policy environment must be in place in order to achieve the intended objectives, particularly for those countries—developed, developing, and post-socialist—that are abandoning failed socialist policies and liberalizing their economies. Privatization should be part of a package of economic reforms. The elements of an ideal policy environment are the familiar ones of a competitive market economy:

- market prices without price controls or subsidies
- the right to own property and to exercise property rights

- no government barriers to entry by competitors and no protectionism
- equal application and enforcement of laws, including the tax code and contract law, within a fair, comprehensive, independent legal system
- no favoritism by government in providing access to credit and foreign exchange
- no favoritism by government in selling raw materials or purchasing products
- market-based interest rates, not preferential rates on government loans
- freedom for the newly privatized firm to hire and fire employees, subject to equal application of labor laws and the privatization agreement
- freedom for the private firm to restructure or change the business, subject to the privatization agreement
- political stability
- currency stability and control of inflation

Needless to say, nowhere is such an ideal policy fully in place, although Hong Kong before reverting to China came closest. But unless accompanied by economic liberalization, privatization of public enterprises is not likely to result in significant gains in economic performance.[29]

The post-socialist countries are privatizing rapidly and often clumsily, but they are only slowly and painfully developing the necessary institutions and laws for a market economy. Most must still establish the basic elements that Westerners take for granted, such as property rights, corporate law, contract law, tax codes, antimonopoly laws, labor and pension laws, bankruptcy law, banking law, disclosure requirements, accounting practices, independent regulatory bodies, and an independent judiciary.

Forms of Privatization

Because privatization can be accomplished by many different techniques, confusion abounds when discussing privatization efforts in different countries and different situations. Various terms have been used: public-private partnerships, contracting out, denationalization, degovernmentalization, destatization, shareization, and divestment, for example. These are synonyms for privatization as defined in this book. Other terms—corporatization, commercialization, and marketization—can refer to privatization or to attempts to make GOEs operate as though in a market environment. Some of these terms are unwieldy in English but not in their own languages. Other terms are unsatisfactory. For example, the privatization of an enterprise or asset owned by a municipality cannot rightly be called denationalization; should it be called demunicipalization?

The preceding chapter, in a static analysis, identified ten arrangements for providing goods and services. The remainder of this chapter presents a dynamic analysis, demonstrating how to go from an arrangement that relies heavily on government to one that relies more on the private sector. This section presents a classification taxonomy that encompasses all the forms I have observed for privatizing government-run services and functions and government-owned enterprises and assets. It has the added virtue of simplicity.[30] Later chapters describe in detail the privatization process for services (chapter 7), enterprises and assets (chapter 8), and infrastructure (chapter 9).

Three general methods are used to privatize government services and activities, government-owned enterprises (GOEs), and other state-owned assets: delegation, divestment, and displacement. Each of these incorporates several specific approaches, which are identified in table 5.2 and discussed in turn

Delegation

The first broad privatization strategy is delegation, which calls for a positive act by government. Sometimes called partial privatization, delegation requires a continuing, active involvement by government, for the state remains entirely responsible for the function but merely delegates the actual production activity to the private sector. Delegation is carried out by contract, franchise, subsidy (by grant or by voucher), or mandate.

Delegation by contract.   Government can privatize an activity by contracting with a private organization, for-profit or nonprofit, to perform the work. This, the most common form of privatization in the United States, is taking place at the federal, state, and local government levels. It is not new: America was discovered more than 500 years ago by a private contractor hired by Queen Isabella of Spain to explore the western ocean. Competitive contracting ("tendering") is compulsory for selected local government services in Britain.

TABLE 5.2—FORMS OF PRIVATIZATION

Delegation	Contract	for part of the service for total management
	Franchise	by concession by lease
	Grant	
	Voucher	
	Mandate	
Divestment	Sale	to joint venture to private buyer to the public to employees to users or customers
	Free transfer	to a joint venture to the public to employees to users or customers to original owner (restitution) to selected recipients
	Liquidation	
Displacement	Default	
	Withdrawal (load shedding)	
	Deregulation	

Local governments contract for direct services such as solid-waste collection, street repair, street cleaning, snow removal, and tree maintenance, as illustrated in chapter 4. Government agencies at all levels often contract for support services such as data processing, loan processing, architecture and civil engineering, training, audiovisual services, food services, employee medical examinations, mail and file services, libraries, laundry and dry cleaning, facilities maintenance, warehousing, transportation, and vehicle maintenance. The average American city contracts out 23 percent of its 64 common municipal services to the private sector.[31] The average American state contracts out 14 percent of its activities.[32] More than 200 different services are being provided by contractors to local governments[33] and the practice has been growing rapidly at both state and local levels, regardless of the political affiliation of elected officials. Between 1982 and 1992 contracting out increased by 121 percent in the 596 cities where comparable data were available.[34]

Although contracting usually involves payment to the contractor by the government, this need not be the case. A growing practice in developing countries is for the state to turn over the management of rural irrigation systems to water-user associations, that is, farmer cooperatives, which have proven to be more effective than government agencies in maintaining such systems. In essence, the association enters into a maintenance contract, but the cooperative does not get paid; its reward is a reliable supply of water.[35] Competitive contracting for public services is discussed fully in the next chapter.

Delegation by franchise.   Franchising is another method of privatization. Under a franchise, government awards a private organization the right (often the exclusive right) to sell a service or a product to the public. The private firm usually pays the government a fee. Two forms of franchising exist. One involves the use of the public domain—airwaves, air space, streets, underground space, and so forth. For example, broadcasters, airlines, bus and taxi companies, and utilities (electricity, gas, water, telephone) use the public domain in the course of carrying out their commercial activities. This arrangement is usually called a *concession.* Infrastructure projects that are built, expanded, or upgraded through public-private partnerships are franchises, usually in the form of concessions; they are discussed in chapter 9.

The second form is a *lease,* in which tangible, government-owned property is used by a private lessee to engage in a commercial enterprise. This is one of the common privatization strategies emerging in post-socialist countries, although it is likely to be temporary until the property can be sold outright. (The others are free transfer of shares to the public, identified previously, and deregulation, discussed later.)

There is no sharp distinction between a lease and a concession. Some differentiate the two in that capital investments under a lease are made by the owner, the government, while under a concession they are made by the concession holder, the franchisee. This is important in some privatizations, but the distinction has little significance with respect to infrastructure privatization, as is evident in chapter 9.

Both franchising and contracting should be carried out in an open, transparent, competitive process.

Delegation by grant.   Delegation is also achieved by awarding grants. Instead of carrying out an activity itself, government arranges for a private entity to do the work and provides a subsidy. In the United States, grants are used for mass transit, low-income housing, maritime shipping, and innumerable other activities. Grants are distinguished from contracts in that grants usually involve only the most general requirements (run a bus service, build houses that rent at below-market prices, conduct research, promote the arts), whereas contracts usually specify in great detail a particular service (sweep the west side of certain north-south streets between 7 A.M. and 9 A.M. on Tuesdays and Fridays).

Delegation by voucher.   Governments can also delegate by issuing vouchers to eligible recipients of formerly state-run services. Instead of subsidizing producers, as grants do, vouchers subsidize eligible consumers. Vouchers, as described in chapter 4, are used for food, housing, education, health care, day care, and transportation. Recipients use vouchers to supplement their own funds when purchasing these goods and services in the marketplace. Chapter 10 deals further with vouchers for education and social services.

Delegation by mandate.   The fifth and final form of privatization by delegation is a government mandate requiring private agencies to provide a service at their expense. Unemployment insurance is a long-standing example of such a mandate in the United States; private employers provide this fringe benefit for their employees. Privatization connotes a change in direction and therefore mandates, like grants, vouchers, franchises and contracts, can be considered forms of privatization only when they lead to a lesser, not a greater, role for government. Thus if the government-run Social Security system in the United States were replaced by mandatory, individual retirement accounts, this would be privatization by mandate, a form of delegation. On the other hand, if market-based health care were replaced by mandatory, employer-provided health care, this would be the opposite of privatization, as it would involve a greater rather than a lesser role for government. A trend in the United States that many consider ominous is to create new social programs (for example, family leave, aid to the handicapped, job training) by imposing government mandates on private employers instead of providing the services directly. The net economic effect, of course, is the same, but the public is forced to pay covertly, through higher prices, rather than openly, through taxes.

Divestment

Divestment means shedding an enterprise, function, or asset. Like delegation, this requires a direct, positive act by government, but unlike delegation, it is generally a one-time affair. The enterprise or asset is either sold or given away as an ongoing business, or an enterprise may be liquidated (that is, closed down and the remaining assets sold). Where state-owned enterprises are abundant, "denationalization" is frequently used to mean divestment. Chapter 8 describes the process of divestment in detail.

Divestment by sale.   Table 5.2 (p. 127) shows that divestment by sale can be carried out in five ways: (1) by joint venture (see later); (2) by selling the enterprise (or asset) to a private buyer, as was done with the Vista Hotel in New York City, which had been owned by a government authority and was sold to a major hotel chain; (3) by issuing and selling shares to the public, as was done with Conrail, the U.S. government-owned freight railroad in 1987; (4) by selling the enterprise to the managers or, more broadly, to employees, as was done with the National Freight Company, the state-owned British trucking company;[36] and (5) by selling the enterprise or asset to its users or its customers. For example, state-owned land may be sold to ranchers or loggers, and a rural electricity or water system may be sold to a cooperative of local users; in Argentina, a freight rail line that served industrial customers was sold to a consortium of users.

Governments in the United States own more than $4 trillion in real estate assets, it is estimated.[37] It is commonplace for government to sell land, buildings, equipment, and other assets that are no longer needed, or to avoid future departmental expansions. The City of New York recently sold its two radio stations and its television station.[38] At the federal level the largest privatization in the United States since the Homestead Act took place: the Clinton administration sold the government-owned uranium enrichment plants; helium plants, power-marketing agencies, and oil fields also went on the block.

The sale of a GOE can be partial, when the government sells most, half, or only some of the GOE. A joint venture can be created, whereby a private firm receives half the shares by supplying investment capital and know-how and assumes operating control; the private capital stays in the joint venture and the government receives no direct compensation for contributing its shares to the private firm. Whether it is a joint venture or any other arrangement, however, unless government cedes control, with or without ceding majority ownership, such a sale can be considered merely a form of raising capital, not privatization. A sale can also be in stages, called "tranches," whereby the government sells a portion of its holdings at a time, as Japan and Germany did with their state-owned telecommunications companies.

Divestment by free transfer. Divestment does not require sale of an enterprise; the latter could be given away, for example, to employees, to users or customers, to the public at large, to the prior owner (restitution), or to a qualified class of people. One could look at a joint venture as an example of free transfer, in that the state transfers its shares into a newly created entity as its contribution and receives no compensation, but it is more logical to look at joint ventures as a partial sale, because the state is still a part owner.

An instance of giving away an enterprise to the employees occurred when the English Channel hovercraft ferry service, formerly owned by British Rail, the state-owned railway, was given to its management, thereby ending the drain on the public purse.[39] A proposal to privatize municipal hospitals in New York City would give them away to newly created, local, nonprofit, community-based boards representing the residents (i.e., users) who rely heavily on that hospital. Proposals to privatize America's air-traffic-control system would give or sell the assets and responsibilities to a consortium of airport users.[40]

In Kenya, the national water agency, responding to complaints about the poor quality and quantity of water, turned over parts of the system to rural water cooperatives; neighbors got together, dug deeper wells, connected more homes to trunk lines, managed the system, and improved their water supply, doing all this with their own money and labor. Because the customers are the owners, the operation is self-regulating and no governmental regulatory apparatus is needed.

A novel example of giving away an SOE to the public took place in Canada. The proposed sale of an enterprise owned by a provincial government, the British Columbia Resources Investment Corporation, led to a prolonged and bitter political debate. To block the sale, opponents questioned the proposed sale price. The dilemma faced by the proponents was that if the price were too low, they would be accused of giving away the people's patrimony; if it were too high, the sale would not succeed. In a stroke of political genius, the provincial premier reasoned that because, in the final analysis, the corporation belonged to the people, and the people had already paid for it once, why should they have to pay for it again? It could be given to them! Despite the complexity, this bold step was carried out successfully by issuing shares to residents of the province.[41]

Giving away SOEs to the public, or selling them at token prices, has been an important privatization strategy in post-socialist countries,[42] as has restitution, restoring property to the original owners from whom it had been confiscated by communist regimes.

Examples of giving away shares of an SOE to a specially designated group can be found in Albania, and also in Haiti, where former political prisoners were given shares as a form of national atonement and compensation for their years of suffering under harsh dictators.

Divestment by liquidation.   Finally, divestment can be carried out by shutting down and liquidating a poorly performing enterprise, that is, selling its assets if no buyer can be found for it as a going enterprise and if the prospects are bleak for ever making it profitable. This is privatization because the assets reenter the marketplace and become available for better uses. Thousands of such enterprises have been liquidated in post-socialist and developing countries, and it is the fate of many more in China.

Displacement

Besides divestment and delegation, privatization can proceed by displacement, as shown in table 5.2. In contrast to the first two methods, which require positive acts by government, displacement is a more passive or indirect process that leads to government being displaced more or less gradually by the private sector—a withering away of the state, so to speak, as markets develop to satisfy people's needs. It has also been called privatization by attrition, or, perjoratively, privatization by stealth.[43] Often unrecognized as a form of privatization, displacement is both commonplace and an extremely important process by which effective privatization often occurs with relatively little political battling.

Displacement occurs by default, by withdrawal, and by deregulation, and it depends ultimately on local initiatives and entrepreneurship. It can be accelerated by imposing market-based user charges on hitherto "free" government goods and services, which makes the cost of government provision clear and invites private competitors.

Displacement by default.   When the public considers government production of goods or services to be inadequate, and the private sector recognizes and satisfies the demand, the process can be termed displacement by default. This process, too, satisfies the definition of privatization, namely, relying more on the private sector and less on the state to satisfy people's needs. Gradually, the public begins to look to the private sector for this activity, and, if the service grows over time and the government-supplied goods or services continue to be neglected or the government role shrinks in relative terms, the private sector will play a larger and larger role. Simply put, customers desert or avoid the public service. A common example is the growth of private transportation where government-provided bus service is deemed unsatisfactory or inadequate by the public. Gypsy cabs, commuter vans, minibus systems and other informal, quasi-legal, or technically illegal transport services have emerged in numerous cities throughout the world. We are also seeing displacement by default in public education in large American cities: even parents of limited means have been withdrawing their children from the public schools in droves, enrolling them in proliferating private schools and schooling them at home.

Private police offer another example. The public's unsatisfied demand for conventional police protection and dissatisfaction with the level of public safety in the United States led to the growth of private guard and patrol services. Although the latter have not displaced the former, in the United States the growth has been primarily in the private sector: by 1990, private police comprised three-fourths of all police.[44]

A similar phenomenon is evident throughout the world as private firms begin to satisfy infrastructure needs that government agencies could not. Thus, the private sector is financing, building, owning, and operating roads, bridges, water systems, and wastewater-treatment plants in poor, developing countries,[45] and also in advanced nations, as evidenced by the English Channel "chunnel" linking England and France. These may be purely private ventures, in effect, franchises, or they may involve some degree of public funds through various complex public-private partnerships, as described later in this book.

Displacement by withdrawal. Whereas default is unintended or inadvertent, government can engage in deliberate withdrawal, or "load shedding,"[46] by constricting an SOE's growth or shrinking its size while the private sector expands into that field. This has also been termed "privatization by extinction."[47] "Mothballing" is yet another term for this process, allowing SOEs to sit idle and waste away over long periods, which diffuses labor unrest.[48] This process has been going on in Russia and China. An official from Thailand referred to it as the "bonsai approach" to privatization. His government stopped giving subsidies to state enterprises, thereby retarding their growth. Starving them of nutrients, so to speak, and pruning back any visible signs of growth tacitly encouraged private-sector competitors to grow and take over the garden. Ultimately, the stunted enterprises, like neglected and diseased bonsai plants, succumbed and were discarded.

In Lesotho, the Lesotho Freight and Bus Services Corporation (LFBSC), an SOE that provided trucking and bus services throughout this mountain kingdom, had received no new vehicles, had cannibalized the old ones, and was gradually being displaced by private operators with new equipment: vans for intracity transportation, buses for intercity travel, and trucks for moving goods. When I visited the country, LFBSC had only 66 employees and 25 vehicles, was losing money, and served only a tiny market niche; I recommended that they liquidate the land, buildings, and remaining rolling stock and withdraw altogether from the business.

Withdrawal often goes hand-in-hand with default. In Britain, private health care is reemerging as the system of socialized health care deteriorates in quality and availability and as funds are cut; people are slowly migrating toward a private alternative.[49]

Load shedding, or withdrawal, can occur by accommodation, that is, informal cooperation between government and private-sector providers. This happens when the latter relieve the former of a function the public agency would rather not perform. For example, private companies provide security inside shelters for the homeless, an unpleasant task, but it is agreed that regular police officers will respond expeditiously to calls for help from such private guards.[50] Some states grant campus police and other private security personnel the power of arrest and give them jurisdiction on public streets in the vicinity of their employer's property. Not-for-profit institutions such as museums, zoos, opera houses, libraries, and social service agencies are being encouraged to rely more on private sponsors and philanthropists and less on government for financial support. It is anomalous, for example, that not-for-profit institutions which do not pay property taxes receive municipal refuse-collection service without charge, but private firms which pay property taxes do not.

Government withdrawal from established services will not be easy, for a new political consensus must be achieved to replace the one that brought about government entry in the first place. Nevertheless, discontent with government services suggests that such a consensus may emerge. This need not involve a bruising battle between opposing ideologies. All that is needed is appropriate encouragement of forces already at work. Evidence concerning the extent to which working adults care for their elderly relatives is instructive. A study of employees in a large American insurance company showed that 28 percent of the full-time employees over the age of thirty provided regular care for elderly relatives and friends; they devoted an average of 10.2 hours per week to such care, and 42 percent of the caregivers had daily contact with the elder.[51] The remarkable aspect of this finding is that this traditional pattern of family care persists and is adhered to even by people holding full-time jobs outside the home. To the extent that this practice can be rewarded, made easier, and encouraged by government, through changes in tax and zoning policies and building codes, for example, the demand for more government provision of such care will be reduced.

The voluntary formation of geographic collective units, in both urban and suburban communities, also leads to withdrawal. A new, very local level of government has emerged in the United States: the condominium. Ranging in size from a single building to a large community, condominiums, neighborhood organizations, civic associations, and business improvement districts—we can call one a voluntary microcollective, a micropolis,[52] or a common-interest community[53]—already provide an array of collective goods, including cleaning and maintaining local streets and parks, removing snow, collecting refuse, operating volunteer ambulance, fire, and patrol services, and providing plantings and attractive "street furniture" (signs, litter baskets, benches, bus shelters, street lights, and consolidated newspaper vending machines).[54] City services have been reduced in these locations. Besides improving the local quality of life, such organizations can forge a desperately needed sense of community and can restore citizenship skills that have atrophied from disuse, skills without which a democracy cannot long survive.

Such collective units can best be formed in established communities that have well-defined geographic boundaries, are relatively homogeneous in terms of income, and have shared values with respect to the services to be provided through this mechanism. Local leadership is necessary, as is an encouraging posture by the local government. The latter can mean giving tax rebates to residents in areas that forego city services. This poses a minor administrative problem for the local government, but many communities do this, including Houston and Kansas City, Missouri. In the latter, local homeowner associations can choose to opt out of municipal refuse collection service and receive a proportional rebate on their property taxes, but they contract with private firms for a higher level of service than the city provides.

Another device to encourage the creation and assure the viability of such self-governing associations is to grant them taxing authority as special assessment districts. New York State has such legislation.[55] An important attribute of such microcollectives, besides honing the citizenship skills of their members, is that the latter have an opportunity to contribute their labor instead of their money. In the days of a barter economy, people could pay their taxes in specie such as grain and livestock. In a market economy they must pay cash. Load shedding to voluntary associations restores to the taxpayer the choice of paying in kind—with labor. "Off the books" earnings in the underground economy would then have their counterpart in "off the books" tax payments, that is, payments in kind for collective goods.

Thus, while government has been growing, some load shedding has also been going on. As the demand for certain collective goods exceeds the ability of government to supply them at a suitable price and quality, particularly in cities that have been experiencing fiscal stress, exasperated citizens form organizations to supplement the municipal service. Default has gone hand-in-hand with civic action, desertion of the municipal service by residents, and continued withdrawal of the city service. The voluntary associations obtain the services they want, custom tailored to their specific local needs and preferences, thereby exercising direct influence over the quality of their surroundings.

Displacement by deregulation.   State-owned enterprises and government activities often exist because they have monopoly status and the private sector is prohibited from competing. Deregulation facilitates privatization if it enables the private sector to challenge a government monopoly and even displace it altogether. In the United States, express mail and parcel delivery services offered by competing private companies have grown rapidly by de facto deregulation, at the expense of the U.S. Postal Service. The latter claims and vigorously defends its exclusive right to handle first-class mail and prohibits its competitors from depositing mail in recipients' mail boxes, but the regulations are under attack and their repeal was advocated by the President's Commission on Privatization.[56] In Guatemala, an estimated 60 to 80 percent of all mail is carried by some 250 private delivery services, which are deemed more reliable than the government mail service. Even government agencies are reported to use private services for important mailings that they cannot afford to lose.[57]

Day care is another good candidate for deregulation. Since time immemorial, parents have arranged for relatives, friends, and neighbors to care for their children, and parents have taken into consideration the character and qualities of individuals to whom they entrust their children and the surroundings in which their children are placed. In recent years, however, day care has become the object of increasing government involvement and financing. The result has been an increasingly complex web of legal restrictions as to who can provide the service, the number and kind of personnel who must be in attendance, the nature and design of the facilities, and so forth. The statement of an incredulous and indignant day-care operator to a zoning board in Washington, D.C., is worth quoting:

"You're telling us we cannot operate a day-care facility in a residentially zoned middle-class neighborhood with a large number of working mothers, but we can operate a center in a commercial zone between two topless bars?"[58] The bizarre result of all the restrictions, however well intended, was that most families and homes would not be certified by government as suitable for child care. In fact, the situation has been changing, with the introduction of vouchers that can be used by the parent to pay any provider of day care.

In many countries, years of state regulatory intervention have produced bureaucratic obstacles and economic stagnation. Hernando de Soto illustrates how much time is wasted in Peru following the labyrinthine official procedures to start a business or build a house: it takes 289 days to register an industrial enterprise and 26 months to license jitney operators, for example. The informal economy (i.e., "black market") encourages far greater productivity than the official sector.[59] (It is dismaying to note that getting a jitney license is even more difficult in New York City![60]). DeSoto advocates deregulation, debureaucratization, and decentralization. *The Economist* succinctly summarizes the situation in developing countries: "[B]ad government is the biggest single reason for poverty in the third world, and less government is the most effective single remedy."[61]

In countries where state-owned agriculture marketing boards are the only authorized buyers and sellers of agricultural products, deregulation allows private markets to develop and displace those SOEs. In Somalia, for example, the state-owned corporation that had a monopoly of agricultural products saw its market share plummet from 100 percent to less than 5 percent within three years after private entrepreneurs were allowed to buy and sell farm products.[62]

Post-socialist countries revived their devastated economies by repealing laws that prohibited private ownership, thereby encouraging entrepreneurs and allowing market mechanisms to prevail. "Marketization" is another term for this process, which aims to achieve economic efficiency through exposure to market discipline. The end result of deregulation is the emergence of demand-driven, market-based arrangements to satisfy unmet needs.

Overall, the People's Republic of China offers the best example of privatization by displacement. The first step was the deregulation of agriculture, in 1978. In effect farmers were able to exercise virtually all property rights customarily associated with ownership of specific parcels of land, provided they paid rent to the state in the form of contracted deliveries of grain. Agricultural production mushroomed, in sharp contrast to the food shortages that occurred under collective farming, leading to famines that killed millions. The resulting rural wealth, coupled with further de facto deregulation, led in turn to the creation of (politically correct) village and township enterprises that engaged in manufacturing that contributed immensely to China's economic boom. Although some may question whether this can be called privatization, such enterprises are analogous to employee stock-ownership plans. In the 1990s this nominally communist country has been withholding support for SOEs, often by failing to pay the workers and thereby hastening their departure from the inactive, moribund enterprises; this is withdrawal. It has also been encouraging the formation and growth of private enterprises instead of forbidding them as in the past; this is deregulation. Displaced workers have been getting jobs and starting businesses in the booming private sector. This process has been accomplished without significant social unrest, due to firm autocratic control.

Comparison of Privatization Methods

Each of these privatization methods has advantages and disadvantages. The principal features of each method listed in table 5.2 (p. 127) are summarized in table 5.3, which is adapted from Daniel Potash.[63] Judging from this summary, the easiest option is sale or free transfer to users or customer cooperatives, although this is rarely an available or meaningful option. The most advantageous options, the ones that are most likely to achieve the privatization objectives listed previously, arouse opposition that must be overcome. Chapter 11 discusses these obstacles.

Examples of Privatization

Thousands of privatizations have been carried out utilizing one or more of these methods. Two examples are given here to illustrate the range of issues that arise even in what appear to be straightforward privatization efforts, as well as the need to use more than one of the methods.

By a Combination of Methods

Several of these different forms of privatization can be illustrated in a single example: the bus system in the capital of a Third World country. The city, with a million inhabitants, had the following transportation system:

(1) A state-owned bus enterprise with the exclusive right to operate

TABLE 5.3—ADVANTAGES AND DISADVANTAGES OF PRIVATIZATION METHODS

Method	Advantages	Disadvantages
Contract	Increases productivity; saves money; is transparent	Probable worker opposition
Franchise by concession	Brings expertise, technology, investment; cuts costs	Probable worker opposition
Franchise by lease	Brings expertise, technology; cuts costs	Probable worker opposition
Grant	Less costly than direct government provision	Continued cost to government; not very transparent
Voucher	Gives recipients choice; saves money; corruption-free	Continued cost to government
Mandate	Imposes full cost on private sector	Imposes full cost on private sector; masks government role
Sale to joint venture	Brings expertise, technology, investment; raises some cash; government retains part ownership	Not very transparent
Sale to private buyer	Brings expertise, technology, investment; raises cash	Possible worker opposition; may not attract buyers; not very transparent
Sale to the public	Popular; transparent; raises cash	Suitable only for low-risk situations; no new investment in the enterprise
Sale to managers and employees	Retains operating experience; popular with employees	No new investment, expertise, or technology brought into the enterprise
Sale to users or customer cooperative	Popular; gets rid of problem; eliminates drain on funds; raises cash; transparent	
Free transfer to joint venture	Brings expertise, technology, investment; government retains part ownership	Raises no revenue
Free transfer to the public	Popular with the public	Retains management; no revenue; no new investment or expertise
Free transfer to employees	Popular with employees	No revenue; no new investment or expertise; unfair to public
Free transfer to users or customer cooperative	Popular; eliminates problem and money drain; transparent	Raises no revenue
Free transfer to original owner	Fair	Raises no revenue; unpopular?
Liquidation	Gets rid of problem; raises some cash	Worker opposition
Default	Subtle solution	Temporary public complaints
Withdrawal	Can do gradually	Public complaints
Deregulation	Good policy	Complex; opposition from vested interests

ordinary (large) buses for public transportation within the city. These buses carried a third of the city's paying passengers. The vehicles were old and poorly maintained, and many were an inappropriate size for their routes. (Buses of the wrong size had been bought because they were the only buses manufactured in the country that provided the foreign aid that made the purchase possible, and purchasing these buses was a condition of the aid.) The buses were garaged and serviced in a large, new depot near the center of the city.

(2) An extensive system of route taxis, that is, private vehicles that ran along fixed routes and picked up and dropped off passengers anywhere along that route (if they had vacant seats), charging a fixed fare. Only sedans could be used for this service; vans, minibuses, and the like were not permitted. Nevertheless, these taxis carried two-thirds of the city's paying passengers.

(3) Privately owned bus companies that used large buses restricted to intercity service, charter service (for example, for tourists), and transporting school children.

The SOE was losing a great deal of money and, having just built the costly depot, was faced with the added need to buy an expensive new bus fleet to replace the aging one that had been poorly maintained. Moreover, there was widespread dissatisfaction with the service. For these reasons, because of the likelihood of a continued drain on this nation's resources, and because the nation's political leaders became convinced that the private sector could do a much better job and relieve the government of a troublesome burden, the decision was made to privatize the SOE.

Immediately numerous policy questions arose. Should the SOE be sold intact? If not, what should be done with it? Which form or forms of privatization should be employed? Which regulations, if any, should be eliminated? What new regulations, if any, should be imposed? Given the government's desire to maintain transport services in some of the outlying, less densely populated areas of the city, how can this best be accomplished? Presumably, one reason for the heavy losses of the SOE is the political desire to keep fares low. Should the fare prices be controlled? Should city transportation continue to be subsidized? Should all passengers be subsidized? Some passengers? Which ones? How, that is, by what mechanism? What is the best way to privatize passenger transportation in this city?

A recommended privatization plan involved the following elements: selling the buses, by auction; selling or leasing the new depot directly, by bidding and negotiation, perhaps to a consortium of private bus or taxi owners; liquidating the SOE; deregulating entry and allowing the private transport industry to use vans, small buses, or any other vehicles; awarding (by competitive bidding) exclusive, fixed-term franchises for major routes (to avoid dangerous, cut-throat competition in the city streets) with price regulation based on profits; contracting for service to the low-density areas by competitive bidding (in effect, subsidizing these routes); establishing safety regulations for driver licensing, vehicle inspection, and mandatory insurance coverage; subsidizing school children and senior citizens at appropriate times of the day, using vouchers (that is, discount passes); otherwise relying on market prices. The support of the current drivers of the GOE buses could be gained if some or all of the buses were given to the drivers, along with franchises of limited duration for certain routes.

Note that this plan includes almost all the forms of privatization shown in table 5.2: sale, free transfer to employees, liquidation, contract, lease, franchise, voucher, and displacement by withdrawal and deregulation.

By Default, Deregulation, and Franchising

My experience in Ukraine illustrates how default, deregulation, and franchising led to the creation of a private bus industry. I arrived in Odessa, Ukraine, in August 1993, under an assistance agreement between the United States and Ukraine, to advise on the privatization of municipal services. As a former "Deputy Vice Mayor" of New York City (this was the Russian approximation of my title, First Deputy City Administrator, when I served under the Deputy Mayor/City Administrator), it was easy to make contact with Odessa's deputy mayor, a dynamic individual who was open to new ideas.

When I explained that my mission was to seek opportunities to privatize municipal services, he encouraged me enthusiastically and arranged meetings with various city and provincial ("oblast") officials. I quickly observed that public transportation—provided by the national Ministry of Transportation, operating at the oblast level—was woefully inadequate, as I counted more than 200 people waiting at each of several bus stops; discussions with ordinary citizens and public officials rapidly confirmed the accuracy of my observations and revealed widespread dissatisfaction with the service. When I raised the idea (over glasses of Slivovitz at his dacha on the banks of the Dniester River one Sunday afternoon) of having private firms provide bus service in the city, however, the deputy mayor was dubious. "Who would be crazy enough to operate a private bus service in Odessa?" he asked. Nevertheless, he suggested that I draft an announcement for the local papers to see if anyone would respond. He translated my draft, had it approved by the City Council, and placed it in the four local Russian and Ukrainian newspapers. The announcement simply stated that the Odessa City Council was interested in having private firms operate buses in the city, and asked interested parties to call for information.

Ultimately eight people showed up at a meeting. Some owned buses used for "shopping tours" to Bulgaria and Istanbul, others were drivers for state-owned enterprises that had buses for transporting enterprise employees between job sites but were underutilized. Of invaluable assistance in this entire project was the city's staff person who kept track of transportation issues, but whose work was widely ignored and even ridiculed as useless, given the City's non-role in bus transportation. He turned out to be an indispensable fount of knowledge, generator of ideas, and enthusiastic supporter of the concept.[64]

Extended discussions resulted in laying out four initial routes for the entrepreneurs (in essence, these were franchises), and an agreement that they would (1) receive no subsidy; but (2) charge a market fare, which was fifty times (!) the fare on the public buses (the customary socialist fare covered only 2 percent of the cost of the service); and (3) pay a franchise fee of about 3 percent to the city, to defray in full the cost of a city dispatcher.

The first private buses started operating in November 1993, exactly three months after my agreement with the deputy mayor. The public was greatly satisfied with the new service, despite the unaccustomed high fare, and profusely thanked the city officials for providing this new and much needed service. (This is a politician's dream: a service that costs the city government nothing yet draws grateful appreciation from the citizens.)

The state-run bus service immediately saw this private service as a threat to its long-standing monopoly and tried to sabotage the fledgling program in various ways (e.g., running along the private routes with similar bus numbers—50A instead of 50—but undercharging the private buses) while at the same time improving its own service (by bringing in buses from other cities!). The city government, however, frustrated and unhappy with the state agency—it had been calling in vain for better service for years and had even purchased buses and given them to the agency—supported the private plan. After extensive negotiations, a truce was arranged and the private buses, now increased in number, entered routine operation. The city government helped bring this about in two crucial ways: (1) by applying a creative interpretation to a national law that might have been used to prohibit private bus services—in effect, they deregulated by treating the private buses as taxis; and (2) by guaranteeing the private operators that if they could not get fuel from their own sources, the city would sell them fuel, at market prices. (Fuel shortages were widespread in Ukraine at the time.) These two acts by the city government, coupled with the city's protection against the hostile state bus agency, proved to be critical to the success of the program.

In January 1994, just six weeks after the start of the program in Odessa, I returned to Ukraine and, together with my successor on the project and Odessa's transportation specialist, went on a 1,400-kilometer road tour, visiting the cities of Nikolaev, Zaparozhye, Donetsk, and Kharkov in a one-week blitz. We met with the mayors of those cities and explained what we had done in Odessa, arousing great interest. At the same time, television stations throughout Ukraine were reporting favorably on Odessa's private bus program; this was part of our carefully planned publicity effort.

The benefits of the program were so obvious and well known that the idea spread like wildfire throughout all of Ukraine. By August 1995, just two years after my first meeting with Odessa's deputy mayor and after overcoming many problems, a private bus industry, complete with an industry trade association, had emerged. No less than 52 private companies were in existence, operating with 1,700 buses in 75 cities. Plans were afoot to establish a bus assembly plant in Ukraine. Subsidiary industries sprouted for bus repair, rehabilitation, customization, and advertising on buses. The state agency learned a lesson from the marketplace: it raised its regular fares, thereby recovering a larger portion of its costs through the fare box, saving about $10 million per year, and reducing the drain on government funds, while the public's demand for more government service abated. In the meantime, an estimated 5,000 new jobs were created and the public began getting vastly better transportation service. The services, the savings, and the job creation were expected to continue growing rapidly. In short, a private bus transportation industry was established where before there was only a malfunctioning and inadequate government monopoly. Postscript: Three years later the mayor of Lviv, another major city in Ukraine, was re-elected primarily because he had introduced private transportation in his city.

The critical factors for success in this case were

- openness by a high-ranking official to the idea of privatized public services, a new idea imported by a foreign expert;
- an internal "champion" of the idea, the city's staff person responsible for transportation;
- government default and an obvious need for more and better service for the public;

- entrepreneurs willing to take a chance;
- creative deregulation by the city government, allowing private firms to enter the field;
- franchise awards by the city government;
- city support for this infant industry by assuring the firms of fuel supplies and protecting them from the predatory state monopolist;
- widespread publicity and reporting of the successes; and
- superb guidance of the project by my successor, working closely with city officials.

There are even more lessons to be learned, however. At one point the private bus firms were bribing public bus drivers to disappear from their routes, so that the private buses would be able to pick up even more passengers. The public drivers were given enough cash to correspond to normal fare receipts, which they would turn in as usual at the end of the day, and also a sizable bribe for abandoning their routes that day. Even rudimentary management oversight in the public bus agency would have prevented this corrupt practice. The moral of the story is that good management, anticorruption watchdogs, and monitoring of franchisees are necessary for proper privatization (and for government operations in general, for that matter).

Managing the Privatization Process

Privatization is more a *political* than an *economic* act. Long-term, incrementalist tactics are needed to implement a privatization strategy, with a research and public relations effort to press for internal and external support respectively, tax reforms to encourage it, legislation to allow it, and strong coalitions of stakeholders—some newly converted—to support it. It may also be necessary to erode antiprivatization coalitions, for example, by selling or giving shares to workers of a GOE that is to be privatized.[65]

Government must organize and manage the process. A useful set of management guidelines for this vital task is summarized here;[66] these are elaborated and discussed in detail in chapter 7 (for contracting) and chapter 8 (for divestment):

1. **Assure that the political will exists and is understood throughout the government;** this is the most important requirement, without which the process is doomed.

2. **Assign unambiguous responsibility for the process,** for it is a complicated one that requires authority, resources, knowledgeable personnel, and often consultants.

3. **Establish clear objectives for the privatization program.** As just noted, because there may be many different desirable but sometimes conflicting objectives, careful attention must be given to this step. Intuitive feelings are not enough.

4. **Select the appropriate form of privatization,** choosing among the many different forms identified previously or crafting a suitable combination of them. The selection should be based on a careful analysis of the sector, sector trends, experiences elsewhere, political factors, employee relations, degree of competition that can be elicited, financial conditions, estimates of the situation-specific economic and other benefits that may be realized, and the privatization objectives.

5. **Enact necessary legal reforms.** Privatization may require new laws to protect private investors and to allow contracting for services, selling state assets such as natural resources, or establishing long-term concessions for infrastructure, for example.

6. **Develop clear and transparent procedures for the process:** competitive bidding, public announcements, disclosure of prices and bidders, and oversight. Chapter 8 discusses bidding in more detail, but suffice it to say that the hallmarks of a good procedure are open and equitable criteria for qualifying bidders and selecting winners, a reasonable timetable, and clear standards for performance, payment, and future investment (if appropriate).

7. **Estimate the values of assets and enterprises** that are slated for divestment by using professional assessment specialists. Different methods may be used, such as discounted cash flow, liquidation value, replacement value, book value, or comparative value, but ultimately the only valid measure is the market price as determined by a competitive process, such as auction, bid, or public share offering. Governments typically have greatly inflated and unrealistic expectations of the value of their troubled enterprises and deteriorating assets. Generally speaking, the ease of gaining support for privatizing an enterprise is inversely proportional to the difficulty of finding a buyer.

8. **Deal fairly with current employees.** This topic is treated at length in chapter 11.

9. **Address fears that privatization will harm the poor.** This topic, too, is dealt with in chapter 11.

10. **Gain public support by educating the public about privatization.** The public must come to understand, however superficially, what privatization is, why it is necessary, the problems it is intended to overcome, the short-term and long-term advantages, how it will be carried out, and how all segments of the public stand to benefit.

Summary

Certain common symptoms help identify privatization candidates. Privatization objectives are varied and sometimes mutually exclusive, and they must be selected thoughtfully. Privatization is not enough, however; a suitable policy environment is needed to achieve the desired goals.

Divestment, delegation, and displacement encompass twenty different specific techniques to privatize services, enterprises, and assets. Each of the techniques has unique characteristics with advantages and disadvantages. Together they comprise an impressive arsenal to be used selectively by discerning public officials. Guidelines for executing privatization programs have been developed based on widespread experiences. Competition is the essential ingredient common to successful privatizations.

CHAPTER SIX

The Results of Privatization

PRIVATIZATION IS POPULAR and growing throughout the world for purely pragmatic reasons. When carried out sensibly, it leads to greater productivity and better economic performance. Numerous convincing studies of competitive contracting and divestment provide overwhelming and unambiguous evidence as to the effectiveness of privatization. Comprehensive studies of public services—typically municipal services—that have been privatized by contracting are numerous and widespread because the services themselves are very similar in different cities and even in different countries: solid-waste collection, bus transport, water supply, and the maintenance of vehicles, parks, and streets, for example. Hence, these studies can be carried out across jurisdictions and aggregated, leading to a large volume of responsible studies. In contrast, every state-owned enterprise is different and operates under a different regime in each country; no country has more than one national airline and one national telephone company. This would appear to make it harder to draw compelling conclusions about divestments of such enterprises, but, in fact, several important studies of such divestments have been conducted and are presented here. First, the principal studies of contracting are reviewed and then the evidence on divestment, comparing public and private enterprises.

Contracting for Public Services

Contracting has been examined in the United States, Canada, England, Germany, Japan, and Switzerland, through surveys of public officials, before-and-after studies, and cross-sectional econometric studies. These studies demonstrate that savings average about 25 percent for the same level and quality of services, after taking into account the cost of administering and monitoring the contract.[1] These three very different kinds of studies are remarkably consistent and mutually corroborative. The results do not mean, of course, that savings are guaranteed—every situation must be examined individually—but the probability of significant savings is very high and therefore a feasibility study is often warranted. In Britain this is more than a recommendation, it is law: local governments cannot merely continue performing their municipal functions using their own municipal work forces year after year. Under the Local Government Act of 1988, as noted in chapter 7, competitive tendering (bidding) is compulsory for an array of common local services, with outside firms able to compete against the in-house labor force.

Surveys of Public Officials

The fact that contracting is commonplace and growing indicates that, on the whole, public officials are satisfied with it. Surveys corroborate this intuitive assessment. Two early surveys of government officials showed that about 60 percent of responding officials considered contracting to be less costly or no more costly than in-house service. By a ratio of about four to one they considered the quality of contracted services to be at least as good as in-house services.[2]

A larger, subsequent study in New Jersey covered every county and one-sixth of all the municipalities, randomly chosen. It was found that public officials are overwhelmingly satisfied with contract services: 61 percent were very satisfied and 28 percent were somewhat satisfied; only 8 percent percent were dissatisfied and the remaining 3 percent had no opinion. Cost savings (41 percent) and in-house limitations (30 percent— insufficient expertise, inadequate facilities, high capital investment required) are the major reasons they cited for contracting out.[3]

A major nationwide survey conducted in 1987 provides further evidence in support of contracting. Three-quarters of U.S. local governments that contract for services reported that cost savings are an advantage of contractin. Of 450 respondents, 11 percent reported savings of 40 percent or more, 41 percent reported savings of 20 percent or more, and 80 percent reported savings of at least 10 percent.[4] Public officials responding to surveys in several states in Australia reported savings of 16 to 19 percent, but the responses were few, ranging from 49 to 116.[5]

The 100 largest cities in the United States were surveyed in 1995. Of the 66 responding cities, 82 percent reported that they were satisfied or very satisfied with privatization, and the remaining 18 percent were neutral; none said they were dissatisfied. Asked why they privatized, 54 percent replied that they had done it to reduce costs and 30 percent to improve service;

they reported an average improvement in service delivery of about 25 percent for each of the four major service areas: public works/transportation, public safety, human services, and parks and recreation. The survey's authors conclude that "[P]rivatization is now firmly entrenched as a viable, alternative service delivery option in most of America's largest cities."[6]

One can and should go beyond the positive attitudes of public officials about contracting to examine carefully executed, comprehensive, comparative studies of contracted services. After all, privatization by contracting out might be no more than a temporary enthusiasm, a fad not unlike many earlier nostrums for improving productivity. Moreover, answers given by public officials to opinion surveys are suspect if they are reporting on privatizations that they themselves initiated.

Before-and-After Studies

There is by now a lengthy list of quantitative studies demonstrating quite conclusively that, in general, contracted services cost less and are at least as good in quality as corresponding services produced in-house by government agencies. Two types of studies lead to this conclusion: before-and-after studies and cross-sectional studies.

By far the most common studies are before-and-after comparisons carried out in individual jurisdictions. The cost and quality of contractual service, provided by a newly hired contractor, is contrasted with the cost and quality of prior in-house work. Such comparisons are numerous; they are easy to do and may be carried out in the normal course of events.

There are drawbacks to such studies, however; the first is that in individual cases it is often extremely difficult to distinguish rigorously between the effect of contracting and other changes that may have taken place simultaneously, such as changes in service guidelines or a changed operating environment. Second, such routine comparisons are sometimes not as systematic or professional as they should be. Third, there is an inevitable reporting bias: when a service is contracted out, it is reported; but, if an in-house study concludes that contracting out would cost more, without a commensurate improvement in service level or quality, the decision to make no change is rarely reported. (And of course, just as contracting is sometimes erroneously adopted because of a poorly executed study, it is sometimes erroneously rejected because of a poorly executed study.)

A fourth shortcoming of such simple comparisons is that they contrast an existing in-house service with service by a newly hired private contractor. A commonly cited concern is that the first contract may result from an artificially low bid, made in order to capture the service, and that the price will subsequently be raised to a much higher level. (This is called lowballing; evidence contradicts this common belief, and, as discussed in the next chapter, is easy to avoid.) Finally, these simple comparisons can be countered by pointing to contrary instances, wherein a contractor was replaced and the government agency took over and began (or resumed) doing the work in-house.

Large-scale studies.   Having identified these possible shortcomings, however, one should not ignore all such evidence. Can so many different jurisdictions be wrong? Several noteworthy large-scale experiences are summarized in table 6.1.

The Los Angeles County Auditor-Controller examined all 651 contracts that had been entered into by the county over an eight-year period for data conversion, grounds maintenance, and custodial, food, laundry, and guard services. The contracts totaled $182 million and saved the county $86 million from its original in-house cost of $268 million; that is, the in-house cost was 47 percent greater than the contract price or, conversely, the contract savings were 32 percent. A total of 2,700 positions were eliminated, or 3.6 percent of the county's total.[7] Los Angeles then

TABLE 6.1—SUMMARY OF BEFORE-AND-AFTER STUDIES

Contracting agency [source of study]	Number of contracts	Cost before contracting (millions)	Savings in percentages
Los Angeles County, 1979–87 [Los Angeles County Auditor-Controller]	651	$268	32
Los Angeles County, 1979–89 [Los Angeles County Auditor-Controller]	812	701	28
U.S. Department of Defense, 1980–82 [same]	285	1,128	31
U.S. Department of Defense, 1983–84 [same]	131	132	33
U.S. Department of Defense, 1978–86 [U.S. General Accounting Office]	1,661	2,270	27
U.S. Department of Defense, 1978–94 [Center for Naval Analyses]	2,138	4,768	31
Wandsworth Borough, London, 1978–87 [Centre for Policy Studies]	23	174	27
GSA Public Buildings Service, FY92 [U.S. General Accounting Office]	576	N.A.	25
State of Western Australia, 1993–94 [University of Sydney]	891	324	20

expanded its privatization program even more aggressively and a subsequent study two years later summarized the county's ten-year experience: a total of 812 contracts costing $508 million resulted in savings of $193 million, or 28 percent; 4,700 positions were eliminated, or 6 percent of the total, yet this was accomplished with only a handful of layoffs.[8] (No information is presented on the relative quality of the work or on the cost of contract administration and monitoring.) This study is particularly compelling because the county official who conducted these studies was independently elected and not part of the county administration that contracted for the services.

At the request of the U.S. Congress, the Department of Defense reported before-and-after comparisons of its contracts for commercial services. The study covered all 285 contracts awarded during a two-year period for support activities such as data processing, food service, and audio-visual services, and revealed that the cost of this work when done in-house prior to the competitions had been 45 percent higher than the cost of the contract work. (Therefore the savings were 31 percent.)[9] A similar study of all 131 contracts awarded the next year showed that the contracts cost $87.5 million but saved $43.9 million; that is, the in-house cost had been 50 percent greater and the savings were 33 percent.[10] (No data on comparative quality are offered nor are the costs of contract administration and monitoring discussed.) The studies cover only the cases in which contracts were *awarded*; presumably there were many cases where no savings could have been realized and, therefore, no contracting took place. Thus, one cannot conclude from these Los Angeles and federal studies that *all* in-house services cost 28 percent to 50 percent more than comparable contract work.

The U.S. General Accounting Office (GAO) examined 1,661 cost-comparison studies (including the 416 studies previously discussed) covering 25 major types of commercial functions performed by the Department of Defense. The original cost of performing the work in-house was compared to the contractor bids and to lower-cost bids made by in-house units that faced the threat of privatization. The GAO found that the original cost had been 37 percent greater than the winning bids, and that an estimated $614 million (27 percent) had been saved by this competitive process.[11] This study was subsequently extended to cover eight more years, a total of 2,138 contracts; the extended data show that savings due to such competition increased to an average of 31 percent over the entire 16-year period.[12] As in the case of Los Angeles County, this study was carried out by an independent agency.

The other three studies shown in table 6.2 reveal similar findings. The Borough of Wandsworth, in London, introduced competition for its munic-

TABLE 6.2—BEFORE-AND-AFTER STUDIES OF BUS SERVICES

Bus system	Savings by contracting (in percentages)
Copenhagen[b]	22
Denver[b]	33
Houston[a]	37
Indianapolis[b]	22
London[b]	46
Las Vegas[b]	33
Los Angeles, 1988[a]	38
Los Angeles, 1989[a]	48
Miami[a]	29
New Orleans[a]	50
San Diego[a]	44
Stockholm[b]	32

Sources: [a]E. S. Savas, "A Comparative Study of Bus Operations in New York City," Report No. FTA NY-11-0040-92-1, Federal Transit Administration, U.S. Department of Transportation, 1992; [b]Wendell Cox et al., "Competitive Contracting in Public Transit: Review of the Experience," 1996 Public Transportation Assessment, Supplemental Report, Legislative Transportation Committee, State of Washington, 1 February 1997.

ipal services. About one-third of the competitions were won by the in-house workforce and two-thirds by private contractors, leading to overall savings of 27 percent.[13] A GAO study of the Public Buildings Service of the U.S. General Services Administration focused on custodial and maintenance contracts for buildings and found that savings averaged 25 percent for the services that were contracted out.[14] The Competitive Tendering and Contracting Research Team at the University of Sydney studied contracting in the State of Western Australia and found that savings averaged 20 percent of the pre-contract cost.[15]

What is most striking about table 6.1 is how similar the results are in the United States, Britain, and Australia; the savings range from 20 to 33 percent. The British situation is unclear, however; the official position is that savings due to compulsory competitive tendering (CCT) averaged only 6 percent, but skeptics assert that quality specifications were raised for contracts (thereby invalidating the cost comparisons) and that the threat of CCT resulted in cost reductions for in-house work, lessening the apparent advantage of outside contractors.[16] A more direct way to force competition between the in-house unit and outside contractors, "managed competition," is discussed in the next chapter. In the studies cited here, one can presume that the responsible officials compared in-house costs with contract bids and chose the least costly, without formally inviting competing bids from their own workers.

Studies of bus service. Table 6.2 summarizes studies of city bus services before and after contracting. Savings tend to be even larger for contracted bus services in the United States than for the functions represented in table 6.1 because federal funding through the Urban Mass Transportation Act has had the effect of driving up the cost of public bus operations.

Other major studies of bus services are summarized in table 6.3. These are not before-and-after studies, strictly speaking, but they are nevertheless instructive. They reinforce the general findings that private bus costs are substantially lower than public bus costs and that contract bus service is highly cost-effective compared to public bus service. The study by Perry and Babitsky finds that cost-plus contracts are not cost-effective; this is consistent with the recommendations on contracting presented in the next chapter.

Cross-Sectional Studies

The before-and-after studies examined in the previous section provide strong support for competitive contracting. For more compelling and definitive evidence one must, however, turn to another type of study: comprehensive, cross-sectional, deliberate, econometric studies that compare in-house and contract services across samples of randomly chosen jurisdictions. Such studies are time-consuming, costly, and difficult to carry out. Nevertheless, enough careful studies of this type have been completed since 1975 to provide definitive evidence on the efficiency of contracting for services. The most extensive summary of these studies covers solid-waste management, street sweeping, street repaving, traffic-signal maintenance, bus transportation, administrative services, custodial work, tree maintenance, lawn maintenance, and corrections. In short, it costs about one-third more to do the work using in-house forces than to use a contractor selected through competitive bidding. In all these studies the cost of contract administration and monitoring was included and the quality of the work was studied and found to be the same for both municipal and contract work.[17] Another important study found no evidence that the greater efficiency of contractors results in lower quality work.[18] Table 6.4 presents data from the most comprehensive single study. These studies do not show the effects of privatization, strictly speaking; they compare results in randomly selected jurisdictions, half of which use public agencies and the other half private contractors to do the work.

TABLE 6.3—COMPARISON OF PUBLIC AND PRIVATE BUS SERVICES

Study authors	Nature of study	Conclusions
Morlok and Viton, 1985[a]	Survey of five major studies in the U.S., U.K., and Australia	Private bus costs are 50% to 60% lower than public bus costs.
Morlok and Moseley, 1986[b]	Survey of 31 bus systems	Average savings by contracting with private firms were 29%.
Perry and Babitsky, 1986[c]	Private vs. cost-plus private contract vs. public bus	Private operators are significantly more efficient. Cost-plus systems contractors and municipal bus lines are less efficient.
Teal et al., 1987[d]	Study of 864 bus systems	For large bus systems, private bus costs are 44% less than public bus costs. A large public bus system (more than 250 buses) should be able to save 36% to 50% by contracting with a private firm to operate more than 25 buses.
Sherlock and Cox, 1987[e]	Survey of 567 private bus systems	From 1970 to 1983, cost per mile for private buses decreased 3% whereas for public buses it increased 52%. The average cost of service by private contractors is 32% less than the cost of public service.
Walters, 1987[f]	Study of bus service in five large cities	Private operators generally appear to be 50% to 65% less expensive than public buses and usually pay large sums of money into government treasuries.

[a]Edward K. Morlok and Philip A. Viton, "The Comparative Costs of Public and Private Providers of Mass Transit," in *Urban Transit: The Private Challenge of Public Transportation,* Charles A. Lave, ed. (Cambridge, Mass.: Ballinger Publishing Co., 1985), 233–53.

[b]Edward K. Morlok and Frederick A. Moseley, *Potential Savings from Competitive Contracting of Bus Transit,* Report R-UP8851-86-1 (Washington, D.C.: Urban Mass Transportation Administration, April 1986).

[c]James Perry and T. Babitsky, "Comparative Performance in Urban Transit," *Public Administration Review,* 46, no. 1 (January/February 1986): 57–66.

[d]Roger F. Teal et al., *Estimating the Cost Impact of Transit Service Contracting,* Report CA-06-0220 (Washington, D.C.: Urban Mass Transportation Administration, December 1987).

[e]Norman Sherlock and Wendell Cox, *The Potential for Optimizing Public Transit through Competitive Bidding* (Washington, D.C.: Urban Mass Transportation Administration, March 1987).

[f]A. A. Walters, "Ownership and Efficiency in Urban Buses," in *Prospects for Privatization,* Steve H. Hanke, ed. (New York: Academy of Political Science, 1987), 83–92.

TABLE 6.4—COMPARATIVE CROSS-SECTIONAL STUDIES

Functional area	Savings by contractors (in percentages)
Solid-waste collection	25
Street construction	49
Street cleaning	30
Building custodial services	42
Traffic light maintenance	36
Tree pruning	27

Source: Barbara J. Stevens, "Comparing Public- and Private-Sector Productive Efficiency: An Analysis of Eight Activities," *National Productivity Review* 3, no. 4 (Autumn 1984): 395–406.

Studies of Other Services

A comprehensive survey of many different studies examining public versus private services was compiled by John Hilke;[19] some of the findings are summarized in table 6.5.

More than 100 independent studies are summarized, representing a wide range of services, including maintenance at military bases, property assessment, nursing home operation, claims processing, postal services, railroad repairs, automobile towing, forestry, slaughterhouses, and weather forecasting. Most of the studies were conducted in the United States, but studies from Germany, Canada, Australia, and Denmark are also included; the U.S. studies examined federal, state, county, and municipal services. These studies are of uneven quality compared to the previous studies cited in detail, and some represent simple, individual, before-and-after studies. Nevertheless, because of their sheer quantity and range, they deserve to be mentioned here. The studies typically found cost reductions of 20 percent to 50 percent resulting from privatization.

Why Contracting Works

The reason that government services are so often both costly and poor is not that the people who work in government are somehow inferior to those who work in the private sector; they are not. In fact, the issue is not public vs. private but monopoly vs. competition. Monopoly is generally inferior to competition in providing high-quality, low-cost goods and services, and most government activities are unnecessarily organized

TABLE 6.5—OTHER STUDIES OF PUBLIC VERSUS PRIVATE SERVICE DELIVERY

Service area	Findings
Maintenance support for air force bases	Contracting reduced cost 13% by use of 25% fewer personnel; achieved improved availability of parts and planes.
Airline operation	Efficiency measures of private airline were 12% to 100% higher.
Airports	Airports subject to market forces had savings of 40%.
Property-tax assessment	Private assessments were 50% less expensive and more accurate.
Cleaning services	In-house work cost 15% to 100% more.
Day care	Private day care cost 45% less because of fewer teachers, fewer non-teaching staff, and lower wages.
Debt collection	Private services were faster and 60% less costly.
Fire protection	Switching to private contract firefighting saved 20% to 50%.
Forestry	Labor cost was twice as much per unit of output for public agency.
Housing	Public agencies cost 20% more than private contractors.
Insurance claims processing	Private insurers' equivalent costs were 15% to 26% lower.
Laundry service	Private costs were 46% lower than public costs.
Legal services	Contract counsel was faster and cost 50% less.
Military support services	Contract costs were lower because of higher productivity and lower wages, but contract costs increased over time.
Motor-vehicle maintenance	Contractor costs were lower because of greater productivity.
Nursing homes	Contract-operated homes cost 45% less per day.
Parking	Contracting costs less because of lower fringe benefits and greater flexibility in staffing.
Parks and recreation	Cost savings of 20% to 31% because of privatizing.
Payroll and data processing	One study found no differences; another found higher-quality data processing and cost savings of 15%.
Postal service	Contractors saved up to 66% on delivery and 88% on window services.
Printing	Private costs were 33% lower for commercial printing.
Prisons	Private construction cost 45% less; operations cost 35% less.
Railroads	Private railroad handled repairs 70% more efficiently; a public railroad increased its efficiency after competition was increased.
Security services	Private security services saved 50% or more.
Ship repair and maintenance	Private ship repair costs averaged 80% less than navy's costs.
Slaughterhouses	Public agencies were significantly more costly because of overcapacity and overstaffing.
Towing of automobiles	Contract towing provided cost savings of more than 40%.
Weather forecasting	Private forecasters provided equivalent service at 35% lower cost.

Source: Derived from John Hilke, *Cost Savings from Privatization: A Compilation of Study Findings* (Los Angeles: Reason Foundation, 1993).

and run as monopolies. Privatization, when properly carried out, gives public officials and the public a choice; choice fosters competition, and competition leads to more cost-effective performance. Thus, as noted, privatization means dissolving public monopolies and introducing competition in the delivery of public services. The public will benefit from this competition, provided that sound, competition-promoting procedures are employed.

The productivity gains through contracting result, in general, from more work performed per employee per unit time, not from lower wages. A study by the National Commission for Employment Policy "found no significant pattern of lower wages" paid by private contractors.[20] This finding is corroborated in a survey of municipal privatization in Illinois, which found that of the city officials who knew the wages paid by their contractors, 78 percent reported that the wages were the same (40 percent) or greater (38 percent) than the municipal wages for that work. Only 10 percent reported that contract wages were lower than their own.[21] Fringe benefits show a mixed pattern but are generally somewhat lower in the private sector; the difference is greatest in pension contributions, holidays, and sick leave.[22] Whether the private-sector benefits are too low or the public-sector benefits too high is a value judgment, of course, but Mayor Edward Rendell of Philadelphia battled the municipal unions in 1993 over the holiday issue: municipal employees enjoyed eighteen paid holidays a year, including Flag Day! Noting that taxpayers who worked in the private sector generally had only nine holidays a year, the mayor saw no reason why they should pay to provide this extravagant benefit to municipal employees.

After an extensive study of municipal services, Barbara J. Stevens concludes that there is no statistically significant difference between municipal and contract work with respect to salaries, service quality,[23] or the cost of fringe benefits. The observed cost difference is accounted for by the factors shown in table 6.6. Contractors (1) provide less paid time off for their employees (less vacation time and fewer paid absences such as unlimited sick leave); (2) use part-time and lower-skilled workers where possible (not shown in this table); (3) are more likely to hold their managers responsible for equipment maintenance as well as worker activities; (4) are more likely to give their first-line managers the authority to hire and fire workers; (5) are more likely to use incentive systems; (6) are less labor intensive (that is, they make greater use of more productive capital equipment); (7) have younger workforces, with less seniority; and (8) have relatively

TABLE 6.6—MANAGEMENT POLICY DIFFERENCES BETWEEN MUNICIPAL AGENCIES AND PRIVATE CONTRACTORS

Management policy	Municipal agency	Private contractor
Direct labor as percentage of total cost	60.2	49.0
Number of pieces of capital equipment	4.54	5.42
Percentage of cities with unionized workforce	48.1	20.0
Average age of workers	36.1	32.1
Average tenure of workers	8.12	5.83
Number of vacation days per year per worker	14.0	10.1
Average number of days absent per year per worker for any reason (other than vacation)	12.85	8.84
Number of management layers between worker and department head	1.91	1.51
Percentage of cities where supervisors can fire workers	16.0	53.7
Percentage of cities using written reprimands for workers	72.5	33.8
Percentage of cities using employee incentive system	12.3	26.9
Percentage of cities where service provider maintains the equipment used in the service	48.1	92.5
Percent of cities holding staff meetings	81.5	53.8

Source: Barbara J. Stevens, ed., *Delivering Municipal Services Efficiently: A Comparison of Municipal and Private Service Delivery* (Washington, D.C.: U.S. Department of Housing and Urban Development, Office of Policy Development and Research, 1984),

more workers and fewer supervisors, that is, more Indians and fewer chiefs. Stevens concludes that

> [I]n the majority of public agencies, the concepts of clear, precise task definitions and job definitions, coupled with easily identifiable responsibility for job requirements, are not enforced as vigorously as in the majority of private enterprises. It is this difference that appears, in general, to be responsible for the very significant public sector–private sector cost differences.[24]

The increased productivity associated with competitive contracting is dramatically illustrated in table 6.7 and table 6.8, for street sweeping and solid-waste collection respectively. The street-sweeping study in Newark, N.J., was carried out in two carefully drawn districts of the city that were similar in virtually every important respect. As is evident in the first row of table 6.7, the streets in the two areas were equally dirty (or clean), with 0.19 tons of litter per curb mile. After that, however, the table shows that the two areas are very different in terms of productivity. The contractor sweeps about 2.5 times as many miles per shift, with the result that

TABLE 6.7 — COMPARISON OF PUBLIC AND CONTRACT STREET SWEEPING

Efficiency measure	Municipal	Contract
Tons collected per curb mile	0.19	0.19
Tons collected per shift per sweeper	1.2	2.9
Cost per ton collected	$449	$179
Curb miles swept per shift per sweeper	6.5	16.3
Cost per curb mile swept	$84	$32

Source: Report on Street Cleaning, Director of Engineering, Newark, N.J., 16 March 1994.

the municipal service costs 162 percent more than contract service, $84 compared to $32.[25]

The comparison of productivity between public and private refuse collection in table 6.8 shows a comparably large difference. The two cities, Mount Vernon, N.Y., and East Orange, N.J., are only twenty-one miles apart in the New York metropolitan area, and each considered the other to be a very similar city, as indicated by population, area, total annual tonnage of solid waste, and service levels (collection frequency and location). The difference in operating practices was immense, however, with four workers in each municipal crew compared to only two per contract crew, and 63 truck shifts a week versus 39. As a result of these differences, contract collection was 2.84 times as productive as municipal collection, in terms of tons collected per man per day, and municipal collection was 34 percent more costly, $39 per household compared to $29.14.

TABLE 6.8 — COMPARISON OF PUBLIC AND CONTRACT SOLID-WASTE COLLECTION

	Mount Vernon, N.Y.	East Orange, N.J.
Collection arrangement	municipal	contract
Population	70,000	74,000
Area (square miles)	4.3	3.8
Tons collected annually	41,973	39,312
Collections per week	3	3
Collection location	curb	curb
Truck shifts per week	63	39
Men per truck	4	2
Man-days per week	237	78
Tons collected per man-day	3.40	9.67
Productivity index	1.00	2.84
Cost per household	$39.00	$29.14

Source: Barbara J. Stevens and E. S. Savas, "An Analysis of the Feasibility of Private Refuse Collection and Disposal in Mount Vernon, New York," report submitted to the Mount Vernon Urban Renewal Agency, January 1977.

The reasons cited here for the relatively low productivity of government can be considered immediate causes. The ultimate cause, as stated previously, is the absence of competition. When a government agency performs the work directly, it usually acts as a monopoly; when an agency is forced to compete with a contractor, it can be made more productive, and even match the contractor's performance,[26] as discussed in chapter 7.

Rowan Miranda went further and examined the effects of contracting on total city expenditures and municipal employment in American cities. He found that the form of city government makes a difference: in council-manager cities, contracting significantly reduces total expenditures and total municipal employment, whereas in mayor-council cities it does not. That is, savings realized from contracting certain services are used to reduce total costs and the number of workers in council-manager cities, but the savings are spent in other ways in mayor-council cities.[27] There is nothing wrong with this of course; for example, Mayor Stephen Goldsmith of Indianapolis made it an explicit policy to use the savings from his aggressive privatization of other municipal services on infrastructure and public safety.[28]

In short, contracting has been found to be superior to in-house service provision in general, but it does not follow that contracting will be advantageous in every single case. Prudent contracting of appropriate services under competitive conditions, preceded by a careful study to gauge the potential benefits and followed by effective monitoring, is the key to success. This self-evident statement has been corroborated empirically by Simon Domberger and David Hensher, who found that contractor-selection procedures and contract-enforcement mechanisms have the greatest influence on contract performance.[29] (Chapter 7 describes in detail how to contract out effectively.) For all the reasons presented here, privatization by competitive contracting is being widely adopted throughout the world.

Privatization of Solid-Waste Collection

It is instructive to look closely at the most studied municipal service in the world: solid-waste collection. Many large research studies were conducted in the 1970s and 1980s, offering a great deal of compelling evidence concerning the efficiency, effectiveness, and equity of contracting out. Privatization of this service is a settled issue; it no longer attracts much attention from researchers. Contracting for this service is a growing phenomenon not only in the United States but also in Europe, South America, and the Middle East. In the United States, 38 percent of all cities were using contract collection for residential refuse collection in 1992,[30] and 50 percent of large cities were doing so.[31]

Efficiency

The comparative efficiency of solid-waste collection arrangements was investigated exhaustively through detailed, nationwide studies in the United States, Canada, Britain, Switzerland, and Japan, as well as in regional studies in Connecticut, California, and the midwestern United States. Ten major studies were conducted by different researchers, some in government and some in academia, over a twelve-year span.[32] The results are strikingly consistent and mutually corroborative, as shown in table 6.9. Examination of these studies leads one to conclude that municipal collection is about 35 percent more costly than contract collection, although a range from 14 to 124 percent is reported. The single report that found no difference had a relatively small sample size and was restricted geographically to only one county in Missouri. (Two other small-scale studies, with sample sizes of 24 and 26 cities, found no difference[33] and greater governmental efficiency[34] respectively; however, these studies failed to distinguish contract collection from free-market arrangements and therefore are not relevant.[35])

The most thorough studies (reported by Savas, by Savas, Stevens, and Berenyi, and by Stevens[36]) included the cities' costs of contract preparation, bidding, monitoring the contractors' performance, contract administration, and the like in the cost of the contract work; they conclude that the cost of municipal collection is about 35 percent greater than the total cost to the city of contract collection. In these studies, municipal collection was monopolistic and not the result of managed competition.

Government is significantly less productive than contractors: it uses more men to do the same amount of work, allows more paid absences by workers, employs less productive vehicles, and therefore services fewer households per hour.[37] These findings in the United States are paralleled in Canada[38] and in Britain.[39]

Municipal collection costs 35 percent more than competitively contracted collection; although this is the relevant figure as far as government budgeting is concerned, the full difference between the two arrangements is even greater. Take into account the following: the cost of contract collection to the city consists of administration costs (4.4 percent of the total) and the price of the contract (95.6 percent of the total).[40] The contract price, in turn, includes both profits and taxes, as well as the actual cost of performing the service. That is, private firms generally pay various fees and taxes—local business licenses, vehicle registration, property taxes, fuel taxes, income taxes—that governments do not. Industry sources in the United States estimate that the sum of all the fees and taxes paid to

TABLE 6.9—COMPARATIVE STUDIES OF PUBLIC AND PRIVATE RESIDENTIAL REFUSE

Author	Study site	Date reported	Data period	Number of cities surveyed	Number of cities analyzed	City size
Savas and Stevens	United States	1975	1974	439	315	2,500– 720,000
Kemper and Quigley	Connecticut	1976	1972–74	N.R.	101	1,100– 158,000
Kitchen	Canada	1976	N.R.	142[a]	48	Over 10,000
Pommerehne and Frey	Switzerland	1977	1970	112	103	5,000– 423,000
Collins and Downes	St. Louis County	1977	N.R.	53	53	Under 500– 65,000
Petrovic and Jaffee	Midwestern United States	1977	1974	149	83	25,000– 180,000
Hamada and Aoki	Japan	1981	1980	N.R.	211	N.R.
McDavid	Canada	1984	1982	N.R.	109	Over 10,000
Stevens	Los Angeles SCSA[d]	1984	1983	20	20	10,000– 200,000
Domberger et al.	Britain	1986	1983–85	610	610	N.R.

Note: N.R. = not reported.

[a]Kitchen reports only that he surveyed all cities over 10,000 in population; there were 142 such cities in 1970.

Source: Adapted from E. S. Savas, "Public vs. Private Refuse Collection: A Critical Review of the Evidence," *Journal of Urban Analysis* 6 (1979): 1–13.

federal, state, and local governments amounts to 15 percent of revenues. The cost of these taxes is, of course, included in the price charged by the firms. Therefore, when a resident pays government $135 for municipal service, he or she gets only that service. But for a price of $100 for equiv-

COLLECTION

Means of data collection	Distinguished private and contract collection?	Distinguished collection and disposal costs?	Findings
Visit, mail, phone	Yes	Yes	Cost of municipal collection is 29% to 37% higher than the price of contract collection in cities larger than 50,000 in population; no difference in effectiveness.
Mail, phone	Yes	Yes	"Cost of municipal collection is 14% to 43% higher than the price of contract collection."
Mail, phone	No[b]	N.R.	"Municipally run refuse collection tends to be much more expensive." "Municipalities could economize by contracting out."
Mail	No	N.R.	"Public production of refuse collection seems to be subject to higher average costs than private production."
Visit	Yes[c]	Yes[c]	"No clear pattern emerges."
Visit, mail	Yes[b]	Yes[c]	"Costs . . . tend to be less for a private firm under contract . . . than for a municipally operated system." Cost of municipal collection is 15% higher than the price.
N.R.	Yes	Yes	Municipal collection costs 124% more than contract collection.
Mail, phone	Yes	Yes	Public collection appears to be 40% to 50% more costly than contract collection.
Visit	Yes	Yes	Municipal collection costs 42% more than contract collection; no quality difference.
City reports	Yes	Yes	Municipal collection costs 28% more than competitive contracting.

[b]McDavid reports that "nearly all private firms operate via contract"; this may also apply to Kitchen's study.

[c]While not stated explicitly, this appears to be the case.

[d]Standard Consolidated Statistical Area.

alent contract service (via the government as purchasing agent), the resident receives not only refuse-collection service but also a bonus of $14.34 (15 percent of $95.60) worth of other, unidentified government services that the firm, in effect, rebates to the resident via its taxes. Taking this rebate into account, the cost to the resident for municipal service is, in fact, 58 percent greater than contract service [$135/(100 − 14.34)].

One further calculation is relevant. Having discussed the effect of taxes included in the price of contract service, let us now examine the effect of profits. The annual reports of several major waste management firms show that profits amount to roughly 10 percent of revenues ($9.56 in this illustration). Therefore, one can conclude that it costs municipal agencies 88 percent more to perform the work than it costs private firms before profits [$135/(95.60 − 14.34 − 9.56)]. To summarize:

1. A municipal budget director has to allocate 35 percent more money for municipal collection than for contract collection of equivalent quality.

2. A resident has to pay 58 percent more for municipal collection than for contract collection, after taking into consideration the tax rebate he or she receives indirectly from the contractor.

3. It costs the municipal agency 88 percent more than it costs the contractor (before taxes and profits) to perform the same work; that is, the agency uses its resources much less productively.

Thus far in this section, we have been comparing the efficiency of government and contract service. What about market and franchise arrangements? Both are common in the United States, as was indicated in chapter 4. Under the market arrangement, each individual household makes its own arrangement with a private firm. One would expect this cost to be higher than the cost of contract collection because of economies of contiguity and billing costs. The contract firm collects from every household in the area, and this is more efficient—because there are more customers per unit area—than a market arrangement where different firms may collect on the same block. A franchised firm operating in a community with mandatory collection—where every household must subscribe to the service—is like a contract firm (and like a municipal agency, for that matter) in that it realizes these economies of contiguity. Billing costs are a significant cost factor for firms operating under either a franchise or a market system; the cost of sending out bills to each household, and losses resulting from unpaid bills, are not incurred by a contract firm, which receives a lump-sum payment from the city in response to a single bill.[41] Contracting is the most efficient arrangement for residential solid-waste collection; the ideal contracting process is through managed competition.

Effectiveness

Contract service is demonstrably more efficient than municipal service, but is it possible that this is achieved because the service is poorer in quality? This question was settled by studying the effectiveness of different service arrangements through a large-scale, nationwide survey of U.S. households. A total of 8,166 telephone interviews were conducted with randomly selected households in eighty-two randomly selected cities. Private collection service, that is, the market arrangement, received the highest evaluation, with 93 percent of respondents rating it good or excellent, compared to 90 percent for municipal service and 89 percent for contract service. From the standpoint of public policy, "The differences among the three collection arrangements are too small to matter, and . . . the decision as to which arrangement to employ should therefore be based on efficiency."[42]

Equity

Contract service is no less equitable than municipal service and may even be more equitable. An important aspect of equity, it will be recalled from chapter 4, is fairness of service allocation or delivery. Because contract and municipal service are both paid for by municipal revenues, there is no difference between them on this score. I have observed the following, however: A municipal agency that could not meet its daily collection schedule because of vehicle breakdown or absenteeism (both are relatively common with municipal service;[43] municipal agencies are 10 percent more likely to miss a collection than are contract firms[44]) and did not want to pay overtime to finish the routes, typically postponed collection to the next day in the poorer sections of the city—which had less political influence and were minority neighborhoods. This practice was discriminatory and inequitable in its effect. In contrast, a city that contracts for service requires the contractor to complete his daily schedule or pay a penalty. The contractor therefore looks at the city as a workload to be completed, rather than as a set of political districts, some with more influence than others.

I can report another personal observation relating to equity that was recounted in chapter 4. A city that switched from municipal to contract collection put a residency clause in its contract requiring that the contractor's workforce match the racial composition of the city's population. This racial parity had never been reached in the city's own sanitation department, but it was readily reached by the contractor.

In these two respects, service quality and employment, contract service was observed to be more equitable than governmental service in its effect on minority groups.

Anticompetitive Behavior

No discussion of the private-sector role in waste collection would be complete without mention of illegal actions in this industry. Numerous instances have been reported over many years, particularly in and around several large cities, and each case attracts widespread attention and notoriety. The issue involves anticompetitive behavior—the allocation of customers or territories among private firms in the waste-hauling business—sometimes involving threats or acts of violence against a firm that attempts to compete against an entrenched firm. Mayor Rudolph Giuliani won nationwide recognition when he successfully ended Mafia dominance of the commercial waste-collection business in New York; the resulting competition reduced costs to local businesses by 30 to 40 percent.[45] Such incidents are not restricted to a single ethnic group—contrary to popular folklore in some parts of the United States—nor are they unique to the United States.

The waste industry points out, with considerable justification, that the entire industry is unfairly smeared when a waste hauler breaks the law, whereas illegal acts by bankers, stockbrokers, doctors, and lawyers are treated as isolated incidents, as are price-fixing conspiracies in other businesses.

There is more to it than that. Traditionally, in all cultures, waste removal has been a low-status occupation. New workers were recruited primarily from a limited labor pool that consisted of family, friends, and others from the same caste or village. Thus, the work was dominated by untouchables in India, Coptic Christians in Egypt, immigrants from southern Italy in the northeastern United States, Armenian immigrants in southern California, Dutch immigrants in Chicago, Albanians from Yugoslavia in Austria, and Turks in Germany. The resulting tight social network made it easy for members to agree on ways to carry out the arduous and unpleasant work in an amicable, cooperative, noncompetitive manner. Still, however innocently the sociological pattern may have evolved, the end result could be viewed by an outsider as a conspiracy in restraint of trade.

In the United States, the industry changed rapidly, in technology, size, sophistication, and business organization. "Mom and Pop" operations, one-truck firms, and family-owned businesses have all but disappeared, as have old patterns of association. The industry is rapidly evolving, and in almost all areas of the country it has long since been clear that its participants are no different from people in other businesses in terms of obeying the law. The argument that solid-waste collection, or municipal services in general, should not be contracted out because of the possibility of corruption is a red herring.

Summary

Conclusive evidence from a number of authoritative studies shows that the contract arrangement is the most efficient. It is more efficient than franchise or free-market service, and substantially more efficient, as effective, and at least as equitable as municipal service. Government service can be thought of as a permanent monopoly and the free-market arrangement as continuous competition; contracting creates a temporary monopoly with periodic competition, and this is the best arrangement for this service.

The best approach for a city with municipal collection is to divide the city into sections and seek competitive bids for each section *both from private firms and from its own department.* This tactic assures the maximum degree of competition and protects the city against possible collusion by contractors.[46] It can be used by any city with a population greater than 100,000 to create sections of at least 30,000 people, which are large enough to achieve economies of scale in refuse collection.[47]

Divestment of State-Owned Enterprises

State enterprises are being sold all over the world. Sales in 1997 totaled $157 billion, with developed countries (OECD members) accounting for $102 billion and developing countries $55 billion. Divestment activity is accelerating in the latter group: sales worldwide increased by 70 percent over 1996, but sales in developing countries increased by 170 percent.[48] This level of activity shows that divestment is widely regarded as a good policy; evidence supports this belief.

Comparing the performance of public agencies with that of contractors, as summarized in the preceding sections, is relatively easy because municipal services and support services are common and generally similar among various governments, and therefore many comparative studies have been carried out. On the other hand, SOEs differ more, as do the precise terms of privatization, and therefore the results of divestment of, for example, state-owned telecommunications enterprises even in neighboring countries may be very different.

Many studies have compared the performance of private and public companies. For example, an interesting comparison was made between a public and a private trunk airline in Australia. The former was operated by a government agency, whereas the latter operated as a franchise service. The airlines were required to fly similar routes, service similar cities, use similar aircraft, and charge equal prices. Three measures of efficiency were used to compare the airlines: tons of freight and mail carried per employee, passengers carried per employee, and earned revenues per employee. By each measure the private airline displayed greater efficiency, with ten-year means of 204 percent, 122 percent, and 113 percent, respectively, of the corresponding measures for the public airline. A complete analysis for sixteen consecutive years found that the private airline outperformed the public one in every measure and in every year.[49] In contrast, a study of the Canadian National Railroad (state owned) and the Canadian Pacific Railroad (privately owned) showed no significant difference in efficiency. This was attributable to the fact that the two railroads compete with each other and therefore achieve similar results.[50]

Many such studies are summarized by Anthony Boardman and Aidan Vining, by Robert Millward and David Parker, and by John Hilke.[51] Several large-scale studies, however, stand out in examining the performance of public and private commercial enterprises, and these are reviewed in the next section.

Comparison of Public and Private Enterprises in Competitive Environments

The 500 largest manufacturing and mining firms outside the United States were studied by Boardman and Vining: 419 were private companies, 58 were SOEs, and 23 were mixed enterprises, that is, ownership was partly private and partly state. This was not a study of the effects of privatization, as none of these enterprises was privatized (or nationalized) during the period under study, but a comparison of public, private, and mixed enterprises in competitive environments, that is, a comparison of ownership arrangements. The principal findings are profound: (1) private firms are both more profitable (return on equity was 14 percent greater) and more efficient (the ratio of sales to assets was 27 percent greater) than SOEs or mixed enterprises; (2) therefore ownership matters, not just competition; and (3) SOEs and mixed enterprises performed equally poorly compared to the private firms.[52] It is not surprising that private control, not merely some private investment, is the relevant factor; therefore selling minority shares in a SOE—a popular practice—is not privatization but merely raising capital, and it may not lead to much improvement.

Of course, the United States, too, has government-owned enterprises, and some have been examined. A study of four U.S. government corporations (AMTRAK, the Postal Service, the Tennessee Valley Authority, and Conrail before it was privatized) found that all were less effective in containing costs and increasing productivity than private enterprises.[53] Another study of the effect of ownership thoroughly examined more than 100 Indonesian public and private companies that were involved in finance, agriculture, distribution, manufacturing, and transportation, among other sectors. The private firms had higher profit margins and lower operating costs than the SOEs.[54]

Study of Monopoly Enterprises before and after Divestment

A study by the World Bank looked at twelve monopoly SOEs—five utilities, four airlines, two other transport enterprises, and a state lottery—in four countries, Great Britain, Chile, Mexico, and Malaysia, both before and after privatization. A counterfactual approach was used, that is, actual results were compared to a sophisticated extrapolation of what would have happened if the enterprises had remained government owned. A complex econometric analysis examined the effects on all beneficiaries—workers, investors, citizens, and owners, and the results of the analysis were expressed as follows: the net gain due to divestment was equal to 26 percent of the pre-divestment sales revenue. Moreover, workers were better off in three of the twelve divestments due to higher wages and/or the increased value of the shares they received, but the workers in the other nine divested enterprises were not worse off because they were able to find other jobs in the full-employment economy or they received adequate severance pay.[55]

Another study looked at the privatization of five state-owned monopolies in Argentina: telephones, electricity, gas, water and wastewater, and energy.[56] Preliminary results indicate that privatization contributed significantly to the government's fiscal position, improved the financial and productivity performance of the firms under private ownership, and benefited most stakeholders.

The government's fiscal condition was improved by revenues from the sales, taxes paid by the privatized enterprises, and value-added taxes resulting from the increased output of the enterprises, and by elimination of government subsidies to the four firms that were losing money before privatization. Every firm improved financially, and in the aggregate they earned $2 billion annually instead of losing $2 billion. Quality of performance and productivity improved dramatically: in four years the number of telephone lines increased by 63 percent; the ratio of lines per employee more than doubled; the number of public phones jumped 143 percent; international call-minutes almost doubled; and domestic long-distance call-completion rates jumped from only 30 percent to 93 and 99 percent in the two franchise areas. With respect to electricity, the output per employee more than doubled, as did the ratio of customers per employee. The quantity of gas distributed increased by 11 percent. Water production capacity increased by 22 percent and water losses were reduced from 40 percent to the contract target of 25 percent; water supply coverage was expanded by 10 percent and sewerage service by 8 percent. The effect on prices is unclear, as some prices went up, others went down, and the government eliminated some subsidies. About 27 percent of the workers lost their jobs but were cushioned by generous severance benefits (in the range of $10,000 U.S.) and various other measures. The employees who were kept on the payroll benefited from renegotiated labor contracts and additional training.[57]

Study of Enterprises in Competitive Businesses before and after Divestment

This study examined the performance before and after divestment of enterprises, previously government-owned, that were engaged in commercial activities subject to competition, in contrast to the government-owned monopolies discussed earlier. There were 61 companies in the study, from 32 industries and 18 countries (6 developing and 12 industrialized). The researchers found significant positive changes after divestment: a 45 percent increase in profit (measured as percent of sales); a 27 percent increase in sales; an 11 percent increase in efficiency (sales per employee); a 45 percent increase in investment; a 96 percent increase in dividends; a 36 percent decrease in the ratio of long-term debt to equity; and a 6 percent increase in the number of workers employed in the enterprises. The last figure was a surprise, given the general observation that government enterprises are seriously overstaffed, but the number of workers increased in two-thirds of the cases and declined in only one-third. The explanation lies in the 46 percent increase in investment: private owners saw and seized opportunities to expand the business, which led to more hiring. The study authors note that the increases in sales, profits, and dividends did not result from price increases.[58]

In another study, the financial and operating performance of seventy-nine companies in twenty-one developing countries that were divested fully or partially between 1980 and 1992 was examined.[59] The sample included firms operating in competitive and noncompetitive markets. The newly privatized firms were found to have significant increases in profitability, operating efficiency, capital investment, dividends, and total employment. These results are similar to those reported in the preceding paragraph. The fact that employment increased in this study as well (observed in about two-thirds of the companies) supports the hypothesis that more investment and greater efficiency leads to increased output and employment.

Study of Enterprises in Post-Socialist Countries

A study of 6,300 firms in seven post-socialist countries (Bulgaria, Czech Republic, Hungary, Poland, Romania, Slovak Republic, and Slovenia) examined both privatized firms and firms that were still government owned. Those that had been privatized for four years—ranging from 8 percent of the firms in Bulgaria to 89 percent of the firms in the Czech Republic—experienced a productivity increase three to five times as great as those that were still in the hands of the state. The authors conclude that "privatization is the key to restructuring state-owned enterprises."[60]

It may be, however, that the firms that were privatized had certain initial advantages—likely to make privatization easier and subsequent success greater—that were lacking in the firms that were still government owned. In other words, they may have been better to begin with, and the study was therefore affected by selection bias. The same criticism could be directed at the Boardman and Vining study discussed previously if, for example, many of the GOEs had been private firms that were taken over because they were failing.

Another study overcame this limitation by a before-and-after examination of about 160 mid-sized manufacturing firms (100 to 1,500 employees) in Poland, Hungary, and the Czech Republic; about half were still government owned and half had been privatized, the latter in 1990, 1991, or 1992. Compared to the government-owned firms, the privatized ones showed a 28 percent increase in the number of employees, a 77 percent revenue increase, and a 40 percent increase in the revenue per employee three years after the transition. Roman Frydman et al., found that "it is the ability to stem revenue losses and often generate revenue increases that most strongly distinguishes privatized (other than worker-owned) firms from their state counterparts. . . . In general, we find that firms with outsider [nonmanager and nonworker] owners significantly outperform the firms with insider owners on most performance measures, and that the employees are particularly ineffective owners (indeed, less effective than the state)."[61] Note the recurring pattern, in study after study, of higher employment after privatization, following an initial drop during the transition.

Country Studies of Divestment

Numerous studies have been made of privatization programs in various countries.[62] Two are singled out here to illustrate the results of large-scale efforts.

United Kingdom. The privatization program in Britain was evaluated and the key results were summarized as follows:

1. Performance has significantly improved where competition has been introduced.
2. Opportunities to introduce competition in the affected industry during the privatization process were frequently overlooked.
3. Surrogate competition through yardstick comparisons is a poor substitute for actual competition.
4. Even where competition has been limited or absent, however, there have been significant improvements in efficiency.
5. The power of both the state and trade unions has been significantly reduced.
6. The regulator has replaced the state as the single most powerful external body, but regulatory control is inefficient, ineffective, and unduly expensive.
7. Assertions that "public sector assets were sold too cheaply" are largely meaningless.[63]

Privatization led to large-scale reductions in the workforce as companies focused more on profits. But the remaining workers were successful in maintaining their wages relative to other comparable workers. Where market power was reduced, however, as a result of liberalization and the resulting entry of more competitors, for instance, relative wages were also reduced.[64]

Another study, of privatized utilities in the UK, challenges the notion that earnings are high because customers are being overcharged for poorer service. Gas charges have fallen by 23 percent in real terms since privatization, telecom prices by more than half, and electricity prices by 12 percent to residential customers and 25 percent to commercial customers. Before privatization, only 74 percent of residential telephone installations were completed on the promised date, compared to 95 percent after privatization.[65]

An analysis of the privatized electricity system in the UK concludes that the net benefits to customers, shareholders, and the government amounted to a permanent cost-reduction equivalent to 3.2 to 7.5 percent of prices, or a 40 percent return on assets.[66]

A more limited study of water-system privatization in the UK focused on the labor issue. The ten water companies that resulted from the privatization of the state-owned monopoly underwent a marked reduction in staffing. A decade before privatization, the workers numbered approximately 60,700. At the time of privatization they numbered approximately 49,500, and a decade later they numbered 37,500—a decline of 38 percent from the original figure and a 24 percent decline since privatization. A drop in staffing immediately before privatization (in this case, 18 percent) has been typical in Britain, apparently a reflection of managerial actions designed to impress the new private boards of directors.[67]

Mexico.   The Mexican government had privatized 361 firms by 1992. Of these, sufficient data were available for 218 nonfinancial firms to allow comparison of their performance after privatization with their average performance for the four years before privatization. Profitability was up 40 percent, costs per unit were down 18 percent, and output was up 54 percent. Unlike some of the other studies, employment was found to be down by 20 percent; however, the remaining workers did very well: blue collar wages were up 120 percent and white collar wages were up 78 percent. Only 15 percent of the increased profits came from higher prices; 33 percent came from employment cuts and the lion's share, 52 percent, came from increased efficiency.[68]

Summary

The evidence is overwhelming that privatization, whether by contracting (or, by extension, franchising) or divestment, leads to large performance improvements—provided that the process is carried out in accordance with good practice. Gains in efficiency and effectiveness are the norm, and while each privatization is unique, valid generalizations can be made. Contracting generally leads to lower costs due to increased worker productivity, that is, the same amount of work is performed by fewer workers who are often better paid. Divestment generally results in better performance and, as a successful company expands, more employees.

CHAPTER SEVEN

Contracting for Public Services

Competitive contracting—the principal means of privatizing by delegation—is the most common form of privatization in the United States and is mandatory for municipal services in Great Britain. As illustrated in chapter 4, many services can be procured from the private sector. Both public officials and the public at large have accepted the idea that under the proper circumstances private contracting results in better and cheaper public services. Chapter 5 provides detailed evidence to support this view. A survey of 596 U.S. cities showed that the level of privatization increased by 121 percent between 1982 and 1992 and that 28 percent of services had been privatized by contracting out.[1]

Competitive contracting does not necessarily lead to privatization, because it may lead to a "contract" with an in-house unit if the latter can win a fair competition against the private sector. "Privatization" is clearly a misnomer if applied to "contracting in" to a public agency; nevertheless, as used in this chapter it should be understood to refer to competitive contracting and to include the possibility of "contracting in" as well as "contracting out." "Managed competition" is a term increasingly being used for this practice.

Robert Poole presents an intriguing scenario of a fictitious city in California that, over twenty years, gradually contracted out all its services.[2] It started with a contract for private fire protection after the city experienced a serious fire while its firemen were on strike. Following a grand jury indictment of the police chief, in Poole's vivid tale, the city entered into a contract with the county sheriff for police services. In short order thereafter, street, park, and vehicle maintenance were contracted to private firms, followed by building inspection, sewage treatment, and water supply. Then a private guard service replaced the county sheriff. Next, the city sold off its docks, beaches, and parking lots to private operators and its parks to local neighborhood associations. Finally, City Hall itself was sold, and the remaining three employees rented a small office to oversee and manage the contracts. (They charged for the time spent with incredulous researchers and outside officials who swarmed in to see how the city achieved such a low per-capita cost and such a high growth rate with full employment.) This fictitious example is not far-fetched: La Mirada, California, a city of 40,000 people, contracted out more than sixty services and had only fifty-five employees.[3] Mayor Stephen Goldsmith of Indianapolis got into trouble with his unions when he said a city could be run with just a mayor, a police chief, a planning director, a purchasing agent, and a handful of contract monitors.[4]

The Contracting Process

The steps involved in carrying out a competitive process for contracting are shown in table 7.1, which is consistent with the guidelines in chapter 5. The process for awarding a franchise or concession is similar, although these are awarded only to private entities and not to in-house units. Each step is discussed in turn here,[5] but some steps can be taken concurrently.

1. Consider the Idea of Contracting Out

While the idea of privatizing a service can be introduced by anyone in an organization, leadership to give the idea serious consideration has to come from the very top, from a mayor or governor, for example, who sponsors the idea, initiates the necessary actions, and motivates managers to adopt and act on the concept. Private-sector task forces can be effective in helping

---

TABLE 7.1—STEPS IN CONTRACTING FOR SERVICES

1. Consider the idea of contracting out
2. Select the service
3. Conduct a feasibility study
4. Foster competition
5. Request expressions of interest or qualifications
6. Plan the employee transition
7. Prepare bid specifications
8. Initiate a public relations campaign
9. Engage in "managed competition"
10. Conduct a fair bidding process
11. Evaluate the bids and award the contract
12. Monitor, evaluate, and enforce contract performance

such a leader,[6] and so are meetings with privatization experts and other officials in similar positions who have carried out such programs. The decision should be made on pragmatic grounds, not ideological ones.

In no sense is the decision to contract for services an admission of failure or an abdication of government's responsibility, although opponents may claim that it is. The experience in waste management, where contracting and other forms of privatization are far advanced, is instructive. Government is not abandoning its concern for solid-waste management; on the contrary, its involvement is growing. But increasingly governments turn to the private sector to collect waste efficiently and effectively, to dispose of wastes at sophisticated, environmentally sound landfills, to extract energy and recyclables from the waste stream in technologically advanced resource recovery facilities, and to treat hazardous wastes. The public sector retains its responsibility but exercises it by calling on the specialized skills of the private sector and taking advantage of the latter's strengths.

Contracting presents the classic principal-agent problem that emerged after the industrial revolution when sole proprietors gave way to owners and hired managers. The objectives of company owners, the principals, may diverge from the objectives of the managers, the agents. The latter may be perfectly willing to forgo profits for owners in favor of more money and better perquisites for themselves. This presents a control problem, exacerbated because the agent generally has more information than the principals. The principal, therefore, must bear (1) the cost of providing incentives to encourage the agent to pursue the goals of the principal; (2) the cost of obtaining information and monitoring the agent to reduce opportunistic behavior; and (3) the cost of any residual opportunistic behavior by the agent.[7]

The principal-agent problem in government arises at three levels. The public, as the principal, has to control its agents, the elected officials, but the public has no common objective, does not speak with one voice, and, in any event, is unable to communicate its diverse wishes effectively. Second, public officials, acting as principals, must exercise control over their agent, the bureaucracy, a task more difficult than in the private sector because of civil-service protection in the public sector. Finally, government (as principal) must control its agent (the contractor) to pursue the organization's goals at minimum cost, to reduce risk, and to encourage innovation and efficiency.

Various policy issues must be addressed before handling the more technical aspects of contracting:[8] Is legislation needed to allow contracting for services? Do regulations limit the use of grants or other revenues for contract services? Will employees need training to carry out the contracting process and to prepare, monitor, and evaluate contracts? Are competitive contractors available and likely to be interested in bidding? How to assure a fair, open bidding process? How will personnel and labor relations issues, including "bumping" of civil servants, affect the outcome? Will the legislature and the community be supportive? Is the reason for contracting strong enough to warrant the necessary political effort?

In order for a unit of government to privatize by contracting, six conditions must generally be satisfied:

1. A leader grasps the idea, initiates action, and provides motivation.
2. An internal champion is prepared to lead the effort.
3. The unit is under serious fiscal stress or otherwise needs to reconsider its present practice.
4. Significant monetary savings or other benefits are achievable by contracting, with no reduction in quality or level of service and with the possibility of improvement.
5. Contracting is politically feasible, taking into consideration the power of the affected employees and other current beneficiaries.
6. A precipitating event makes it impossible to avoid change and maintain the status quo.

The political leader must find and support a strong internal champion of the idea who has to carry the argument and sell the idea on an ongoing basis;[9] as is true of any major change in any organization. This champion may be an assistant to the chief executive, a budget director, or a professional public administrator. Rarely does the head of the affected department take the lead in promoting privatization in his or her agency. On the contrary, persons in such positions are often found either leading the opposition or quietly sabotaging the effort. A business community in favor of privatization can be a powerful ally, although some parochial business interests may be opposed, for example, those that currently have comfortable relations with the target agency, perhaps as vendors.

The decision to contract out has been studied by James M. Ferris.[10] A government with serious budget problems is a good candidate for a privatization program, as large potential savings are a great motivator. In my experience, however, the mere availability of large and much-needed savings, although necessary, is rarely sufficient to assure that privatization will be implemented; a precipitating event is needed to tip the scales in favor of contracting out. Such events often originate at higher levels or in other branches of government. For example, a state agency may threaten a county hospital with loss of accreditation because of poor conditions in the hospital. A court may order the closure of a municipal landfill because it presents an environmental hazard. These actions necessitate responses by the affected government unit, and privatization—of the hospital or of solid-waste management—may be the best option, or the path of least resistance.

Other events that demand action, often culminating in privatization, are employee strikes that arouse strong public indignation. In an interesting variation on this theme, St. Louis took the step of contracting out its municipal hospital after the physicians, who were themselves on contract from the local university medical school, went on strike in part because the civil servants neglected or refused to perform their patient-care functions, thereby forcing physicians to work as orderlies. When the city contracted out, nonmedical staff became employees of the private firm, and the problem disappeared.

Yet another kind of event that often precipitates privatization is the sudden need for a large and unanticipated capital expenditure for facilities, equipment, or new technology. A major water-main break in Atlanta opened the floodgates, ultimately, to the largest privatized water-supply system in the country. A new hospital, prison, water-supply system, wastewater-treatment plant, truck fleet, sanitary landfill, or modern computer system is an example of such a capital need; a government may resort to privatization of the service instead of raising taxes or borrowing money to build the facility or buy the equipment. Even a large increase in insurance premiums can tip the scales. Elected officials can seize such a precipitating event as an opportunity to create the political consensus that makes privatization feasible.

If these conditions are satisfied, it is likely that the decision will be to privatize. Implementation is not automatic, however; opposition and barriers to privatization are inevitable, as is discussed in detail in chapter 11. This should not daunt the would-be privatizer. The decision process was examined in a series of case studies in which contracting was carried out with surprising ease; political leaders were readily able to overcome the resistance to change.[11]

Table 7.2 summarizes the exemplary process and timetable followed under Mayor Stephen Goldsmith's leadership in Indianapolis, Indiana, in contracting for the maintenance and operation of the city's two 125-million-gallon-per-day (475,000 cubic meters per day each) wastewater-treatment plants. The remarkable feature about this privatization was that the plants were considered well run by the government, and a major consulting firm hired to examine the economic feasibility of privatizing the plants concluded that no more than 5 percent savings could be realized. Mayor Goldsmith asserted, however, that one would never know how much could

TABLE 7.2—PROCESS FOR PRIVATIZING WASTEWATER TREATMENT PLANTS IN INDIANAPOLIS

May 1993	Mayor creates Review Committee (6 mayoral appointees and 2 from City Council)
May 1993	Committee issues Request for Qualifications (RFQ) to 28 companies
June 1993	7 responses are received, including one from the current management of the plants
June 1993	Committee reviews the responses and culls them to 5, including current management
July 1993	City provides $15,000 for consultants to help current management prepare its bid
July 1993	Request for Proposals (RFP) are issued to the 5 firms found to be qualified
July 1993	Teams from the qualifying firms separately visit and study the plants
August 1993	The 5 qualifiers submit proposals and prices
August 1993	A technical consultant and a financial consultant are hired to assist the committee
September 1993	3 of the 5 proposals are rejected, including management's bid for $27 million, down from the current cost of $33 million; the 2 surviving bids are both for $17 million per year for a 5-year, fixed-price contract.
October 1993	Each finalist gives detailed briefings to the Review Committee
October 1993	Review Committee visits plants operated under contract by the 2 finalists
November 1993	Review Committee picks the winner unanimously
January 1994	Winner starts contract operation

be saved without a market test, that is, competitive bidding. Ultimately the management and operation of the plants was privatized and the results were astonishing: savings were 44 percent, effluent water quality was higher, the number of employees required was almost halved, the accident rate was reduced to one-tenth the national average for wastewater treatment plants, and the number of employee grievances dropped from 38 to 1 in a single year although the employees belonged to the same union before and after privatization.[12]

2. Select the Service

Services that satisfy some or all of the following criteria are preferred candidates for competitive contracting.[13] Different weights could be assigned to each of these in a formal analysis:

- services with no legal or contractual impediments to contracting
- services for which it is easy to carry out competitive contracting, and present minimal risk

- hard services rather than soft services, as it is easier to write enforceable specifications
- stand-alone services, because they are easier to manage under contracts than services that are highly interrelated with other services
- services that can be segmented by location into two or more contracts, as it is easier to create a permanent competitive environment
- services that have been successfully privatized by competitive contracting elsewhere
- services for which there are experienced, willing, and responsible bidders, "the Yellow Pages test"
- services in which part-time employees can be used to a significant extent, as larger savings may be realized because government agencies cannot readily employ part-time workers
- services that offer opportunities for large savings, because they are overstaffed, poorly managed, or can be restructured or re-engineered
- services that are the subject of many public complaints
- services where employee or union resistance can be overcome, and where legitimate employee concerns can be dealt with satisfactorily
- services whose privatization will not generate overpowering political opposition
- services for which necessary in-house expertise can be retained and the ability to monitor the contractor's performance would not be dissipated

One has to set exact boundaries for the service being considered for contracting, that is, to identify the precise activities to be included in the contract. This can be illustrated by reference to solid-waste collection: What services is the contractor to perform? Collect from residences only or from commercial establishments as well? From multifamily dwellings of any size or only from buildings with fewer than six units? Collect trash separately from garbage? Collect recyclables? What about bulky objects, such as discarded major appliances and mattresses; are they to be collected? If so, how often? Only during spring and fall cleanups? What about yard waste and leaves? What about litter baskets on city sidewalks?

Analogous issues arise with respect to infrastructure privatization: If the contract is for maintenance and operation of a city's water-treatment plant, for instance, how are necessary capital replacements to be handled? Who will be responsible for maintaining water mains? For reading water meters? For billing water users? For operating the water-quality-control laboratory? All these questions must be addressed and dealt with in carefully drawn specifications.

3. Conduct a Feasibility Study

Once a service has been designated as a candidate for privatization (or managed competition), the next step is a feasibility study to see if it is worth doing. As mentioned repeatedly, one of the principal reasons for contracting is the potential for large cost savings. Therefore, one must examine the current cost to establish a baseline against which a subsequent contract price can be compared. The quality of the current in-house work should also be assessed, for example, by looking at complaints, measuring performance, and conducting surveys.

A reliable cost comparison is not as easy to make as it might appear, for there are some serious errors to be avoided. The first and most flagrant fallacy is that "government can do it cheaper because it doesn't make a profit." This incantation is supposed to ward off privatization and was intoned even by a Speaker of the U.S. House of Representatives.[14] Unfortunately, the phrase reveals serious economic ignorance. The quest for profits leads to greater efficiency, and the resulting gain to the public far offsets the profit. The studies reviewed in chapter 6 show convincingly that the price of for-profit contract work, on average, is substantially lower than the cost of non-profit, in-house work.

Another common error in determining the cost of in-house government service is excessive reliance on published budgets. The problem with budget documents is that they are not designed as cost-accounting reports, but merely reflect established conventions and bookkeeping practices. A detailed examination of the matter, covering sixty-eight jurisdictions, revealed that the true cost of a particular government service, measured properly using valid cost-accounting procedures, was 30 percent greater than the cost nominally ascribed to that service in the formal budget. Given the magnitude of this misperception, incorrect conclusions will often result from analyses that rely on budgets to compare the cost of government and contract services; the cards are likely to be stacked in favor of the government producer, unless the comparison is carried out correctly.[15] What is needed is activity-based costing, which assembles and compiles all costs associated with a particular activity.

The following are the principal factors responsible for understating the cost of government-produced services; these must all be taken into consideration when determining the full cost of a government activity:

1. Capital expenditures for facilities, vehicles, and other equipment do not appear in conventional operating budgets.

2. Interest costs on capital expenditures are rarely allocated to the operations that incur them. Departments should be charged interest—at the rate the government pays to borrow money—for the use of fixed assets such as buildings and land.

3. Costs of supplies, such as fuel for vehicles, are often included in budgets of supporting agencies instead of the operating agency; the same is true of maintenance labor.

4. Fringe benefits, including pension contributions, are often entered in an overhead category.

5. If pension funds are underfunded, the government has incurred a liability that it will someday have to pay, even though it makes no provision for this in the current budget.

6. The cost of labor borrowed from other agencies or hired seasonally may not be attributed to the activity being studied.

7. The costs of operating and maintaining the buildings used in the activity are often neglected.

8. The opportunity cost of land and buildings used by the agency should be charged to the activity; foregone property tax should be included here.

9. The cost of premiums paid for liability and fire insurance, or the cost of claims paid under a program of self-insurance, should be apportioned to the activity.

10. Overhead costs of executive and staff agencies should also be apportioned correctly to the activity,[16] although this is subject to debate; this cost would not be eliminated by contracting, but, it is argued, executive attention would be directed at other functions of government, thereby improving them, and therefore credit should be taken for this.

The privatization of prisons reveals another area of undercounting government costs. Many attorneys budgeted under the Department of Justice work full time defending the Bureau of Prisons against suits brought by litigious prisoners, but these expenses are not included when calculating the total cost of a prison. Private firms that operate prisons, in contrast, must pay their own lawyers for this activity. Hidden costs such as these should be uncovered and entered into the calculation.

Yet another frequent error made by government employees arguing against contracting is to estimate the cost of producing a single unit of the activity and then to extrapolate it. I witnessed this, for example, in connection with a city's proposal to contract for street-sign installation. The supervisor of the city agency, who opposed the plan, estimated that it required only ten minutes to install each sign and calculated the labor cost for ten minutes and the cost of the sign materials, which came to a total of $15.27 per sign, compared to a contractor's bid of $30 per sign.

The supervisor's implicit assumption was that 12,000 signs a year were installed (10 minutes per sign = six signs per hour x 2,000 hours per year). In fact only 2,000 signs were being installed annually by his unit, an average of one sign per hour, and the true cost for materials and direct labor alone were $46.57 per sign. Thus, instead of the contractor's price being twice the in-house price, it was one-third less. Rigorous analysis is needed to guard against such errors; a useful primer and worksheets for calculating in-house costs are available.[17] Table 7.3 illustrates one such form.

The true cost of service emerged as a major point of contention in early efforts to contract more federal government functions. Before 1976, for the purpose of comparing government to contract costs, the total cost of retirement benefits for federal employees was considered to be 7 percent of gross pay. This implausibly low figure was recalculated in 1976, and the true figure was found to be 24.7 percent of gross pay. Federal employees fought vigorously against this realistic guideline and actually succeeded a year later in getting this figure (but not their benefits) reduced to 14.1 percent of gross wages; later it was raised to 20.4 percent and in the 1979 and 1983 guidelines it was 26 percent.[18]

The objective of competitive contracting should be to minimize the cost of delivering a given quantity and quality of service. The cost is the sum of the production cost (contract price), the one-time transition cost, and the cost of contract governance, which include the administrative cost of preparing and negotiating the contract; the cost of monitoring; the cost of negotiating changes to the original contract due to unforeseen circumstances; and the cost of disputes.

TABLE 7.3—ILLUSTRATIVE FORMS FOR CALCULATING IN-HOUSE COSTS

Salaries

Position title	No. of employees	Percentage in this activity	No. of FTEs[a]	Annual salary	Cost
Supervisor	1	50	0.5	$50,000	$25,000
Foreman	2	100	2.0	40,000	80,000
Driver	25	100	25	30,000	750,000
Laborer	50	100	50	25,000	1,250,000
Secretary	2	100	1.5	28,000	42,000
Clerk	2	100	2.0	18,000	36,000
Subtotal					$2,183,000

Fringe Benefits

Social Security	$153,000
Pension fund, uniforms, insurance	619,000
Subtotal	$772,000

Other Operating Expenses

Vehicle operation and maintenance	$350,000
Office supplies and expenses	13,000
Liability insurance, interest	102,000
Contractual services and miscellaneous	18,000
Subtotal	$483,000

Overhead

Overhead Agency	Salaries and Fringes	Other	Percentage in this Activity	Net Cost
Chief executive	$130,000	$20,000	2	$3,000
Finance, controller, budget	90,000	10,000	2	2,000
Clerk, attorney, others	245,000	15,000	3	7,800
Subtotal				$12,800

Equipment

Type of Equipment	Number (1)	Cost (2)	Percent usage (3)	Total $1 \times 2 \times 3$	Depreciated (8-yr life)
Trucks	20	$100,000	100	2,000,000	$250,000
Pickup trucks	2	36,000	100	72,000	9,000
Sedan	1	15,000	50	7,500	938
Subtotal					$259,938

Grand Total	$3,710,738

[a]The number of employees expressed as full-time equivalents (FTEs)

Most of these costs can be anticipated.[19] The cost of production can generally be obtained from potential bidders; although this is not a bid and is likely to be lower than a subsequent formal bid, it does provide a sense of potential savings. Estimates may also be obtained from other jurisdictions that contracted out. The cost of preparing the contract and monitoring the contractor's performance can be estimated. (In my experience, the cost of monitoring public works contracts has ranged from 1 percent to 7 percent of the price of the contract.) The quality of the contractor's work can be assessed from his performance elsewhere. Transaction costs,[20] political costs, and transition costs, enter into the calculus here even though they may not all be fully quantifiable. Together with the information obtained in the earlier steps, the decision can be made whether or not to proceed with competitive contracting.

4. Foster Competition

When contracting is properly done, it creates and institutionalizes competition, the underlying factor that encourages better performance. True competitive bidding, with multiple suppliers who desire to do the job, is preferred. At times, however, when it is difficult to disqualify marginally competent bidders, it may be best to negotiate bids with a handful of clearly eligible contractors after a preliminary qualifying round. This may also be the best approach for contracting prisons, hospitals, social services, and professional services. State laws differ in their requirements for formal competitive bidding, depending on the nature of the service. (Interestingly, there is some empirical evidence that negotiated and competitive bids do not differ in price.[21]) Sole-source procurement is not a good idea but may be unavoidable in some circumstances, as when a higher level of government is footing the bill.

One of the barriers to contracting for services may be a shortage of prospective bidders. This is a major problem in developing countries but is not unknown in industrial nations, particularly in smaller communities. Sometimes private firms believe that the jurisdiction asking for bids is not serious, and that the process is merely a negotiating tactic aimed at its unionized employees. Sometimes the number of interested bidders is low because a government has a reputation for being slow to pay its bills. Consider a city that, over the past century, has constructed an elaborate, time-consuming, costly, bureaucratic system of checks and balances designed to assure that it receives fair value in its purchases and is protected against corruption in contracting for supplies and equipment. The consequence, however, is a long delay in securing bids, ordering goods, and paying bills. Requests are prepared and sent to bidders on an approved list. Sealed bids are received and analyzed, contracts are awarded, purchase orders are prepared and issued, goods are received, several different agencies check to see that goods really were delivered and were not phantom purchases and that the right goods were delivered in good condition to the right place at the right time, payment is authorized after a proper invoice is received and then cross-checked, and finally a check for payment is grudgingly issued by the city treasury months later.

The result of all this red tape is that many potential bidders refuse to do business with the city, while those who do must charge higher prices to make up for their additional cost and trouble.[22] Thus, a strategy intended to increase competition and reduce the cost of goods has the opposite effect of reducing competition and increasing costs. Fair, open, honest, and competent treatment of vendors is the best way to encourage potential bidders to compete for the business.

One way to attract many bidders, in the case of a service that is geographically dispersed, is to divide the contract area into small zones, leaving each zone large enough to allow economies of scale. If the service does not permit geographic subdivision, it may be divisible into small functional units; clerical work and data processing can be segmented in this manner. Indeed, bundling services into one large contract has an anticompetitive effect. The policy should be to offer several small contracts, without sacrificing economies of scale; give a long lead time to bidders; publicize the bid widely; give enough information to bidders; award enough contracts both to avoid excessive reliance on a single supplier and to permit a significant fraction of the bidders to succeed in their quest, thereby encouraging the losers to try again next time; stagger the contracts so that some are awarded every year and bidders' interest is sustained; establish a low upper limit on the number of contracts that any one bidder may be awarded at one time; and handle problems fairly and pay bills promptly to keep suppliers interested in keeping the business.

Potential participants may be deterred from bidding by the belief that an incumbent contractor has an insurmountable advantage because of his knowledge and experience in that specific activity in that jurisdiction. This "incumbent advantage" can be minimized, as Philadelphia did when contracting out the maintenance of its street lights. The incumbent had to provide, and the city included in its bid package, operational details such as the number and type of vehicles used by the contractor; the contractor's route, schedule, and staffing; and the contractor's experience as to the number of lights, by type, that had to be replaced.

Yet another deterrent to potential private bidders is a request for detailed and sensitive business information that is not essential to the procurement. Generally speaking, there is no need to request information on profits, wages, the number of employees, and so on.

Contracting for social services is commonplace, but competition is often lacking for a variety of reasons.[23] Contracts awarded without competition to nonprofit neighborhood groups may be merely the latest manifestation of local political patronage. When contracts are restricted to nonprofit organizations, including religious ones, a quota system may be in effect, for example, when assigning children to Catholic, Protestant, or Jewish foster-care agencies for placement. However well-intended, this practice is not likely to provide the most efficient, effective, and loving care to those in need.

Sometimes competition to provide social services is limited if the service is site based, for example, a senior center or a homeless shelter. An incumbent who owns such a facility may have an insuperable advantage over potential competitors. Offering the use of government-owned or government-leased facilities to potential bidders (at a price) can reduce the incumbent's advantage and lead to more competition. Another approach is to have the bid specifications require that incumbents rent their facilities to the winning bidder, at a fair price, if the incumbent fails to win the bid. For instance, the bid price could consist of two parts, the rent for the facility and the price of the service. The contract would be awarded based on the sum of the two prices, but the low bidder would have the choice of renting the owner's facility at the rent bid by the owner or arranging for his own facility.

5. Request Expressions of Interest or Qualifications

Often a government agency is unsure about what to include in a bid document, what terms to impose, what the scope of the contract should be, what features will attract bidders, what will repel them, and so on. The best way to proceed is to announce to potential participants that privatization is being considered and to prepare and issue a Request for Expressions of Interest (RFEI) to prospective bidders. Then, a pre-bid conference to which all respondents are invited is held to discuss the issues in an open and transparent process. Each participant may seek a proprietary advantage, and the group as a whole may have a common bias, but the process is a wholesome one that provides valuable information to the agency and maximizes the probability of success.

If a complex function is being considered for privatization, such as infrastructure or contract management of a GOE, it is necessary to restrict the competition initially to qualified firms. In this case a Request for Qualifications (RFQ) should be prepared and issued. Firms respond, giving their experiences and qualifications. Checking the submissions is a crucial step and leads to a list of firms qualified to participate further. (In complex cases, a Request for Proposals [RFP] should be issued subsequently, not an Invitation to Bid.) Planning discussions can take place as under the RFEI process.

6. Plan the Employee Transition

As noted frequently, the biggest problem in privatization, or managed competition for that matter, is how to handle the problem posed by redundant workers, for redundancy is common whether contracting out to a private firm or contracting in to the agency group whose winning low bid is predicated on a smaller workforce. Attrition, redeployment, early retirement, hiring by the private contractor, preferential hiring in filling future vacancies, and severance pay are among the most common approaches for dealing with this problem, as addressed in detail in chapter 11. This issue must be dealt with early in the process because it may be decided that the contractor should follow certain policies, such as retaining workers, and these constraints have to be identified in the bid specifications.

7. Prepare Bid Specifications

Contracts will achieve their intended purpose only if the terms are clear, thorough, accurate, and unambiguous. This seems obvious, but I saw one contract awarded for street sweeping that failed to name the streets to be swept or the frequency of sweeping! Contract specifications must be expressed in ordinary language. If many suppliers are to be encouraged to bid, they must not be confronted with massive and impenetrable documents that require legions of lawyers and accountants to comprehend. Many potential bidders can do the job well enough, although they are relatively small and lack the sophisticated bureaucratic apparatus that government agencies assume to be universal.[24] A contractor cannot respond intelligently to a poorly drawn invitation to bid, and, if he does, subsequent misunderstandings are inevitable. In one instance, a federal government facility ostensibly sought to contract its entire laundry operation, but did not know and could not tell prospective bidders how many pieces were to be ironed.[25] How could a contractor calculate his bid price without this information?

Contract specifications should avoid unnecessary restrictions. Some agencies prepare specifications that go beyond stating performance requirements to specify in detail just how the contractor should carry out the work. For example, some misguided specifications for public works contracts call for particular kinds of vehicles to be used, the number of men to work on each truck, and the wages to be paid. In another instance, a municipal parking garage in Cincinnati stated in its bid specifications that "a bidder must agree to employ City personnel in their present positions at present pay rates and provide a comparable benefits package for a minimum of two years." Considering that the term of the contract was only three years and that labor is the overwhelming cost of operating this facility, no savings could possibly be achieved. Clearly, such specifications go beyond the bounds of management prerogatives and obviate the entire purpose of contracting—which is sometimes the underlying intention of those who draw up such self-defeating contracts. This is one of the barriers to contracting—setting specifications whose hidden purpose or ultimate effect is to make contracting out as costly as government service, thereby eliminating the incentive to change.

Outright sabotage can also take place, for example, by planting a time bomb in the specifications. I know of the following case: A department head in New Orleans, reluctant to contract but ordered to do so, wrote service specifications for a lower level of service than the community was used to. The winning bidder, naturally enough, started providing service at the level called for in the contract. A public uproar ensued, much to the consternation of the unsuspecting contractor, to the embarrassment of elected officials, and to the satisfaction of the vengeful department head— who was on the verge of retirement anyway.

Other obstacles to contracting include the difficulty of writing specifications for some services and possible legal restrictions with respect to matching funds. For example, a local government that receives a federal matching grant for a program may wish to use city overhead expenditures as part of its matching contribution. This may or may not be acceptable to federal auditors if the service is contracted to a private organization.

Having already preached the virtues of specificity, we must also acknowledge that while desirable in general, specificity can result in problems in case of a sudden change in circumstances; ambiguity, inadvertent or otherwise, may then turn out to be a virtue. Also, it is relatively easy to write specifications that seem proper and tightly drawn but are in fact proprietary and favor a particular bidder, hence providing an opportunity for bribery or extortion.

"Hard" services, those involving tangible and visible physical results, are generally easier to write specifications for than the kind of "soft" services provided by social workers to clients. That is why the former lend themselves to contracting and some of the latter are more amenable to vouchers. But even the former can be difficult to specify clearly. For example, whereas street paving is a good candidate for competitive contracting, repair of potholes is not as good because information on the location and frequency of pothole occurrence and on the expected life of repaved streets is virtually nonexistent in many cities. How, then, can one write specifications for such work? A contractor cannot respond sensibly to a specification that calls for "the repair of all potholes that may occur on a given street" nor to a broader specification "to maintain a given street free of potholes," for in the latter case he cannot intelligently weigh the tradeoffs of repaving the entire street or repairing individual potholes. Finally, because it is technically difficult to identify particular potholes, letting a contract on a "per pothole" basis may be inviting trouble.

John Marlin offers illustrative specifications for sixty-five different municipal services,[26] briefly identifying both quantity and quality factors, as well as typical outputs. The listing goes awry, however, by suggesting that input resources should be included in the specifications; government agencies should focus on outputs and leave the configuration of input resources to the contractor in order to allow creativity and innovation in service delivery. The specifications should also identify the standards that are to be maintained and the penalties for violations. Sample specifications and standards for building custodial services appear in table 7.4; contract terms for local bus service in Houston, Texas, including specifications and penalties, are shown in table 7.5 (p. 193).

Contracting for a service that requires long-lived capital assets presents a challenge, although not an insurmountable one. How will someone awarded a contract for three years amortize a facility that has a twenty-year life? The most direct approach would be to set the term of the contract equal to the life of the assets, but this approach is tantamount to granting a long-term monopoly, which is appropriate for franchises or concessions. Another approach is to recognize that the asset can be depreciated over time, has a value at any point in time, and can be sold to the new service producer if the original one is unsuccessful in bidding for a successor contract. Yet another approach is to have the government own the

TABLE 7.4—WORK SPECIFICATIONS AND STANDARDS FOR CUSTODIAL SERVICES

Tasks	Standards
1. Empties wastebaskets and trash cans daily and inserts new liner as needed.	1a. Empties wastebaskets and trash cans usually with no spillage. 1b. Empties all assigned wastebaskets and trash cans. 1c. Completes work according to schedule set by supervisor.
2. Cleans and dusts office furniture and window-sills daily.	2a. Cleans and dusts with minimal disturbance to papers, other items, and furniture. 2b. Performs work assignment with minimum supervision. 2c. Completes work according to schedule set by supervisor. 2d. Furniture and windowsills are free of soot and look clean.
3. Cleans washbasins, toilet bowls, urinals, and mirrors; replaces towels, tissue paper, and soap; and damp mops and disinfects restrooms daily.	3a. Performs work assignment with minimum supervision. 3b. Completes work according to schedule set by supervisor. 3c. Bathroom fixtures look clean and smell fresh. 3d. Bathrooms are almost never lacking tissue paper, soap, etc. 3e. Employee complaints about cleanliness and maintenance of bathroom facilities are minimal.
4. Tells supervisor of plumbing and lighting problems, etc.	4a Informs supervisor immediately and usually with clear and accurate details of the problem.
5. Cleans lunchroom counters, tables, chairs, and appliance tops.	5a. Performs cleaning assignment with minimal supervision. 5b. Completes work according to schedule set by supervisor. 5c. Lunchroom tables, chairs, counters, and appliances are free of spots and present a clean appearance.
6. Washes and waxes and/or polishes desks and other office furniture weekly.	6a. Performs work assignment with minimal supervision. 6b. Completes work according to schedule set by supervisor. 6c. Furniture appears clean and polished.
7. Washes walls, tiles, and glass partitions to shoulder-high level on weekly basis.	7a. Performs washing assignment with minimum supervision. 7b. Completes work according to schedule set by supervisor. 7c. Walls, tiles, and glass partitions present a clean appearance.
8. Polishes brightwork on a weekly basis.	8a. Follows established procedures for polishing brightwork. 8b. Completes work according to schedule set by supervisor.

(table continues)

TABLE 7.4—(CONTINUED)

Tasks	Standards
9. Opens up building, performing functions such as turning on lights, opening doors, checking boilers and elevators to assure proper functioning, sweeping or plowing sidewalks when necessary, hoisting national and city flags at the appropriate time, taking out refuse each day.	9a. Opens up building on time as directed by supervisor. 9b. Checks building completely as per work assignment with minimal supervision. 9c. Sidewalks are clear, allowing safe passage to and from building. 9d. Reports malfunctions and major problems immediately to supervisor. 9e. Takes out refuse and performs other assigned tasks with minimal supervision.
10. Scrubs, strips, and waxes floors monthly.	10a. Performs work to standards with minimum supervision. 10b. Completes work according to schedule set by supervisor. 10c. Floors look clean and waxed.

long-lived asset and lease it to the successful bidder at a price stated in the request for bids. This could be done for garages, restaurants and service stations on turnpikes, and facilities for concessions in parks and stadiums.

Contracts that call for private construction and ownership of complex facilities, such as resource-recovery plants, wastewater-treatment plants, and prisons, present intricate problems in several domains: legal,[27] including the antitrust field,[28] financial,[29] and insurance.[30] These require specialized expertise to avoid lengthy delays and unanticipated consequences. Infrastructure privatization is discussed in chapter 9.

As to the contractual basis for payment, there are several ways to provide incentives for good performance and to handle uncertainties. Cost-plus-fixed-fee is at one end of the spectrum of contract types, and firm, fixed price is at the other.[31] The former may appear at first glance to lead to minimal price, but it has no incentive to encourage efficiency and much disincentive; it is useful only when the function to be performed is not fully identifiable at the outset, specifications are inexact, and changes are expected. Such a situation may arise in the case of support services for military installations. A variant of this is cost-plus-fee, wherein the size of the fee, up to a maximum, is awarded by the government. A firm fixed price is desirable but can be utilized only when the specifications are clear and changes are unlikely. As an intermediate form of contract payment, to encourage effective, informal cooperation between a government agency

TABLE 7.5—CONTRACT SPECIFICATIONS FOR BUS SERVICE IN HOUSTON, TEXAS

Service specification: By individual route, with number of trips and starting times for each trip

Basis of payment (Bid price):   Price per revenue hour (i.e., hours of operation in passenger service)

Contract term: Three years

Penalties: $100/day for failure to provide scheduled trips

$100/day for failure to maintain current maintenance records on buses

$100/day for late Passenger Counts, Accident Reports, Road Call Reports, Contract Discrepancy Reports, or data required for UMTA Reports

$50/day per occurrence for

Interior and/or exterior of bus not washed and cleaned daily

Interior or exterior damage not repaired

Air-conditioning not functioning to Metro standards

Operator not in uniform

Passenger counts not taken

Fare collection procedures not followed

Operator observed smoking, eating, or drinking on bus.

Bonding: Bid bond equal to 2 percent of bid price is required; performance bond equal to 5 percent of the contract amount is required

If contractor fails to meet 94 percent on-time performance (on time defined as 0 to 5 minutes late) over a three-month period, the following percentages will be deducted from each of the three monthly invoices:

Criteria	Damages
less than 90 percent	minus 1 percent per month
90–91.9 percent	minus 0.5 percent per month
92–94 percent	no penalty

If contractor has more than 1.9 accidents per 100,000 miles in passenger service over a three-month period, the following percentages will be deducted from each of the three monthly invoices:

Criteria	Damages
More than 3.0	minus 1 percent per month
2.5–2.9	minus 0.5 percent per month
1.9–2.4	no penalty

Source: Request for Bids issued in 1990 by Houston Metro for service to the Texas Medical Center.

and a contractor working on a complex, one-of-a-kind, first-time project, an extra fee in addition to the fixed price could be awarded to the contractor based on a unilateral judgment by the government buyer about the contractor's performance;[32] this requires a defense against corruption, however. An incentive or penalty could be included to encourage on-time or

within-budget performance. Table 7.6 summarizes the principal characteristics of different payment methods.[33]

Depending on the particular service, unit pricing or an hourly rate may
be appropriate. The former makes sense for maintaining streetlights and
traffic lights, at so much per currently installed light; an hourly rate may
be best for snow removal work, while bus operations might be contracted
on a per-mile basis, for example.

Allowances for inflation during the term of the contract are appropriate, but they should be based on official measures; mere increases in the
contractor's cost of doing business should not be sufficient to trigger a
price increase. For example, owners of firms have been known to get
together with their employees and demand an increase in the contract price
to pay for "unanticipated" wage increases, under the threat of a strike. A
private-sector union sometimes serves as the vehicle for assuring noncompetitive practices and conspiratorial, collusive bidding. The best defense
against such occurrences and against collusive bidding in general is to have
part of the work done by a government agency and part by contractors,
where this is possible.

Occasionally a dispute will arise between the contractor and the
agency. The bid document, which includes a copy of the contract signed
by the winner, should specify the dispute-resolution process in case the
contractor disagrees with a penalty that is imposed or with the meaning
of certain terms of the contract.

8. Initiate a Public Relations Campaign

Strong opposition to privatization is almost certain to surface, whether
from public employee unions, private firms that want to avoid competition, or special-interest groups who fear the loss of privileges. In the face
of this opposition, proponents of contracting have to develop supportive
coalitions.[34] They can be amalgams of civic associations seeking better government, neighborhood groups dissatisfied with poor services, disgruntled
taxpayers, trade associations of private-sector providers, and business
groups. As noted in chapter 4, associations of minority businessowners
can be particularly effective because privatization, particularly of municipal services, offers entrepreneurial opportunities uniquely suited for their
members. Chapter 11 discusses opposition arguments and how they may
be addressed.

An aggressive campaign should be carried out through the media, at
public meetings, through advertising, and wherever the opportunity pre-

TABLE 7.6—FORMS OF CONTRACT PAYMENT

	Firm, fixed price (FFP)	Fixed-price-plus-award (FPPA)	Cost-plus fee
Description	Fixed price with no adjustment based on contractor cost or performance	Fixed price plus award for excellent performance based on evaluation by government	Government pays for level of effort plus a fee up to a predetermined maximum; could have incentive for on-time completion or avoiding cost overrun
Applications	Simple functions; exact specifications; minimal expected changes	Like FFP but high level of performance is desired	Functions and specifications are inexact; changes in scope are expected; high level of performance is needed
Advantages	Low risk to government; easy to administer; incentive to control costs	Low risk to government; improved relationship between government and contractor; incentive to control costs; stimulates better performance	No need to define activities precisely; some incentive for cost control to receive maximum fee, realize economies of scale
Disadvantages	Requires exact specifications; limits contractor's flexibility; contractor may sacrifice quality to avoid losses	Like FFP but may be difficult to decide on size of award; risk of prejudice and corruption	Higher risk to government than FFP; must monitor and verify contractor costs; little incentive for high efficiency
Limitations		Contractor needs a good cost accounting system; useful only for negotiated procurements	No point using this if objective measurement is possible

Source: Derived from Douglas K. Ault and John B. Handy, *Smarter Contracting for Installation Support Services* (Bethesda, Md.: Logistics Management Institute, May 1986.)

sents itself. The concept of privatization has to be articulated, explaining why it makes sense for the government and how the public will benefit. An early start to the campaign is necessary before the opposition sets the stage and captures the agenda. Chapter 8 describes public relations programs used effectively in developing countries.

9. Engage in Managed Competition

Instead of deciding at the outset to contract with a private firm, public officials can allow the public agency to compete explicitly with private firms for a contract if the issue is cost. Ideally, the government agency is invited to submit a bid at the same time and in response to the same specifications as any outside bidder. This is called "managed competition," a strategy that is gaining growing acceptance. It cannot, however, be used effectively for long-term contracts (e.g., more than about five years) or where capital expenditures may be required, as in wastewater treatment plants, because a public agency cannot realistically make and honor such commitments. Nor can it be used if the reason for privatizing is to acquire a capability that is lacking or if a new program must be started quickly, for example.

Managed competition has several advantages over pure privatization in principle, because it (1) allows an agency's operating management to work together with labor against a common rival, the private sector; (2) improves employee morale and builds community support if the public body wins; (3) reduces the possibility of collusion among private firms; (4) induces private firms to submit better bids if they believe the process is honest and not just a bargaining tactic to beat the public-employee union in a labor negotiation.

Managed competition has been introduced in many jurisdictions where public services were monopolies, but private firms often complain that the competitions are unfair for the following reasons:

1. Public units do not include all their costs. Care must be taken to assure full pricing in the agency's bid, as previously discussed, and therefore it is generally necessary to use an independent unit, such as the management or budget office, to validate the agency's bid and assure that all costs are included and no hidden subsidy exists.

2. A performance guarantee is required of the private provider but not of the public provider. What happens under managed competition if the contract is awarded to an in-house unit that then fails to satisfy the terms of the contract? For instance, the unit submits a bid lower than its traditional cost because it says it will adopt more productive work practices, but it does not change its ways and its costs remain too high? Or the quality of service is poor and fails to satisfy the performance standards called for in the contract? Private firms must post a performance bond; it would be fair but impractical to require

the union to post one. "Loss sharing" has been suggested, that is, imposing a cost on the group of workers that won the bid, but this, too, is impractical, because in-house employees cannot assume risk and cannot pay penalties for poor performance. The best way to handle this situation is to monitor the service closely, weekly or monthly, to see if the contractually promised results are being realized. If not, the arrangement should be aborted and the contract awarded to the outside firm that submitted the best bid in the competition. To assure that this firm's bid remains in effect despite the award to the in-house unit, a modest fee might be paid to retain the firm on standby. (This would also be an incentive for the in-house unit to honor its commitment.)

3. Risk is assumed by the winning private provider but no value is credited for it, whereas if the public agency wins the risk is borne by the jurisdiction, not the agency that submits the bid. A private firm must be credited for the value of the risk it assumes, or conversely the public agency must have that value added to its bid price. For environmental services, for example, the private sector bears the risk of compliance with environmental regulations and must pay any fines for failure to comply. If a public agency fails to comply, the fine is paid by taxpayers, not the agency. If the risks are large and shifting them away from the public sector is important, the service may not be appropriate for managed competition, but should be reserved for a private bidder. Alternatively, the cost of insurance can be added to the price of the public bid, as was done in San Diego in a managed competition to operate a wastewater treatment plant.[35]

4. Private firms must pay taxes and comply with regulations from which the public sector is exempt.[36] The value of taxes paid by the private firm should be subtracted from its bid price or added to the public bid.

5. In-house departments are sometimes allowed to delay their submission until the private bids are in, or to adjust their bids after seeing the private-sector bids. Instead of managed competition, this is mismanaged competition.[37] Unless these biases are addressed, this approach will ultimately fail, in that no private bidders will respond and the jurisdiction will remain at the mercy of its in-house monopoly. The in-house bid must be

submitted and opened at the same time as all other bids, and no adjustments after the fact should be allowed; any other practice is blatantly unfair. Public-employee unions complain, in contrast, that it is unfair to expect them to engage in competitive bidding when they have no experience in that process. They need training to compensate for this lack of experience, but it should not be financed by taxpayers; it should be provided as a local service by the parent national unions such as the American Federation of State, Local, and Municipal Employees and the American Federation of Government Employees. The cost of any public expenditures for consulting assistance to help the agency prepare its bid or proposal should be added to the agency's bid price.

Competition can be sharpened further when both the public and private sectors deliver the same service at the same time in the same jurisdiction; that is, when multiple arrangements are utilized. In such cases the results are likely to be particularly beneficial to the public. For example, Montreal, Minneapolis, Phoenix, New Orleans, Kansas City, Newark, and Oklahoma City have had such systems for residential refuse collection. They employ contracts with private firms to service several districts of the city and a municipal department to service the remainder. The resulting competition has been successful in producing operating efficiencies and costs that are remarkably low by national standards. In Minneapolis, city officials assiduously cultivated a competitive climate and, by pointing to the superior practices of the private crews, were able to get the city crews to adopt similar practices and ultimately to match the private firms' performance.[38]

Competition can be turned upside down. I am familiar with a case in El Paso, Texas, where the city agency was selling its containerized commercial refuse-collection service to local businesses, in competition with private firms. It was temporarily successful because its prices were lower; however, its true cost was higher than the price it charged, and private firms had to pay disposal fees at the municipal landfill while the city agency did not. Moreover, private firms paid various other taxes and fees from which the city was exempt. The competition was manifestly unfair, and, in the final analysis, city residents as a whole were subsidizing the agency's customers. Indeed, the city was accused in a court case of discriminatory and predatory pricing.

When fair competition is taking place, the performance of the public agency can serve as a yardstick to measure the performance of the private agency, and vice versa. If the private sector shows signs that its competitive spirit is waning, government can expand the size and scope of its unit's work and reduce the size of the next contract correspondingly. In fact, the threat of greatly reducing the role of either the public or private producer is a most effective check on both, as is the ability to use one to intervene on an emergency basis to do the work of the other if the latter is unable or unwilling to perform (e.g., because of strikes or equipment malfunction). Montreal has developed this technique to a fine art, posting a well-defined rate schedule to cover the cost of municipal intervention if a contractor fails to collect refuse or clear snow on schedule in its assigned area. The plausible threat of municipal intervention, and the occasional need to do so—for a day or two every couple of years—has been sufficient to guarantee excellent performance by the city's fifty-odd contractors, while the fact that the municipal agency does only 10 percent of the work means that the city can readily have a contractor substitute for the city agency if necessary.

The practice of *mandatory* competitive bidding by government agencies for routine functions was introduced in the United Kingdom. Major improvements have been realized in road maintenance since legislation in 1981 required road-repair agencies to compete with private firms, to maintain separate accounts of income and expenditures, and to achieve a prescribed rate of return on the capital equipment they employ.[39] The Local Government Act, passed under Prime Minister Thatcher in 1988, imposed compulsory competitive tendering (bidding) on local governments. Local authorities could no longer simply continue to provide certain common municipal functions using their own employees; they were required to have a competitive process, allowing private firms to compete with their own labor force. The initial set of services covered by this act were refuse collection, street cleaning, cleaning of public buildings, vehicle maintenance, grounds maintenance, and food service. Most competitions have been won by the in-house departments but only by reducing the number of employees by 20 to 30 percent. Recent estimates put the average savings at 20 percent.[40]

10. Conduct a Fair Bidding Process

The bidding procedure will influence the number and quality of bidders who will participate. In addition to the factors discussed earlier, the following guidelines are recommended:

1. Advertise the Request for Bids (also called an Invitation to Bid, ITB, or Request for Proposals, RFP) as broadly as

possible, being sure to go well beyond the minimal requirement of placing a legal notice in a particular newspaper; use vendor lists drawn from trade associations, telephone directories, industry publications, experiences of other jurisdictions, and the like. Mail the request for bids individually to firms on the list.

2. Allow enough time between the announcement date and the bid-due date for preparation of responsible bids.

3. Hold a bidders' conference to answer the questions of prospective bidders. After the conference, send a written summary of the questions and answers to interested parties.

4. If proposals have been submitted in response to an RFP to develop infrastructure, for instance, have an internal team, possibly strengthened with an outside consultant, evaluate, rate, and rank the proposals using clear criteria and an agreed-upon scoring system. If there is more than one satisfactory proposal after the evaluation, ask for bid prices or initiate negotiations with each finalist to arrive at his "best and final offer."

5. Avoid asking for too many bid prices in a request for bids. If many bid combinations are called for (e.g., price for one year, price for two years, price for three years, and other combinations), it is likely that there will be several "low bidders," perhaps one for each pricing combination. Selecting the low bidder in this circumstance leaves too much room for favoritism and improper influence, and it tends to discredit the process. Astute bidders will generally spot this possibility and may not bother participating. (I was an expert witness in a court case where 122 different prices were asked for in the bid!)

6. Avoid rejecting competitive bids on inappropriate grounds and then negotiating with one of the bidders. This damages the credibility of future requests for bids from the offending jurisdiction. Beware of possible corrupt practices even after a properly conducted sealed bidding procedure, such as holding up the award in order to extract a payment to "expedite" the process, or setting new conditions after the bidding is over.

7. Avoid rebidding if one of the bidders is deficient in his response (e.g., omits a required document). If any bids that are

in full conformance with the bid request are disclosed, an award should be made. To do otherwise is manifestly unfair and might encourage bidders to offer incomplete responses deliberately in order to see what others have bid before submitting their own. But imagine a scenario where the bidders are present in a room at the time of bid opening. When the low bidder is announced, another bidder jumps up and says, "My God, I submitted the wrong envelope! Here is the one I meant to submit!" This envelope has a lower price than the lowest bid previously announced. When this belated bid is properly rejected, the late bidder says that his bid is the lowest and accuses the presiding official of rejecting his low bid because he has been bribed. He vows to go to the media with this accusation. What is the hapless official to do? The mayor (governor, etc.) would be faced with the unpleasant choice of supporting the integrity of the process and paying more for the service, or pulling the rug out from under the official and requesting a rebid, so as not to be accused of wasting the taxpayers' money. (I would argue for supporting the integrity of the process, but it is admittedly a tough call for an elected official.)

8. In the request for bids, announce when the award will be made. Allow sufficient time (the length could be discussed at the bidders' conference) between the date of award and the contract starting date to allow the winner time to mobilize for the work.

9. Bid bonds and performance bonds are commonly required to assure serious bidding and effective contract performance. The former is forfeited if the bidder declines the award, and the latter is forfeited if the contractor defaults during the contract period. A certified check submitted with a bid often substitutes for a bid bond. The size of a performance bond should not be set at a punitively high level, for this simply increases the cost of the contract unnecessarily; it should be sufficient merely to defray the cost of making other arrangements to have the work done.[41] Besides, a large bond has the undesirable effect of screening out small contractors. A performance bond is best thought of as an insurance policy whose premium is ultimately paid, indirectly, by the contracting authority.

An appropriate committee should be created to evaluate the bids. Membership could include personnel from the chief executive's office, the budget office, the agency for that service, the labor office, and perhaps legislators. If this is not a simple bid to be awarded to the lowest bidder but a proposal for a more complicated undertaking, the criteria for selecting the winner should be announced in the bid document. A sample proposal evaluation form appears in table 7.7.

11. Evaluate the Bids and Award the Contract

When the full cost of the current in-house work is known, and the bids (including the in-house bid, if any) are in hand, costs can be compared. Table 7.8 presents the factors to include in making the cost comparison.

Some argue that the in-house cost is simply the marginal cost, also called variable cost, avoidable cost, or "going away" cost. In table 7.8 this is the sum of the in-house direct operating cost and the capital expenses and charges that will be avoided if the service is contracted out. The reasoning is that the overhead costs in the table will not be reduced by contracting out. Using this variable cost favors keeping the work in-house, but it underestimates the true cost of service. Using the full cost, including overhead, makes the outside contractor look less expensive but can increase total government

TABLE 7.7 — SAMPLE FORM FOR EVALUATING A PROPOSAL

Factor	Factor weight	Score	Weighted score
Qualifications of firm			
Relevant experience	3	10	30
Reputation	3	10	30
Qualifications of personnel to be assigned	4	25	100
Technical approach			
Meets or exceeds specifications	4	25	100
Clearly communicates plans	4	10	40
Cost compared to other bidders	2	20	40
Total score		100	
Total weighted score of proposal			340

Source: J.T. Marlin, ed., *Contracting Municipal Services* (New York: John Wiley & Sons, 1984), 78.

Note: The factor weights and maximum scores are established beforehand. Each evaluator assigns a score independently and calculates the weighted score. In this illustration, the maximum possible score for a proposal is 340.

costs after contracting. I believe it is best to deal with total costs but to recognize the individual cost components as in table 7.8. Overhead costs are not likely to change much upon privatization, for although the costs of personnel administration and payroll processing will decline, there will be legal costs for preparing contracts and administrative costs for conducting the bidding process, evaluating bids, and awarding the contract. One could argue that with fewer operational responsibilities, government personnel will do a better job on their remaining tasks, and this has a value which in principle should be credited to the contract. The table distinguishes between unavoidable overhead (e.g., the mayor's salary) and semi-avoidable overhead, such as personnel costs in the human resources department; the latter will decline gradually because fewer staff members will be needed as the number of employees in the privatized service is reduced by contracting out.

Costs will be incurred to monitor the performance of the contractor. In my experience, the cost of systematic and thorough monitoring of public works functions typically ranges from 2 percent to 7 percent of the contract price. But current in-house work should already be monitored; if it is not, but the contract work will be, then the cost of monitoring should be reflected in higher quality work by the contractor and the comparison should take this into consideration.

The issue of risk and the charge for fixed capital are discussed in the section on managed competition. Operating revenues come from fares, user fees, and other such sources, depending on the service. The government may receive revenue from the sale of equipment (e.g., vehicles) it may no longer need if it contracts out. This reduces the effective cost of the contract, as shown in table 7.8.

Federal guidelines set a savings threshold for contracting out federal government services: contracting should be done only if the expected savings exceed 10 percent of the personnel-related costs of performing the work in-house. At the same time, agencies that wish to assume functions performed by a contractor must demonstrate that they could save at least 10 percent on personnel costs and 25 percent on the cost of required facilities and materials. Agencies are further required to take into consideration the federal taxes paid by a contractor; these constitute a rebate, in effect, and lead to a lower net cost to the government than the stated bid. There is nothing holy about this 10-percent figure; I have seen proposed thresholds ranging from 0 percent to 30 percent, the former from a business group and the latter from a public employee union in New York intent on preventing any privatization.

TABLE 7.8—COMPARING IN-HOUSE AND CONTRACTOR COSTS

In-house cost	Cost of contracting out
Direct operating cost (salaries, wages, fringe benefits, supplies, materials, equipment maintenance, leases, office expenses, other)	Bid price (including capital expenses, profit, and operating revenues)
+ Total overhead (supervision, department overhead, government overhead, central services)	+ Unavoidable overhead
+ Capital expenses (including depreciation)	+ Semi-avoidable overhead (costs which will gradually be reduced)
+ Charge for fixed capital used (for land, buildings, etc.)	+ One-time transition costs (start-up, vacation payouts, early retirement, etc.)
+ Current monitoring cost (if not included	+ Contract management and monitoring above)
+ Cost of bearing the risk that the contractor bears and includes in his bid price	- Taxes paid
- Operating revenues (fees, etc.)	- Net revenue from sale of government assets
Total cost of retaining the work in house	Total cost of contracting out the work

Source: Derived from David L. Seader, "Implementing Managed Competition: Service Selection/Cost Comparison," in *Proceedings of the Annual Conference of the National Council for Public-Private Partnerships,* St. Louis, Mo., 15–17 October 1997.

Tax treatment.   The proper treatment of taxes is an important point and the source of much confused thinking. Private firms pay many taxes and fees that government agencies do not. Sometimes those who oppose contracting will exclaim triumphantly that the agency's cost is lower precisely because it does not have to pay taxes. This is shoddy thinking. If the firm does not collect taxes and pass them along to government, the public will inevitably have to pay those same taxes through another tax collector; the people's total taxes will not decline merely because the work is retained in-house, although that is the logical implication of the faulty reasoning. Taxes and fees paid by a contractor to all government units constitute a rebate to the public and should properly be subtracted from the bid price so it can be compared correctly with the cost of the government service. (The only grain of truth in the otherwise fallacious reasoning is that some of the firm's taxes, the federal ones, are a rebate to taxpayers throughout the country instead of only to local ones. This makes a difference in the thinking of the contracting agency if it is a state or local government unit because it means that taxpayers elsewhere subsidize the local in-house service.)

Chapter 6 illustrates this issue by reference to the solid-waste industry; taxes total 15 percent of revenues, and therefore contracting for this service arguably results in a 15-percent rebate from the bid price. This factor, too, is shown in table 7.8. After addressing all these issues, the bottom lines of the two alternatives in table 7.8 can be compared, with or without a threshold, to decide whether to contract out or retain the work in-house.

Social welfare costs. One can anticipate imaginative arguments by opponents. For example, in order to limit the contracting of federal functions, a representative of civil servants ingeniously noted that the Social Security Administration is seriously underfunded and therefore, since additional Social Security costs will ultimately be incurred by the government when workers retire from the private sector, this amount should be added to the price of the contract for the purpose of making comparisons between government and contract work. He also asked that the cost of unemployment compensation for displaced federal workers be added to the contract price, assuming that every one would be unemployed, but failed to note that, conversely, unemployment compensation should be subtracted from the contract price for every worker hired by the private contractor.[42]

Some argue that when privatization results in fewer workers doing the same amount of work, the missing workers will collect welfare payments and food stamps, or show up in homeless shelters, and otherwise "will drain funds from the local social safety net budget"; therefore, the cost of these social services should be added to the contract cost to arrive at the full cost of privatization.[43] I disagree. If the "expense" of these "lost jobs" is to be considered, then one must also include the effect of the new jobs *created* in the private sector by the money that remains in the hands of private individuals as a result of more efficient, privatized, lower-cost government.

Low-ball bids. Much concern is expressed about "low-ball bids," that is, very low bids submitted by contractors whose intention is to win the award, make the government dependent on them, and then raise the price drastically when it is time to renew the contract. This is a troubling scenario, and it may occur from time to time, but the empirical evidence shows that it is not common, and in any event a good defense is readily at hand.

The low-ball theory is refuted by the findings of detailed studies reviewed in chapter 6. When contract prices were determined in those studies, some of the contracts were first-time ones and therefore subject to low-ball pricing according to this theory, but most were well into their second, third, and even more advanced cycle of contracting and thus would have experienced the drastic increases predicted by the theory. After all, in any randomly drawn sample of contracts, as in a large-scale study I did,[44] only a few contracts will be new ones. But the studies show that contract prices on average are substantially lower than government in-house costs. How can this be if most of the contracts have matured into the post-low-ball stage? The theory is plainly inconsistent with the facts and cannot be generally true. Proponents of this theory accept the empirical evidence as it pertains to contract *renewals,* but fall back to the theoretical argument that a low-ball bidder can demand price adjustments, change orders, and extras during the *initial* contract period, before renewal.[45] This is a legitimate concern for one-time projects, but not for ongoing service contracts.

Having concluded that low-balling is not a pervasive problem, we must nevertheless address the possibility of it happening in a particular instance. A moment's reflection shows that low-balling can occur only if the bidder is confident that once he wins the contract, he will have no future competitor. The contracting agency can thwart this hope by the simple expedient of fostering competition, as previously discussed. If the nature of the service is such that a private monopoly is unavoidably created upon contracting, the agency can make sure that it is only a temporary one and that it remains contestable in the future. Once a contract is awarded, of course, the incumbent becomes familiar with the work and may naturally gain a competitive advantage over a future competitor. The agency can minimize even this legitimate advantage and reduce the height of this entry barrier to future bidders, by making available to them in the subsequent round of bidding as much useful operational information as possible, such as work plans and schedules, manning levels, output measurements, and performance data, as also noted previously. Incidentally, *internal* low-balling, i.e., an artificially low price by the in-house unit in the hope that hidden subsidies can be arranged, is at least as great a danger.

Quality and performance. Cost is only half the equation. The bidder's qualifications, the probability that he will perform in accordance with the quality and performance specifications, and his past track record must all be taken into account. With several bidders capable of delivering the promised performance, the lowest qualified bidder should be awarded the contract. Those who feel that the low bidder cannot deliver, that quality must necessarily suffer, should be aware of the remark I heard astronaut Neil Armstrong make on the steps of City Hall in New York after a ticker-tape parade celebrating his walk on the moon: "You have no idea what it feels like to go to the moon and back in a spacecraft where every single part was made by the lowest bidder!" What this means, of course, is that good specifications were written and quality control was enforced.

12. Monitor, Evaluate, and Enforce Contractor Performance

Contracting requires monitoring and enforcement, that is, a systematic procedure to monitor the performance of the contractor, compare it to the standards in the contract, and enforce the contract terms. Close monitoring is recommended but can deteriorate into micromanagement; in contrast, loose monitoring can lead to poor quality of service. A balance must be struck. In addition to regular monitoring at a frequency appropriate for the particular function, a detailed evaluation should be carried out, for example, when it is nearing time to rebid.

A contract manager should be in charge of the contract and responsible for contractor relations, which should not be adversarial. Monitoring should not be turned into a game of "gotcha." The objective is to assure good service at a fair price. The contract manager should do the following:[46]

- Ensure that the contractor has the required permits, bonding, and insurance for his work
- Verify that services were delivered, inspect the work, and have the contractor correct any unsatisfactory work
- Monitor work performance to assure conformance to budget, schedule, and safety rules
- Assure that that contractor's reports are complete and timely
- Review the contractor's invoices for accuracy and completeness:
  - if the contract is for a fixed price, assure that the percentage of billing is equal to the percentage of work performed
  - verify that any charges for equipment, labor, and supplies are in accordance with the contract
  - verify withholding of any penalties or other contractor funds
- Check that the contractor is paying suppliers and subcontractors
- Initiate any necessary changes in the scope of the contract

Sometimes agencies contract for a service and use carefully drawn performance specifications but fail to monitor the work and so essentially abdicate their role. New York City, for example, had stringent performance standards for its street-light maintenance contractor, requiring that all lights be restored to working order within ten days of being reported, or a daily penalty charge would be levied. This was an eminently sensible standard, but the city, unfortunately, kept no records and had no idea whether the standard was being met. Subsequently the city followed a much better approach, involving computerized tracking of all reported light outages and random checking in the field, coupled with an arrangement whereby the city was divided into eight roughly equal-sized zones (equal in terms of the number of street lights) with no more than two zones awarded per contractor.

In another example, not until 1997 did New York City finally revise its contract with the eminent teaching hospital that provided doctors for one of the municipal hospitals; for more than thirty years the city paid for services but exercised only the most cursory oversight. The new contract sets forth specific performance targets, such as Pap tests on a certain fraction of female patients, with monetary penalties if the target is not met. It also establishes productivity standards as to the number of patients seen per specialist; in the past, the city would pay the same amount of money per anesthesiologist per year, for instance, whether she treated one patient per day or fifteen. The new contract pays more if more patients are treated.[47]

Service monitoring can consist of complaint monitoring, examination of the contractor's work records, scheduled field observations (e.g., at critical points in construction projects), unscheduled field inspections (e.g., of social service institutions), inspections triggered by customer complaints, and periodic sampling and evaluation, for example, of the thoroughness of janitorial cleaning, quality of tree pruning, timeliness of bus service, and condition of repaved roads. With respect to the contract standards for bus service in table 7.5 (p. 193), monitoring relies on examination of contractor records and field inspection. Less frequent but more detailed evaluations could involve citizen surveys, in-depth field studies, and cost comparisons—with past performance if a baseline has prudently been identified beforehand, or with current operations if several contractors are involved or if part of the work is being performed in-house.

Monitoring of some activities, such as residential refuse collection and street light repairs, does not require full-time employees and lends itself instead to citizen monitoring, perhaps by retired persons and homemakers.[48] Complaint monitoring is important and cost effective, as poor service is reflected immediately in complaints. The crucial aspect of monitoring contracts by examining the history of complaints is to be sure that complaints are directed to the government agency, not to the contractor. If this is done, good performance records can be compiled easily and inexpensively. Sad to say, some agencies are oblivious to this opportunity and advertise the contractor's telephone number for complaints instead of the agency's. They think they are being efficient by eliminating the intermediary who relays the complaint from the citizen to the contractor, but this is shortsighted.

Citizen surveys have been developed as a useful tool for monitoring satisfaction with public services. Harry Hatry has written extensively on this issue and has designed suitable survey instruments.[49] It is unreasonable to use these for imposing penalties, but they can be used to modify the contracted service and to shape future specifications.

It is a mistake to use as monitors any personnel from an in-house agency that opposed privatization or bid for the work and lost, despite their familiarity with the service. Harassment of the contractor and reporting bias are all but inevitable. Under compulsory competitive contracting in England, an overhead management unit does the monitoring; this is by far the preferred arrangement.

For the City of Newark, New Jersey, I utilized a combination of monitoring methods to compare the performance of municipal waste collection in one part of the city with contract collection in another, similar part. City costs were analyzed both for the in-house service and for the contract work, and the costs of the city's complaint handling and contract monitoring were included. Citizen opinion surveys were conducted, both by random telephone calls and by mail-back questionnaires distributed on selected blocks. Street cleanliness was measured by trained observers using photographic scales. Both municipal and private crews were followed discreetly and their work performance (number of stops per hour, tons collected per hour, etc.) was observed and recorded directly.

Contract monitoring requires careful planning beforehand as to what and how to measure, suitable training of inspectors, and appropriate recordkeeping and analysis. The monitoring plan will require the contractor to compile and provide certain reports, which must be stated in the bid specifications.

Monitoring itself can be contracted out. The environmental protection agency of Buenos Aires contracted with an international firm for cleaning services, and also contracted with an engineering firm to monitor the contractor. (In turn, the firm contracted with me to advise it on monitoring methods.)

Summary

Contracting for services is well known and widely used. It can be implemented if the following conditions are satisfied: (1) There is political leadership and (2) an internal champion promoting the idea; (3) the government is under fiscal stress or otherwise has to reconsider its present practices; (4) large cost savings or other valued improvements are likely; (5) the act is politically feasible; and (6) a precipitating event upsets the status quo and requires change. The major opposition to any form of privatization comes from public-employee unions, whose greatest concern is the loss of jobs and the erosion of above-market wages and benefits. The strongest arguments they raise publicly are the specter of corruption and the assertion that private, profit-seeking contractors are not as devoted to the public interest as they are. Skilled political leaders can generally create coalitions to overcome unreasonable opposition, however, and can develop techniques for tempering the impact on employees affected by contracting.

Various techniques can attract potential contractors to compete, and "contracting in" can supplement "contracting out." The former term refers to "managed competition," having government agencies bid for the work on a fair and equitable basis against private contractors. Dividing the work among several contractors and an in-house unit, where feasible, assures effective competition, knowledgeable contract supervision, defense against possible collusion, and certainty of service.

Contract specifications must be clear and comprehensive because they will affect the number and quality of bids and the overall success. They can, however, be manipulated to undermine a decision to contract or to favor a particular bidder. Bidding procedures will affect the outcome, for better or worse. Comparing in-house and contract costs must be carried out astutely, as there are many pitfalls for the unwary. Low-ball bids are not common, but in any event they are easy to guard against.

Once a contract is in effect, performance must be monitored systematically, using complaint monitoring, citizen surveys, field observations and measurements, and examination of records, for example. Ample experience in making and implementing the decision to privatize is readily available, and a large body of practical knowledge has been developed to help government officials and give them confidence in taking this step.[50]

CHAPTER EIGHT

Divesting Enterprises and Assets

A government-owned enterprise (GOE) is a distinct legal entity that is owned by government; has an accounting system separate from the government unit that controls or supervises it; and is engaged in commercial, industrial, or financial activities involving the production of economic goods or services from which it is expected to earn a significant portion of its revenues.[1] Assets are passive properties such as land or buildings, as distinguished from enterprises. Land may be vacant or used for farming, grazing, mining, or logging, for example.

Divesting, one of the principal forms of privatization (the others are delegation and displacement), is the method of choice for privatizing government enterprises and assets. It is carried out by selling, giving away, or liquidating GOEs and assets, as discussed in chapter 5. Divestment is used in the United States at the federal, state, and local levels, and in developed, developing, and post-socialist countries.

Compared to other countries, the United States has relatively few government-owned businesses, yet many examples of divestment can be cited. The federal government sold Conrail, the freight railroad,[2] the Naval Air Warfare Center in Indianapolis (it produces advanced electronics and was bought by Hughes Electronics),[3] the Construction Loan Insurance Corporation (Connie Lee),[4] and the Student Loan Marketing Association (Sallie Mae).[5] The largest divestment of government property in the history of the United States was the sale in 1998, for $3.65 billion, of the Elk Hills Naval Petroleum Reserve, a giant oil and gas field in California.[6] The government sold the national helium reserve[7] and the United States Enrichment Corporation, which prepares uranium for fuel in nuclear-powered generating plants.[8] There are calls to sell the Tennessee Valley Authority and four power marketing administrations, the Bonneville, Southwestern, Southeastern, and Western Area; these would sell for $45 billion to $62 billion.[9]

Governments plan to relinquish their role in the international, treaty-based, satellite organizations, INTELSAT[10] and INMARSAT.[11]

Divestment at the state level is illustrated by New York's sale of the freight operations of the Long Island Railroad, which is primarily a commuter railroad run by a state authority. New York will sell its sprawling array of unused mental health facilities—twenty properties totaling ten square miles—that were emptied by the deinstitutionalization movement.[12] Michigan sold its Accident Fund, the workers' compensation insurance business, for $255 million.

At the local level, some of the more unusual divestments also took place in New York, where the city government sold its television station to a consortium of Dow Jones and ITT for $207 million,[13] sold its two radio stations at a discount price of $20 million to a nonprofit foundation supported by listeners,[14] sold its United Nations Plaza Hotel to a Hong Kong–based chain for $85 million,[15] and sought a nonprofit buyer for the last city-owned cemetery that was still accepting new burials,[16] while the Port Authority of New York and New Jersey sold the Vista Hotel at the World Trade Center to the Marriott Hotel chain for $141.5 million.[17] These were not exactly core functions of government.

Governments find themselves in a bewildering variety of businesses, some of them bizarre. In Egypt, for example, a Moslem country in which alcohol is nominally prohibited, the government owned and operated a brewery! (It also owned and operated a Coca-Cola plant.) In the United States, governments owned golf courses, radio stations, cemeteries, hotels, and, briefly, an adult bookstore and a brothel. Governments have gotten into business in several ways: (1) in the (usually vain) hope that they would serve as engines of rapid economic development and job growth; (2) for reasons of socialist ideology; (3) by nationalizing existing private companies (which accounts for the beer and Coke in Egypt); (4) to save jobs in failing private firms (hence AMTRAK in the United States); (5) taking over firms that could not (or would not, as in the case of former Philippines President Marcos's cronies) pay back their government loans (this explains the adult bookstore and brothel); (6) because of tradition, for example, providing public markets; (7) assuming control of natural monopolies, or unnatural ones created by government regulation.

Because of the profusion of state-owned enterprises and business functions abroad, divestment has been widespread. In Great Britain scores of state enterprises were divested under Prime Minister Thatcher, mostly by public sale of shares, including British Petroleum (in 1979), British Aerospace (1981), Britoil (1982), Cable and Wireless (1983), Jaguar (1984),

British Telecom (1984), British Gas (1986), British Airways (1987), Rolls Royce (1987), and the British Airports Authority (1987).[18] Even more far-reaching sales followed: water authorities (1989), electricity supply and generation (1990), and British Rail (1994).[19] The ecumenical nature of privatization is indicated by the fact that the Labour government is considering privatizing the London Underground (subway system),[20] an idea raised earlier by the Conservative government.[21] The cumulative sales proceeds of the divestments in the UK from 1979 to 1991 alone amounted to a remarkable 11.9 percent of the average annual gross domestic product (GDP) during that period. New Zealand had the most aggressive divestment program among industrial nations, with sales amounting to 14.1 percent of its average annual GDP from 1987 to 1991.[22]

State-owned enterprises (SOEs) played a large role in the economies of most developing countries, a legacy of socialist thinking that this was the fast track to economic development. In 1980 the average contribution of SOEs to GDP in developing countries was about 10 percent, with variations ranging from 3 percent in Paraguay and Nepal to 38 percent in Ghana and Zambia.[23] Often, however, SOEs were retarding economic development rather than promoting it. Not surprisingly, therefore, in order to overcome the problems of SOEs cataloged in chapter 6, these countries undertook major divestment efforts. Accurate figures are difficult to compile, but an early World Bank survey of eighty-seven countries found that 1,269 divestments had already been completed through 1987, about 80 percent of them in developing countries.[24]

The post-socialist countries represent a different situation entirely. SOEs accounted for an average of about 85 percent of GDP, ranging up to 97 percent in Czechoslovakia (it was 96 percent in the Soviet Union) before the collapse of socialism.[25] Since then divestment has been rapid, often by mass privatization, as discussed later.

Divestment Methods

Table 8.1 is an elaboration of table 5.2 (p. 127), showing in greater detail the features of divestment plans.

By Sale

Divestment of government-owned real property—the sale of land and buildings—is easy to do and attractive for several important reasons: (1) it brings in sales revenue; (2) it brings in tax revenue by restoring property to the

TABLE 8.1—DIVESTMENT OF GOVERNMENT ASSETS AND ENTERPRISES

Sale	*Method of sale*	to private firm	by auction	
			by negotiation	
		to the public	by public offering	
		to employees	by employee buyout	
		to users or customers	by sale to cooperative	
	Scope of sale	partial sale	government majority	government control
				private control
			joint venture (50-50)	private control
			government minority	private control
		full sale	in one step	
			in several steps (stages, tranches)	
	Buyer	domestic		
		foreign		
		mixed domestic and foreign		
Free transfer	to a joint venture			
	to the public			
	to employees			
	to users or customers			
	to original owner (restitution)			
	to selected classes of recipients			
Liquidation				

tax rolls; (3) it eliminates ownership and maintenance expenses; (4) it precludes requests to give away the property to lower-level governments or nonprofit organizations; (5) it foils efforts by government agencies to expand into temptingly convenient space.

Divestment of enterprises by sale can be looked at in terms of the method of sale: to a private firm (a strategic investor, one who knows the business) by auction or negotiation in a trade sale; to the public by a stock offering ("share flotation"); to employees and management via a buyout; or to a cooperative of users or customers.

The sale can also be viewed in terms of its scope: the enterprise can be sold to a strategic investor in its entirety or only partially, in effect, a joint venture, with the government retaining a majority, a minority, or half the shares. The key is giving control to the private partner and bringing into the enterprise the partner's management, financial resources, experience, technology, and access to markets. A sale of shares to the public instead of to a company can also be partial, en route to subsequent full divestment; that is, the sale can be in stages, also called "tranches." Japan and Germany sold their state-owned telephone companies this way.[26] Unless government's control of the enterprise is relinquished, however, this cannot be considered real privatization—the transaction merely raises revenue for the state. This is a good strategy to follow if it is difficult to establish a value for the enterprise and the government is afraid of criticism that the enterprise is being sold too cheaply; the share price in later sales can be more closely attuned to the value as determined by the market after the partial sale and after operation in the private sector.

Often the identity of the buyer is politically important. Xenophobia is rampant in many countries, particularly those with a colonial past, and it is a matter of grave concern whether the enterprise or asset is bought by foreigners or by fellow countrymen. But often there are no local companies or citizens with the qualifications or the capital to buy and invest in improving the enterprise. A common way around this problem is to set a limit on the fraction of shares to be owned by foreigners, even if control is to be exercised by them. For example, a 40-percent share could be sold to a foreign buyer and 60 percent retained (at least temporarily) in the hands of the state or sold (or given away) to the public, but operating control would belong to the foreign private buyer. Another approach is to create a so-called "golden share" for the government, which is essentially a veto that the state can exercise in certain enumerated circumstances, such as reselling the enterprise, selling the enterprise's assets, closing it, or changing the business. The process of selling state enterprises and assets is discussed later in detail.

By Free Transfer

As noted in chapter 5 and as shown in tables 5.2 (p. 127) and 8.1, government can transfer ownership to the public, to employees, to users or customers, to the original owner from whom the property had been taken, or to other selected classes of recipients, or it can contribute its shares to transform an enterprise into a joint venture.

A historic example of free transfer of government assets, on a huge scale, took place in the United States: the Homestead Act of 1862 gave land in the West to anyone who satisfied simple requirements; over the next forty years 80 million acres were given to 600,000 farmers.[27]

In the post-socialist countries free transfers figure prominently in mass privatization, a speedy process of transferring large numbers of GOEs to private hands so they can be restructured, so capital markets can develop, and so the country can move rapidly to a market economy.

The basic problems of privatization in those countries are aptly summarized in a witty aphorism by Janusz Lewandowski, Poland's Minister of Ownership Transformation in 1991: "Privatization is the sale of enterprises that no one owns, and whose value no one knows, to people who have no money."[28] The need for mass privatization in these circumstances in Eastern Europe and the former Soviet Union was evident. With 8,500 large- and medium-sized SOEs in Poland, for example, conventional case-by-case divestment as in Great Britain would have taken more than 700 years, and the 25,000 GOEs in Russia more than 2,000 years!

Michael McLindon points to three forms of mass privatization: (1) rapid case-by-case divestment, as in East Germany. This was a special case of trade sales to buyers, mostly West German companies, who often paid nothing but merely had to keep the current workforce employed at current wages for a year or two; this unique and costly program was part of the process of integrating East Germany quickly into the wealthy Federal Republic of Germany; (2) free transfers of shares in SOEs to the public at large indirectly, through intermediary investment (or mutual) funds; and (3) free transfers of shares to the public directly, through ownership vouchers.[29]

Giving away shares to the general public is fair because under socialism the SOEs were paid for by the people and "the people" were the nominal owners. It avoids the problem of a lack of capital in people's hands, is relatively rapid, does not require prior valuation of the enterprise, is not inflationary, and can be done partially, allowing markets to develop and market values to be established, whereupon the remaining shares can be sold.

Ownership vouchers can be tradable or nontradable, have a nominal value or not, and be distributed to all current citizens young or old, or only to citizens over the age of eighteen, or only to citizens as of a certain date, and so on. Policies differ by country. In Russia, workers and managers received 51 percent of the vouchers, a high price necessary to gain their acquiescence; in Moldova, 20 percent; and in the Czech and Slovak Federal Republic (CSFR), less than 10 percent.

As tangible certificates, vouchers are easy to understand and represent the first exposure to security ownership for people who were never allowed this freedom. Different approaches and auction mechanisms have been employed, ranging from a simple one in Russia to a complex one in the CSFR.[30]

Mass privatization has been very successful by some important measures: in the CSFR, three-quarters of the 6,000 SOEs were privatized within two years; in Russia, 14,000 of the 25,000 SOEs were privatized and an estimated 40 million Russians are now stockholders.[31] Mass privatization can be described whimsically but aptly as expropriation of state-owned enterprises by the people, a neat inversion of communist dogma.

The major shortcoming of mass privatization through free transfer is that the same management—with all its socialist-era failings—remains in power, because the resulting ownership is too widely dispersed to permit effective control. Others point out that giving away shares is no way to establish a market economy: people will not value shares any more than they valued the SOEs that they nominally owned under socialism.[32]

A pernicious form of free transfer to managers and employees is spontaneous or self-privatization. Commonplace in the former Soviet Union and in other post-socialist countries, this process amounted to outright theft of state enterprises by insiders. This has also been called "nomenklatura capitalism"—the *nomenklatura* was the roster of the Communist Party faithful who were managers in state-owned enterprises.

By Liquidation

Liquidating the enterprise and selling the assets is a common method of divestment in the following circumstances: (1) the purpose for which the enterprise was initially established is no longer relevant; (2) private investors are not interested in the enterprise as an ongoing business; (3) creditors are likely to initiate legal proceedings; (4) the value of the physical assets, such as the site, is greater than the value of the business enterprise; or (5) the overall economy would be strengthened if certain parts of the SOE are sold off, thus allowing resources to be recycled and put to productive use.

In some countries the bankruptcy laws do not apply to SOEs and will have to be extended. If the government wants any of the assets to be put to a specified use, this condition should be stipulated explicitly and supported by enforcement and verification procedures. Of course, such conditions often reduce the attractiveness of the assets to the buyer and reduce the sale proceeds. The sale should be conducted by open bidding; the market price is unambiguous, as it does not depend on estimates of the earning power of the SOE.[33]

By a Combination of Methods

Several of these methods are commonly used in a single divestment. For example, selling shares to a private firm and to the public and giving away shares to employees or selling shares at a discount to them; or giving shares to a joint venture and to the public. Such combinations, with carefully prescribed proportions of shares to go to each category, are devised to overcome opposition and gain public support.

Divestment Strategy

When planning the divestiture of a GOE, investing further before selling it is generally not a good idea. I have often heard the following seductive line of reasoning: "If we spend a little money to make some obvious improvements, we will get a much higher price when we sell it." There are several things wrong with this approach: (1) The state has been mismanaging the enterprise so far; why would the future be any different? (2) The enterprise is generally in a sorry state despite prior government investments; why would this investment yield any better result? (3) A private buyer would make the investment that suits his strategy for the enterprise; for example, a state-owned hotel being privatized could be made into a business hotel, a tourist hotel, a family hotel, a casino, a catering establishment, a fancy club, and so on. Different buyers would make different kinds of investments depending on their purpose. Without a particular buyer's plan in mind, further government expenditures prior to sale would be pointless and wasteful.

In my experience, arguments for such expenditures are often intended to delay privatization until a different government comes to power and perhaps drops the whole idea. If the investment is made and the enterprise starts doing better, be aware that the next argument will be, "The enterprise is now doing well so we don't have to sell it," ignoring the likelihood that the enterprise will soon go downhill again. I've heard this reasoning in places as diverse as New York, Venezuela, Greece, Hungary, Egypt, India, and Lesotho.

A useful strategic framework for analyzing divestment candidates is offered by Jacquillat.[34] Government enterprises are classified according to their profitability and to the extent that they have competitors in their industry. Two variables, the profitability of the enterprise and the degree of competitiveness in its industry or sector, form the simple, two-by-two matrix of figure 8.1.

All enterprises can be mapped into one or another quadrant. The enterprises in the upper-right quadrant are profitable and have many competitors; therefore, they are easy to sell. They can attract investors because they earn profits but are not monopolies and so do not pose legal or economic problems for the buyer or the seller, the government.

In contrast to profitable enterprises, consider the organizations located in the lower-left quadrant of figure 8.1. They lose money despite their monopoly status, presumably because they are forced to operate under price controls, are inefficient, are deliberately subsidized as a matter of policy, or

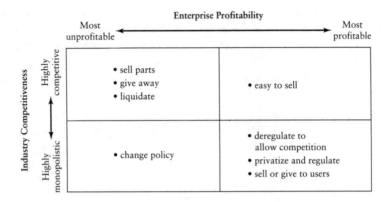

FIGURE 8.1—CLASSIFYING AND RESTRUCTURING ENTERPRISES FOR DIFFERENT DIVESTMENT STRATEGIES

Source: Adapted from B. Jacquillat, *Désétatiser* (Paris: Editions Robert Laffont, 1985), 138.

have little demand for their products or services. Unless their policy environment is changed significantly, they are unlikely sale candidates.

If an unprofitable enterprise in a competitive industry (the upper-left quadrant in figure 8.1) consists of several different businesses or activities, one approach to divestment is to unbundle it, that is, break it up into its components, some of which may be profitable and viable if not entangled in the entire SOE. Other parts of that SOE could be given away to the workers to see if they can make a go of it; this was done with the retail establishments of large state-owned enterprises in post-socialist Russia. Still other parts, which have no future as ongoing businesses, could be liquidated and the assets sold.

Divesting the monopolistic, profitable SOEs in the lower-right quadrant may require restructuring. These SOEs are profitable monopolies. A so-called "natural monopoly" can best be divested by (1) selling and regulating it, or (2) selling or giving it to users or customers, in which case it would be self-regulating. For example, a rural electric, water, or telephone company owned cooperatively by its subscribers is self-regulating because if it were to charge excessively high prices, the profits would go right back to the customer-owners; privatization of profitable monopolies by selling them to the users is a good approach where possible.

Another approach to selling such monopolies is to auction them at a price equal to the appraised (or replacement) value of their capital assets plus the highest bid for the percentage of annual profits that will be paid to the government making the sale. Because part of the profits will be recouped by government, some measure of self-regulation by the buyer can be expected.

If an SOE in this quadrant is not a natural monopoly, either it has been created by regulation, in which case deregulation is recommended, with restructuring of the industry if necessary, or it must be a monopoly by virtue of its being the sole producer in a limited market. In this case, deregulation to allow competition from imports would be an appropriate method to follow.

While these prescriptions for deregulation to break up state monopolies and allow competition in the private sector are compelling, the sad reality is that sometimes political leaders will sell monopolies intact in order to get a higher sale price, although their citizens will ultimately have to pay for this policy in terms of higher prices for the goods or services they buy from the monopoly. Politicians benefit from the immediate revenue, but the citizens pay later. I realized that this was behind the plan for telecom privatization in Panama. The only existing cellular network would be sold to the buyer of the land-line system many months before a second cellular system would be allowed to enter the field, that is, after the market had been locked up by the first buyer. Assured of monopoly profits, the buyer can afford to pay a high price, thereby giving the incumbent politicians a windfall to spend.

Divestment Guidelines

A government saddled with underperforming assets and enterprises can undertake incremental divestments, grappling with opportunities as they arise, or it can initiate a comprehensive divestment program. Many nations have chosen the latter. The elements of a comprehensive program are shown in table 8.2, which operationalizes the broad management guidelines described in chapter 5.

The discussion of the steps in the table that follows draws on my experiences in forty-seven countries and many cities and states in the United States and on experiences reported by others.[35] The table should not be interpreted as requiring this rigid sequence of steps; many of them should proceed concurrently; indeed, a critical-path diagram should be developed for each case of privatization. These steps apply in developed, developing, and post-socialist countries, although the emphasis and details will differ in the various settings.

TABLE 8.2—ELEMENTS OF A COMPREHENSIVE PROGRAM FOR PRIVATIZATION BY DIVESTMENT

1. Make political commitment to privatization
2. Organize for privatization
3. Train the privatization unit
4. Establish overall objectives for the program
5. Develop the proper legal framework
6. Guard against corruption
7. Identify GOE targets and establish individual objectives
8. Gain public support
9. Restructure the GOE
10. Select the divestment method
11. Address concerns of workers
12. Address concerns of the poor
13. Design regulatory regime
14. Prepare enterprise for divestment
15. Create a supportive policy environment
16. Appraise the enterprise or asset
17. Market the enterprise or asset
18. Finance the transaction
19. Execute the transaction
20. Monitor and evaluate post-privatization phase

1. Make Political Commitment to Privatization

It is worth stressing once again that privatization is an intensely political act; that is, a full-scale privatization program has broad and profound implications and generally arouses opposition, for there are winners and losers in the short term. In order to succeed, therefore, it requires strong political leadership and a commitment that is communicated and felt throughout the entire government. The starting point is clear recognition of the shortcomings of existing GOEs, as summarized in chapter 5. This recognition can be gained by analytical evaluations as well as anecdotal observations. The latter should not be underrated, as the continued failings of GOEs are often highly visible and the subject of popular derision, and they can provide public support for a major change like privatization. Outside help is often called for in developing and post-socialist countries to study GOEs, and to enhance the understanding, buttress the confidence, and engage the commitment of national leaders. Once the government's leading officials come to accept that privatization and a greater emphasis on markets is the most promising path to improved, long-term economic performance, an effective coalition that has the necessary will and authority must be created, assembled, or cobbled together.

2. Organize for Privatization

Chief executives have found it valuable to initiate the process by appointing a commission of outside business and labor leaders, officials from other levels of government, politicians, good-government groups, and the like, for fact-finding and making recommendations about a privatization program. President Reagan established the President's Commission on Privatization, which produced a far-sighted and influential report.[36] Many state governors in the United States have created and used such commissions.[37]

A centralized approach is most common.[38] A high-level official, with good access to the political leaders, should be selected to direct the process throughout the government, and this individual must be given the rank, authority, and resources to do the job. The person may be a vice-president, an established cabinet officer, a finance director, a budget director, or the head of a special privatization unit in the Office of the President, for example. President Reagan's privatization program was directed by an associate director of the Office of Management and Budget, which is part of the Office of the President. President Clinton's privatization program was primarily in the hands of Vice-President Al Gore's National Performance Review. In New York, Governor George Pataki entrusted the task to a close associate who directed the state's development authority. Many different centralized models exist and can work. Decentralization has its appeal, but it is not likely to be successful, because experience is not accumulated and not all agency heads have the necessary degree of commitment. An ongoing advisory group, such as a commission, can be useful to the official responsible for the program, as can qualified consultants.

3. Train the Privatization Unit

Staff members of the privatization unit will generally require training, which can be obtained from the voluminous and growing literature on the subject and in special courses. The U.S. Agency for International Development (USAID), for one, has sponsored many such training programs for mid-level officials from developing and post-socialist countries. The National Council for Public-Private Partnerships and many other organizations and universities do this in the United States. Under a centralized approach, a stable staff develops expertise that can be applied to many different privatization targets regardless of the latter's place in their organization, and works closely with subject-matter experts in the selected target. The reason to start the training early is to bring that knowledge to bear in the next steps.

4. Establish Overall Objectives for the Program

One must choose among the many desirable objectives listed in chapter 5 for privatization programs, for many are mutually exclusive: generate revenue, broaden ownership, reduce government's role, and so on. It may be possible, however, to accommodate multiple objectives in a large-scale program that will involve many GOEs by setting different objectives for particular GOE privatizations, thereby creating a portfolio of privatization objectives. This should be planned beforehand, and the different divestments should be executed in a suitable sequence to build and retain public support.

5. Create Proper Legal Framework

GOEs are founded in legislative authorization, and therefore legislation—general or specific—is needed for divestment;[39] the political battle is generally joined at this point. Specific legislative authority may be required for the government to get out of certain businesses, and sometimes the national constitution itself might require amendment if certain GOEs are to be privatized. In the Philippines, for example, contract maintenance and operation of water distribution systems can be done only by firms that are at least 60 percent Filipino-owned. This constraint may be good policy, but as it limits the number of bidders for such work, it may be worth reviewing.

6. Guard against Corruption

Privatization leads to less corruption because the government controls fewer resources.[40] Procedures should be put in place to minimize corruption in the divestment program. Unless this is done persuasively, public cynicism is likely to undermine privatization efforts in countries with a culture of corruption, for opponents will be quick to wield this weapon.

Opportunities for corruption can be minimized by (1) speeding the process, which leaves less time to arrange a corrupt transaction; (2) following a standard procedure that reduces administrative discretion (i.e., don't change the rules during the process); (3) ensuring transparency, that is, providing broad access to information about the process, the value of the enterprise, and the result (in effect, creating thousands of auditors); and (4) having independent control of the process, not control by the agency that previously owned the enterprise and may allow exploitation of old relationships.[41]

Voucher-based mass privatization and privatization by liquidation are least vulnerable to corruption; management and employee buyouts and spontaneous privatization are most at risk. Privatization by the public sale of shares and by trade sales are intermediate in vulnerability to corruption because of their slow pace and the relatively high degree of administrative discretion, despite transparency and independent control of the process.[42]

7. Identify Privatization Targets and Establish Individual GOE Objectives

Unless the social value under continued government ownership is greater than the social value of selling,[43] the enterprise is a candidate for divestment. Potential candidates have to satisfy the objectives of the privatization program, and the political, social, and economic feasibility of its privatization should be assessed. Each candidate GOE should be examined with respect to its performance, costs, financial condition, organizational structure, technical and physical condition, legal status, and workforce. The basic principle is "pick the low-hanging fruit," that is, choose those that are easiest to privatize yet will yield meaningful results. "Easy to privatize" means politically feasible, adequate control over the GOE, a commercially viable enterprise, investor interest, no legal impediments, and no worker problems that cannot be handled satisfactorily. "Meaningful results" means that the economic, budgetary, and other positive impacts are large enough to make the effort worthwhile. As noted previously, individual objectives should be set for particular divestment candidates so that the resulting portfolio of objectives (attract new investment, develop a capital market, satisfy foreign lenders, etc.) satisfies the objectives of the overall program.

Assets (land, buildings, leased enterprises) will generally be easier to privatize than operating enterprises that have significant numbers of public employees. One reason to sell underutilized land and buildings is to deprive expansion-minded government agencies, now or in the future, of the argument that a proposed new program will be inexpensive because the necessary space is already in hand.

8. Gain Public Support

The effect of privatization on the public must be assessed and steps taken early in the design of the program to eliminate harmful consequences and gain public support. Steps may have to be taken to ameliorate any negative impact on the poor, through vouchers or by otherwise spreading a social safety net. If the economy as a whole, spurred by privatization, prospers while tax collecting—which can be used to buffer the impact on the poor—is neglected, widespread suffering with political as well as human consequences may result, as in Argentina.[44]

Programs in Great Britain, Sri Lanka, and Zambia were successful in explaining privatization to the public and gaining widespread support despite strong opposition. In Britain, a massive advertising program featured a ubiquitous character, Sid, who appeared on television, billboards, radio, and print, extolling the virtues of divestment (denationalization) and encouraging first-time and small investors to buy shares. The sales process emphasized small lots and low prices for the average buyer.[45] In Sri Lanka, a conservative government that succeeded a socialist government conducted a year-long publicity campaign in all three common languages and in all media, with a careful sequencing of messages to explain what privatization is, why it was needed, how it would operate, and what benefits would accrue.[46] The publicity program in Zambia featured the country's most popular TV personality in a graduated series of saturation advertisements.[47] Public support can also be gained by creating private-sector coalitions consisting of probable beneficiaries of the process to undertake publicity campaigns. Such communication efforts are particularly important in post-socialist countries where the public has had no exposure to privately owned companies in generations.[48] The purpose of such programs is to rebut tendentious arguments, correct erroneous information disseminated by opponents, inform the public, explain the benefits, and gain support for the leaders who assume political risk to promote privatization. (One wonders whether thwarted privatization efforts in American state and local governments might have succeeded if elected officials had aggressively sought public support instead of allowing antiprivatization unions to make quiet deals with their supporters in state and local legislatures.)

Public support for a broad divestment program will be vitiated if early privatizations are blamed for price increases or other negative consequences. For example, the price of electric power in Pakistan and of liquefied natural gas in Sri Lanka rose immediately after those utilities were privatized, which soured the public mood for privatization. The government never adequately explained why, preferring to let the public blame the private buyers. The explanation was that in both cases the former state subsidies or cross subsidies (from industrial to residential users) were withdrawn and the government fully expected the increases in real, unsubsidized market prices. In fact, it was primarily to stop the losses due to the subsidies that the GOEs were divested.

To garner public support, it is a good idea to announce what could or would be done with the anticipated savings and what other specific benefits the public should expect. In Mexico, Jacques Rogozinski, who was in charge of the privatization of Aeromexico, the state-owned airline, repeatedly announced that the airline was losing $100 million a year, which was enough to supply water and electricity to thousands of small towns. In Puerto Rico, the president stated that privatization of the telephone company would reduce the wait for a phone to less than a year and that the proceeds would be spent on water systems, a state retirement fund, and continued pension benefits for telephone company workers. In the United States, it was announced that money from the privatization of Sallie Mae, the student loan program, would go to the Washington, D.C., school system.

9. Restructure the SOE

GOEs generally have to be "corporatized," that is, transformed into joint-stock companies. The number of shares and their book value has to be established. The enterprise may need further reorganizing before the sale, pruning worthless appendages and tumorous growths or breaking it up and selling parts that in total may be worth more than the whole. Massive, diverse, overly integrated government-owned behemoths are excellent candidates for such treatment. The upper-left and lower-right quadrants of figure 8.1 (p. 219) illustrate such restructuring.

10. Select the Divestment Method

The entire array of privatization tools discussed above is available, singly or in combination, to be chosen for the selected divestment candidate. The preceding section on restructuring and figure 8.1 illustrate the relation between the attributes of the GOE—its profitability and the competitiveness of its industry—and the divestment method.

11. Address Concerns of Workers

Generally the most difficult problem to deal with is the fear of redundancy—job loss—among workers. Given the overstaffing that is so common in government operations, this is an understandable concern, and it must be addressed. While temporary loss of jobs is not uncommon, this is not always the case and in any event there are many ways to deal with the matter. The fear of lower wages is also a serious concern. Because of the importance of the labor issue, it is dealt with at length in chapter 11.

12. Address Concerns of the Poor

If divestment is likely to lead to higher prices for hitherto subsidized services, attention must be paid to the impact on the poor. Water supply is a good example. Many countries have a shortage of safe drinking water. Much of the water that is supplied, however, as in Buenos Aires, Jakarta, and Manila, is pilfered through illegal taps and not paid for. Privatization of water systems, intended to improve access to clean water, inevitably leads to large reductions in the amount of water lost through pilferage. Many poor people find their supply of "free" water cut off. This presents both a political and a humane problem. The government may have to arrange for cross subsidies, vouchers, discounts, rationing, or other means to ameliorate the plight of those affected, but it is important to remember that the end result is more clean water for all.

Market forces are better for growth than government development plans, and better for the poor as well. Public spending in developing countries is financed in part by crippling taxes on agriculture, which provides a living in rural areas where most of the poor live. Overspending by governments slows growth and directly harms the poor at the same time. As *The Economist* put it: "[I]t is much easier for governments to intervene badly than to intervene well. . . . The impolite truth remains: bad government is the biggest single reason for poverty in the third world, and less government is the most effective single remedy."[49] To put it plainly, privatization is good for the poor.

13. Design Regulatory Regime

If the candidate enterprise or asset is a natural monopoly or is subject to monopolization, an appropriate regulatory regime must be designed and put into place to protect the public. Much experience, good and bad, was gained in Britain about how to go about this.[50] A starting point is to minimize the extent of the problem by restructuring the industry—separating monopoly parts from potentially competing parts, where possible. The electricity sector in Britain was restructured by breaking apart the three segments that were previously considered an inviolable and integral unit: generation, transmission, and distribution: competition was introduced in generation. The telecommunications and water sectors lend themselves to somewhat similar restructuring. Hungary, for example, did a much better job in splitting its oil, gas, and power companies into several independent units than did Russia and the Czech Republic.[51]

The second line of defense consists of appropriate contract terms. An example of an *unsatisfactory* contract in this respect can be found in Togo. A government-owned steel mill was leased (not sold) to a private firm. The government was desperate to get out of this money-losing business and agreed to very generous terms for the lease as an alternative to liquidation. Among other things, the private operator was guaranteed high tariffs on competing imports and was thus protected from external competition, and it would have to pay no duties on its own imports or exports. As this was the only steel producer in the country, the domestic sales price was regulated, but the terms were particularly favorable for the firm.[52] Although this is an example of a lease rather than a divestiture, it illustrates how contract terms can affect the competitive climate for better or for worse and create or weaken monopoly conditions. Buyers of GOEs often seek protection against future competitors. This should generally be avoided, as the objective of privatization is to improve efficiency by creating competition, and the whole idea of divestment is to move the enterprise into a competitive market environment. If, however, the GOE is a utility such as telecommunications, for which major expansion and therefore investment by the buyer is desired, it may be reasonable to provide protection for a limited period.

The third line of defense of the public interest is price regulation, which requires appropriate laws and institutions for setting and changing prices, including formulas for automatic price changes based on specified inflation measures such as the cost of living. Prices may be based on profits or, alternatively, on price caps. Profit regulation is the common way that utilities are regulated in the United States. Total costs are calculated and scrutinized, and the regulator approves a price intended to provide an acceptable rate of return (instead of a monopoly rate) on the invested capital. Such profit regulation, however, is very complicated and time-consuming, tends to lag well behind necessary investment decisions, and creates an incentive to overinvest capital. Another approach to price regulation is a price cap. Developed in Britain at the time of its major divestment program, this method allows prices to be increased only at the rate of price inflation minus a fixed percentage; for example, utility rates could increase by only 85 percent of the rate of inflation. This percentage is intended to reflect the expected improvement in efficiency of the privatized enterprise. Predicting efficiency improvements may be easier than predicting profits, and price-cap regulation is more flexible, less restrictive, less time consuming, and allows more operating discretion for managers.[53]

In any event, the regulatory process and policies must be established beforehand so that the buyer knows what he is getting into and what policies will affect his bid, and so that the people recognize that they are protected from monopoly pricing and need not fear divestment of government-owned utilities.

14. Prepare Enterprise for Divestment

An enterprise has to be prepared for divestment—legally, financially, organizationally, managerially. It may have to be transformed into a corporation before it can be sold, for example. Financially, a host of issues have to be cleared up. Who owns the land under the enterprise? (In the post-socialist countries this is a nightmare to sort out.) Who will assume the debt obligations? (Usually the government.) It is no easy task sometimes to determine just what the debt obligations are, that is, who owes what to whom. GOEs often are far behind in loan repayments, tax payments, and contributions to employee retirement plans or social security systems. Contaminated land presents an environmental liability. There may be some disputed liabilities. All these issues have to be cleared up and government funds may have to be infused into the enterprise to improve the capital base. At the same time, GOEs may have hidden assets, such as undervalued property, landing rights, port facilities, and patents. These, too, should be uncovered and the balance sheet cleaned up so that it presents an accurate picture of the financial position.

The boundaries and assets of the GOE have to be delineated. If a government-owned airline is to be divested, should the catering subsidiary be included, or divested separately? Should offices owned by the airline in foreign cities be included? Is the buyer to be granted the exclusive rights for domestic routes currently held by the national carrier?

If the GOE is to be privatized by a public sale of shares, new management may have to be installed to improve efficiency, inject a market-driven philosophy, and prepare for the sale. As for redundant workers, if the magnitude of the problem is large, the government itself should assume the task of shedding workers rather than leaving it to a private buyer—otherwise none may be interested.

15. *Create a Supportive Policy Environment*

The regulatory and tax environment of the newly privatized firm will affect its profitability and therefore its attractiveness to potential buyers. The policies under which the enterprise will operate must be determined and understood at the outset. Will prices be controlled? Will duties have to be paid on capital equipment imported to modernize the enterprise? Can profits be repatriated by a foreign buyer? Will a tax holiday (no taxes for a fixed period) be in effect? Conditions that repel would-be buyers should be avoided. For instance, government restrictions on the sale of factories and hotels that require the buyer to employ the same number of workers and not to change the use of the properties are anathema.

16. *Appraise the Enterprise or Asset*

With regard to price, the buyer and the seller of an asset or a GOE have diametrically opposed positions. The private buyer wants to pay as little as possible, and may be anticipating a real bargain. The government selling the property wants a high price, or at least wants to avoid a loss, so that it cannot be accused of giving away a valuable national treasure to rapacious businessmen, particularly foreigners, even if the property in question is a decrepit white elephant with an insatiable appetite for government subsidies.

Both the seller and the buyer have to estimate the value of the asset or enterprise being offered for sale. This is often done by hiring independent firms with valuation capabilities such as investment banks, consulting firms, or valuation firms. They employ a variety of standards:

- liquidation value, which estimates the value of the GOE's assets if each were to be sold to the highest bidder
- income value, which estimates the value based on the enterprise's expected performance as measured by future income and cash flow
- replacement value, which estimates the cost of replacing the assets
- book value, which tracks the investments and depreciation in the enterprise

Replacement value may be logically appealing as a method, but it suffers from the fact that rarely would one build an exact replacement. Book value is attractive to accountants but may be little more than a bookkeeping artifact with little relation to reality. For an enterprise with little or no future as an operating company, liquidation may be best, as it recognizes that the GOE is worth more dead than alive; that is, the assets are worth more to others than to the enterprise itself. For enterprises with a more promising future, the income approach is best because it calculates the present value by discounting the estimated future profitability and cash flow under new owners.[54] The valuation must take into account not only the current financial situation of a GOE, but past and future policies as well; for example, objectives may have been imposed on the GOE that limited its performance but will no longer apply. Also, if a prolonged legal and political battle is envisioned before a sale can be finalized, the price will be lower. These and other similar factors have to be resolved before a realistic valuation can be made and before a buyer will bid.[55]

17. Market the Enterprise or Asset

For a trade sale, that is, sale to a firm in the same business, a sales brochure or information memorandum should be prepared for the enterprise. It should be readable, and attractively illustrated. In countries with regulated securities markets, a formal prospectus is required for the sale of shares to the public. It should present all the information that a knowledgeable buyer would want, including past history and a discussion of possible future activities under private management. It should include data on physical facilities, technology, productivity, pricing policy, marketing strategy, and managerial effectiveness, and on financial performance presented in accordance with international accounting standards.[56] It should describe the extent of competition that the enterprise will face, the protection, if any, that the government will provide, the implications of expected economic liberalization and of applicable regulations, the tax and regulatory environment (as discussed previously), details on pension obligations, any preferential arrangements on shares for employees and others, and outstanding contractual obligations.[57]

If the enterprise is a relatively large one, it is desirable to seek many possible buyers—the more the better. Discussions should be held with prospective qualified buyers, and competition should be stimulated. Confidentiality is vital in these discussions, so interested parties should sign standard confidentiality agreements. Investment bankers or other advisers should be used as agents of the seller; they are in the business of facilitating the buying and selling of businesses. For small enterprises, such as the retail shops in post-socialist countries, such help is not required.

18. Finance the Transaction

Two aspects of financing need to be considered: financing the divestment transaction and financing the enterprise afterwards. Both are affected by the following features of the local financial environment:

- receptivity to the free flow of capital, foreign and domestic
- availability of domestic private capital to purchase shares of the enterprise
- existence of a viable and regulated securities market
- connection of the capital markets with the rest of the world, and the credit worthiness of the country for access to medium- and long-term international capital, for example, via investment bank underwriting and loans by international development banks and the International Finance Corporation[58]

Existing capital markets should be used to the maximum extent, as the public sale of shares is most transparent and least subject to corruption; they have the added advantage of giving access to local investors and thereby gaining support for the privatization program. This is a limited option in less developed countries but by no means impossible: in Jamaica, two GOEs were privatized very successfully by public share offerings although the stock exchange was open only twice a week for two hours per session and generally had thin and erratic trading.[59]

The timing of divestment transactions by public flotation of shares is important. In Argentina and the Philippines, for example, the governments put GOEs on the market at the same time that they offered particularly attractive government bonds; the poor timing dampened investor interest in the GOE shares.[60]

Despite the shortage of domestic capital, some developing countries restrict foreign buyers, which deprives the countries of capital, needed skills, access to new markets, and modern technology. Some countries further discriminate against their own prosperous minority groups, as Malaysia and Indonesia have done against ethnic Chinese and Kenya against people whose origins are in the Indian subcontinent. These actions must be recognized as serious, self-inflicted handicaps whose social worth must be questioned.

Sale of GOEs should be for cash, not credit, even if it means a lower price. If a significant portion of the sale is on credit, the buyer is in a position to let the enterprise return to the government's hands or to request more loans in the future under the not-very-veiled threat of going under if such support is not forthcoming. In Chile, 70 percent of the firms that had been privatized with only 10 or 20 percent down payments went into bankruptcy and reverted to state hands when hit by a recession.[61] Some GOEs privatized in Pakistan in 1991 were still not meeting their payments in 1997. Private competitors rightly complained that the privatized GOEs had an unfair advantage because they were using public capital at no cost.[62]

The buyer will have to raise the funds to finance the transaction, but the government should not force local financial institutions to make loans or purchase shares, as Brazil tried to do.[63] Leveraged buyouts, guaranteed and convertible bonds, traditional bank loans, venture-capital funds, debt-equity swaps, and joint ventures with international financing institutions can be used to finance divestments.[64]

Debt-equity swaps may be particularly useful instruments for heavily indebted developing countries. Someone who wishes to buy an enterprise can purchase debt at a large discount on the secondary market and trade it for shares in the enterprise. Argentina privatized its national telecommunications company this way. The fiscal illusion provided by debt-equity swaps benefits both buyer and seller: if debt is selling at 25 cents on the dollar, a buyer can claim that he is paying only $2.5 million and getting a bargain, while the seller, the government, can claim it is getting $10 million for the GOE. In some cases, however, the country may be better off selling the GOE for cash and using the money to retire debt, as Mexico did.[65]

Financing management and employee buyouts and employee stock ownership plans (ESOPs) presents a significant challenge. Private sources of finance for these groups—savings and pension funds—are rarely enough to purchase any but the smallest enterprises. Therefore, these are highly leveraged transactions that require government loans or credit arrangements, such as a company-sponsored trust fund for an ESOP. Management and employee buyouts are susceptible to manipulation and corruption, however, and create the impression that these insiders exploited their positions and stole the enterprises for a song. Few pure buyouts of this type have occurred, but it is common to sell some shares—perhaps 10 percent—to employees, often at a discount, to gain their support for the divestment.

As for the financing needed to modernize and expand the enterprise after privatization, profits and internally generated cash flow are the best sources but these may not be enough in the near future. Local and expatriate capital can be raised if investors have confidence in their country's macroeconomic and regulatory policies; assistance may be available from international agencies and bilateral donors.

19. Execute the Transaction

Several issues arise when executing the actual transaction, depending on the method of sale.

Public Sale of Shares. If shares are to be sold to the public, the following policy questions have to be answered:[66]

- Will shares be allocated between domestic and foreign applicants?
- Will shares for domestic applicants be allocated between institutions and individuals?
- Will shares be allocated between employees, pensioners, and others?
- Will a limit be imposed on the number of shares an individual can buy?
- Will prices differ for different classes of investors, such as small, domestic buyers?
- Will shares be reallocated among applicant types if the demand so warrants?
- Will an investor be obliged to hold onto his shares for a certain period?
- Will all shares be alike or will some differ in terms of dividends and voting rights?
- Will listing on foreign stock exchanges be sought for the shares?
- Will debt-equity swaps be allowed?
- How will over- or under-subscriptions be handled?

When the government sets a price on a GOE, it must satisfy various interests: institutional investors, retail investors, taxpayers, and the company's managers, workers, and customers. These interests often conflict. Raising money, broadening share ownership, promoting the development of capital markets, and placating current managers and workers are inherently inconsistent goals, as noted in chapter 5.

If an important objective of the divestment program is to encourage purchase by many small investors, the offering price may be set below the valuation to help assure an early rise in share value after the initial offering. This would be a policy decision to forgo the higher sales revenue in favor of broader national objectives. As additional encouragement for small investors, a "put" option could be made available to them, as in the privatization of Repsol, a Spanish oil and chemical enterprise. Retail investors were offered a 4 percent discount on their purchase of shares, with a possible rebate of 10 percent if the share price fell in the first year.[67] Discounts, guarantees, and promises of profits and dividends may be successful in getting small investors to buy shares, but what is the point, one may ask, of teaching potential investors that owning shares is all profit and no risk?[68]

Auction.   Ownership can be transferred without using a stock market by the process of open public bidding. After appraisal by independent valuators, a minimum bid price is announced and bidders are invited to submit bids. The process can be in two steps: first, interested bidders submit their technical and financial qualifications for review, and then the selected finalists submit sealed monetary bids.

Negotiation.   Another method of transfer is by negotiated sale of the GOE to qualified buyers. The process is similar to the auction method above, but instead of culminating in sealed bids, confidential negotiations are carried out with the selected finalist to establish the terms of sale and the purchase price. This method suffers from the serious disadvantage of not being transparent and therefore being prone to corruption, but it can lead to the best arrangement in countries where corruption is not a way of life because fine details can be pursued to satisfy complex local needs.

20. Monitor and Evaluate the Post-Privatization Phase

Monitoring is needed to assure that the terms of the sale agreement with respect to post-privatization actions are being followed. One should avoid the temptation to have monitoring or regulation controlled by someone loyal to the pre-privatized GOE. Two kinds of biases have been observed: the monitor/regulator (1) engages in vindictive behavior against the newly privatized entity, or (2) favors his alma mater, so to speak, by protecting it against other private competitors. I observed the latter in Sri Lanka where, after it was privatized, the telecommunications company was favored by the regulator and its private cellular competitors were discriminated against in gaining access to the telecommunication company's lines, despite their explicit legal right to such access.

Agreements with respect to worker benefits, for example, or the rate of expansion of telephone lines, water supplies, electric power, and transportation facilities must be monitored and enforced. The original agreement should cover how to deal with any unexcused failure to achieve specified benchmarks on time. Public antipathy is aroused and future divestments are threatened if the newly divested company raises its prices. If the reason for the price increase is that service has been improved or state subsidies eliminated, this should be carefully and repeatedly explained to the populace.

A word of warning: if the enterprise does poorly after divestment and threatens to close down, it should not be rescued as this could well be the first step toward inevitable renationalization. Bad business decisions should not be insulated from the disciplining force of the market.

Summary

Divestment of GOEs can be carried out by sale, free transfer, and liquidation. The principal features of each approach are summarized. The strategy for divesting a particular GOE depends on many factors; among the most important are the profitability of the enterprise and the degree of competition in its industry. A comprehensive, twenty-step divestment strategy is outlined and is summarized in table 8.2.

CHAPTER NINE

Public-Private Partnerships
for Infrastructure

How shall we build our infrastructure? In the past, roads, water systems, and other infrastructure have been financed, owned, and operated in most countries by government agencies with the notable exception of the telephone system and most electric utilities in the United States. The implicit justification for this practice was that infrastructure is so important, benefits so many people, and requires so much capital that the private sector could not be entrusted with this responsibility and in any event lacks the resources. This is curious reasoning. Facilities so vital to a nation's economy should be encouraged with incentives to attract investment in viable projects, priced according to supply and demand rather than politics, operated efficiently, and maintained in good condition. This is a prescription for private rather than government ownership.

The need for infrastructure—particularly in capital-starved former socialist countries and developing countries, but also in U.S. state and local governments—has outstripped the supply of conventional public funds. Increasingly, therefore, we see private groups financing, designing, building, operating, and even owning infrastructure via innovative public-private partnerships. Transportation facilities (roads, bridges, tunnels, rail systems, ports, and airports), water-supply systems and wastewater treatment plants, telecommunications systems, electricity generation and distribution systems, public buildings, and solid-waste and hazardous-waste disposal facilities are being built, expanded, rehabilitated, operated, and maintained around the world through privatized arrangements, relying more on the private sector and less on government to satisfy people's needs.

The distinguishing characteristic of such facilities is that, being toll goods (see Chapter 3), they lend themselves to user charges, because end users or government intermediaries can pay directly according to usage.

Therefore market forces can come into play: private capital can be raised, thereby reducing or obviating the need for government borrowing, and operating costs can be paid for by users, which is more equitable than tax-subsidized services and generally less expensive than government production of the services.

Advantages of Infrastructure Privatization

A large-scale survey of city and county officials in the United States sheds light on the empirical reasons for privatizing infrastructure. Asked why they were privatizing, the officials responded as shown in table 9.1, which summarizes the responses for different kinds of facilities. Lack of expertise and savings in capital costs are the most frequently cited reasons for privatizing infrastructure facilities, while savings in operating costs ranks third.[1] Similar results were obtained in a survey of state officials.[2] Other reasons cited in the two studies are speedier implementation, providing services otherwise unavailable, solving political and labor problems, and sharing risks.

The situation with respect to many existing facilities is depicted in figure 9.1, which illustrates a dismaying but common cycle of events in railroads, telephone systems, and electric power systems. In the entrepreneurial stage,

TABLE 9.1.—REASONS FOR PRIVATIZING LOCAL INFRASTRUCTURE

Type of facility	Capital savings	Lack of expertise	Need for facilities	Operating savings	Means of financing	Better service
Airports	4	1	2			3
Correctional facilities	1	2	2	2		
Hazardous waste	2	2	1	2		2
Hospitals	1	2	2		2	2
Housing	3	2	1		2	
Mass transit	1	3		2		4
Municipal buildings	3	1	4		2	
Pollution control	1		2			
Roads and bridges	1	2	3			4
Solid-waste facilities	3		1	2	4	
Stadiums, etc.	3	2		1	4	
Street lights	1	1	3	1		2
Telecommunications	3	1	4	2		3
Wastewater systems	1	3	2	4		
Water systems	1	3	2	4	4	

Note: A "1" denotes the most frequently cited reason for privatizing that type of facility.

Source: Adapted from T. Irwin David, *Privatization in America* (Washington, D.C.: Touche Ross, 1987), fig. 11.

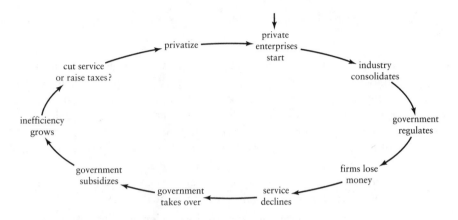

FIGURE 9.1—THE NATIONALIZATION-PRIVATIZATION CYCLE

Source: Jose Gomez-Ibanez and John R. Meyer, *Going Private: The International Experience with Transport Privatization* (Washington, D.C.: Brookings Institution, 1993.) This chart was originally drawn to illustrate the cycle in urban bus services.

many small firms start up and provide service. As the new industry grows, mergers and consolidation take place, followed inexorably by government regulation of fees and franchises in response to complaints about fares and in an effort to control perceived "chaotic" competition. Thereafter, costs gradually rise because of inflation and the need for increased maintenance as the facilities age, but, in the name of "protecting the public," politicians refuse to authorize rate increases or service adjustments. As a result, revenues are insufficient and firms start losing money. This in turn leads to reduced expenditures on maintenance and repair, no further investment in new equipment, increasingly erratic and interrupted service, calls for government action, government takeover, public subsidies for what is now a government-run system, and declining efficiency under public operation. At length the point is reached beyond which subsidies cannot be sustained, and therefore either service must be cut back or user charges or taxes must be raised. (Bus service in New York City has followed this pattern faithfully.) Ultimately, the wheel comes full circle as privatization is called upon to cure the problem.[3]

Public-private partnerships for infrastructure satisfy the needs (1) to upgrade systems to accommodate population growth, to satisfy tightened regulatory requirements (e.g., for cleaner water), or to attract investment and development; (2) to minimize the cost of new infrastructure and consequent "rate shock" among citizens; and (3) to raise capital for other desired projects by receiving an up-front payment for the infrastructure concession.

The private sector helps governments address infrastructure needs in several ways:[4]

1. It helps identify and develop new, innovatively designed, user-financed, profit-making facilities or existing facilities in need of rehabilitation, renovation, or expansion. Private, profit-oriented businesses have a direct financial incentive to seek and carry out new projects that will satisfy public needs at prices the public can pay, projects that would otherwise have to wait until government funds became available. Government-sponsored projects, in contrast, are often uneconomical, grandiose monuments that satisfy personal egos or political needs.

2. By involving private sponsors and experienced commercial lenders, it assures in-depth review of the technical and financial feasibility of the project.

3. It accesses private capital markets to supplement or substitute for hard-to-get government resources. New capital comes from a large and previously untapped pool of investors interested in higher-risk, higher-return investments than traditional municipal bonds; this can leverage limited public funds and may improve the government's credit rating.

4. It builds more quickly and more cost effectively than government usually can, and therefore satisfies public needs more quickly at lower cost. Construction is generally more rapid because private developers are more flexible and do not have to observe government procurement rules and bureaucratic constraints that delay planning and construction schedules.

5. It operates facilities more efficiently than government usually can, while complying with regulatory standards, such as those for water quality.

6. Taxpaying private firms provide a new source of tax revenue. Privately developed projects are estimated to pay over two dollars in new tax and franchise revenue for every dollar in project cost; if the new infrastructure generates ancillary real-estate development or opportunities for concessions, for instance, even greater revenues will be realized.[5]

7. It accepts risks that would otherwise have to be borne by the public sector.

8. It transfers technology and trains government personnel during the course of a project.

9. It establishes a private benchmark against which to measure the efficiency of similar projects and enhances public management of future projects.[6]

Government's vital role is to identify and plan to satisfy the fundamental need for particular infrastructure projects; investigate project feasibility; execute the myriad tasks involved in contract letting (see later discussion); assign monopoly rights (by the act of choosing the private partner); regulate prices in the public interest (inasmuch as the facility is usually a classical toll good, subject to monopoly); establish and monitor performance standards; and (usually) contribute to the financing.

The Spectrum of Public-Private Partnerships

Public-private partnerships for infrastructure take many forms. Table 9.2 shows the spectrum of principal models, ranging from fully public to fully private.[7] In the terminology of chapters 4 and 5, the public-private forms are contracts, franchises, and divestments. The rankings of the models in the right half of the table, that is, their relative degree of "privateness," should not be interpreted too rigidly, as the differences are subtle and depend on individual cases.

Government Department

The traditional method of providing infrastructure-based services is directly through government departments. The government, which owns the facility, is responsible for designing, financing, building, and operating it. A common example is a municipal water department.

TABLE 9.2—THE SPECTRUM OF PUBLIC-PRIVATE PARTNERSHIPS

Government Department	Public Authority	Service Contract	Operations and Maintenance (O&M) Contract	Cooperative	Lease-Build-Operate (LBO)	Build-Transfer Operate (BTO)	Build-(Own)-Operate-Transfer (BOT or BOOT)	Wrap around Addition	Buy-Build Operate (BBO)	Build-Own Operate (BOO)

Fully Public ◄――――――――――――――――――――――――――►Fully Private

Public Authority

In both developed and developing countries public authorities are common for power, water, transportation, and telecommunications services. These are being reformed by commercialization (managerial and financial autonomy and separate budgets based on user charges) and corporatization (legal company status with separation of ownership and management). The intentions of such changes are to achieve efficiency and accountability and to have the entity act like a business rather than a political body. An evaluation of public authorities in the water business concluded that the most successful ones had (1) good managers and stability in mid-management and professional positions; (2) financial strength, with reasonable tariffs that covered costs; (3) good customer relations; (4) in some cases, private contractors for operations and maintenance, private capital, good cost-accounting systems, and clearly defined roles for government, the board of directors, and management.[8] Regional transportation authorities exemplify this form.

Service Contract

Specific services associated with infrastructure may be contracted out to private firms, as is discussed in chapter 7. Examples here are ticketing, cleaning, and food catering for railroads; meter reading, billing and collection for water; and cleaning and snow removal from public highways. The public agency retains overall responsibility for operation and maintenance of the system except for the particular contracted services, and it bears all of the commercial risk. It must finance fixed assets and provide working capital. Compensation to the contractor may be on the basis of time, lump-sum, fixed fee, or cost-plus, or on the basis of a physical parameter (number of water bills sent out). Service contracts are generally for periods of less than five years.

Operations and Maintenance Contract or Lease

A private partner operates and maintains a publicly owned facility under a management contract with the sponsoring government, which owns the facility. This arrangement is similar to a service contract, but in this case the private partner has overall responsibility for operating and maintaining the system (commonly called an O&M contract) and makes the day-to-day decisions; it does not assume any of the capital risks. The objective is greater efficiency and effectiveness of service. This arrangement is used to supply water to Jersey City and to treat wastewater in Milwaukee.[9] The facility could be leased to the private firm, which pays a lease fee and collects user charges; the French term *affermage* is commonly used for this arrangement. An example of the process used to award an O&M contract for wastewater treatment appears in chapter 7.

Cooperative

A nonprofit, voluntary, cooperative association assumes responsibility for the service. Rural cooperatives in countries as diverse as the United States, Canada, and Finland successfully expanded local telephone systems. Kenya, India, and China are among the many developing countries where irrigation management transfer is taking place, whereby water-user associations take over and operate local irrigation works. Using their own labor and monetary contributions, these associations often succeed in maintaining the network of canals and ditches, and even dams, used in local distribution systems where centralized operation by the government water authority was failing.[10] Examples are also found in other services.[11]

Lease-Build-Operate (LBO)

A private firm is given a long-term lease to develop (with its own funds) and operate an expanded facility. It recovers its investment plus a reasonable return over the term of the lease and pays a rental fee. Because the facility remains publicly owned, this arrangement avoids possible legal problems associated with private ownership of a facility that was publicly financed originally. The largest public-private airport partnership in the United States is that for Stewart Airport, a huge but underdeveloped facility located eighty-five miles north of New York City; it is being leased by the state for ninety-nine years to a British company.

Build-Transfer-Operate (BTO)

A private developer finances and builds a facility and, upon completion, transfers legal ownership to the sponsoring government agency. The agency then leases the facility back to the developer under a long-term lease, during which the developer operates the facility and has the opportunity to recover his investment and earn a reasonable return from user charges and commercial activities.

Build-Operate-Transfer (BOT)

A private developer is awarded a franchise (concession) to finance, build, own, and operate a facility (hence this is sometimes referred to as BOOT— build, own, operate, and transfer), and to collect user fees for a specified period, after which ownership of the facility is transferred to the public sector. This arrangement is similar to BTO but may encounter legal, regulatory, and liability issues arising during the long period of private ownership before the transfer. Nevertheless, this is perhaps the most common form of public-private partnership for building new infrastructure. In contrast to a sale or permanent concession, government retains strategic control over the project—which is often a political plus.

Wraparound Addition

A private developer finances and constructs an addition to an existing public facility, and then operates the combined facility either for a fixed period or until he recovers costs plus a reasonable return on his invested capital. He may own the addition. The objective of this arrangement is to expand the facility despite the government's lack of resources or expertise to do so entirely with its own funds.

Buy-Build-Operate (BBO)

An existing public facility is sold to a private partner who renovates or expands it and operates it in perpetuity under a franchise. This is equivalent to divesting a company, which then operates under a franchise. As in other franchise models, during the negotiations prior to the sale, the public owner can use the franchise agreement to exercise public control over pricing, access, noise, safety, quality, and future capacity expansion, for example. The first sale in recent history of a wastewater treatment plant in the United States was carried out in Franklin, Ohio, using this arrangement. In Japan and Germany government-owned telephone systems were sold in order to make them more modern, efficient, and internationally competitive through the infusion of private investment; in Argentina and Peru they were sold in order to expand and improve service. (It is hard to believe, but before privatization one had to wait an average of seventeen *years* to have a phone installed in Argentina!)

Build-Own-Operate (BOO)

A private developer finances, builds, owns, and operates a facility in perpetuity under a franchise, subject to regulatory constraints on pricing and operations. The long-term property rights provide a significant financial incentive for capital investment in the facility. Examples of this model are private toll roads in Virginia and California, the toll road in China connecting Hong Kong and Macao with Guangzhou, the new terminal at New York's JFK Airport, and the "chunnel" under the English Channel. Numerous power projects in the Philippines and Indonesia, as well as ports in the region, are also public-private partnerships. The U.S. Department of Energy departed from its conventional approach of government-owned, contractor-operated facilities (M&O contracts) and changed to a contractor-owned, contractor-operated facility (BOO) to address one of its thorniest problems: remediating 54 million gallons of highly radioactive waste at its plutonium plant in Hanford, Washington. By making this change, and also switching from cost-plus contracts to fixed-price (per unit of treated waste) contracts, the department expects to save money and get faster results.

Many of these models are extremely complicated and time consuming to arrange, and they may call for explicit or implicit guarantees from government, of volumes (of traffic, for toll-road projects or of water usage, for water or wastewater projects, for instance), revenues, input prices, and so on, so that the government is left with significant contingent liabilities after all.[12]

Moreover, the differences between some of these models can be subtle. Concessions always involve operations and maintenance by the concessionaire, and they must last long enough to recoup investments; therefore, if major investments by the private sector are needed (LBO, BTO, BOT, BBO, BOO), the concessions will require longer duration, perhaps more than thirty years. In contrast, if the public sector is responsible for investment, as in a lease-and-operate arrangement (*affermage*), the period can be as little as five to fifteen years.

These models and their variants can be used to develop new infrastructure, to rehabilitate or expand existing infrastructure, or to improve the performance of existing infrastructure. Table 9.3 shows their applicability in each of these circumstances.

Development of a new, expanded, or rehabilitated facility through a public-private partnership is preferred when there is a clear, unmet need for the project, sufficient public funds are not available, and there are benefits to be gained from new revenue sources, faster construction, innovative design, and efficient operation. Sale or lease of an existing facility is indicated when the government wants to recapture its original investment and realize any increase in value, or if it recognizes that significant new investment will

TABLE 9.3—MODELS OF INFRASTRUCTURE PRIVATIZATION

Type of facility	Model	Description
Existing facility	Sale	Private firm buys facility, operates it under a franchise, and collects user fees
	Lease	Government leases facility to a private firm, which operates it under a franchise and collects user fees
	Operations and Maintenance (O&M) Contract	Private firm maintains and operates a government-owned facility; government pays private firm a fee
Existing facility that requires capital investment for expansion or rehabilitation	Lease-Build-Operate (LBO) Buy-Build-Operate (BBO)	Private firm leases or buys facility from government, operates it under a concession, and expands or rehabilitates it, collecting user fees and paying a franchise fee
	Wraparound addition	Private firm expands a government-owned facility, owns only the expansion, but operates the whole facility, collecting fees
New facility to be built	Build-Transfer-Operate (BTO)	Private firm finances and builds new facility, transfers it to public ownership, then operates it for 20 to 40 years, collecting user fees
	Build-Own-Operate-Transfer (BOOT), also called Build-Operate-Transfer (BOT)	Same as BTO, but facility is transferred to public ownership after 20 to 40 years
	Build-Own-Operate (BOO)	Private firm finances, builds, owns, and operates facility and collects fees, under perpetual franchise

Source: Adapted from Steve Steckler and Lavinia Payson, "Infrastructure," in *Privatization for New York: Competing for a Better Future,* E. S. Savas, ed., Report of the New York State Senate Advisory Commission on Privatization, 1992, p. 194.

be needed. Contract maintenance and operation is recommended if current operating costs are too high or if service quality is too low.

The build-own-operate-transfer model (BOOT or BOT) illustrates public-private partnerships for infrastructure. Having identified the need for a particular facility, a government announces its intention to award a long-term franchise or concession to a private firm. It conducts a worldwide competition in an open, transparent process, selects a winner, and negotiates an agreement. If the project is sound, by definition the concessionaire will be able to borrow money and raise equity, and the resulting revenues from tolls after the facility is completed and goes into routine operation will be sufficient to pay off the debt, cover the operating costs, and yield a profit. When the concession expires in twenty to forty years, the facility is turned over to the government free of debt, and the government can operate it itself or competitively select a contractor to operate it.

Infrastructure facilities require continuous investments that obviously cannot be predicted accurately years in advance, and some investments will have to be made near the end of the concession period when they cannot reasonably be amortized. Moreover, the true worth of the concessionaire's business includes not only this unamortized value but also intangible assets, know-how, reputation, and subsidiary systems such as billing procedures; therefore the concessionaire may be tempted to practice "strategic maintenance," that is, nonmaintenance or minimal maintenance near the end of the concession period. Incentives should be designed both to avoid strategic maintenance and, in fairness, to pay the concessionaire for assets that have not been fully amortized. For instance, independent experts can place a value on the unamortized investment, which is then paid by the government to the private firm. Another approach is to have the concession rebid periodically. For example, in Argentina the power distribution concession is let for ninety-five years, but it is rebid after the first fifteen years and every ten years thereafter. If the incumbent bids the highest price, he retains the concession; if he doesn't, the high bidder pays his bid price to the incumbent directly, not the government, so that the assets are valued by the market, not by the state or its regulator.[13]

In monopolistic sectors even BOO projects and full divestment do not guarantee a permanent arrangement for the private partner, although the latter does have indefinite ownership of the assets. The private firm requires a license or franchise, which the government can withdraw, not renew, or revoke for noncompliance, because the government generally reserves the right to terminate the arrangement before the end of its term. Hence, the difference between a traditional fixed-term concession and a permanent one (BOO and BBO—which includes divestment) is not as great as initially appears.[14]

Between 1984 and 1994, an estimated 1,121 infrastructure privatizations took place throughout the world, with investments totaling approximately $665 billion, an average of $60 billion a year; roughly half the public-private partnerships were for new construction and half for existing facilities.[15]

Strategic Issues

Utilizing public-private partnerships requires dealing with several strategic issues: the roles of the different parties, competition, regulation, risks, procurement, and financing.

Roles and Functions

The responsibility for important roles and functions has to be allocated: owning the assets, providing capital financing, providing working capital, making additional capital investments, operating and maintaining the facility, exercising day-to-day managerial authority, and bearing commercial risk. Other vital factors to be identified and resolved are the basis of compensation to the private partner and the duration of the arrangement. The different major service arrangements call for different roles of the participants in these functions; they are summarized in table 9.4. The concession arrangement in the last column of the table encompasses LBO, BTO, BOT, BBO, and BOO, except that the last two, BBO and BOO, are of unlimited duration, that is, in perpetuity.

The private member of the public-private partnership is likely to be a consortium of firms and a constellation of advisers, including design engineers, construction companies, bankers, investment bankers, lawyers, operations specialists, equipment manufacturers, technology suppliers, real-estate developers, financial consultants, marketers, and public relations specialists.

Competition

The benefits of competition are well known: lower costs, lower prices, greater innovation, increased investment, and better service. Nevertheless, it is often argued that infrastructure-based services of the type discussed in this chapter are natural monopolies and only exclusive franchises will be successful, for stability and higher profits are a prerequisite for investment. ("No one will invest unless you grant them a monopoly.") This is not necessarily the case, although in developing countries it may be a sensible practice for a very limited period in difficult circumstances.[16] Restructuring the industry is a way to create competition, as explained in chapter 8.

So-called natural monopolies, that is, infrastructure that has high sunk costs (such as water-supply systems), can nevertheless be subjected to competition for the right to operate the monopoly—competition *for* the market

TABLE 9.4—ASSIGNMENT OF INFRASTRUCTURE DEVELOPMENT FUNCTIONS BY SERVICE ARRANGEMENT

Functions	Service arrangement					
	Government agency	Public authority	Service contracting	Management contracting	Leasing	Concession
Ownership of assets	State	State	State or mixed		State or mixed	
Capital financing (fixed assets)	Government	Public authority (limited subsidy)	Public agency	Public partner	Public partner	Private firm
Current financing (working capital)	Government	Market based	Public agency	Public partner	Private firm	Private firm
Making additional capital investments	Government	Public authority	Private firm for specific items	Public partner	Public partner	Private firm
Operation and maintenance	Government	Public authority	Private firm for specific items	Private firm	Private firm	Private firm
Managerial authority	Government	Public Authority	Public partner	Private firm	Private firm	Private firm
Bearer of commercial risk	Government	Public Authority	Public partner	Mainly public partner	Private firm	Private firm
Basis of private party compensation	Not applicable	Not applicable	For services rendered	For services and results	Based on results, net of contractor payment for use of existing assets	
Typical duration of arrangement	No limit	No limit	Less than 5 years	3 to 5 years	5 to 10 years	10 to 30 years

Source: Adapted from Christine Kessides, "Institutional Options for the Provision of Infrastructure," *World Bank Discussion Paper* 212, Washington, D.C. 1993, 19.

rather than competition *in* the market. If monopolies are natural, however, surely they do not need government protection. Sometimes governments create monopolies unnecessarily and deny entrepreneurs the opportunity to compete fairly with established service providers by erecting entry barriers, blocking credit and access to foreign exchange, taxing dividends and profits inequitably, imposing unfair import duties, and establishing bureaucratic hurdles.[17] Such barriers should be eliminated if the best results are to be achieved.

Regulation

In any event, privatized infrastructure concessions require effective government regulation, which should be based on a stable and trusted system of enforceable laws concerning property rights, contracts, disputes, and liability. Regulations should be designed and administered to protect both the public users of the service and the private partner. Key elements of a regulatory framework include rates, performance, reliability, degree of competition, and access to interconnection with other systems in the case of such services as telecommunications, electric power, water supply, and airline operation. The process of regulation should be as straightforward and predictable as possible, with automatic price adjustments based on predetermined formulas and minimal reporting requirements; price regulation should allow producers to benefit from efficiency improvements. Interested parties, including users of the service, should be encouraged to present their views at hearings and should have access to the decisions, and regulatory rulings should be enforceable, with the right of appeal. Self-regulation can play a significant role, inasmuch as qualified infrastructure operators want to protect their reputations (hence the importance of screening potential bidders at the outset).

These conditions are generally to be found in the United States and in other developed countries, but they are just emerging in many developing nations and in the post-socialist countries. Nevertheless, it is useful to note the principal elements of regulation because infrastructure privatization in the United States is occurring mostly at the local government level, where there is often little experience in such regulation.

The following basic and general design questions for regulation are raised and discussed by Bernard Tenenbaum:[18]

- Should there be a single regulator or a commission?
- Should the regulatory body have jurisdiction over only one sector (e.g., rail, power, telecommunications) or several?

- What activities or parameters should be regulated?
- What are the control mechanisms for price and quality? (Inspection of accounting and operating records, customer surveys, observation?)
- How are regulatory rules created and enforced?
- What are the desired political and legal attributes in terms of independence and transparency? Is the regulatory body autonomous with respect to tariff changes or do the latter require approval by the executive or legislature?
- Who regulates the regulator? Can decisions be appealed to the courts?
- How should responsibility be divided between the regulatory body and other government authorities?

These issues are particularly important in the case of divestment, when a formal regulatory agency may be required. In the case of contracts, leases, and concessions, however, the contract document itself might serve as the regulatory device, setting performance standards, tariffs, and the process and frequency of adjusting tariffs. Monitoring the private partner is essential, of course, as discussed in the preceding chapters, but contractual oversight is not free.

Price regulation of infrastructure services such as telecommunications, transportation, and power was traditionally based on the rate of return earned by the private firm. The shortcomings of this approach are that it encourages excessive and unnecessary capital investment and, like cost-plus procurement, has no incentive to cut costs or improve efficiency. This practice is being replaced by price-cap regulation, which uses a predetermined formula to set prices for several years in advance. During this period, the firm may keep the benefits of its productivity gains. Customers, too, benefit because prices may rise less rapidly and the firm may be encouraged to offer innovative new services. One drawback of price caps is the danger of erosion of service quality, and therefore vigilant oversight is necessary. Moreover, during the relatively long term of the cap period, fundamental changes may occur that render the contract inappropriate.[19] Finally, there is evidence that price caps subject firms to greater risk and therefore raise their cost of capital; this means that they must be permitted to earn higher returns.[20]

The greatest deterrent to private participation in a public-private partnership for infrastructure is the regulatory environment and attitude. Private investors will be repelled and will seek a more hospitable place to invest if regulation is unlimited in scope, unclear in operation, and inclined toward micromanagement. The regulatory regime must be limited, transparent, fair, and consistent, and government must keep its promises. Investors are wary not only of expropriation but also of many small regulatory actions that together constitute incremental expropriation, depriving the private partner of legitimate recovery of costs and of profit commensurate with the risks undertaken. In a particularly egregious case, a French firm operating a provincial water system in Argentina was losing $2.8 million a month due to nonpayment by 80 percent of its customers, while the government refused to enforce payment and even encouraged nonpayment; yet, the firm had to stay on for eighteen months, prohibited by the governor from canceling its contract.[21]

Regardless of the process or principle, the danger of regulatory capture is ever present. In the past, the principal concern was that the regulator might be captured by the "regulatee"; more recently, the growing problem is that the regulator is captured by an advocacy group with a special interest. In either case, instead of being an impartial referee working to maximize total output, the government regulator reflects the interests of powerful electoral groups in order to maximize votes.[22]

Risks, Rewards, and Responsibilities

Infrastructure privatization presents significant risks that are shared between the public and private partners. Along with the risks come rewards and responsibilities that are allocated correspondingly. Total project costs are minimized if each risk is assigned to the partner who can best handle it. Many of the risks can be identified and allocated in the basic contract document that establishes the public-private partnership. The risks can be categorized in three main groups: business, financial, and political.[23]

Business risk.   *Cost-overrun risk* is the risk that construction delays, design changes, belated discovery of site problems, failure to obtain (or issue) permits, and so on, will result in costs greater than expected. Fixed-price construction contracts like those often used in all-private projects protect investors from contractor-caused cost overruns but not those caused by the government itself; the latter should bear the risk of delays due to site problems, government-desired design changes, and so on. *Operating risk* is the risk that the operating costs of the enterprise will be greater than expected or that quality or capacity will fall short of desired or mandated levels. This risk should generally be borne by the private sector, although the public sector can mitigate the danger of strikes and sabotage by reducing redundant labor prior to privatization, for example, or by agreeing to provide severance pay for workers who are not needed by the private operator. *Revenue risk* is the risk that demand will be insufficient or the rates will be too low to generate the expected revenue. The government can reduce this risk by guaranteeing a minimum level of demand at agreed-upon rates ("take or pay"). For private development of new facilities, the government may agree not to build or not to allow competing infrastructure for the term of the concession. Sometimes private operators are unable to enforce payment of bills by customers who are public agencies. (A newly privatized power company in Russia cut off electricity to a military base that had not paid its bill. The base commander dispatched his tanks, with cannons leveled, to the power plant, which promptly restored service.)

Financial risk. *Debt-service coverage risk* is the risk that operating cash flows will not be enough to cover the required principal and interest payments for the debt used to finance the project. The private investors may bear this risk alone, or the government may guarantee a portion of the debt. *Exchange rate risk* is the risk that local currency earnings will not be convertible to a foreign currency at an expected rate of exchange, either because the value of the currency has declined or because the government requires exchange at an artificially low official rate. This reduces the value of the earnings. The private partner may bear this risk alone, or the government agency may guarantee exchange at a fixed rate.

Purely public provision of infrastructure appears to lower the financial risk compared to private provision because of government's lower cost of capital. This is an illusion, however, as the risk is simply shifted to a third party, namely, taxpayers.[24]

Political risk. *Rate regulation risk* is the risk that the government regulator will not allow sufficient or timely rate increases to provide a reasonable return on investment, or will even mandate a reduction in rates. This risk can be mitigated by establishing a specific regulatory mechanism to allow increases in accordance with an agreed-upon formula without further government approval. *Expropriation risk* is the risk that the government will renationalize the facility or impose taxes or regulations that severely diminish the value of the enterprise. The government usually agrees not to expropriate the enterprise without paying fair compensation to the private party; an arbitration mechanism is often specified for determining the compensation if it is not established beforehand by formula. *Repatriation risk* is the risk that investors will not be able to transfer their earnings out of the country. The host government usually agrees to allow such repatriation. Investors can also obtain insurance against this risk through third-party government agencies such as the U.S. Overseas Private Investment Corporation (OPIC) and international agencies such as the Multilateral Investment Guarantee Agency (MIGA). *Dispute resolution risk* is the risk that contract disputes between the private developer and sponsoring government will not be settled fairly in a neutral jurisdiction. Private partners may require that contracts be enforceable in a third country and can insure themselves against breach of contract through investment insurers such as OPIC or MIGA.

Other risks. *Technology risk* is the risk that new technology being utilized will encounter unexpected problems that will slow or even halt a project. Early resource-recovery plants that were to recover materials and generate energy from solid waste are examples of projects that stumbled badly. *Environmental risk* is the risk that the enterprise, while still in government hands, caused environmental damage that the new private owners or operators will be required to correct. The government will usually agree to rectify all such damage. *Force majeure risk* is the risk that events beyond the control of the public or private partner, such as flood or war, will impair the ability of the enterprise to earn money. This risk could be covered by private or government insurance.

Procurement

Three common bidding procedures are used to select the private partner: advertised procurement, competitive negotiation, and a three-step process.

Advertised procurement. The public sponsor issues and advertises an invitation to bid (ITB), evaluates the bids, eliminates the bids that fail to satisfy the stated requirements, and awards the contract to the qualified bidder who submitted the lowest bid price. While this method is perfectly transparent, it may not be satisfactory in a complex procurement when including all possible details and anticipating all factors in the bid invitation is impossible and extensive discussion and revised thinking may be necessary before reaching a complete understanding between the public sponsor and the private partner. Also, a superior bid whose price is only slightly higher would have to be rejected.

Competitive negotiation. The sponsor issues a request for proposals (RFP), receives and evaluates the proposals, negotiates with the bidders, and awards the contract to the one who has the best proposal, although not necessarily the lowest price. The principal shortcoming of this approach is that it lacks transparency, and therefore it may appear that the procurement was subject to undue influence and possibly even corruption.

Three-step procurement. The public sponsor first issues a request for qualifications (RFQ) and scrutinizes the financial condition of the private firm to assure the latter's ability to complete the project. The second step is a request, to those found qualified, for technical and economic proposals— in separate envelopes. The technical proposals that score below a cutoff are eliminated and the envelopes with the economic proposals are opened; the contract is awarded to the bidder with the best proposal, balancing both price and technical merit. (See chapter 7 for more details on competitive procurement.) Alternatively, all proposals that score above the technical minimum might be treated equally, with the lowest bidder winning the project.

Key strategic issues in the procurement terms include the following:[25]

- rate-setting and adjustment mechanism: how to protect ratepayers from "excessive tariffs" while protecting the bidder from detrimental denial of reasonable rate changes
- funding of future capital upgrading and expansions: timing, levels, sources, and recovery rights
- restriction of ownership transfer: reconciling the government's desire to "lock in" its selected strategic partner vs. the private party's desire to preserve flexibility in long-range capital investments
- tax concessions: stipulated tax rates and exemptions, electricity tariffs (for state-owned power supply used in the project), credits or waivers for certain outstanding liabilities
- labor understandings: balancing the drive for greater economic efficiency against the government's political desire to avoid drastic workforce and wage reductions
- investment protection: neutral forums for dispute resolution, opportunity for the government to repurchase or the private partner to sell if certain events occur

Financing

The demand for infrastructure is huge. New York City's infrastructure needs have been estimated at $9 billion per year for a ten-year period.[26] I estimate that developing countries alone need more than a trillion dollars for water, power, transportation, and telecommunications projects. Infrastructure can be financed publicly, privately, or through mixed public-private means. The advantage of public financing is that it allows access to tax-exempt debt and government grants, reducing project costs (although ultimately at taxpayers' expense). Debt service is then paid from project revenues. Public financing is most appropriate for projects that offer little commercial potential. International lenders can finance projects in developing countries.

For private financing, the private partner secures project financing and then pays the costs from project revenues. Private financing provides access to a wide range of flexible financial instruments. It is most appropriate for speculative projects that have significant profit potential.

The third alternative, mixed public and private financing, provides the widest range of options, although legal, legislative, and political restrictions may be encountered.

Public-private partnerships for infrastructure rely on the independent financial feasibility of the undertaking. Adequate capital for construction and sufficient revenues to cover operating costs are needed for a viable project, and profit potential is necessary to attract private investors.

Capital costs. The feasibility of a project depends to a great extent on obtaining capital funding on satisfactory terms. Government financing may include tax-exempt bonds, taxable bonds, revenue bonds, and grants. Private financing may include debt and equity securities, loans, and financing (loans or equity) by contractors and vendors on the project. Government can reduce the costs of the project by allowing free or discounted use of public land or right-of-way for the project; providing law enforcement services; delaying bills for services provided by the government until after construction financing is arranged; establishing a trust fund with the sales tax receivables on supplies, equipment, land, labor, and so forth used in the project, such trust fund to be used as secondary credit support for the project; exempting or deferring local property taxes until project debt is retired; setting limits on tort liability at least to the level borne by similar government-owned infrastructure; and offering active government assistance in planning, permitting, and land acquisition, as well as help in overcoming intergovernmental and interagency disputes.

Revenue sources.   There are several sources of incoming revenue after the project is in operation: (1) user charges, in the form of fares and tolls for transportation infrastructure, fees for water, wastewater, and solid-waste services, and prices for telephone service and electricity, for example; (2) government subsidies; (3) special dedicated taxes, such as fuel taxes earmarked for road maintenance; (4) value capture, which includes tax-increment financing, where the increase in property-tax collections due to the increase in property values caused by the project is devoted to the project; (5) other forms of publicly implemented value capture, such as impact fees and special-benefit assessments, which, like tax-increments, are also real-estate related revenues intended to capture the increase in property values due solely to the project; (6) the sale of air rights, right-of-way (e.g., for telecommunication lines or pipelines along a toll highway), and other project development rights created by or associated with the project; (7) collateral revenue from advertising, services, and more intensive development of the facility (e.g., innovatively thinking of an airport as a shopping mall that happens to have parking spaces for airplanes as well as automobiles!).[27]

The financial arrangements for a public-private partnership to expand a wastewater treatment system under a wraparound arrangement (defined in table 9.3) are illustrated in figure 9.2. The city issues bonds for the project and the private partner borrows from banks and offers equity.

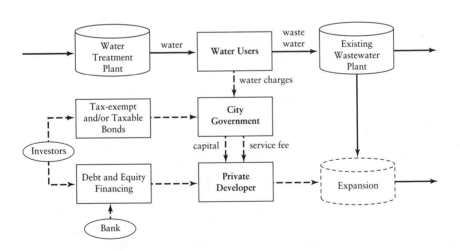

FIGURE 9.2—PROJECT STRUCTURE

Source: Adapted from Larry J. Scully, "Structuring and Financing Successful Privatization Projects," presented at Third Annual Water Industry Summit, 1 May 1996, Washington, D.C.

Investors buy municipal bonds and equity in the project. Water users pay a fee for the service, and taxes may also be applied by the municipality. The developer services the debts and loans from operating revenues.

Summary

Public-private partnerships offer a solution for governments that are seeking funds to develop the infrastructure needed to satisfy people's needs and promote economic development. Billions of dollars of infrastructure are needed in developed and in developing countries. The benefits are substantial, but the roles of the two sectors must be carefully defined and maintained. There are many different models for the arrangements; all are complex and require expertise on both sides to succeed. Most involve concessions of natural monopolies, and therefore regulation is necessary. Competition is a crucial element but it takes skill to apply it in these settings. Substantial risks exist and must be allocated appropriately, commensurate with the rewards. Legal and financial intricacies dominate the decisions, but knowledge and experience have been gained throughout the world, and the satisfactory results justify the effort.

CHAPTER TEN

Reforming Education and Privatizing the Welfare State

Major policy debates are raging in the United States at the dawn of the twenty-first century about three fundamental areas of societal concern: educating the young, assisting the needy, and supporting the elderly. These debates, conducted under the banners of education reform, welfare reform, and Social Security reform, center on the respective roles of government and the private institutions of society in addressing needs in these areas.

Competition and Choice in Education

Primary and secondary education is the largest function of state and local government in terms of budget and the number of employees. U.S. schools are near the top in spending but near the bottom in pupil achievement among industrial nations, according to a study by the Organization for Economic Cooperation and Development.[1] In the past twenty-five years, per-pupil spending has increased, student achievement has declined, and, incidentally, the size of teachers' unions has quadrupled.[2] The monopolistic nature of public schools is arguably to blame for this situation. Nowhere is the problem of monopoly more serious and competition more needed, reformers say, than in big-city schools, where most students are below the national average in reading and mathematics, and the dropout rate is high. Teachers attribute the problem to conditions in the home. Parents blame uncaring or incompetent teachers. The education establishment wants more money to spend. The situation is ripe for a drastic change in policy—privatization.

There is not yet a consensus on a prescription for teaching inner-city children. There are advocates for higher teacher salaries, merit pay, designation of master teachers, less emphasis on pedagogical credentials and more on subject-matter expertise, larger school budgets, magnet schools, greater business involvement in the curriculum, back-to-basics curriculum reform, more discipline in the classroom, and, increasingly, greater parental choice of schools for their children.

Question: What should you do when you don't know what to do? *Answer*: Do many different things. Nature's incessant experimentation through mutations forces competition for survival that enables species to adapt to environmental change. Similarly, various educational approaches should be tried to see which prove capable of educating inner-city children today. But the existing government education monopoly resists competition from real alternatives. The monolithic public school system is inadequate, yet, its critics charge, it won't facilitate broad experimentation or tolerate alternative pedagogical approaches. Diversity has never been the strong suit of government.

A comparison of ancient Athens and Sparta with respect to education monopolies is instructive. In Sparta there was no scope for parental choice. The state went so far as to remove children from their homes and place them in schools designed to shape them in the Spartan mold. By contrast, in democratic Athens education was the responsibility of the parents and subject to parental choice and control. Schools were private, often owned by the teachers. The state's role was to specify minimal standards and provide military training. Rather than destroy the family, as in Sparta, Athens preserved it as a means of developing and reshaping personality and made it responsible for education. Athenians understood that this was vital in promoting a healthy sense of involvement in the community.[3] In America, advocates of educational reform would say, the Athenian ideal is much to be preferred over the Spartan.

Gabriel Roth provides a fascinating look at public and private education in developing countries.[4] At the dawn of civilization on the Indian subcontinent, the Aryans required at least eight years of broad schooling for every child; this was a matter of religious practice, not state legislation. It was the British who injected government fully into education in India, and they did so for political reasons, namely, to control the curriculum. Public schools are vulnerable to government whim, as can be seen in the exploitation of public schools that occurred in Uganda during the dictatorship of Idi Amin: schools had to purchase all their supplies from a central office and had to pay in advance, even though often the supplies were not delivered. In Malta, in 1973, the government imposed politically mandated changes in the public schools, causing a large-scale withdrawal of children from those schools and transfers to private schools. The government relentlessly sought to recapture the children by freezing the fees the private schools could charge in 1982 and by abolishing fees in 1984. By thus starving the private schools, the government hoped to force all Maltese children into its school monopoly.

The United States has also seen heavy-handed attempts to monopolize education. A 1922 Oregon law, subsequently overturned by the U.S. Supreme Court, compelled all children to attend government schools, in effect banning all private schools. The impetus for this law came from the Ku Klux Klan, which abhorred what it considered the alien influences of Catholic schools.[5]

Government does not have a complete monopoly on primary and secondary education in the United States. There are public schools and private schools—the latter operating in the educational marketplace as for-profit, nonprofit, religious, or secular institutions; 5 million children, 11 percent of the total, are enrolled in private schools. There is also self-service education: "home schooling" is legal in thirty-eight states, allowing more than a million children to be taught at home.[6] Another arrangement is education through intergovernmental agreements, whereby children in one jurisdiction go to public schools in another and the sending town pays the receiving one. In yet another arrangement, a suburban family that prefers the public school in a nearby town over its own often can send its children there and pay tuition privately. There are vouchers, scholarships, or tuition tax credits for private education; charter schools; and contracts with private firms to run schools. Some of these offer parental choice and escape from government education monopolies.

The typical public school system operates as a local government monopoly, a stifling one in that, for the most part, pupils must attend a particular school; they are not free even to attend another school within the monopoly. Such a policy is designed for administrative convenience rather than the educational development of the child. The parents may have no choice in the matter unless they want to place the child in a private school, in which case they have a very wide choice limited only by cost and distance (and any selection criteria the school may have for the children it accepts—bright, slow, artistic, athletic, science-oriented, from prominent families, from alumni, etc.). If a family chooses to use a private school, it must pay tuition, but it receives no rebate on its taxes even though its choice saves money for the public school system. In effect, the family pays twice, once in tuition for the school it wants, and once in taxes for the school it shuns. Surely this is unfair, and "it is [even more] unjust to compel poor children to attend bad schools."[7] Milton Friedman recognized the problem long ago and, in 1955, proposed vouchers as an equitable means to introduce competition and improve education.[8]

Parental choice increasingly is viewed as an essential lever for reforming education.[9] "Choice, not assignment" is the watchword of the movement. Several different approaches have been proposed to enhance parental choice, some more effective than others: open enrollments, charter schools, vouchers, tuition tax credits, and tax-free savings accounts for education.[10]

Open Enrollment

Many parents eager to send their children to a good school go to great lengths to pretend they live in such a school's district; in turn, popular districts try to find and expel illegally enrolled students because such students consume local taxes. Other parents withdraw their children from their own school districts and send them to neighboring ones; however, these parents have to pay individually just as if they were sending their children to private schools.

Parents could be allowed to send their child to any school in the district or to a school in another district. The parents' own school district would transfer funds accordingly, including any state aid to which the district would be entitled. In a manner of speaking, the child would deliver a bundle of tax funds when she went to the chosen school. This inevitably means that the funds would *not* go to a school she was *not* attending, not even the public school nearest her home.

Minnesota took the lead and enacted legislation in 1984 to facilitate interdistrict enrollment in public schools. Such open enrollment alters the current monopolistic practices of most school systems. Allowing public funds to accompany the child enhances choice and promotes competition at least to some degree, with the objective of producing better educated children. This approach has adverse consequences for any school that could not attract enough pupils to stay in business, for it could no longer compel enrollment of the neighborhood children. But existing open-enrollment programs are often feeble in practice: the school that is shunned rarely loses much of its budget (and may even be rewarded with more money, to improve itself), and the school that gains a good reputation is rarely expanded—its waiting list is lengthened instead.

Charter Schools

Public schools in the United States customarily have been run politically, that is, by elected school boards. But, critics say, the only personnel required for schools are teachers, principals, and pupils; politicians need not apply. In belated recognition of this truism, a new model is emerging for public schools, namely, charter schools. This model is intended to address numerous shortcomings, including lack of accountability for pupil performance, unresponsive school bureaucracies, restrictive rules, and limited choices among public schools. Charter schools typically operate under charters or contracts with school districts or other government education agencies. They are designed by groups of parents, teachers, school administrators, community members, or private firms, and they usually operate with considerable autonomy from external controls such as district, state, and union contract provisions. They exercise their autonomy in such areas as curriculum, instruction, budget, and personnel in exchange for being held accountable for pupil performance. As of 1995, eleven states had legislation allowing charter schools, and 134 such schools were in operation, with the number growing rapidly.[11] A study of charter schools in Massachusetts found a high satisfaction rate among parents of children in such schools; other early results are also promising.[12]

The key objectives of effective statutes for establishing charter schools are listed by Theodore Rebarber:[13]

- Allow charter schools to be fully independent and avoid prescriptions for their internal governance
- Give blanket waivers of state statutes and regulations except for those addressing performance goals and assessments and those relating to health, safety, civil rights, and certification requirements
- Create new entities or authorize existing ones to approve charters; charters approved by local school boards should be subject to state review
- Protect the integrity of the charter-approval process and insulate it from political influence
- Establish direct state funding for charter schools at a level equivalent to the average of state expenditures for schools, including both capital and operating funds

- Ensure that charter schools have access to adequate capital for facility and other major initial costs that require long-term repayment schedules

- Avoid limiting provisions that treat charter schools as experimental rather than as a basic reform

Milton Friedman warns that charter schools are not enough: parents need to control the funds, for as long as government controls the money, competition is available only on the demand side, not the supply side.[14] Myron Lieberman argues persuasively that choice restricted to public schools, whether through open enrollment or charter schools, is a hollow choice. Only if parents can choose from a wide variety of public and private schools, religious and secular, for-profit and nonprofit, do they have a meaningful choice.[15]

Vouchers

Vouchers have been used in higher education in the United States for many years, under four different federal programs: the G.I. Bill, federally sponsored student loans, Pell Grants, and tuition tax credits (enacted in 1997).[16] Some states also have voucher programs for college; for example, New York State Regents Scholarships are awarded competitively to state residents who can use them in any approved college in the state, provided they gain admission. Now the idea is to extend the voucher concept to elementary and secondary education.

Under a pure voucher system, parents of a school-age child would receive a voucher to send their child to the school of their choice—conventional public, charter, or private; they would give the voucher to the school, which would turn it in to the issuing jurisdiction and receive money for it.

There are five main arguments for education vouchers, and they are interrelated:

1. Competition for students will force schools to be more effective and responsive.

2. Entrepreneurship by teachers and principals will produce much needed innovation in teaching methods.

3. Competition for teachers will lead to a more flexible, professional employment relationship and better teaching.

4. Stifling and unnecessary bureaucratic controls will be greatly diminished.

5. Morality and religion, which are avoided in public schools (much to society's detriment), can be reintroduced into children's education in private schools.[17]

Table 10.1 shows that there are many choices in designing a voucher system.[18] Student eligibility, school eligibility, admissions policy, and subsidy level are among the crucial design factors that have to be specified; extensive public debate can be expected about each of them. Voucher plans that allow a broad choice of private schools, including religious schools, are strongly opposed by an education establishment composed of teacher unions, school boards, parent-teacher organizations, teachers' colleges, and miscellaneous groups who fear they will lose power, jobs, or both. Vouchers are also opposed by those who see them as breaching the wall separating church and state, and by vendors who are used to making effortless sales to established school systems. The teachers' position seems hypocritical in light of a study of nine cities that found that teachers were 62 percent more likely than average parents to enroll their own children in private schools.[19] President Clinton was accused of similar hypocrisy for enrolling his daughter in a private school while blocking choice for other parents in Washington, D.C.

On the other hand, voucher advocates worry that if vouchers were adopted and then used in private schools, legislation, regulation, and bureau-

TABLE 10.1—DESIGN ALTERNATIVES FOR SCHOOL VOUCHER PLANS

Factor	Illustrative range of alternatives
Student eligibility	Universal vs. means tested (low-income only)
School eligibility	All private including religious? All private except religious? More or less regulated? Subject only to market forces or lose accreditation for failure to perform?
Admissions	According to schools' own criteria (subject to civil rights laws) or by lottery?
Value of voucher	Equal to or less than current per-pupil spending? Related to family income or achievement gains?
Information	Parents provided with information on school rank and performance? Parents inform themselves? Counseling available?
Transportation	Subsidized completely, partially, or not at all?

Source: Derived from Isabel V. Sawhill with Shannon L. Smith, "Vouchers for Elementary and Secondary Education," in *Vouchers and Related Delivery Mechanisms: Consumer Choice in the Provision of Public Services*, conference papers, Brookings Institution, Washington, D.C., October 2–3, 1998, pp. 136–67, table 2.

cratization would soon follow and would so transform private schools that they would resemble today's public schools.[20] This happened with the voucher-like system in the Netherlands, where private schools are fully state financed but are regulated as to inputs, for example, teacher salaries and curriculum. Financial equality with the public schools is achieved, but at the expense of the very choice that the system was originally intended to ensure.[21] Friedman argues that vouchers should not cover the full cost of tuition; parents should pay some of the cost of private schools so they are conscious of the price. Inasmuch as private schools usually cost less than government schools, why give the private schools an incentive to raise tuition?[22]

The two largest publicly funded voucher systems in the United States are in Milwaukee, with 15,000 students in the program in 1997, and Cleveland, with 3,000. Reading and math scores improved for children participating in both programs.[23] A negative initial report on the Milwaukee program was seized upon by opponents, until a subsequent analysis discredited that report and found that students enrolled in a choice school showed substantial gains in performance after two years.[24] That analysis, however, has itself been challenged,[25] demonstrating that more experience may have to be gained and more research may have to be done to confirm claims that positive results are accumulating.[26] The case for vouchers and tuition tax credits was significantly bolstered by James Coleman's famous 1982 education study, which found that private high schools, including Catholic schools, provide a better education than public high schools and are less segregated as well.[27]

Privately funded voucher plans are multiplying rapidly, although they are still small. Fed up with the decline of public schools, private donors have financed small-scale voucher systems in New York City, Albany, and elsewhere. By the end of 1997, thirty such systems—scholarship programs, in essence—were operating around the country, and 42,000 families were waiting to participate.[28] The programs are spreading. A business group in San Antonio, Texas, is providing $50 million for vouchers for all students in a poor, mostly Hispanic school district.[29] A group of business leaders is raising $200 million for a nationwide voucher program that would enable 50,000 inner-city public school children to attend parochial and other private schools for four years.[30]

Vouchers are popular. When a group of private firms, philanthropists, and foundations raised funds to support a modest voucher program in New York City, 22,700 children applied for the 1,300 openings.[31] In Washington, D.C., 4,725 children from poor and working-class families applied for 1,000 private vouchers.[32] Early results from a voucher program in Cleveland showed that after a year, two-thirds of the families who had transferred their children to choice schools reported being very satisfied with the academic quality, compared with less than 30 percent for parents of children who remained in the public schools.[33] Such a survey is not conclusive, as people tend to ratify their prior decisions, but surely it is encouraging.

Tuition Tax Credits and Other Tax-Based Methods

Tax credits for tuition paid to private schools, within limits, have an effect similar to that of vouchers. They permit parents to take a dollar-for-dollar reduction in their taxes, up to a certain limit, for tuition paid to private schools. Three states—Arizona, Iowa, and Minnesota—offer parents tax credits, and more are considering it. Tax deduction for tuition is another, less generous approach, and tax-free savings accounts for education are yet another. These approaches are not particularly useful for low-income families, however.

Given all these approaches to parental choice, it might seem unnecessary to privatize education in order to introduce competition. Allowing parents to choose among public and charter schools should lead to competition, provided the schools have sufficient autonomy and independence to become distinctive. This is analogous to managed competition in contracting, discussed in chapter 7, and it has had some positive effect in New York City, for example.[34] Advocates of school choice argue, however, that only competition from private schools, via vouchers and tuition tax credits, can bring about the necessary diversity among public schools within a single district. Moreover, education needs research and development, just like any other industry; private, for-profit schools are logical leaders in this direction. One such private enterprise, the Edison Project, is investing in research and development with the aim of designing a new primary education process and perhaps becoming the Microsoft of the industry and the market leader. Advocates insist that only vouchers, usable anywhere, are equitable for families of all income classes and can introduce the kind of competition that can bring about lasting improvements in elementary and secondary education.

Arguments against Parental Choice

Critics of vouchers and tuition tax credits raise several arguments, the foremost of which is that vouchers represent an impermissible establishment of religion by government. When the issue reached the U.S. Supreme Court, however, the justices let stand a ruling by the Supreme Court of Wisconsin that Milwaukee's vouchers, when redeemed at religious schools, do not violate the separation of church and state.[35] The Wisconsin Supreme Court stated, "[N]ot one cent flows from the state to a sectarian private school . . . except as a result of the necessary and intervening choices of individual parents."[36] A tuition tax-deduction measure in Minnesota withstood the highest level of judicial scrutiny when Justice William Rehnquist stated for the U.S. Supreme Court that a tax deduction "to defray the cost of educational expenses incurred by parents—regardless of the type of schools their children attend . . . serves [the] purpose of ensuring that the state's citizenry is well educated."[37]

The G.I. Bill of Rights, a federal voucher program that provided college education for veterans of World War II and the Korean War, was very successful. John Norquist, the Democratic mayor of Milwaukee, once pointed out that under the G.I. Bill a veteran could enroll in Notre Dame University to become a Catholic priest, or in Yeshiva University to become a rabbi. Pell Grants flow through college students to religious schools. The New York State Regents Scholarship preceded the G.I. Bill by many years and operated the same way. Voucher plans merely extend the concept to elementary and secondary education.

One criticism is that choice systems will destroy public schools. Several points have been made in rebuttal: (1) what is important is that education be universal and offered without charge, not the public or private character of the teacher's employer; (2) if a school is doing a poor job, it *should* go out of business—the adjective "public" in its name should not immunize it from the consequences of poor performance; and (3) competition from private schools may actually save public schools if it succeeds in waking them from their torpor.[38] Following the introduction of vouchers, for example, the motto of Milwaukee's public schools became, "We want to be Milwaukee's schools of choice."[39]

A second criticism of parental choice is the "cream-skimming" argument; that is, the private schools would skim the best students, and the public schools would be a dumping ground for the leavings. Advocates of parental choice, however, cite evidence that contradicts this assumption. Applicants for a voluntary voucher program in New York City were not top achievers: only 18 percent scored at or above level in math and only 26 percent of the 6-to-9-year-olds were reading at grade level.[40] Advocates argue, further, that gifted students should not be deprived of the opportunity to develop their innate abilities to the fullest or sacrificed to enrich the environment of others. Moreover, this criticism can be turned around: a vigorously competitive environment can be expected to create schools with specialized "market niches," including schools for children with discipline problems. Richard Milburn High School, which, despite its name, is a corporation with headquarters in Woodbridge, Virginia, performs such a role and serves 50,000 students annually in more than sixty locations, providing alternative education that includes elementary remediation and skill development for former dropouts and offering a recognized, standard high school diploma.

A third criticism is that private schools promote segregation. Coleman found, however, that private schools are less segregated than public ones because so many suburban public schools are highly segregated.[41] Defenders of parental choice thus counter that local-school monopolies result in government-imposed segregation. A study of ten large American cities found that their schools were much more segregated in 1995 than in 1968; the fraction of whites in central-city public schools had dropped dramatically from an average of 51 to 16 percent.[42] This statistic corroborates and expands on an earlier study in California, which found that private Catholic schools have a higher population (40 percent) of minority pupils than public schools do.[43] Marsha Levine and Denis Doyle report that for many inner-city black families, few of whom are Catholic, the Catholic schools are an affordable alternative to unsatisfactory public schools. Enrollment figures reveal that Catholic schools are responding to this demand, as Gallup polls show inner-city blacks to be the most dissatisfied with urban public schools.[44] The assumption that whites will take advantage of choice and that blacks will not is condescending and inaccurate. Again, evidence from New York City shows that minority families are more likely than Caucasians to avail themselves of choice systems: about 47 percent of the applicants were Latino, a level higher than their proportion of the public-school population, and the same was true of blacks.[45] Another study shows that blacks and Hispanics are twice as likely as whites to utilize such a credit.[46]

A fourth criticism is that choice systems benefit the rich. The American Federation of Teachers cites a study of private schooling in Europe, which found that those who took advantage of subsidized private schools were primarily middle- and higher-income families, who were better informed of the opportunities than working-class families, with the result that class differences were magnified. The study's author notes that where the dissemination of information is dependent on press releases and the cooperation of resistant public-school administrators, most working-class parents remain uninformed, but he points to successful programs in

Scotland, Paris, and New York that successfully informed working-class parents about school choice.[47] Additional evidence shows that the situation in the United States is very different. In Washington, D.C., 4,725 children applied for 1,000 newly announced private scholarships offered to poor and working class families; 11 percent of the eligible population jumped at the chance to leave the public schools.[48] In the United States in general, many poor, inner-city blacks scrimp and save to enroll their children in neighborhood-based private schools.[49] A survey in the 1980s showed that people making less than $15,000 a year were more than twice as likely as those making more than $25,000 to say they would use a $500 tuition tax credit.[50] Applicants for New York's private voucher system had an average annual family income about 30 percent below the national poverty level; they came from the bottom 15 percent of New York households, and over two-thirds came from families that were receiving food stamps and Medicaid.[51] One in four families with children in private schools have incomes under $35,000, and almost half have incomes under $50,000. Two-thirds of families with children in Catholic elementary schools have incomes under $35,000, and 72 percent of families with children in Catholic high schools have incomes of $50,000 or less.[52] A Massachusetts survey found that charter-school parents had lower incomes and less education than district-school parents.[53]

The likely explanation of the American pattern is that low-income minority groups located in large cities are more dependent on monolithic public schools, which they find unsatisfactory, than higher-income groups, who can find a satisfactory school by moving to a suburban community. Hence, low-income families and minority groups constitute an important constituency for vouchers and tuition tax credits. In other words, the situation in the United States differs markedly from the one in Europe cited by the teachers' union as a warning about the harmful effects of choice; class differences may be reduced, not magnified, if working-class parents can give their children a better education by availing themselves of choice.

A fifth criticism is that if many more children attend independent private schools, we soon will have a nation of adults who lack any common educational background and may even lack basic exposure to the nation's history and basic democratic values. This hypothetical shortcoming is easy to avoid. State education authorities can require certain common curriculum elements at a minimum, and they should administer common achievement examinations to all students, as some already do.[54] The results of the examinations would serve at least three purposes: (1) to inform parents about their child's progress, (2) to provide evaluative data for accreditation, and (3) properly summarized, to help parents assess and choose schools for their children. Rating services are springing up, providing parents with analyses of local schools by publishing what are, in effect, hybrids of *Lovejoy's College Guide* and *Consumer Reports*. New York issued its first statewide, school-by-school rankings in 1996.[55] Such reports differ from state to state, but in general they give information on enrollments, cost per student, average class size, graduation rate, dropout rate, standardized test scores, percentage of students achieving at or above grade level, and the fraction of seniors with four or more years of math and science.[56]

A sixth criticism is that the weakening of community schools means the weakening of communities. An empirical study of paired suburban school districts and paired inner-city school districts sheds light on this issue. Far from atomizing citizens or turning them into mere consumers, it found, "school choice ... helps build communities of concerned and engaged parents. School choice can do this in suburban communities, where most Americans now live, and in inner-city neighborhoods, where the stock of social capital may be most depleted and where its absence may have the most deleterious effects."[57]

The Case for Vouchers

To summarize, one can have *universal* education without *public* schools and *markets* in education without charging parents for their children's schooling. As long as every child attends school at common expense financed by general taxes, the public interest can be satisfied. Arguments that vouchers will draw off the better students, the richer students, and white students can be refuted by the available data.

Minority groups are recognizing that the heavily Democratic teacher unions—they endorsed 250 Democrats and only one Republican in the 1996 congressional election[58]—are not their ally on this issue. Black leaders are endorsing vouchers as national polls reveal that 72 percent of black respondents favor them. Another survey showed vouchers were supported by 65 percent of Hispanics, 56 percent of blacks, and 47 percent of whites.[59] These results are easy to understand, considering that Hispanics and blacks are the principal victims of bad inner-city schools, which whites have been able to flee more readily by enrolling in private schools or moving to suburbs.

The political winds are shifting in favor of vouchers, despite intense opposition by the teacher unions and their mostly Democratic allies. Republicans made vouchers ("opportunity scholarships") part of their national platform in 1996 and attacked the National Education Association, the largest of the two teachers' unions, for opposing vouchers. Governor Arne Carlson Anderson of Minnesota, Governor Tommy Thompson of Wisconsin, Mayor Michael White of Cleveland, Mayor John Norquist of Milwaukee, and Mayor Bret Schundler of Jersey City are among the political leaders of both parties who had implemented school choice programs by 1998. Mainstream education leaders, having seen their preferred solutions fail, are reluctantly beginning to back vouchers.[60]

Parental choice advocates argue that if competition is to be real and effective, for-profit schools are required. They can create incentives for students, teachers, and parents, perform the necessary research and development, innovate, and find new and better ways to prepare students for the world they will inhabit. Vouchers are seen as an effective means of promoting competition by allowing unfettered parental choice.

Although there is much talk about the voucher "experiments" cited previously, to date they have been no more than demonstrations. They are too narrow in scope: the number of students is limited, as is student eligibility; the choice of schools is restricted; and the value of each voucher is less than the per-student expenditure in the public schools. Hostile unions and the unknown life of a particular "experiment" add to the uncertainty. All these factors compromise the validity of any "findings," but the results nevertheless are impressive. Moreover, the studies have been couched only in terms of improvements in pupil performance, not in terms of cost-effectiveness (price vs. performance). Surely no evaluation of competitive education is meaningful unless the cost part of the equation is also considered. If voucher students in a private school do no better than those in public schools, but the per-pupil cost is lower by a third (as in other service privatizations), this is a sign that vouchers work, not that they don't, and it would be a persuasive case for more vouchers.[61]

Contracting for Educational Services

In addition to parental choice through vouchers, tuition tax credits, charters, and similar mechanisms, choice can also be exercised by school boards, through contracts awarded competitively to private, for-profit firms. Contracts can be awarded to operate a single school or a whole school district. The cities of Baltimore, Miami, and Hartford, Connecticut, contracted with a private firm to run their schools, but the contracts floundered under unremitting opposition from teacher unions, misunderstandings about contract terms, and the lack of authority to make changes.[62]

A somewhat different approach has been more successful. The Edison Project, an ambitious for-profit educational venture, has assumed control over twenty-five public schools since 1995. Most students showed measurable improvements in reading and math during the first two years compared to their earlier scores and to the scores of similar students in other public schools in the same district. The Edison *modus operandi* is as follows: it takes over one or more schools in a district, generally with the agreement of the teachers' union, and pays premium salaries (and sometimes even stock options)[63] to teachers that Edison selects from the school system. At a school in Wichita, Kansas, where three-quarters of the students live below the poverty level, Edison has installed a computer in the home of every student. Parents and teachers e-mail one another, and students can turn in their assignments by e-mail. One result is that more parents volunteer to help in the school as tutors, and an expected side benefit is greater parental involvement in the education process at home. The school day has been extended by an hour and classes are divided in half according to ability, permitting more time for more specialized attention. By 1997 Edison had taken over three schools in the district and the waiting list was over 1,000 just two years after the program began.[64]

A school system might increase its appeal and compete for students by contracting out the teaching of some courses and the education of some categories of students. For example, colleges could be hired to run programs for gifted children, private firms for vocational education and driver training, and special private schools for handicapped children. One school district could contract with another for certain programs under an intergovernmental contract. In a bold proposal, Boston University offered to operate the troubled Boston public schools under a contractual arrangement.

Entrepreneurial teachers and administrators might form a group teaching practice, in the manner of a group medical practice. The group could contract with a school district to teach a subject or grade, or, in a more ambitious step, it might assume complete responsibility to manage an entire school and strive to attract a growing clientele by the excellence of its education.

In response to the explosive growth of special education, and the wasteful process of evaluating children referred to the program, New York's Mayor Rudolph W. Giuliani proposed privatizing the evaluation process and saving money by contracting with private psychologists.[65] Contracting is widespread for support functions in a school, such as pupil transportation, buildings and grounds maintenance, and food, medical, administrative, and janitorial services.[66] The process of contracting is described in chapter 7, and the results are similar to those reported in chapter 6.

Other Forms of Privatized Education

Enrollment in public and private elementary and secondary schools in the United States was 52 million in 1997, and more than $600 billion was being spent annually, 10 percent of GNP. It is no wonder then that private firms, spurred by broad dissatisfaction with public schools, are emerging and discovering specialized market niches where they can help solve America's educational problems. An investment firm has cataloged sixty firms in this broad, newly defined industry.[67]

For example, a different form of private schooling is appearing at the periphery of traditional public schooling: for-profit learning centers where children are tutored after their regular classes.[68] Tutoring is hardly a new concept, but doing it under a corporate form of organization, as a business, dates only to 1979. It is related to the commercial enterprises that prepare students to take Scholastic Aptitude Tests. The latter business aims mostly at high school juniors and seniors, whereas commercial tutoring concerns market their services mostly to upper elementary and junior high school pupils. Both represent private-sector initiatives to improve educational performance. Radio advertisements for reading and math tutoring by learning companies are omnipresent; their market is young school children.

Public schools are also learning about education markets. Tuition-charging summer school programs sprang up throughout California after Proposition 13 caused a shutdown of what was called the world's largest baby-sitting service, the summer program in public schools that was free for everyone. It was finally recognized that summer programs cost money, relatively few children need academic remediation during the summer, and the vast majority of families can afford to pay for recreation and enrichment programs to occupy their children during the vacation period.[69]

Private education programs have their flaws too. In New York City, the numerous proprietary schools that offer training to would-be barbers, beauticians, computer programmers, cashiers, secretaries, truck drivers, and other job seekers are sometimes accused of flagrant abuses; they are charged with enrolling students who are incapable of doing the work and failing to find jobs for them. Likewise, when political powers forced an open-admissions program on the city's own university, the latter also accepted students unable to do the work, as was demonstrated by the high failure rate.[70] Moreover, one wonders whether the placement results of proprietary schools are any worse than those of public vocational schools. Advocates of choice, therefore suspect the motives of those who would impose rigid restrictions on proprietary schools that charge tuition, ostensibly to protect individuals from wasting their private funds, while ignoring similar shortcomings in the public schools that waste public funds. The focus of concern should not be whether private schools have faults—of course they do—but how they compare with public schools in terms of price and performance.

Reinventing Welfare

Welfare reform came as a sudden, and controversial, change of direction in the United States in the mid-1990s, after the high-water mark of the welfare state was reached in the early 1980s. Before that, social problems were being aggregated and shifted to the highest and most distant level of government for solution. The traditional emphasis on self-help and community effort had given way to a large, paternalistic welfare apparatus that saw recipients as helpless victims rather than as citizens needing assistance. The private, nonprofit, charitable organizations that historically had been dealing with troubled people were transformed into auxiliaries of the state[71] while the government programs designed to deal with the problems, were both ineffective and unmanageable. Well-meaning programs often made matters worse for the intended beneficiaries, the poor and minorities, as Charles Murray demonstrates in *Losing Ground*.[72] In retrospect, it appears that the problem of the so-called permanent underclass ("transgenerational welfare dependence") was created by the state, at least in part.

Supporters of welfare reform contend that there is little that government—federal, state or local—can do to solve the underlying problems of cities, for instance, although well-intentioned politicians have spent a great deal of money on programs that purport to do so. The "underlying problems"—dropping out of school, teenage pregnancy, irresponsible insemination (males are to blame, too), illegitimate births, and drug and alcohol addiction—produce generations of social misfits who are seemingly unable to participate in the world of work, doomed to a marginal existence, and dependent on support obtained either legally through welfare or illegally through crime.

Reformers argue that the private institutions of society—family, neighborhood, church, community—can best change these destructive patterns of behavior and prevent their development. The participation of local citizens is deemed necessary, for they ultimately have the opportunity and resources and will benefit most from the well-being of their neighbors, while state power is limited, paradoxically, because it can only issue orders. By contrast, a member of the clergy can suggest that an alcoholic getting support from the church also receive counseling to "clean up his act;" he may be entitled to help, but he must also assume the social obligations of citizenship, as Lawrence Mead points out.[73] A decentralized, localized system allows fine-grained judgments based on personal knowledge about an individual and his changing circumstances.

A vivid illustration from New York supports the reformers' case. A Catholic church in Brooklyn announced that it was terminating its twelve-year-long operation of a twenty-five-bed shelter for homeless men, because the city government had opened two huge shelters nearby, which drew away the church's clientele. The church's program had required that in order to be accepted, a man had to give up drugs and alcohol, clean himself up, get dressed in the new clothing that the church provided, and take a job. In striking contrast, the city shelters made no such demands; they merely provided food and shelter with no questions asked and no change in behavior required.[74] Reformers of the government's welfare system could point to this as an instance in which bad social programs drive out good ones, just as Gresham's Law says that bad money drives out good.

John Goodman and Michael Stroup succinctly summarized the situation before welfare reforms were put into effect:

> Entitlement programs for welfare are structured so that benefits are granted solely on the basis of personal circumstances. Applicants do not have to give the reasons for their circumstances, nor are they required to explain how they plan to change them in the future. They don't even have to show a willingness to change. In the AFDC [Aid for Dependent Children] program, for example, the requirements for eligibility essentially amount to: (1) low income, (2) very few assets, (3) dependent children, (4) no man in the household. Anyone satisfying these requirements is entitled to benefits. And the word entitlement means [that] "right" benefits cannot be withdrawn simply because the recipient refuses to modify behavior.
>
> The philosophy of the private sector is quite different. Because of the emphasis on a behavioral approach to the problem of poverty, our best private charities do not view the giving of assistance as a "duty" or the receipt of assistance as a "right." Instead, charitable assistance is viewed as a tool which can be used intelli-

gently, not only to provide relief but to change behavior. At many private charities, for example, the level of assistance varies considerably from individual to individual. Private agencies usually reserve the right to reduce the level of assistance or withdraw assistance altogether if recipients do not show behavioral changes.[75]

Long before the advent of the welfare state, Americans practiced mutual aid, commonly through benefit or benevolent societies formed along religious, ethnic, or occupational lines. For a modest fee that was within reach of even the poorest workers, members had sick benefits, proper funerals, and support for widows and children, a combination of unemployment, health, and life insurance. These societies ran orphanages and old-age homes, and many still do. The disappearance of most of them has been attributed principally to the emergence and growth of the welfare state.[76]

Growing recognition of the potential of "mediating structures"[77] is evident in dealing with the alarming rise in births among unmarried teenagers, particularly blacks. The initial, reflexive reaction among many policy advocates was to call for a government program to "solve the problem." That approach—offered more out of habit than conviction—stalled because of a growing consensus that government programs, no matter how well intended and well financed, are essentially unavailing for this kind of problem. Reformers noted that illegitimate births increased at the same time that sex education became widespread, while contraceptives and abortion were legalized and made readily available, safe, and cheap. Because births among teenagers cannot result from ignorance about birth control, reformers point out that more government-sponsored instructional programs and clinics are not the answer.

Leaders in the black community recognize that creative local initiatives, informal person-to-person efforts, recognizable role models, and intracommunity pressures are more likely to be effective than bureaucrats following federal guidelines.[78] For example, Black Muslims arguably have done more to discourage drug abuse than government programs have. The family, not a government agency, is the societal institution most capable of providing the detailed, long-term attention and the concern, love, care, support, guidance, admonition, restriction, control, and punishment necessary to reduce teenage pregnancy and yet do so in a way that is acceptable to society and consistent with the community's values.[79] In fact, births to black teenagers declined for the first time in the late 1990s, a result attributed in part to community and family pressures that stressed personal responsibility and abstinence.

Government did not always occupy a dominant role in welfare. Its role as a supplement to private charity was articulated by President Thiers of France in the mid-nineteenth century:

> Some general diseases, affecting an entire social class, must be treated by the collective charity of everybody, in fact, by public assistance. But it is important that this virtue, when it changes from individual to collective, retains its virtuous character, which is to remain spontaneous, voluntary, and free. It must not become a constraint. Therefore, there must be public charity, to complete the private or religious charity, acting where some good remains to be done.[80]

Today's welfare reformers would add that the challenge facing governments at the dawn of the twenty-first century is to strike a better balance between state and private charity, bearing in mind the great value to society of having its members behave as willing philanthropists instead of reluctant taxpayers. Compassion is an emotion unique to individual humans, not organizations.[81]

Organized charities have slipped gradually into the role of lobbyists distinguished mainly by their lofty moral purpose. Volunteers of America receives 94 percent of its funding from government; Catholic Charities, 62 percent.[82] Termed "nonprofitization" by Richard Nathan,[83] this practice deeply affects the very nature of these organizations.[84] Is government needed as the middleman, collecting taxes and distributing them for charitable purposes either directly to the needy or to charitable institutions? Critics of government welfare programs answer that question with a negative, urging instead that private charities should reclaim their traditional direct role in helping the poor and the afflicted. Goodman and Stroup advocate privatizing the welfare state by allowing taxpayers to allocate up to a third of their federal income taxes to private charities; this would be a tax credit, not merely a tax-exempt contribution. The operative feature of this plan is that for every dollar allocated in this manner, the federal government would be required to reduce its poverty budget by one dollar.[85] Legislation along these lines was introduced in Congress in 1996 but it did not pass. Another plan, "Jobs Plus," installed in Oregon in 1994, took the funds being spent on Aid to Families with Dependent Children (AFDC), food stamps, and unemployment insurance and used them instead to subsidize jobs for welfare recipients in the private sector.[86]

The tradition of American giving continues. Charitable contributions increased by 75 percent in inflation-adjusted terms between 1967 and 1997, in parallel with the growth in GNP.[87] Despite dire predictions that giving would decline sharply because a reduction in the marginal tax rate during the Reagan administration made contributions much more costly—two-thirds more costly for someone in the top bracket—private individuals, prompted by moral considerations and acting through voluntary associations, continued to help those less fortunate and thereby assumed part of the social burden amassed by government. Opponents of government involvement believe that these private philanthropists point the way to restoration of civil society.[88] But even though these opponents claim that government action may have worsened dependency and its attendant ills, they are equally convinced that its belated retreat and its displacement by private institutions may not eliminate the condition, because social pathology has economic and demographic causes too.

Welfare Reform

Growing public outrage at the excesses and failures of the welfare system emboldened political leaders at the state level to demand the freedom to reform their systems and, with surprising ease, they persuaded Congress and the Clinton administration to grant it in the Welfare Reform Act of 1996. The act decentralized the welfare process and allowed states to design their own systems to a considerable degree: imposing work requirements, setting limits on how long one can be on welfare, tightening eligibility standards, examining eligibility much more stringently, and turning welfare centers into job centers. The result was a striking reduction in the size of the welfare rolls, 37 percent from 1993 to 1998, without an increase in homelessness or in lines at soup kitchens, to the surprise of welfare advocates. As the welfare rolls melted away, the question arose as to what happened to those previously on welfare. Opponents of welfare reform predicted a disastrous "race to the bottom" as states competed to cut benefits and adopt measures to keep poor people away. The answer, according to one study, was that they found jobs during a period of unparalleled economic prosperity.[89] "Welfare to work" works, said the reformers. In New York City, welfare recipients unable or unwilling to find jobs on their own were put to work in city agencies, earning their welfare allowances at the minimum-wage rate. Another factor was reduction in fraud; many who were working and illegally receiving welfare payments, or were enrolled in more than one jurisdiction in a metropolitan area, failed to show up in face-to-face recertification interviews. New York's Mayor Giuliani made a bold promise:

> We will end welfare by the dawn of the new century. We will replace dependency with work in exchange for earnings. This means that by the year 2000, all adults and heads of families who are now on welfare will be working in a private job or, if necessary, in a public job. ... New York will be the first city in the nation, on its own, to end welfare. ... When family heads come in looking for help, we will offer it in exchange for participation in a full-time 35-hour workweek, with usually 20 hours engaged in actual work and the balance of the week spent in training or other activities leading to the earliest possible full-time private employment.[90]

Other Western democracies, suffering from the excesses of the welfare state, are also struggling to make long-overdue changes. Generous benefits in Europe made it comfortable for people to stay unemployed, but this practice is under attack. Britain, for example, is following America's footsteps in coaxing, prodding, and pushing unemployed youths into the marketplace for jobs. The Netherlands is terminating a program under which the government bought the paintings and sculptures of would-be artists.[91]

Privatized Social Services

The preceding discussion about reinventing welfare emphasizes privatizing the welfare state by displacement: government withdrawal from failed activities; resumption of traditional roles by local community groups and the family because government programs are in default; and deregulation to facilitate the latter, such as the tax-law changes mentioned previously and advocated by Goodman and Stroup.

Privatization by delegation is also occurring, with contracts and with vouchers. Contracting with nonprofits has long been practiced, although it has been attacked for altering—if not deforming—the basic nature of those organizations.[92] More recently, however, contracting with for-profit organizations is a growing phenomenon. Private firms are administrating social service programs[93] and delivering social services directly to clients: they operate day-care centers, senior-citizen centers, homeless shelters, and job-training programs for the hard-to-employ. They track "dead-beat dads,"[94] and they are being considered for managing child-welfare cases.[95] A private, for-profit firm, America Works, has attracted well-deserved attention by finding jobs for welfare recipients at a cost to taxpayers far less than government programs that have the same objective.[96]

Between 1990 and 1996, more than half the state and local governments surveyed by the General Accounting Office increased their contracting for selected social services—child care, child welfare, child-support enforcement, and temporary assistance to needy families. Many of them are engaging in managed competition and deliberately encouraging ongoing competition between public agencies and private nonprofit and for-profit contractors. The challenges they face are (1) to attract enough qualified bidders, particularly in rural areas; (2) to develop sufficiently detailed contract specifications; and (3) to monitor the contractor effectively.[97] These are the usual requirements for successful contracting.

Contracting is not the only way social services are being privatized. Vouchers are used to some extent for home care for disabled persons and are increasingly employed for child day care: in New York City, vouchers were used for 46 percent of the 87,000 children in day care at the end of 1998. The Joint Partnership Training Act (1989) encouraged the use of vouchers for dislocated workers. Programs under the Economic Dislocation and Worker Adjustment Assistance Act use vouchers as well as contracts. An experienced, displaced worker can use a voucher to select the training program she deems best for her circumstances. Vouchers account for about 7 percent of the $27 million spent by New York City for such retraining.[98]

Privatizing Social Security

No topic arouses more intense discussion than Social Security. This venerable system, which in recent decades has been likened to a government-sponsored chain letter, is in serious financial straits. The Social Security system is not an actuarially sound pension plan but rather a "pay as you go" plan, in which contributions from current workers are paid immediately to current beneficiaries. Payments out of the so-called trust fund will exceed payments into it by about 2014, and the fund will be depleted altogether by about 2034 if major changes are not made. As the system presently stands, "baby boomers are projected to lose [to the system] roughly five cents of every dollar they earn . . . in taxes net of benefits. Generation-Xers will lose more than seven cents of every dollar they earn in net taxes."[99]

Various proposals are offered to "save" Social Security. They include raising the retirement age, reducing benefits, increasing the Social Security tax, diverting general tax revenues, and investing in the stock market, the last intended to increase the rate of return on the system's assets. (In fact, there are no assets, only IOUs in the trust fund; that is, government promises to repay the money that has been collected through the Social Security payroll tax but has been spent for other purposes.)

The Social Security trust fund has a historic annual return of under 2 percent compared to the stock market's return over a comparably long period of about 7 percent. Therefore, turning to the marketplace and investing in U.S. securities is recommended as a way to generate more income for retirees. Two very different plans have been proposed, however. In one plan, the government would buy shares of U.S. companies for the Social Security trust fund, in effect, *nationalizing* a portion of U.S. industry; President Clinton espoused this approach in his 1999 State of the Union address. In the other—diametrically opposed—plan, individuals would be allowed to put a portion—or even all—of their Social Security taxes into approved mutual funds under their control, just as they currently manage their Individual Retirement Accounts (IRAs), in effect, *privatizing* a portion of the Social Security system.[100]

The Clinton approach could be called partial privatization of the Social Security trust fund and, simultaneously, partial nationalization of private companies. This proposal for nationalization—astonishing to some—is put forth at a time when the rest of the world is moving in the opposite direction, privatization. In 1981 Chile was the first country to establish a privatized retirement system, and numerous countries have followed its lead. Australia and Sweden have privatized at least part of their state-run pension systems. Britain over the last two decades shifted primary responsibility for retirement income from government to individuals by requiring forced savings and private investment by employees—privatization by self-service.

Opponents of the Clinton plan fear that government manipulation of purchases and sales of company shares for political purposes will be inevitable, and that government would have an unavoidable and insurmountable conflict of interest. Government-controlled investment invites crony capitalism, state-directed industrial policy, politically correct decisions, and the steering of funds toward well-connected interest groups or corporate contributors, all at the expense of retirees.[101] Moreover, studies show that pension funds managed by political entities, such as those of state employees, earn rates of return that are lower by 1.9 percent to 2.4 percent than funds run by managers who do not face demands to use the funds to support political objectives.[102] Supporters of the Clinton plan who oppose privatization claim that the administrative cost of maintaining individual accounts would be high and therefore retirees would have larger pensions if the government were to invest directly.[103] Others scoff at the notion that government could have low administrative costs. The argument that "government can do it cheaper" was found wanting in chapter

6. The outcome of this historic debate is uncertain, but any change would involve a complex and lengthy transition and substantial transition costs.

Summary

Societal forces are demanding major reforms of education, welfare, and social security. The abysmal state of inner-city schools is driving demands for change, principally the end of government monopolization of schooling paid for by taxes. Choice and competition are the rallying cries for reform. The principal alternatives that allow parental choice are vouchers, tax credits for tuition, tax-free savings accounts, and charter schools. School boards can encourage competition for school-support functions—transportation, food service, and custodial work—by competitive contracting.

The education establishment fiercely opposes these reforms; powerful teacher unions have been called "the principal obstruction to educational reform."[104] But the change in public mood is bolstering the courage of political leaders, who recognize the futility of reforms within the existing monopoly arrangements and the need for structural change.

Long-standing private efforts to help the needy were nationalized, that is, they gave way to government programs whose shortcomings can no longer be hidden behind the shield of good intentions. Welfare reform minimizes government guarantees and substitutes market incentives to get people to work. Privatization of social services is proceeding both by displacement—rediscovering the positive role of private institutions—and by delegation—contracting with nonprofit and for-profit organizations and vouchers. As always in contracting, the challenges are to find qualified bidders, to prepare contract specifications, and to monitor contractor performance. Vouchers are increasingly being used for child day care, home care, and job training.

Social Security reform is in the wind, as other countries turn to market and self-service arrangements to deal with the looming problems of pensions. In the United States the growing debate is between two polar extremes: (1) government purchases of stocks and bonds of private companies—partial nationalization—in order to increase the returns of the Social Security trust fund; and (2) self-managed individual retirement accounts financed by at least a portion of the payroll deductions that at present go to the government—partial privatization of the Social Security system. Opponents deem the former dangerous and the latter costly.

Reforms in education, the welfare state, and Social Security remain as dominant public policy issues at the start of the second millennium.

CHAPTER ELEVEN

Obstacles to Privatization

Privatization is like dismantling a bomb—it must be done *very* carefully,[1] for wrong decisions can have nasty consequences. There are obstacles to be overcome, arguments to be rebutted, proponents to be mobilized, and opponents to be thwarted.

Operational Barriers

Several surveys in the United States inquired about the principal operational barriers to privatization. In 1987 a survey was conducted of city officials in all cities with populations of more than 5,000 and county officials in all counties with populations greater than 25,000; the response rate was 19 percent. The responses differed by type of privatization: contracting, infrastructure development, or asset sales. The greatest impediment to privatization by contracting is the fear of loss of control, which was named by 51 percent of the responding officials. Employee (and union) resistance is second, identified by 47 percent of respondents, and politics is third, named by 42 percent. Politics and loss of control are named most frequently as impediments to infrastructure privatization and to the sale of government assets—each is cited by about 38 percent of the respondents.[2] The labor issue is not as significant in asset sales, because the number of workers affected is relatively small.

A similar survey of U.S. state governments in 1992 drew 158 responses. Loss of control and labor problems are ranked by state officials as the principal impediments to contracting for services, the same as their ranking by local officials. The need for enabling legislation, the fear of loss of control, and the lack of awareness of methods are the main impediments to privatization of infrastructure and to the sale of government assets.[3]

Another survey looked at social services and health services.[4] Contracting is the principal mechanism for privatization of these services;

vouchers are used to a much lesser extent. Labor issues, loss of control, and bureaucratic inertia were identified as the main barriers. In a 216-city study of municipal water and wastewater systems, 94 percent of the respondents reported that labor issues were far and away the largest impediment to public-private partnerships.[5] A sector-specific survey of bus services found that the principal reasons for not contracting were union political pressures and labor contracts and concern about service quality, safety, and reliability.[6]

A consistent pattern emerges from these studies: with respect to contracting, the major stumbling blocks are labor issues and loss of control. I would place the labor issue firmly in first place (although it is not a major problem in small towns[7]). My own more recent observations lead me to believe that the fear of loss of control has subsided as more knowledge and experience have been gained and publicized. For example, Mayor Stephen Goldsmith of Indianapolis (quoted later in this chapter) asserts that he has much more control over contractors than he ever had over his own, in-house workforce; he can fire a contractor for poor performance but cannot do much with or to a malfunctioning city department. This increased control is gained because governments have to write careful specifications for contracts, which they rarely do when the work is routinely done in-house, and because the legendary rigidity of civil service systems, reinforced by union contracts, limits an official's managerial authority.

Legislative Barriers

These surveys focus on operational barriers, but among the greatest obstacles are legislative barriers. Some countries are saddled with constitutional requirements that protect GOEs and seem to prevent their privatization unless the constitution is amended. In the United States various legislative obstacles impede privatization. State laws can prohibit negotiated bids and limit the length of contracts; the latter provision thwarts long-term contracts for infrastructure projects. Other states have laws that prohibit contracting with private firms for certain social services and ban for-profit hospitals.

Under federal law, municipal bonds are tax exempt but private bonds issued for the same purpose are not, for example, bonds for water supply and wastewater treatment plants and for transportation projects such as roads, tunnels, and bridges. Grants given by the federal government to localities for infrastructure projects have required that state and local governments return any undepreciated portions of the grants to the federal government; this makes privatization of such facilities more expensive and effectively has blocked contracting with private firms for maintenance and operation.

Other federal regulations inhibit private investment—for example, by prohibiting tolls on most interstate highways. Without tolls, there is no way that investors can raise funds for such undertakings. Tax policies that subsidize government-owned enterprises but not private companies in the same business prevent fair competition and make government agencies appear more efficient than they really are. The cost of solid-waste management services in cities is deductible if paid for by property taxes but not if paid directly to private waste-management companies by homeowners. Federal laws make bus privatization almost impossible because of the infamous clause 12(c) in the Urban Mass Transportation Act, which requires public bus agencies to continue paying bus drivers for six years if they lose their jobs due to privatization.

These obstacles interfere with the privatization of infrastructure, which is otherwise attractive to state and local governments as a means of reducing their operating costs while receiving a one-time cash windfall that they can use to reduce their debt burden or finance other needed long-term projects. Moreover, infrastructure privatization can put formerly government-owned property on local tax rolls, leading to an ongoing stream of tax revenues. Besides stifling new investment in infrastructure and reducing operating costs of existing facilities, these legislative barriers force state and local governments to forgo about $3 billion annually in property tax revenues, and the federal government itself loses up to $7.7 billion annually in corporate income tax receipts.[8]

Sources of Opposition

Practical political leaders who initiate privatization programs in order to overcome the problems and achieve the benefits identified in chapter 6 encounter only four sources of opposition—to put it whimsically: workers, public officials, business interests, and the general public.

Opposition by Workers

My experiences with contracting and divestment in forty-seven countries are that labor redundancy and the concern about jobs are by far the principal impediments. Workers understandably feel threatened by privatization, just as they are apprehensive about other major changes in the workplace. They are concerned about job losses, lower wages, fewer benefits, a changed work environment, bigger workloads, moving to a new location, different schedules, new bosses, and so on. Almost invariably they oppose privatization, at least initially. In the United States, the American Federation of State, County, and Municipal Employees (AFSCME), the nation's largest public-employee union with 1.3 million members, raised its dues by $7 million a year primarily to fight privatization.[9]

Robert Kuttner asserts that privatization results in lower wages and reduced benefits.[10] He is mistaken. The principal reason why privatization leads to increased efficiency is not lower wages and benefits but greater productivity, that is, fewer workers needed to do the same amount of work, as was illustrated in chapters 6 and 7 and is further demonstrated in the next section and later in this chapter with respect to the Indianapolis experience. Indeed, buyers of divested GOEs and contractors find it profitable to provide more training for their workers and can afford to pay them more, precisely because such workers are more productive. The *total* bill for wages and benefits declines, but only because there are fewer workers, not because each one gets less.

Redundant labor.   Policymakers the world over recognize redundancy in government agencies and GOEs as a self-evident fact of life and a thorny issue that must be dealt with. Redundancy was inevitable when government hired workers for make-work activities to "create jobs" or took over failing private concerns "in order to save jobs." Long-standing paternalistic and patronage policies toward public employment became rooted in the culture and now frustrate newly elected, change-oriented leaders. This is the single greatest problem in implementing privatization.

There is overwhelming evidence from scores of countries that government agencies and enterprises in general are seriously overstaffed. Tables 6.8 and 6.9 (pp. 159, 162) in chapter 6 show that public- and private-sector productivity rates in solid-waste management services in the United States differ by factors of 2.5 and 2.8 respectively; that is, the public agencies required 2.5 and 2.8 times as many workers to do the same amount of work. A wastewater treatment plant in Indianapolis, after maintenance and operation was contracted out, needed fewer than half the number of employees yet achieved better operating performance.[11] After privatization, a steel mill in Togo needed only one-sixth as many workers per ton of steel produced. The private firm that is paying the Argentine government $102 million annually for twenty years to take over and operate the postal system as a concession knows that it can reduce personnel and costs drastically: under government operation the system delivers 18,000 pieces of mail annually per employee, compared to 225,000 in the U.S. Postal Service, which is not often hailed as a paragon of productivity.[12] The Buenos Aires water system had eight employees per thousand connections whereas efficient systems have two to three;[13] privatization by franchise led to layoffs of more than half the employees.[14] Similarly, the privatized Argentine railroad system required only 780 employees instead of 3,000 for the same freight volume.[15] The Chile Telecommunications Company was privatized and the number of employees per 1,000 lines, a standard measure of productivity in that industry, declined from 13.7 to 6.2 within four years.[16]

A careful study in the United Kingdom concluded that privatization led to large-scale labor shedding as enterprises changed their objectives and became more profit oriented. The fourteen large SOEs that were examined had been overstaffed by a third, on average, and therefore employment was reduced by a quarter after privatization. The remaining workers were successful in maintaining their wages relative to other groups, however, except where the market power of the company was reduced as a result of deregulation and liberalization.[17]

Even when workers can benefit directly from increased productivity, their union may object. In 1992 the town of Arlington, Massachusetts, wanted to reduce personnel and change from three-man to two-man trucks for refuse collection, with the savings to be shared with the unionized employees. Redundant workers were to be shed by attrition and early retirement. The workers were willing to go along with this, but the union at the state and national levels refused to allow it. In the end, the town contracted out the service and all the workers lost their city jobs.[18]

It is not unusual to find that privatization is good for unionized workers but bad for their union leaders. The workers may be guaranteed jobs with the private contractor, join a (different) union, and be better off in terms of wages and promotion opportunities, but labor leaders see a loss of membership in their union and a loss of dues.

Government inefficiency as a full-employment program. Many people apparently believe that inefficiency in government constitutes a full-employment program; at least they act on this belief. In every developing country I have visited on privatization matters, I have heard the same argument: "Yes, we know that the agency (or GOE) is very inefficient, and the work can be done with far fewer workers, but they need the work; what would they do if they were to lose these jobs?"

The short-sightedness of this reasoning struck me when, as a consultant to the World Bank, I found myself in the middle of a debate between two different groups. The issue concerned a Bank-financed road construction project in a poor Central American country—building a simple gravel road into the interior. The transportation group in the Bank wanted to force the country to privatize the work because under the national public works agency the funds were being squandered and progress was abysmally slow. "For every one shovel they had five workers," they complained. Another unit in the Bank agreed with the numbers but argued that this was a poor country, people needed work, and therefore it was acceptable to treat the project as partly a welfare program. "Wait a minute," I interrupted, "What's the better route to economic development and prosperity in this poor country—building one kilometer or building five kilometers of road for the same amount of money?" Clearly, the country would benefit by linking the rural agricultural areas with the cities by this road. Development was being hindered by this seemingly kind but fundamentally pernicious policy. Inefficiency is the route to impoverishment, not development. Rich countries may be able to afford inefficient and ineffective government services, but they, too, are wasting resources that could be put to better use by society.

If putting unneeded workers on the public payroll is an inescapable political necessity, at least the redundant workers should be assigned to do more work, giving the public more for its money. For example, if streets are being swept once a week, they should be swept twice a week, or daily, or maybe even continuously. And the work should be real, so as not to create a culture that cannot distinguish make-work from productive activity.

Because redundancy is so common, so great, and so well known, workers facing the prospect of privatization have two fears: some are afraid they will have no work, while others are afraid they will have to work. The result, unsurprisingly, is strong opposition led by employee unions. Privatization is not anti-union, however. Private contractors' employees are themselves often unionized, and so from the overall perspective of the union movement, the losses of some union leaders are balanced by the gains of others.

Legal challenges. Lawsuits aimed at blocking contracts on the grounds that they violate civil service statutes have been rejected in numerous court cases. Other legal challenges are possible, based on labor contracts or on myriad other grounds. Labor agreements handle contracting in several different ways: (1) by not mentioning it and assuming it to be an inherent right of management; (2) by explicitly mentioning it as a management right; (3) by mentioning it as a management right with certain restrictions, typically, that no layoffs occur; or (4) by prohibiting it.[19]

In India the unions offered the interesting argument that the state-owned scooter-manufacturing company was losing money because of gross mismanagement, bad government policies, and the government's failure to invest sufficient capital, particularly in technology. They demanded more government intervention, not less, and succeeded in getting all the major opposition parties in the Upper House of the Indian Parliament to walk out, protesting that privatization was "only a first step in handing over sick public sector units to the private sector."[20]

Bureaucratic barriers.   Public employee unions and their allies sometimes try to impose cumbersome bureaucratic barriers in the contracting process to discourage managers from undertaking the effort, for example, calling for the creation of a central agency to oversee all proposed contracts and the preparation of social-impact statements for each proposal.[21] In 1993, after a new governor had initiated thirty-six privatization efforts in two-and-a-half years that saved an estimated $273 million, the Massachusetts legislature passed an antiprivatization law over the governor's veto. On the face of it the law seemed innocent enough, and even a sign of good government, calling for cost-benefit analysis to document expected savings from proposed privatizations. The actual intention, however, was

> to protect state jobs by erecting unscalable procedural barriers to privatization. The law requires that bids by private providers be compared not with the current cost of delivering a service, but the cost if state employees were to work "in the most cost-efficient manner." Private bidders must provide their employees with both wages and benefit plans that match those of the state employees who would perform the work. Each quarter, a company must satisfy three separate state agencies that they have met this requirement. At the end of the process, a final adjustment is made. The agency must add lost tax revenues to the private sector bids if any part of the work is to be performed outside Massachusetts. Conversely, no addition is made to the estimated cost of foregone tax revenue. A private company would be taxed by the state on the revenue earned, while public agencies pay no taxes on amounts they are allocated in the state's budget. Even if a proposal scales these barriers, the State Auditor could strike it down for reasons as ambiguous as not being "in the public interest."[22]

This mischievous law essentially prevents privatization. The New York City Council passed an ordinance that had a similar effect, establishing an impossible bureaucratic gauntlet.[23] Another New York ordinance calls for "a living wage," arbitrarily requiring some city contractors to pay double the minimum wage.[24] No wonder that contractors no longer bother bidding some jobs. Baltimore and Los Angeles also passed "living wage" laws, and Massachusetts, New York, and Pittsburgh have each given veto power over privatization to another official after the chief executives' vetoes were overridden in each case. "Proven savings" and mandated benefits to be paid by contractors have also been erected as barriers.[25]

Gaining worker support.   In fact, workers can become supporters of privatization. If their jobs are reasonably secure, promotions are possible, working conditions are attractive, the private company plans to invest in the activity, and workers can gain public respect instead of being the butt of complaints, workers may drop their initial opposition and endorse the process. Many approaches have been utilized throughout the world to establish employee adjustment plans that address legitimate concerns of the affected workers and overcome their opposition. Among them are the following:

1. *Allowing competition* between the in-house workforce and outside contractors is inherently fair and gains public support; from the union perspective a decision to have managed competition is far better than a decision to privatize (see chapter 7).

2. *Attrition* can solve the problem if privatization can be partial instead of total. This is often the case with services, such as solid-waste collection and bus operations, where a few routes at a time can be contracted out at a rate lower than the normal rate of attrition, which is generally in the range of 5 to 8 percent per year. Contracting out fewer routes than that every year allows workers to be reassigned to different routes so that no one loses a job. This approach is applicable to a wide array of maintenance and other services.

3. *"Banking" openings and absorbing workers* is a possible strategy. When a privatization is planned, the government can impose a broad hiring freeze, *"banking" normal vacancies* as they occur in agencies where the affected workers could be placed; for example, workers in street repair crews could be assigned to work in parks, sanitation, or water departments.

When the privatization takes place, redundant workers are transferred to fill the banked vacancies. In the interim, any necessary work is performed by temporary workers or by regular workers on overtime.

4. *Hiring by the contractor or buyer* can be required. A condition of the sale or contracting agreement can be that the winning bidder must hire a certain number (or all) of the affected employees. Of course this means that the sale price will be lower or the contract price higher than it would be without this requirement. A major study of the issue by the National Commission on Employment in 1989 found that 93 percent of affected employees were satisfactorily taken care of through one or the other of these methods and only 7 percent lost their jobs as a result of privatization.[26]

5. *"Leasing" employees* is another option. The workers remain on the government payroll as employees but they work for the private firm, which reimburses the agency for their salaries and fringe benefits. This approach might be utilized for older workers who are close to retirement and would otherwise lose their pension benefits, but problems of supervision may arise. The firm would have the right to return unsatisfactory workers to the government agency.

6. *By hiring with a "put" option,* the private firm can agree to hire the workers for a fixed period, perhaps six months, but have the right to terminate workers after that time. Rejected workers can return to the government, where by this time more attrition will have occurred and openings will be available for them.

7. *The right of first refusal* may be given to affected workers. The successful contractor or buyer will hire only as many workers as he wishes but must first give affected employees the opportunity to fill the available openings.

8. *First choice in rehiring* is another solution, whereby workers laid off due to the privatization are the first ones to be called back when openings arise, as they inevitably do.

9. *Preserving pensions* may be a viable option. For the sake of continuity, a private contractor wanted current employees to stay when it took over a prison in Washington, D.C., but those who had eighteen years of service did not want to leave

city employment because in two more years they would qualify for a significantly increased pension upon retirement. The contractor hired and purchased annuities for each of these workers so that, together with the pension represented by the vested rights, the workers were guaranteed a pension equivalent to the one they would have gotten had they remained city employees.

10. *Retraining programs,* based on expertise, ability, education, and ambition, could be used to prepare redundant workers for new job opportunities. The workers can look forward to continued employment and better prospects in a different area.

11. A *social safety net*—severance pay, early retirement benefits, unemployment insurance—can be provided to workers who depart voluntarily. Lesser amounts can be given to those who do not accept the initial offer but are subsequently laid off. In Tunisia, 90 percent of the redundant employees accepted the severance package and only 10 percent were laid off.[27] The money for these payments may come from the proceeds of divestment, but if these are not enough to pay for overly generous commitments made rashly in the heat of political battle, an entire privatization program can stall, as in Ghana, where 22,000 redundant employees remained on the government payroll and no private buyers were willing to bid for those enterprises.[28]

12. *Outplacement assistance* in the form of retraining, information about job openings, assistance in job searches and, resume writing, information on benefits, and so on can be provided either by the government or by the contractor/buyer if required in the privatization agreement. Again, placing this responsibility on the private firm makes the transaction less attractive to the private sector. Table 11.1 shows the experience of Indianapolis after it contracted out the operation and maintenance of its wastewater treatment plants. Despite starting out with twice as many workers as were necessary, the contractor had successfully accounted for all the workers within eight months after privatization.

13. *Better job opportunities* are possible for workers who choose to leave the security of a government job and go to work for the private contractor or buyer after privatization. When the container terminal at Port Klang in Malaysia was privatized,

TABLE 11.1—WHAT HAPPENED TO WORKERS AFTER PRIVATIZATION OF WASTEWATER TREATMENT PLANTS IN INDIANAPOLIS?

Number of employees before privatization	322
Retired	5
Found jobs elsewhere on their own	10
Hired by contractor and used in plant	170
Hired by contractor and used elsewhere	27
Filled "banked" vacancies in city agencies	67
Outplaced after assistance by contractor[a]	43
Total number accounted for	322
Number of employees after privatization[b]	176

[a]Completed within eight months after privatization.

[b]Including six managerial employees brought in from outside.

Source: Derived from city reports.

99 percent of the 800 workers chose to work for the new private company instead of exercising their option either to stay at the Port Authority with no loss of pay or benefits, or to take a generous, lump-sum severance or early-retirement package.[29] In the United States this is most evident in water and wastewater privatization where a municipal employee is generally stuck in a real backwater department and has little opportunity to advance to a better job; private firms in this business have more plants and offer many more opportunities for advancement than even the largest city. Research shows that outsourced public technology workers end up on better career paths, make more money, and are happier in their private-sector jobs.[30]

14. *More workers may be hired* if a divested GOE is in a growth industry such as telecommunications. Although the government-owned telephone company in Chile had twice as many workers as were needed (based on international productivity standards in the industry), the demand for more telephone lines led to a rapid doubling of the number after privatization and consequently no workers were laid off; the excess workers were retrained and gradually absorbed. This was a requirement in the sale contract and resulted in a sales price lower than it would have been had the buyer been allowed to scale down the number of workers, but the government deemed this

a reasonable course of action that avoided powerful opposition to the privatization.[31] A similar policy was followed in Mexico with respect to Telmex, the national telecommunications company, which had 15,000 redundant workers; they were also absorbed during the rapid expansion called for in the sale agreement.[32]

More workers are also hired if the buyer invests in the enterprise and dynamic expansion occurs. A comparison of sixty-one enterprises before and after privatization showed an average increase of 6 percent in the number of employees, with increases in two-thirds of the companies and reductions in only one-third. This was due to a 45 percent increase in investment.[33] Increases in company employment after privatization are realized in both developed and developing countries: employment increased in the British Airports Authority and in a moribund textile firm in Niger; in the Mexican auto parts industry, employment rose by 30 percent following privatization.[34] Broadly speaking, jobs will be created in an economy revitalized by privatization, liberalization, and deregulation.

15. *Employee ownership* to one degree or another is a common approach to gaining worker support for divestment. One method is to give (or sell at a discount) 3 to 20 percent of the shares to employees. Another is an employee stock ownership plan (ESOP), a technique for allowing the employees to buy the company by gradually paying for the shares, which are being held in escrow for them; favorable tax laws are needed to facilitate this. Still another approach is to encourage current employees to form their own company, which initially is awarded a contract on a noncompetitive basis, although subsequent awards would be strictly competitive. Legislation may be needed to allow such a process. The State of Virginia studied the possibility of privatizing state functions through ESOPs; it found no impediments, and it now recommends this as a good approach.[35]

16. *Entrepreneurship programs* could screen workers for entrepreneurship potential, help develop suitable business opportunities, and provide basic training in business skills. Special arrangements could be made to use severance pay to enable workers to start their own small businesses. In Mali, modest

grants—a few hundred dollars each—were given to redundant workers who submitted winning proposals in a competition.

17. *Tax-free earnings in a new job* is the incentive in Romania and Turkey to encourage workers to find new jobs quickly if they are laid off because of privatization. When a worker loses a job because of privatization, he or she gets severance pay of six months' wages, and any subsequent earnings for two years are tax free. This is a great stimulus to get another job quickly and far better than the U.S. system of unemployment insurance, which provides a fixed stipend for several months. Studies show that people receiving such payments in the United States tend to find jobs disproportionately during their final month of eligibility, whereas the system in Romania and Turkey promotes immediate searches for jobs.

18. *Other support mechanisms* can be found in all societies. That is, officials need not fear that layoffs from government jobs will automatically result in people starving in the streets. Many workers have second jobs in the informal economy, and help is generally available from immediate or extended families, tribes, clans (in Polynesia), and charitable organizations.

19. *Liquidation* may be the only alternative to privatization. This inescapable fact is the ultimate trump card in the debate to overcome worker opposition.

Opposition by Public Officials and Bureaucrats

Despite high-level support for privatization, some officials see their empires threatened, power waning, status dropping, patronage opportunities dwindling, and perquisites of office disappearing. Officials who are chairmen of state enterprises as well as heads of government agencies may have airplanes at their disposal and not merely chauffeured limousines. In one country I was told of an official heading an agency who was also chairman of several GOEs, with a mistress ensconced in each. Such influential positions also attract monetary emoluments (i.e., bribes). In Thailand, strong opposition to privatization came from the military, because its control over GOEs meant that high-ranking officers could look forward to well-paid positions after retirement.[36] It is not surprising to find hidden opposition by high officials to official privatization policies.

Bureaucrats see their roles eliminated and often struggle to keep up with changed policies that they do not understand, so different are they from the experiences of a lifetime. People resist change. ("Only wet babies are in favor of change.") Sometimes the barriers put up by bureaucrats are comical. A consultant hired by a U.S. federal agency to sell its underutilized real-estate assets could not get the property appraisals from the agency until he filed a request under the Freedom of Information Act![37]

Middle managers have many legitimate concerns that cannot be dismissed. Civilian managers in the federal government who face closing of military bases or other federal facilities are understandably reluctant to end their careers or diminish their responsibilities without being able to envision an alternative future. They need answers to questions about the reality of employee stock-ownership plans, pensions, and training for other government positions, for example. The poor portability of the civil service retirement system is a significant obstacle; rules should be changed to allow early retirement without penalty for those over 55 years of age who are affected by privatization. Many of the privatization opportunities exist in facilities, laboratories, and programs of the Defense and Energy Departments that are impacted by national security issues such as access to intellectual property, equipment, and expertise. These complications need to be reviewed and addressed expeditiously.[38]

But the picture is far from bleak. Management ranks in government also produce stars who champion privatization, succeed at it, and may go on to lucrative consulting careers. Privatization can provide job enrichment for public-sector managers, effectively promoting someone into a position where she handles make-or-buy decisions, like the automobile executive who has to decide whether to manufacture windshield-wiper motors or buy them.

One scholar explored why it was possible to privatize city services and reduce the number of patronage workers in Chicago, a city legendary for its patronage politics. He attributed the results to three changes in the political environment: (1) Campaigning now requires large amounts of money, not large amounts of labor, which in the days of machine politics was supplied by patronage employees. (2) Changing demographics resulted in a decrease in the proportion of the population consisting of ethnic groups that in the past were employed in great numbers by the city. (3) The city's financial problems required the mayor to find more efficient ways to deliver services, hence, to privatize.[39]

Opposition by Business Interests

In some countries the first thing that has to be privatized is the private sector! Some firms are accustomed to easy profits and state subsidies in markets protected by the government, and they may demand a free market in public but then lobby in private to maintain their privileges.[40]

Some private companies are perfectly happy with the GOEs and want them preserved. They may have very profitable relations with a GOE to which they sell goods or services at high prices, or from which they buy goods or services at low prices. The last thing they want is a change in these cozy arrangements because of new management in these entities and a competitive marketplace. In Pakistan, private firms in the polyester and cooking oil businesses were pleased to have GOEs in the same fields because the GOEs were inefficient and charged high prices for their products, thereby establishing a price umbrella under which the more efficient private competitors could make huge profits while still charging less than the GOEs. Divestment of these GOEs led to greater competition and lower profits.

In general, however, many elements in the private sector support and advocate privatization in order to promote economic development, reduce government expenditures, and encourage greater efficiency.

Opposition by the Public

The public may oppose privatization if its members fear that prices will rise or that they will have to pay for services that were "free." This is particularly true of basic commodities such as water, fuel, and electricity. Political opponents of privatization can play upon these fears. Privatization programs have been harmed if an early divestment leads to a rise in the price of a GOE's goods or services; this may happen if at the same time the government seizes this opportunity to stop subsidizing that enterprise. To the public these simultaneous acts make it seem that privatization is bad and rapacious capitalists are exploiting the people. Once again it must be stressed that privatization does not necessarily mean market prices for all: vouchers, contracts, and other forms of consumer subsidies can be employed if desired.

In contrast, good-government groups and taxpayer organizations can generally be counted on to support prudent privatization, and so will ordinary citizens who feel victimized by an unresponsive and ineffective bureaucracy. Proponents of privatization will seek out these groups and enlist their backing.

Opposition Tactics

Opposition tactics range from inertia to violence and assassination. Among the tactics I have seen are delaying action in the hope that a new government will abandon privatization plans; extracting campaign promises from candidates that they will not privatize; testifying at public hearings to oppose privatization plans; waging anti-privatization campaigns on radio and television and in newspapers; advertising against privatization on billboards; negotiating anticontracting clauses into labor agreements; bringing lawsuits to block privatization; lobbying compliant legislatures for laws that create procedural thickets that effectively bar privatization; conducting public demonstrations; calling sickouts and strikes; and hurling accusations of corruption. Committed ideologues have planted bombs and sabotaged telephone cables in Puerto Rico, bombed privatized companies in Peru,[41] telephoned threats at all hours to a Mexican official and his family,[42] issued a death threat to a Greek government official in charge of privatization,[43] and assassinated Detlef Rohwedder, the director of Treuhandanstalt, the German government agency administering the privatization program in East Germany in 1991.

Opposition Arguments and Rebuttals

Would-be privatizers must deal with a number of common opposition arguments and find workable solutions to carry out their programs. These obstacles, sources of opposition, and principal arguments are listed here and discussed in turn. Some of them apply to divestment, some to delegation (primarily contracting out), and others to both.

Ideology

Some people believe that government is morally superior to the private sector and instinctively oppose privatization. Others, adherents to a failed economic philosophy, continue to tend the dying flame of socialism despite its universal collapse. Crypto-socialists instinctively abhor privatization and are unremittingly suspicious of the private sector; with reflexive antipathy toward markets and visceral opposition to capitalism, they fan public hostility toward successful entrepreneurs and recognize market forces only as an evil to be subdued.

To a misguided few, the very word *privatize* summons forth images from emotional depths and causes misunderstanding and polarization.

Numerous public officials throughout the world have told me, in frustration, that they wished another word could be found. For that reason I started using the term *alternative service delivery* for municipal government audiences in the United States as a circumlocution to avoid using *privatization*.[44] More recently, to newly elected governors and mayors in the United States, I recommended avoidance of the word and substitution of the phrase "introducing competition in the delivery of public services," admittedly a mouthful. A linguistic outgrowth of this concept is *managed competition*. The euphemism *productivity enhancement* was employed early in the Reagan administration to minimize reflexive employee opposition. Because the word may conjure up an old image of a small, ruling elite and a large lower class, less controversial terms have been artfully chosen by political leaders: de-statization in Greece (this awkward English word is more euphonious in Greek), socialist privatization in Spain, renewal in Hungary, people-ization in Sri Lanka, people's capitalism in Latin America, renovation in Vietnam, and economic reform in China, which gave way in 1997 to share ownership system, meaning individual share ownership.

Some tend to read into privatization a plot to establish a completely free market, with overtones of dog-eat-dog, survival of the fittest, and culling of the weakest. Others interpret the word as an attack on government, government programs, and direct beneficiaries of government programs, including employees; therefore they defend these interests by attacking privatization. Still others are provoked by the term because they see it as an attack on the ideals they cherish: *public* to them denotes brotherhood, sharing, caring, and community, and they interpret *private* to mean abandoning these vital values.

But privatization can be profoundly compassionate and humane. Vouchers, for example, can provide more benefits, greater dignity, more choice, and a greater sense of personal responsibility than government programs. Indeed, the legitimate societal aspirations once thought attainable only by big government have proven illusory but may be achievable by smaller but better government, through privatization. Besides, the societal savings achieved through privatization can be applied to the very ends desired by the advocates for the needy—albeit by very different means.

Here is a fundamental paradox: privatization as a *means* can be employed effectively even by the welfare state, but privatization as an end is inimical to the welfare state. Thus, even socialist governments (e.g., the USSR and China in the 1980s) turned to privatization in a last, pragmatic effort to salvage their economies; but to anachronistic socialists who continue to exalt the role of the state, privatization remains an evil.

This same paradox also explains why some proponents of privatization differ from and even berate other proponents: Libertarians who believe in much less government want to encourage only market, voluntary, and self-service arrangements and often challenge privatizers who also advocate contract, voucher, and franchise arrangements, which involve a substantial role for government. To the former, only the withdrawal of government and the sale of government assets count as real privatization; contracting hardly merits inclusion within the same concept. (Some of my earlier writings were occasionally attacked from this quarter for this reason.)

Loss of Control

The surveys cited previously reveal that officials fear that they will lose control if they privatize. With contracting, however, even greater control is achievable. When public officials contract for services they have to specify desired results, monitor performance, and impose penalties if necessary; this is more than they typically do with their in-house work. Contractors can perform poorly, of course, but so can government agencies.

Mayor Goldsmith of Indianapolis, who has privatized scores of services, has this to say on the subject:

> Because privatization means many things, it is easy for adversaries
> to threaten the public with "loss of control," presumably suggesting
> that vendors will not be responsive to the public. The truth is that
> we possess many more tools to control the quality and price of a
> private contractor or winning public employees than we do those
> employees acting in a typical government bureaucracy. As a result
> of the bidding procedure, we can impose fines for poor quality or
> missed deadlines, more easily reward performance, and if necessary
> simply cancel the contract rather than navigate the excruciating pro-
> cedures required to actually fire a civil service employee. In each of
> our competitive initiatives, the city retained and even enhanced its
> control over services. In all too many American cities, mayors and
> city managers operating in monopolistic governments have very
> little control. Competition and marketization dramatically increased
> government control by giving policymakers more tools for putting

their policies into effect and better yardsticks for measuring performance. The only control politicians lose is the ability to hire workers on the basis of patronage instead of productivity.[45]

Furthermore, a government agency is not automatically under effective government control. For example, the government-sponsored Tennessee Valley Authority has been defying air pollution control standards of environmental control agencies,[46] and was accused of filing a misleading report to the Nuclear Regulatory Commission about an accident at one of its nuclear generating plants.[47] Another example of a government agency out of control is provided by two frustrated representatives: exasperated by evidence that the U.S. Postal Service practiced deceptive advertising with respect to its airmail and special delivery services, and calling it fraud, they called for an investigation, but the Federal Trade Commission declined because it cannot investigate another government agency.[48]

A telling Cold War experience provides yet another illustration of the "loss of control" fallacy. Soviet submarines had a serious weakness in that they had noisy propellers and could be tracked easily by underwater listening devices, while American submarines had comparatively silent propellers because they were designed by computer and produced by numerically controlled machine tools. By agreement among the NATO countries, it was forbidden to sell this technology to the Soviet Union. Nevertheless, the latter was able to buy the equipment and technology, partly from a Japanese electronics firm, Toshiba, and partly from a Norwegian firm, Koningsberg Vaapenfabrik. *The Norwegian firm was a government-owned enterprise!* It violated the nation's security laws while Norway was being plagued by repeated incursions into its national waters by Soviet submarines; the state had lost control of its own agency.

In some countries, those who hope to advance their social goals want GOEs to occupy "the commanding heights of the economy," thus serving as ideal instruments for their purposes. Government control of these sectors, it is thought, can be used to stimulate growth and economic development and influence prices and wages.[49] Despite repeated disappointments, this policy illusion—reflected in continued control of basic industries—is particularly pervasive in developing countries, especially those with a colonial past, but I observe a waning of this failed practice. Note the irony: given the worldwide evidence of the poor performance of GOEs, the "commanding heights" policy means that bad management is reserved for a nation's most important industries. Upon close examination, the "loss of control" argument often means merely loss of patronage, loss of power, and loss of budgetary empire.

Nationalism

A common argument raised against privatization is based on nationalism, and it arises in various guises. One is national security, the last refuge of antiprivatization forces. I encountered this tactic in Israel when officials opposed to the privatization of El Al, the state-owned airline, argued that it was needed for national defense. I suggested that the Israeli air force, not the commercial airline, was needed for national defense, but if the airline pilots were cross-trained to fly fighters and were needed, they could be mobilized at once. The best defense is a strong economy, and privatization can strengthen an economy. Ten years later, El Al was privatized.[50]

Closely related is the argument that foreigners will buy the national patrimony, the family jewels. A list of the family jewels, however, usually includes ordinary businesses, often moribund and losing money. The nation would be lucky if it were able to find a buyer, foreign or domestic, for these so-called jewels.

A more serious objection, particularly in developing countries that were once colonies of foreign powers, is the fear of foreign domination, namely, that foreign firms will buy crucial government-owned enterprises and thereby be able to exercise strategic control and diminish the hard-won national autonomy. Privatization of telecommunications, water, electricity, and ports poses the greatest threats and raises the strongest fears. Foreign participation, however, is generally desirable because it can bring capital, experienced management, technical knowledge, and access to new markets. It is therefore sensible to facilitate foreign participation in privatization[51] while allaying these legitimate fears by requiring majority ownership by nationals ("indigenization"), and retaining the government's right (through a "golden share"), after privatization, to veto a subsequent sale to a foreign entity. Consortiums of foreign and domestic firms can usually be organized to satisfy these requirements. It is useful to recall that the United States, too, was once an underdeveloped country, and foreign capital—notably from its former colonial ruler, England—played a significant role in its development.

Minority Domination

In some countries privatization is stymied or slowed because the dominant population group fears the economic prowess of a minority group in the country, even though the latter may consist of native-born citizens. This has been the case in Malaysia, where the official policy has been to favor the majority Bumiputra population over the ethnic Chinese.[52] In East Africa privatization has been slow because the government reflects the fears of the black majority that the relatively prosperous citizens of South Asian ancestry will be the principal buyers of GOEs.

Discrimination cannot be condoned and it results in economic harm, for it deprives a country of the full utilization of all its citizens, squanders talent, and wastes productive resources. Discrimination on grounds of race, color, creed, sex, or national origin is not good for economic development.

Shortage of Capital and Weak Capital Markets

It is sometimes argued that privatization cannot be carried out because nationals lack the capital to participate effectively and therefore foreign or minority domination would be inevitable. But often capital is available in the hands of expatriates, or hidden as "mattress money," or banked safely abroad. Rather than a shortage of capital, there is a shortage of confidence in the government or in the privatization process, manifested in a lack of interest or demand for shares. By following proper, transparent policies and establishing investor-friendly market policies, the government can overcome the skepticism of its own people and encourage them to invest in their homeland. When new leaders in Mexico and Argentina in the early 1990s initiated major reforms and transformed their economies, money came pouring in from the overseas bank accounts of their citizens.

Even primitive capital markets can be used to carry out the sale of shares to the public, if the public trusts the government. The Commercial Bank of Jamaica was successfully privatized by public offering of shares although the Kingston Stock Exchange was open only two afternoons a week for two hours each time and daily turnover averaged only $30,000.[53] Privatization is fostering the growth of capital markets throughout the world.[54]

Profitability

"Why should we sell it, it's making money?" This logic is frequently trumpeted as a reason to hold on to a GOE, but it is a poor one. In the first place, the enterprise may not continue making money; a gradual slide into the red is more likely than not, so it may be advisable to sell it now while it can still fetch a good price. Second, inasmuch as the private sector is able to obtain a greater return than the government for a given set of assets (see chapter 6), the enterprise is worth more to the private sector than to the state (i.e., the net present value is greater). Therefore the state will be richer if it sells it than if it keeps it.

"Government can do it cheaper because it doesn't make a profit." This remark was uttered by a former Speaker of the U.S. House of Representatives, "Tip" O'Neill.[55] Chapter 6 summarizes the evidence to the contrary. (Someone exhibiting this degree of economic ignorance should not be allowed to vote, I believe, much less hold public office!)

The desire to tax and regulate the profits of private enterprises can smother privatization and development in their infancy. Rondinelli notes that private firms in post-socialist countries pay huge taxes and must also make large payments for social services. In the Czech Republic, for example, there is a turnover tax of 22 percent on businesses that sell goods and a tax on profits that ranges from 15 to 55 percent; in addition, there is a 30 percent tax on many export goods.[56] Such confiscatory practices deter would-be buyers of GOEs. Economic instability and uncertainty, unchecked inflation, and political instability all serve to keep buyers and investors away, thus thwarting privatization. Policies favorable to the development of private enterprises are needed.

Concentration of Wealth

Privatization is opposed in some countries because it is feared that the same few, rich families will become even richer. "Familization" it has been called, derisively. Ramanadham cites disturbing statistics about the concentration of wealth in Pakistan and Sri Lanka.[57] Prime Minister Margaret Thatcher's privatization program in Britain avoided this problem by limiting the number of shares per buyer and promoting purchases by workers and all members of the public. This is more difficult to do in a developing country or in a country such as Albania, where two generations of isolation from a market economy have left the public confused and unable to make sound investment judgments.

Private Monopolies and the Lack of Competition

As discussed in prior chapters, vigilance is needed to guard against the creation of uncontrolled private monopolies via privatization. A public monopoly might merely be transformed into a private one that can exploit the public. Opponents will quite properly seize upon this shortcoming and demand that it be addressed before privatization can proceed. Although, as noted previously, private monopolies may be easier to control than public ones, it is nevertheless a bad idea to privatize a monopolistic GOE without restructuring the industry to create a more competitive climate, passing appropriate and effective anti-monopoly legislation, promulgating suitable regulations to be in effect from the outset, and establishing a regulatory body with enforcement powers and the capability to exercise them.

With respect to contracting, Donald Kettl cautions that competition may not be easy to promote, particularly in small jurisdictions, and that it requires effort to sustain. He reports that almost a tenth of the jurisdictions in a survey said they had difficulty finding enough contractors.[58] This means that even though enough contractors can be found in more than 90 percent of jurisdictions, privatization may not be applicable or appropriate in some cases, a valid point stressed also in chapter 7. Every contemplated privatization must be treated as a unique case and not a foregone conclusion.

Kettl further warns that competition's capacity to reduce the size of government and increase efficiency is exaggerated, for three reasons: (1) the goods and services that government buys are highly specialized and the markets for them are imperfect; (2) the transactions are riddled with uncertainty, making competitive procurement an elusive concept; and (3) the endemic nature of the principal-agent problem.[59] He acknowledges, however, that in the final analysis competition works: contracting out saves money, and suppliers who fail to meet the buyer's expectations can be replaced.[60]

Corruption

Corruption can occur at the boundary between the public and private sectors, and in some places corruption is so widespread and deeply ingrained that the public is hostile to the idea of privatization, assuming with good reason that well-placed officials and wealthy families will use it to line their pockets.

People instinctively feel that it is better to keep GOEs in the hands of the government even though they are losing money than to sell them for a song to favored buyers even if this stops the drain of public funds; "crony capitalism," it has been called. Some developing countries are in this unfortunate situation, as are some post-socialist countries. In one developing country I visited, privatization is derisively termed "pocketization." In Russia, "*nomenklatura* capitalism" ran rampant; that is, the *nomenklatura*, Communist Party members who managed GOEs, took over valuable government properties for trivial sums or stole them through "spontaneous privatization" or "self privatization."[61] Vietnam is experiencing serious corruption problems, and similar fears abound in China as that country embarks on its program of "public ownership," that is, private ownership.

Corruption can occur not only in the sale of GOEs but also in providing government services. The awarding of government contracts, franchises, and grants is obviously susceptible to bribery, collusion, and extortion. Vouchers are vulnerable to a variety of fraudulent schemes, as evidenced by the counterfeiting, theft, sale, and illegal redemption of food stamps. A would-be contractor might offer a bribe (or a campaign contribution) to a public official to influence the award in his favor, or the official might take the initiative and solicit or extort a payment. This is one of the arguments exploited by public employee unions. A publication issued by the American Federation of State, County, and Municipal Employees (AFSCME) stresses this point, and, despite its strident tone and obvious self-interest, it performs a public service by describing numerous instances of corruption in contracting.[62] By drawing attention to the problem, unions exert pressure on public officials to adopt good, honest, competitive procurement practices.

But corrupt behavior is not unique to contract arrangements and other forms of privatization. It occurs even in direct government activities without any involvement of the private sector. Consider the situations wherein public-sector employee unions give endorsements, make campaign contributions, and supply campaign workers to favored candidates for public office. They can be quite explicit about their expectations when their candidate is elected;[63] they expect—and frequently obtain—a quid pro quo in the form of greater expenditures for the service their union performs, more jobs, agency shops, fat pay raises, more generous retirement plans, and tilted collective-bargaining rules that will lead to more favorable outcomes for them in subsequent labor negotiations. When Mario Cuomo won a close primary prior to winning the governorship of New York, he explicitly credited support from the teacher unions for his victory: "After his reelection . . . Cuomo signed legislation that provided state aid to New York schools, but only for teacher salaries. . . . [T]he amounts appropriated reached about $160 million. At the same time, the New York City schools were in wretched physical condition."[64] Cuomo delivered an even larger payoff later when he signed legislation requiring all teachers to pay service fees to the union as a condition of employment.[65] While such an exchange of favors is legal at present, one can ask if the end result differs significantly from a bribe or contribution by a private firm to secure a contract. The result in either case is a higher price paid by the public.

Government pension plans can also be perverted into rewards from public officials to public employees in return for political support, as was demonstrated in Boston. The son of a former mayor, holding the post of city clerk, applied for an annual pension of $28,000 because of the emotional damage he claimed he suffered by acting as parliamentarian to the fractious city council. The city censor applied for a $21,000 yearly disability pension on the grounds that he had been traumatized by two rock concerts he had attended on official duty. "There is no doubt in my mind that the [pension] system was designed . . . to serve the alliance of politicians and public employees," said the city auditor.[66]

Consider another villain, the official who tries to extort money from an honest contractor by threatening to delay or deny proper payments to him. If this service had not been contracted out, would such extortion be conceivable? Can there be anything analogous to such reprehensible behavior entirely within a pure governmental arrangement? Yes indeed: there have been numerous instances in which public officials extracted money from their subordinates, demanding kickbacks from them in return for allowing them to keep their jobs, get raises, or be promoted.

Yet another form of fraud is collusion, where prospective bidders coordinate their bids in order to keep prices high. How common is such behavior? It is impossible to tell, but if it were widespread, one might expect the cost of contract services to be higher than the cost of government services. But chapter 6 presents overwhelming evidence to the contrary, which indicates that this practice is rare or ineffective. Moreover, government agencies can protect themselves by creating and maintaining a competitive environment and process, and by competing directly with the private sector for some or all of the work, as detailed in chapter 7.

I am familiar with the following instructive case: a city awarded a contract competitively for a particular municipal service and realized net savings of 22 percent per year, along with higher-quality service and greater citizen satisfaction; these improvements were carefully measured and documented by outsiders. A year later, legal proceedings were started because there were allegations of collusive bidding, and, it was averred, the bid price was 10 percent higher than it would have been in the absence of such collusion. Ponder the irony: residents in this city had been paying $100, let's say, for a municipal service, and then paid 22 percent less, or $78, for a contractor to provide the same service. In the absence of the alleged collusion, the price would have been $71. Significant media attention was directed to the $7 overcharge (the difference between the alleged collusive price and the theoretical market price), but none was paid to the $22 overcharge (the out-of-pocket difference that the public had been paying for years). Collusion in the contracting process cannot be condoned or excused, but one cannot help but be struck by the media's blithe indifference to the larger loss. Contracting proved to be much cheaper than municipal service, and would have been even cheaper if no collusion had occurred.

This example is not unique. In a much-publicized scandal wherein New York City officials accepted money in exchange for awarding contracts to collect fines for parking violations, little note was taken of the fact that collections actually increased under the contract;[67] in narrow, economic terms the city was better off than it had been when a municipal agency was collecting the fines.

As a final dispiriting point, one must acknowledge that embezzling and theft of property and services by employees occurs in both the public and private sectors. For example, one can count on regular exposés of public-works officials who arrange for public employees to perform private construction work for them. One may correctly conclude from this discussion that direct government operations, as well as all methods of privatization, including sale of GOEs, displacement, and delegation by contract, voucher, grant and franchise, are subject to various forms of illegality. No arrangement has a monopoly on virtue or knavery, saints or sinners.

Looking at the issue more broadly, the level of corruption depends on the magnitude of the available benefits, the risk of exposure and punishment, and the honesty and integrity of public officials and private individuals. Bribes are paid by contractors or by buyers of GOEs—or extorted by public officials—for benefits such as inclusion on bidders' lists; favorable bid specifications or terms of sale; award of a contract, franchise, or sale; getting away with overcharging, underpaying, or underperforming; winning subsidies; and paying below-market rates for government supplies, loans, and foreign exchange. Bribes (and their mirror image, extortion) are also paid to avoid costs, for example, to evade regulations and taxes and to avoid delays.[68]

As noted repeatedly throughout this book, open and transparent processes with strong external monitoring and stern enforcement of sound laws are necessary to establish a climate in which corruption is minimized and the public can, with confidence, support a privatization program.

Going beyond the privatization issue, a broad strategy to decrease corruption requires deregulation, including elimination of price controls and subsidies in order to reduce opportunities for illicit payments; civil service reform to reduce gross disparities between public- and private-sector compensation; strong financial and auditing systems with open reporting; watchdog and good-government groups; "whistleblower" protection; freedom-of-information laws; a free press; independent review and investigatory bodies; an honest and independent judiciary; and penalties for both briber and bribee (extorter and extortee) that are related to the amount gained, not the amount paid. Total elimination of corruption is unrealistic, but a significant reduction in the extent and level of corruption can be realized by adopting these elements, leading to a basic improvement in the honesty, efficiency, fairness, and political legitimacy of government and its programs.[69]

Lack of Managerial Skills

Privatization increases the need for well-educated public managers and reduces the need for low-skilled public employees. This is especially true of contracting for goods and services. Kettl, for example, stresses that contracting will fail unless government is a "smart buyer," able to figure out what to buy, who to buy from, and how to determine what it has bought.[70] This is a crisp summary of the steps in chapter 7, but Kettl emphasizes how complex this becomes as market imperfections increase and as buyer and seller become interdependent. He is certainly correct that contracting changes the relation between program managers, program outputs, political appointees, elected officials, citizens, and government, but the problems of implementing policy arise even under direct government production of service. As noted in chapter 7, the principal-agent problem arises *within* government as well as *between* an agency and its contractor. A government that is not a smart buyer of contract services cannot be a smart buyer of in-house services either, and if government were to be restricted only to activities it does well, it would do very little.

Surely the answer is to train government personnel to be good articulators of demand, purchasers of services, and monitors of performance; given the obstacles of civil service systems, it is easier to do that than to continue to manage a department of unionized, tenured civil servants. Kettl adds his recommendations for building a smart-buying government:

- Hire and reward front-line bureaucrats trained to manage contracts
- Retrain mid-level bureaucrats
- Make political appointees aware of the issues in contracting
- Do not contract out core government functions
- Recognize that market methods raise new issues for governance.[71]

Insulated from market forces throughout their careers, managers of government agencies and GOEs understandably resist being thrust into the maelstrom of the marketplace. They generally lack experience in marketing, sales, advertising, customer relations, personnel management, recruitment, worker discipline, purchasing, cost consciousness, and efficiency measures such as redesigning work processes, reassigning workers to new tasks, raising productivity, and trimming the workforce in order to cut costs and compete against rivals.

Public-sector managers cannot effectively engage in managed competition because of this inexperience; they generally need outside help to prepare proposals and carry out the operational changes they promise. Managers of former SOEs in post-socialist countries, in addition to these shortcomings, are used to fulfilling quotas in a command system and are unused to accepting responsibility and taking risks; therefore, they can rarely carry out effectively the restructuring that is so desperately needed.[72] As a result, divestment of such SOEs through mass privatization or by management or worker buyouts—strategies that were adopted to gain public support and reduce opposition from managers and workers—has serious limitations and may not produce the desired outcome, a viable company.

A managerial approach advocated instead of privatization or as an intermediate step prior to privatization is "corporatization," whereby the agency is forced to operate on commercial principles and to survive by earning money while paying its bills.[73] It may even be formally transformed into a corporation, free of civil service rules. This is a practical step for departments that can charge for their services, such as utilities, airports, seaports, business development agencies, and public bus companies.

Less "Social Justice"

Advocates for the poor fear that privatization will make life even harsher for those at the bottom of the social ladder.[74] This fear is based on the misapprehension that privatization automatically means paying market prices for public services and terminating unprofitable ones: abandoning bus service in low-income areas; paying directly for children's education and for inoculations, health clinics, and social services; and paying for waste collection and street cleaning in their neighborhoods. As has been noted several times throughout this book, any desired degree of subsidization of the poor is compatible with and can be achieved by privatization if so desired: vouchers, grants, and contract services can all be used for that purpose.

"Cream Skimming"

Yet another argument raised against privatization is that "cream skim-ming" will occur. That is, the private sector will be interested only in the best opportunities and will not bid on the others. For example, with respect to health care, private firms will select only the most profitable patients or services, leaving government agencies to provide care for the most expen-sive and least desirable ones.[75] Kuttner complains that ambulances were privatized in Boston's suburbs but not in Boston itself.[76] Similarly, with respect to bus service, the private sector will bid on franchises for profitable routes only, leaving the public bus agency to serve the loss-making routes. With respect to GOEs, buyers will be interested only in the best ones and will leave the rest in the hands of the state.

This argument requires skeptical examination. It is not much of an exaggeration to say that everyone always practices cream skimming. We do it when we pick out fruit in the store, or shop for clothing, cars, or housing. We select the best buy for the money and pass up that which does not meet our implicit cost-benefit criterion. If bus routes are to be priva-tized, bidders will pay for profitable ones but will require subsidies for unprofitable ones. Government will have to pay job-training contractors more to find jobs for the hard-to-employ than for the easy-to-employ. There is a price at which even the worst GOE can be liquidated.

It is possible to have both cream skimming and the lowest total cost to the public. This will occur whenever the per-client price charged by the private firm is less than the per-client cost of the public agency. Table 11.2 illustrates how so-called cream skimming by the private sector can never-theless reduce the total cost to the public. The public sector can contract

TABLE 11.2—"CREAM SKIMMING" CAN REDUCE PUBLIC COSTS

A. Costs and prices per client	Easy to serve	Hard to serve
Cost of public service	$200	$400
Contractor's cost	$100	$400
Contractor's price	$125	$500

B. Alternatives (assuming one easy-to-serve and one hard-to-serve client)	Total cost
Alternative 1: Both clients served by public agency	$600
Alternative 2: Both clients served by contractor	$625
Alternative 3: Cream skimming—contractor serves only easy client	$525

C. Net savings to public by selecting alternative 3	$75

with a profit-making private firm to serve the easy clients and take advantage of the savings, even while it retains the difficult-to-serve clients. In this hypothetical case, the public saves $75 (12.5 percent), even though the private firm earns a profit of $25 (25 percent).

This can be a sensitive issue, however. If the public agency contracts with a private firm to serve the easy clients (alternative 3 in table 11.2), a superficial comparison would reveal that the per-client cost to the public is $400 for the agency but only $125 for contract service. One can imagine quite a fuss being made about this striking difference, because the private contractor is much cheaper than the public agency; but the invidious comparison would be inappropriate, and the agency would be maligned unfairly. Rather than try to explain this outcome, a cautious bureaucrat might choose to avoid this potential problem altogether by doing all the work in-house, despite its greater cost. This simple illustration also reinforces the point made in chapter 7 about the importance of careful and valid comparisons between public and private providers.

What about cream skimming when there is a user charge? In this circumstance, if a private firm takes over the profitable part, government is left with the unprofitable part and is deprived of the opportunity to cross-subsidize the latter with the profit from the former. Can this possibly be beneficial to the public? Yes indeed: the savings to the public at large may outweigh the loss to the government. This is an interesting situation in which a policy that is good for the public is bad for the public agency, and vice versa.

Table 11.3 offers a hypothetical case of a public bus system that charges a uniform fare and serves both a profitable, high-density area and an unprofitable, low-density area. It is assumed that the number of passengers is the same in both areas. So-called cream skimming occurs, wherein a private bus line takes over the profitable area under a free-market or franchise arrangement and charges a lower fare. In this circumstance, alternative 2, the agency budget must be increased from 70 cents to 75 cents per rider, with this extra cost presumably paid by a tax subsidy. But the total cost to the public, fare plus tax subsidy, declines from $1.70 to $1.65 per rider because of the lower fare charged by the private firm. The public agency is worse off because it must seek a bigger budget, but the public as a whole is better off.

Every situation must be scrutinized to determine what is best for the public, not best for the public agency, as their interests often diverge. One can conclude from these simple analyses that—despite the pejorative use of the term—cream skimming may be good public policy. The private

TABLE 11.3—"CREAM SKIMMING" WITH A USER CHARGE

A. Per-rider costs and fares	Low-cost area	High-cost area
Cost for public agency	$ .90	$2.50
Fare charged by public agency	1.00	1.00
Cost for private firm	.50	N.A.
Fare charged by private firm	.80	N.A.

B. Cost of alternatives	For two riders[a]	Average per rider
Alternative 1: All riders served by public agency		
Fares paid by riders	$2.00	$1.00
Subsidy paid by taxes (cost minus fares, $3.40 - 2.00)	1.40	.70
Total cost to the public	3.40	1.70
Alternative 2: Cream skimming— private firm serves low-cost area government serves high-cost area		
Fares paid by riders	$1.80	$ .90
Subsidy paid by taxes (cost minus fare, $2.50 - 1.00)	1.50	.75
Total cost to the public	3.30	1.65
Savings by choosing alternative 2 ($3.40 - $3.30)	.10	.05

[a]One from each of the two areas

sector can find niches that the public sector ignores. Upon closer examination, cream skimming is nothing more than market segmentation.

Summary

Privatization programs inevitably encounter obstacles that can slow down or abort the process. Principal opposition comes from workers who fear the loss of jobs, but fair and sensitive employee adjustment plans have been developed and successfully put into practice. Other sources of opposition are public officials themselves, certain business interests, and the general public. The principal opposition arguments are based on ideology; nationalism; the fear of foreign ownership, minority ownership, and loss of control; shortage of capital; current profitability of an SOE; and concern that privatization will lead to a concentration of wealth, decline in social justice, corruption, private monopolies, and cream skimming. These arguments should be heard but most can be rebutted and overcome with good managerial practices and preventive actions.

CHAPTER TWELVE

The Future of Privatization

Privatization is now commonplace throughout the world, in communist, socialist, and capitalist countries, in developed and developing countries, in democracies and dictatorships; more than one hundred countries have officially endorsed privatization and more are considering it.[1] In the United States it is being practiced by Democrats and Republicans, liberals and conservatives, blacks and whites. It is no longer a partisan or ideological issue but a pragmatic and increasingly routine approach to governing and to managing public services.[2]

The Leading Edge of Privatization

Privatization by contracting out conventional government services and selling off government-owned businesses and assets continues at a brisk pace, but the practice has advanced far beyond that. Private towing services rescue floundering pleasure boats for a fee, something the Coast Guard used to do at taxpayers' expense.[3] Privatized approaches are protecting the environment: North Atlantic salmon are being protected by private environmental entrepreneurs who use market forces to buy and retire fishing rights, an improvement over government conservation efforts.[4] Private groups are saving open space: in ten years, 1,200 local land trusts permanently protected 2.7 million new acres from development.[5] A market-based approach, namely, international emissions trading, is called for in the Kyoto Agreement to reduce pollution that is said to contribute to global warming.[6]

State parks and resorts in New Hampshire and Georgia are leased to private firms.[7] Churches in Indianapolis maintain neighborhood parks under city contracts.[8] Bryant Park, in the middle of Manhattan, was transformed from a crime-ridden, addicts' haven to a six-acre jewel by a local business association, while nearby Central Park, one of the world's most famous urban open spaces, is managed by another nonprofit organization.[9] New York sold its popular convention center, the Coliseum, to developers who will take advantage of its premier location[10] and is selling hundreds of millions of dollars of other prime real estate.[11] The federal government is auctioning 27,000 acres of land near Las Vegas, Nevada, worth $500 million to $1 billion.[12]

A relatively new area for local-government contracting can be found in Riverside County, California, which contracts with a private company to manage its 25-branch library system, and Jersey City, New Jersey, is considering doing the same.[13] Whereas contracting out individual services such as solid-waste management is by now standard practice, a private firm, appropriately named City Municipal Services, Inc., is serving as a public works department for several towns in Michigan, performing the entire array of traditional public works functions.[14] Municipal parking is also being privatized in interesting ways: the city of Richmond, Virginia, contracted with a company to manage its on-street parking program, including enforcement.[15] Parking tickets in New York City can be paid automatically by credit card twenty-four hours a day via a toll-free number from any telephone in the United States. A computer checks the validity of the card and the availability of funds during the transaction. This approach, provided by an innovative private contractor, is convenient for ticketed car owners and highly cost-effective for the city, reducing handling and processing of about 5 million checks a year. Similar responsive technology will be applied to collect many other kinds of fees and payments from the public.[16]

Ending one of the most archaic arrangements imaginable, the United States Naval Academy in Annapolis is selling its 865-acre dairy farm, which has supplied milk to midshipmen ever since 1911, when a typhoid fever epidemic in the academy was traced to tainted milk from a local distributor.[17] This absurd situation is rivaled by one in Pakistan, where the national airline owns a poultry farm in order to provide chicken and turkey dinners to its passengers.

The last government-owned vaccine laboratory in the United States, which makes anthrax and rabies vaccine and was losing millions of dollars annually, was finally sold by the State of Michigan.[18] The United States is turning over governance of the Internet to a private, nonprofit, multinational corporation to assure a hands-off, market-driven approach to regulation instead of risking a slowdown in the Internet's growth under government intervention.[19] American embassies abroad are guarded not only by U.S. Marines, but also by private firms under contract to the State Department.[20] NASA turned to private contractors to manage its numerous unmanned satellites in space at a cost of $3 billion over ten years;[21] the work includes data acquisition from spacecraft, data transmission to the end user, data processing and storage, ground and space communications, and operations at the mission-control center. The International Telecommunications Satellite Organization (INTELSAT) is being privatized.[22] The Department of Defense is teaming with the private sector to build, renovate, and manage military housing,[23] although the expected savings have been questioned.[24] U.S. Army ammunition plants, managed by private contractors, are being used in part by various manufacturers for commercial purposes under the Armament Retooling and Manufacturing Support (ARMS) initiative enacted by Congress; sixteen plants with 187 commercial tenants employing 2,882 workers were in the program by 1998.[25] Surplus military materièl—equipment, building materials, electrical supplies—worth more than $8 billion when initially acquired, is being sold for the Defense Department by one of the nation's largest disposition firms.[26]

The St. Lawrence Seaway, owned by the Canadian government, is now being managed by a private group comprised of the major users, who hope to restore the waterway's fortunes by making it more competitive with other forms of transportation.[27] (The U.S. government, however, continues to own the corporation that operates and maintains the part of the Seaway that is in U.S. waters.)

China, still nominally a communist country, is privatizing one of the most basic of all services, housing. Most urban residents will have to buy their homes or pay much higher rents as work units withdraw from supplying housing and social services as workplace benefits. This profound economic reform is radical and far-reaching, another nail in the socialist coffin. The emerging housing market will create a whole new industry of mortgage institutions, real-estate brokers, architects, home decoration, and home repair.[28]

In Britain, the first Labour government in almost twenty years stunned some of its supporters by abandoning the party's economic creed of nationalization and continuing the privatization policy initiated by the former Conservative prime minister, Margaret Thatcher. It announced plans to sell $4.9 billion of state assets over three years by divesting 51 percent of the air traffic control system and entering into public-private partnerships for the government-owned betting service and for the Royal Mint, which produces coins and banknotes.[29] It was also proceeding with plans to privatize the Underground, London's subway system. As a final, striking example of the limitless opportunities for privatization, the British Defense Ministry is seeking proposals to privatize the Queen's airline, that is, the

Royal Air Force squadron that transports the royal family, government ministers, and VIPs around the world.[30]

Privatization is also being carried out by the private sector itself, in a manner of speaking: "outsourcing" is a growing phenomenon in the United States as companies subcontract with specialized firms to operate their computers; handle their logistics (warehousing and delivery); assemble parts; run their company cafeterias; process their mail; provide their advertising, marketing, and public relations services; staff their telephone order and help lines; administer their payrolls; manage employee benefits; and perform other mission-critical functions, thereby becoming virtual corporations. They strip to the bare essentials, even leasing employees. When done properly, this does not "hollow out" the corporation; it reduces internal bureaucracies, flattens the organization, and affords greater strategic focus. In other words, outsourcing brings many of the same benefits to private corporations that privatization brings to governments.

New Directions

Privatization has advanced beyond the point of no return, and the examples cited illustrate the continuing inventiveness of public officials in applying the concepts in new ways. The next major areas to benefit from privatization, I believe, are government-owned businesses, infrastructure, and social insurance. The three are radically different and therefore so are the ways that their privatization is likely to evolve. Before discussing these, however, it is appropriate to review the major changes that are underway in the ever-evolving field of public management, changes that bear directly on privatization.

The New Public Management

Public-administration reforms are underway in many countries, and they have common characteristics. "New Public Management" is the label applied to this set of innovative reforms, whose defining feature is the infusion of market principles into the political world. Specifically, this means (1) striving for efficiency in the face of unresponsive bureaucracies; (2) utilizing economic market models for political and administrative relationships: public choice, negotiated contracts, transaction costs, and principal-agent theory; and (3) applying the concepts of competition, performance-based contracting, service delivery, customer satisfaction, market incentives, and deregulation.[31]

Privatization is obviously in the mainstream of the New Public Management, exhibiting all these characteristics. Public managers operating in this environment are introducing managed competition and are contracting competitively with the private sector to deliver services more efficiently and effectively. They are expanding customer choice by introducing voucher systems, and they are creating public-private partnerships to satisfy public needs. They are selling off real property, getting rid of government-owned businesses, and deregulating to allow market forces to achieve the benefits expected of regulation. Privatization *is* the New Public Management.

Public managers and decision makers face complex choices about which public services and functions should be kept in the public sector and which should be privatized, how privatization should be carried out, and what kind of supervision they should exercise over the private sector. They can no longer monopolize, or even concentrate on, program delivery alone. They require private and nongovernmental organizations to participate if services are to reach people effectively and efficiently.

A critical challenge is to manage the process for eliciting the participation of the private sector in ways that protect public interests while allowing businesses to earn a reasonable return on their investments. Public- and private-sector managers will have to both gain a better understanding of the changing roles of government and find effective ways to forge public-private partnerships that can provide services and infrastructure for which neither sector alone has sufficient resources. Governments must be restructured to authorize, partially finance, oversee, or supervise and assure access to many types of services and infrastructure rather than deliver them directly.

Governments now more than ever must persuade and motivate citizens to secure their support. Furthermore, because many societies, even in advanced market economies, are becoming less coherent and unified, and have less respect for political authority, public officials must bring together the various stakeholders and gain consensus on common action. They will have to spend less time managing service delivery and more time communicating, persuading, and negotiating with their citizens, and then articulating the demand for services.

They must develop the capacity to manage contractual relationships and public-private partnerships. As functions shift from government enterprises and public agencies to the private sector, governments must take on more responsibility for enforcing regulations that protect the collective welfare, ensure open competition, and take advantage of market discipline without imposing unrealistic controls and constraining businesses unnecessarily.

Public officials and employees must be trained in negotiation and interaction, in effective regulation, and in how private companies operate. They are responsible for overseeing privatized enterprises that are "natural monopolies" or that provide services that directly affect the social and economic well-being of citizens. Finally, they must play an essential role in mitigating any temporary negative impacts of the transition.[32]

Government-Owned Businesses

In the United States there are numerous government corporations, generally described as state or federally chartered entities created to serve public functions of a predominantly business nature. The estimated number of federal corporations has ranged from twelve to forty-seven, depending on the definition that is employed and who does the counting.[33] Overlooking this curious state of affairs, which invites serious examination, it does not require much imagination to predict that many of them should and will be privatized. A list of thirty-one U.S. government business enterprises appears in table 12.1. One of these, the U.S. Postal Service (USPS), has already started to privatize. In 1997 it awarded a five-year, $1.7 billion contract to Emery Worldwide Airlines to create a network of ten Priority Mail processing centers along the East Coast, as the first step in contracting out the processing of all such mail.[34] Additional entities engaged in business exist within government departments and are not on this list; they may have to be corporatized prior to sale, as indicated in chapter 8. Similar privatizations can be expected for government corporations at the state and local level. Some of the corporations might best be privatized by withdrawing and allowing the private sector to handle the function, if it is needed at all.

Infrastructure

Developing countries need more telecommunications, more electric power, more water, more roads, more railroads, and, in general, more of all kinds of physical infrastructure to promote economic development, although this is a chicken-and-egg proposition. In the advanced industrialized nations, ever more stringent environmental controls on water, air, and land dictate new, more expensive efforts for the prevention and treatment of pollution. In both cases, this means large capital investments in water supply and wastewater-treatment systems, in power-generation systems that are less polluting, and so forth. It also means greater emphasis on research and development and on applying advanced technology, in which there are economies of scale.

TABLE 12.1—PARTIAL LIST OF U. S. GOVERNMENT CORPORATIONS

African Development Foundation
Bonneville Power Administration
Commodity Credit Corporation
Community Development Financial Institutions Fund
Corporation for National and Community Service
Corporation for Public Broadcasting
Export-Import Bank of the United States
Federal Crop Insurance Corporation
Federal Deposit Insurance Corporation
Federal Housing Administration
Federal Prison Industries, Inc.
Government National Mortgage Association ("Ginnie May")
Inter-American Foundation
Legal Services Corporation
National Credit Union Administration Central Liquidity Facility
National Railroad Passenger Corporation (AMTRAK)
Neighborhood Reinvestment Corporation
Overseas Private Investment Corporation (OPIC)
Pennsylvania Avenue Development Corporation
Pension Benefit Guaranty Corporation
Power Marketing Administrations
Resolution Funding Corporation
Rural Electrification Corporation
Rural Telephone Bank
Southeastern Power Administration
Southwestern Power Administration
St. Lawrence Seaway Development Corporation
Tennessee Valley Authority
The Financing Corporation
United States Postal Service
Western Area Power Administration

Source: Derived in part from *Government Corporations: Profiles of Existing Government Corporations*, GAO/GGD-96-14, (Washington, D.C.: General Accounting Office, December 1995).

This is a prescription for private-sector involvement, for competition, and for the capital and in-house expertise that are generally beyond the capacity of local governments. Public-private partnerships are ideal in these circumstances, as discussed in chapter 9, and undoubtedly they will proliferate.

Transportation is another good target. Continued suburbanization is straining the capacity of current transportation infrastructure in developed countries, and the situation calls for more efficient use of that infrastructure as well as for new and improved transportation modes. Privatized toll roads and the addition of toll lanes to existing roads, with automated toll collection and time-of-day pricing, are of proven value in reducing congestion. An added innovation is "congestion tolling," a system of dynamic pricing whereby prices change every few minutes in response to changing traffic patterns and are flashed to drivers. This is being done in California, where it maximizes highway throughput because drivers can use a toll lane or a free lane depending on traffic conditions and on the value they place on their time.[35] Private capital and public-private partnerships are fueling these capital-intensive improvements, and additional revenue is generated by sharing rights-of-way with fiberoptic communication lines.[36] More private roads can be expected.

Burgeoning air travel throughout the world is crowding existing airports and endangering air traffic control systems. It is no surprise, therefore, that privatized airports are being built (Greece) and existing public ones are being sold (Germany, Britain, New Zealand, Mexico) or turned over to private management for operation and expansion (New York, San Diego, Indianapolis, Puerto Rico). Air traffic control systems have been privatized in New Zealand, Switzerland, and Canada,[37] are being privatized in Britain,[38] and have been advocated[39] and planned for[40] in the United States.

Prisons are another kind of infrastructure in which privatization is growing through several different models.[41] First introduced in the United States, private prisons can also be found now in Canada, Australia, and Great Britain, and they are being introduced elsewhere. At the end of 1996, the seventeen firms in this "business" housed 85,000 inmates in 132 secure adult facilities, including maximum-security prisons and large prisons with more than 2,000 inmates. The number of inmates in private prisons had increased by a third in that year, and continued rapid expansion in the number of such facilities was forecast;[42] as only 3 percent of U.S. inmates were in privatized prisons, this is an area that offers great growth potential, to put the best face on it. States are accepting out-of-state prisoners in such prisons, which are seen as economic salvation for declining communities because of the jobs they generate.[43] Given the success of incarceration in reducing crime, more private prisons are in the offing because the private sector can build them more rapidly and at lower cost through design-finance-build-leaseback arrangements. Real-estate investment trusts (REITs) that specialize in prison properties are being created, making it easier to raise private capital for this purpose.[44]

Social Insurance

For more than a century, people have increasingly looked to government for retirement income, health care, and assistance in case of poverty, which together can be called social insurance. The resulting system is the welfare state (the term is not meant pejoratively here), which is widely perceived as being in crisis:

> Twenty years ago, selling state-run businesses . . . to the private sector seemed politically impossible. Now governments everywhere are privatising, whether they lean right or left. It is the commercial enterprises run by the state that seem to be out of place today, not the privatised ones.
>
> Will the next two decades bring a similar change in attitudes to the privatisation of social insurance? There are at least three striking similarities between nationalised industries then and welfare states now: a widespread conviction that the old way has failed; plenty of good reasons to suppose that privatisation could help solve at least some of the problems; and hostility to that apparently promising solution from a majority of the public.[45]

Policymakers in wealthy nations have avoided reconsidering the state's role in social insurance, but the time is right for doing so, as the system was designed for yesterday's world where poor health and poverty were the norm and life expectancy was forty-five years:[46]

> The most sensible way to rethink social insurance . . . is to ask, what works? . . . Answering that question means being open-minded about the possibility that the private sector may replace much of what is now done by government, while admitting that there may be things that government can do better than private business, or even that only government can do. . . . [The part played by private firms] should be large. Although they do not shout about it, governments are keen to shift more welfare provision into private hands to keep public spending under control and to avoid having to raise taxes or cut benefits. In many rich countries the private share of social insurance has been edging up in recent years.[47]

The social area in the United States that is very likely to be partially privatized, as discussed in chapter 10, is Social Security, the government-run retirement system. A major policy debate has been triggered because this is a pay-as-you-go system in which payments from current workers go to retirees. Because the system operates on faith instead of actuarial soundness, it has been disparaged as a government-run pyramid scheme. The looming problem is that there will not be enough workers in the future to pay similar benefits to today's workers when they retire. Individual retirement accounts (IRAs) in the United States and enforced private pension plans, as pioneered in Chile and copied in more and more countries, have the twin virtues of being actuarially sound and providing a much higher payoff to the worker on retirement. The problems are how to manage the transition fairly, over several decades, for those who have contributed to the current system but are far from retirement; how to provide income transfers to those who could not save enough; whether and how to add income support for those who neglected to save enough; and what kind of government regulation is needed for privatized pension systems.

Privatization of other social insurance programs has proceeded in several ways. As noted in chapter 10, social services have long been contracted out to the private sector—to nonprofit organizations. This has been a "fatal embrace," because private, nonprofit organizations with distinguished histories have become, in effect, government surrogates subject to coercive regulations that sap their initiative and thwart their efforts to find better ways to help the needy;[48] they have lost their independence in the scramble for government dollars. Increasingly, however, for-profit firms have entered the field and are both providing services such as child care and job training directly and administering social programs under government contracts. Examples of the latter are determining eligibility for benefits, administering welfare-to-work programs, handling child-welfare functions from foster care to adoption to family services, and tracking down "dead-beat dads" to collect support payments.

As the evidence mounts that for-profit firms can deliver equally high-quality services more cost-effectively than nonprofits, much more contracting will take place. This outcome should come as no surprise, as chapter 6 shows that for-profit firms generally provide quality services at a lower cost than nonprofit governments. The ideological ethos and the anti-market, anti-profit bias of the social-services professions, however, often combined with holier-than-thou attitudes, have blinded the nonprofit establishment, just as government officials thirty years ago scoffed at the notion that for-profit private firms could undersell and outperform nonprofit government agencies.

Vouchers are emerging as the preferred privatization method for those social-welfare services that satisfy the prerequisites identified in chapter 4. This is happening for two reasons: (1) Social services have been monopolistic, and vouchers introduce competition, which destroys monopolies and improves services[49]—nonprofits deplore vouchers as much as public-sector unions deplore contracting out, and for the same reason. (2) It is difficult to specify quality standards in social-service contracts, but vouchers offer a solution because standards do not have to be articulated; voucher recipients simply choose the program they like among the available suppliers. For example, child care has been "voucherized" in two ways: with vouchers that permit parents to enroll their children in approved day-care facilities, and with cash allowances that allow parents to hire relatives or friends to care for their children. Education vouchers work the same way: parents do not have to be professional educators, or even literate, to select the schools that they deem best, on the whole, for their children. Services for which vouchers can be used include food, housing, education, health care, health insurance, child care, home care, elder care, job training, and family services.

Yet a third way for privatizing social-welfare functions, beyond contracting with firms for direct service delivery and introducing vouchers, appears on the horizon—default and displacement. The first sentence in this book names the family and voluntary groups—religious, charitable, neighborhood, civic, and so on—as two of the principal institutions of the private sector (the market is the third). These voluntary groups are also called NGOs, nongovernmental organizations.

Two of the first ten amendments to the Constitution of the United States emphasize that government is to be limited and that people have power, too. The Ninth Amendment says, "The enumeration in the Constitution, of certain rights, shall not be construed to deny or disparage others retained *by the people*" (emphasis added). The Tenth Amendment goes further: "The powers not delegated to the United States by the Constitution, nor prohibited to the States, are reserved to the States respectively, *or to the people*" (emphasis added). Implicit in these founding principles is recognition of the vital role of voluntary groups and families.

The remarkable Alexis de Tocqueville, in the 1830s, already observed something unique in the American character:

> Americans of all ages, all stations in life, and all types of disposition constantly form associations. They have . . . associations of a thousand . . . kinds,—religious, moral, serious, futile, general or restricted, enormous or diminutive. The Americans make associations to give entertainments, to found seminaries, to build inns, to construct churches, to diffuse books, and send missionaries to the antipodes; they found in this manner hospitals, prisons, and schools. . . . Wherever, at the head of some new undertaking, you see a government in France, or a man of rank in England, in the United States you will be sure to find an association.[50]

"Mediating institutions" are found among such associations, standing between the individual in his private life and the large institutions of public life.[51] But the critical functions of these local institutions were nationalized, centralized, and governmentalized. Now, as confidence that government can solve social problems has waned and disillusionment has set in, mediating institutions have been rediscovered and accorded new respect as the best hope for the future. Political leaders are discovering the virtues of decentralization and the power of family and community values and of faith-based institutions.

The Alliance for National Renewal, which is active in promoting this approach, illustrates the philosophy this way:

> [M]ore than 5 million at-risk children . . . are growing up
> in severely distressed neighborhoods, communities beset by . . .
> "family-crushing variables" like drugs and violence. Faced
> with mounting concern about the future these children face,
> communities are focusing on integrated, multi-partner efforts
> to improve neighborhoods as the chief vehicle for stabilizing
> families and improving the chances that today's children will sur-
> vive tomorrow.
>
> Increasingly, these initiatives are being supported by partner-
> ships among government agencies, businesses, foundations, and
> non-profit organizations that break down old barriers. Where fami-
> lies and communities are concerned, these organizations have con-
> cluded that innovation is required. And they are discovering that
> when they forge strong working relationships with one another,
> they can help even the most modest neighborhood uncover hidden
> assets and create hope.[52]

The interrelated social problems that bedevil America today—school truancy and dropping out, promiscuity, teen pregnancy, illegitimate births (the politically correct terms are "out-of-wedlock births" and "nonmarital childbearing," thereby avoiding any hint of impropriety), child and spousal abuse, drug and alcohol addiction, and crime and public disorder, with all their attendant consequences—have resisted government solutions. School dropouts can barely survive in an information age, and young men raised without fathers dominate the ranks of violent criminals.

The re-creation of civil society is of paramount importance.[53] This means encouraging families, promoting responsible fatherhood, inculcating moral values,[54] reversing the normalization of teen pregnancy, sustaining mediating institutions without suffocating them, and supporting religion. On this last point Theodore Roosevelt said, in 1902,

> The forces for evil, as our cities grow, become more concentrated, more menacing to the community, and if the community is to go forward and not backward they must be met and overcome by forces for good that have grown in corresponding degree. More and more in the future our churches must take the lead in shaping those forces for good.[55]

Family-based programs strengthened by community and neighborhood efforts and faith-based programs guided by religious groups offer great promise. For example, inner-city ministers have succeeded in increasing marriage rates among their flocks, sending forth more college-bound youngsters from their communities, and reducing unemployment, addiction, crime, and other antisocial pathologies.[56]

Another hopeful sign is a survey showing growing youth involvement in community and religion, its focus on family, and increased volunteerism. Moreover, youth volunteer activities take the form of social service in a one-to-one setting, such as soup kitchens, hospitals, and schools, rather than public service. While the sponsors of this survey—an association of state-government officials—seem dismayed at the individualism indicated by these preferences and at the low voter turnout among 18- to 24-year-olds, it seems to me worth celebrating the fact that young people express their compassion personally and directly rather than by voting to spend other people's money to buy synthetic compassion for the needy from a government agency.[57]

There will be more efforts, I believe, marshaling the power of mediating institutions, families, individual volunteers, and communities, sometimes with government in supporting roles, in partnerships to achieve a higher level of social welfare.

A New Public Philosophy

Throughout the world we are experiencing a reorientation of government, a redirection away from a top-down approach, an abandonment of the reigning assumption that a powerful, active, and interventionist government, manned by a caring intellectual elite and driven by good intentions, is the basis for a good society. This change is most evident in the United States, which is a pioneer in such trends. Between the overwhelming rejection of

Barry Goldwater, the Republican candidate for president in 1964, and the resounding triumph of President Reagan, the Republican candidate in 1984, a scant twenty years later, a dramatic change had occurred in public attitudes. So profound was this change that when President Clinton in 1996 became only the third incumbent Democratic president to be re-elected in 160 years, he did so by dropping the pet programs of the left, shifting toward the right, adopting the more centrist programs of his Republican adversaries, and declaring an end to the era of big government.

As Everett Carll Ladd put it,

> From the beginnings of Franklin Roosevelt's presidency on through the Great Society, those advocating expanded governmental programs domestically often found the winds of public sentiment at their backs. "More government" was progress. Now, in contrast, while most Americans aren't antigovernment, a majority no longer believes that expanding the state is the answer. Those advocating big new government programs, especially ones centered in Washington, encounter resistance far greater than they did in the New Deal and Great Society years. The results of the health-care debate of 1993–94 are a case in point. Ideological fundamentals [such as] confidence in private initiatives and the importance of policies that encourage them are [not changing].[58]

Privatization is in the ascendancy, even in unlikely settings. A paean of victory is not needed, however, for those who have advocated prudent privatization for the past thirty years. Will this success continue? Will privatization be overtaken by other forces? Is it merely another management nostrum, having its day in the sun but doomed to be supplanted? I think not. Privatization as defined in this book is not merely a management tool but a basic strategy of societal governance. It is based on a fundamental philosophy of government and of government's role in relation to the other essential institutions of a free and healthy society. Privatization is a means, not an end; the end is better government and a better society.

Notes

CHAPTER ONE

1. E.S. Savas, *Privatization: The Key to Better Government* (Chatham, NJ: Chatham House, 1987), 3.
2. E.S. Savas, quoted in David Osborne and Ted Gaebler, *Reinventing Government* (Reading, MA: Addison-Wesley, 1992), 25.
3. Nathan Glazer, *The Limits of Social Policy* (Cambridge, MA: Harvard University Press, 1988), 126.
4. Ibid.
5. S.M. Lipset and W. Schneider, *The Confidence Gap* (New York: Free Press, 1983), 83.
6. Robert J. Blendon, et al., "Changing Attitudes in America," in *Why People Don't Trust Government*, Joseph S. Nye, Jr., et al., eds. (Cambridge, MA: Harvard University Press, 1997), 205–216. See also Al Gore, *Creating a Government That Works Better and Costs Less*, Report of the National Performance Review (Washington, DC: Government Printing Office, 7 September 1993), 1.
7. *New Millennium Project, Part 1: American Youth Attitudes on Politics, Citizenship, Government and Voting* (Lexington, KY: National Association of Secretaries of State, 1999), 19.
8. Gore, *Creating a Government That Works Better*, 1.
9. Lipset and Schneider, *Confidence Gap*, 75. No more recent poll results on this exact subject were found.
10. "Groceries' Service Rated High," *New York Times*, 10 March 1986.
11. Gore, *Creating a Government That Works Better*, chap 2.
12. Milton Friedman, *Capitalism and Freedom* (Chicago, IL: University of Chicago Press, 1962).
13. David Blankenhorn, Steven Bayme, and Jean B. Elshtain, eds., *Rebuilding the Nest: A New Commitment to the American Family* (Milwaukee, WI: Family Service America, 1993).
14. Amitai Etzioni, *The Spirit of Community* (New York: Simon & Schuster, 1994).
15. Ted Kolderie, *An Equitable and Competitive Public Sector* (Minneapolis: Hubert H. Humphrey Institute of Public Affairs, University of Minnesota, 1984).
16. Richard C. Cornuelle, *Reclaiming the American Dream: The Role of Private Individuals and Voluntary Associations* (New Brunswick, NJ: Transaction, 1993).
17. Friedman, *Capitalism and Freedom*.
18. Peter F. Drucker, *The Age of Discontinuity* (New York: Harper & Row, 1969). Poole shortened the term to *privatization* and used it in his newsletters beginning in 1976 (see note 21). The earliest dictionary definition of the word appeared in *Webster's New Collegiate Dictionary*, 9th ed. (Springfield, MA: Merriam, 1983), 936.

19. R. Phalon, "City May Use Private Refuse Haulers," *New York Times*, 6 April 1971, 1; E.S. Savas, "Municipal Monopoly, Uncivil Servants—There Are No Culprits, Only Scapegoats," *Harper's*, December 1971, 55–60; idem, "Privatization from the Top Down and from the Outside In," in *Privatization*, ed. J.C. Goodman (Dallas: National Center for Policy Analysis, 1985), vii–ix, 69–77; idem, *Privatization: The Key to Better Government*, 291.

20. E.S. Savas, "Municipal Monopolies versus Competition in Delivering Urban Services," in *Improving the Quality of Urban Management*, ed. W.D. Hawley and D. Rogers (Beverly Hills, CA: Sage Publications, 1974), 473–500; idem, *Alternatives for Delivering Public Services* (Boulder, CO: Westview Press, 1977); idem, *The Organization and Efficiency of Solid Waste Collection* (Lexington, MA: DC Heath, 1977); idem, "An Empirical Study of Competition in Municipal Service Delivery," *Public Administration Review* 37 (1977): 717–24; idem, "Policy Analysis for Local Government: Public versus Private Refuse Collection," *Policy Analysis* 3, no. 1 (1977): 49–74.

21. R.W. Poole, Jr., *Cut Local Taxes without Reducing Essential Services* (Santa Barbara, CA: Reason Press, 1976).

22. R.M. Spann, "Public versus Private Provision of Governmental Services," in *Budgets and Bureaucrats: The Sources of Government Growth*, ed. T.E. Borcherding (Durham, NC: Duke University Press, 1977).

23. M.N. Rothbard, *For a New Liberty: The Libertarian Manifesto*, (New York: Collier Macmillan, 1978).

24. Donald Fisk, H. Kiesling, and T. Muller, *Private Provision of Public Services: An Overview* (Washington, DC: Urban Institute, 1978).

25. Robert W. Poole, Jr., *Fiscal Watchdog* (Los Angeles: Reason Foundation). In February 1988 the name of this newsletter was changed to *Privatization Watch*.

26. Savas, *Privatization: The Key to Better Government*, 122.

27. E.S. Savas, *Privatizing the Public Sector: How to Shrink Government* (Chatham, NJ: Chatham House, 1982).

28. Jeffrey R. Henig, "Privatization in the United States: Theory and Practice," *Political Science Quarterly*, 104, 4 (1989–90), 649–670.

29. Matthew Bishop and John Kay, *Does Privatization Work?* (London: London Business School, 1988), 5–6.

30. Ibid.; V.V. Ramanadham, ed., *Privatisation in the UK*, (London: Routledge, 1988).

31. R. Candoy-Sekse, *Techniques of Privatization of State-Owned Enterprises*, vol. 3: *Inventory of Country Experience and Reference Materials*, technical paper no. 90, (Washington, DC: World Bank, 1988).

32. Gore, *Creating a Government That Works Better*, chap 2.

CHAPTER TWO

1. Patrick Fleenor, ed., *Facts and Figures on Government Finance*, 31st ed. (Washington, DC: Tax Foundation, 1997), table A4.

2. Stephen Moore, *Government: America's #1 Growth Industry* (Lewisville, TX: Institute for Policy Innovation, 1993), 26.

3. "The Entitlement Cuckoo in the Congressional Nest," *The Economist*, 30 May 1992, 23–24.

4. Helene Cooper and Thomas Kamm, "Much of Europe Eases Its Rigid Labor Laws, and Temps Proliferate," *Wall Street Journal*, 4 June 1998, A1

5. Thomas Kamm, "Continental Shift: Au Revoir, Malaise, Europe's Economies are Back in Business," *Wall Street Journal*, 9 April 1998, A1.

6. Lester M. Salamon, *Beyond Privatization: The Tools of Government Action* (Washington, DC: Urban Institute Press, 1989), 10.

7. Alan Schenker, "Zero Employee Governments," *Small Town* 16, no. 7 (September/October 1985).
8. Charles Brecher, *Where Have All the Dollars Gone?* (New York: Praeger, 1974).
9. Thomas E. Borcherding, ed., *Budgets and Bureaucrats: The Sources of Government Growth* (Durham, NC: Duke University Press, 1977), 50.
10. Allan H. Meltzer and Scott F. Richard, "Why Government Grows (and Grows) in a Democracy," *Public Interest*, no. 52 (Summer 1978): 111–18.
11. Mancur Olson, *The Rise and Decline of Nations: Economic Growth, Stagflation, and Social Rigidities* (New Haven, CT: Yale University Press, 1982), 69–73.
12. James L Payne, *The Culture of Spending: Why Congress Lives Beyond Our Means* (San Francisco, CA: ICS Press, 1991), 28–46.
13. Charles Wolf, Jr., "A Theory of Non-market Failure," *Public Interest*, no. 55 (Spring 1979): 114–33.
14. Karen W. Arenson, "To Graduate Sunday, CUNY Students Must Pass Test," *New York Times*, 28 May 1997, B3; Russ Buettner, "CUNY Chief Hits Hostos, Says Many Students Barely Do College-Level Work," *Daily News*, 31 July 1997, 28.
15. For an excellent discussion of risk in the context of health, see Aaron Wildavsky, "Richer Is Safer," *Public Interest*, no. 60 (Summer 1980): 23–39.
16. For example, see E.S. Savas, "Public vs. Private Refuse Collection: A Critical Review of the Evidence," *Journal of Urban Analysis* 6 (1979): 1–13.
17. Morris P. Fiorina, *Congress: Keystone of the Washington Establishment* (New Haven: Yale University Press, 1977).
18. Richard E. Wagner, "Revenue Structure, Fiscal Illusion, and Budgetary Choice," *Public Choice* 25 (Spring 1976): 45–61. Also, James M. Buchanan, "Why Does Government Grow?" in Borcherding, *Budgets and Bureaucrats*.
19. Madsen Pirie, *Dismantling the State* (Dallas: National Center for Policy Analysis, 1985), 20–21.
20. James Q. Wilson, *Political Organizations* (New York: Basic Books, 1973), 330–33.
21. Odgen Nash, *I'm a Stranger Here Myself* (Boston: Little, Brown, 1938), 193. Reprinted with permission.
22. Gordon Tullock, "Why Politicians Won't Cut Taxes," *Taxing and Spending*, October/November 1978, 12–14.
23. Fiorina, *Congress: Keystone of the Washington Establishment*.
24. Buchanan, "Why Does Government Grow?," 13.
25. Robert J. Staaf, "The Public School System in Transition: Consolidation and Parental Choice," in Borcherding, *Budgets and Bureaucrats*, 143–46.
26. Tom Bethell, "The Wealth of Washington," *Harper's*, June 1978, 41–60.
27. William A. Niskanen, Jr., *Bureaucracy and Representative Government* (Chicago: Aldine-Atherton, 1971), 36–42.
28. Bethell, "Wealth of Washington."
29. E.S. Savas, "New Directions for Urban Analysis," *Interfaces* 6 (November 1975): 1–9.
30. John W. Kingdon, *Agendas, Alternatives, and Public Policies*, 2nd ed. (New York: HarperCollins, 1995), 122.
31. Nathan Glazer, "How Social Problems are Born," *Public Interest*, (Spring 1994): 42.
32. James L. Nolan, Jr., *The Therapeutic State: Justifying Government at Century's End* (New York: New York University Press, 1998).
33. George F. Will, "The Triumph of the Therapy Culture," *New York Post*, 7 February 1999, 53.
34. E.S. Savas, "Municipal Monopoly: Uncivil Servants—There Are No Culprits, Only Scapegoats," *Harper's*, December 1971, 55–60.
35. Robert L. Bish and Robert Warren, "Scale and Monopoly Problems in Urban Government Services," *Urban Affairs Quarterly* 8 (September 1972): 97–122.

36. A study by William D. Berry and David Lowery, *Understanding United States Government Growth: An Empirical Analysis of Postwar Data* (New York: Praeger, 1987), found little support for the theory that public-sector monopoly power caused excessive government growth, but the evidence that competition reduces the size and cost of government is powerful, as shown in chapter 6.

37. *City of Lafayette, Louisiana, and City of Plaquemine, Louisiana v. Louisiana Power & Light Company*, 435 U.S. 389 (1978).

38. Edward Gramlich, "The Size of Government," *Journal of Policy Analysis and Management*, 8, no. 3 (Summer 1989); Richard Rose and Terence Karrran, *Taxation by Political Inertia* (London: Allen & Unwin, 1987).

39. Thomas E. Borcherding, Winston C. Bush, and Robert M. Spann, "The Effects on Public Spending of the Divisibility of Public Outputs in Consumption, Bureaucratic Power, and the Size of the Tax-Sharing Group," in Borcherding, *Budgets and Bureaucrats*, 219.

40. Tom Topousis, "Garbage Jobs Are an Offer Many Can't Refuse," *New York Post*, 14 June 1998, 26.

41. E.S. Savas, *The Organization and Efficiency of Solid Waste Collection* (Lexington, MA: Lexington Books, 1977), 67–78.

42. William J. Baumol, *Performing Arts: The Economic Dilemma* (Cambridge, MA: MIT Press, 1966).

43. Savas, "Municipal Monopoly."

44. Jane Hannaway, "Supply Creates Demands: An Organizational Process View of Administrative Expansion," *Journal of Policy Analysis and Management*, 7, no. 1 (1987). 118–134.

45. For example, see Sharmila Choudhury, "New Evidence on Public-Sector Wage Differentials," *Applied Economics*, March 1994, 259; Wendell Cox and Samuel A. Brunelli, "America's Protected Class III, the Unfair Pay Advantage of Public Employees," *The State Factor*, April 1994, 1–34; Bradley R. Braden and Stephanie L. Hyland, "Cost of Employee Compensation in Public and Private Sectors," *Monthly Labor Review*, May 1993, 14–21.

46. Michael A. Miller, "The Public-Private Pay Debate: What Do the Data Show?" *Monthly Labor Review*, May 1996, 18–29.

47. Bureau of Labor Statistics, "Employee Compensation in the Professional, Administrative, Technical, and Clerical Survey," *Industry Surveys*, no. 464 (Washington, DC: 1975).

48. Madhu S. Mohanty, "Union Premiums in the Federal and Private Sector," *Journal of Labor Research*, 15 (Winter 1994): 73–81.

49. Giovanni De Fraja, "Unions and Wages in Public and Private Firms," *Oxford Economic Papers*, 45 (July 1993): 457–69.

50. E.S. Savas, "Analysis of Daily Compensation of Police," unpublished report on police salaries in a suburban town in New Jersey.

51. Savas, "Municipal Monopoly."

52. Robert M. Spann, "Rates of Productivity Change and the Growth of State and Local Governmental Expenditures," in Borcherding, *Budgets and Bureaucrats*, 100–129.

53. Brecher, *Where Have All the Dollars Gone?* 99.

54. I am grateful to Edward V. Regan, former Comptroller of the State of New York, for this lucid and insightful observation.

55. Stuart M. Butler, *Privatizing Federal Spending: A Strategy to Eliminate the Deficit* (New York: Universe Books, 1985), 9–28.

56. John Noble Wilford, "Space Mission Is Rescued at the Brink," *New York Times*, 4 May 1994, A18.

57. James Gwartney, "Less Government, More Growth," *Wall Street Journal*, 10 April 1998, A10.
58. Ibid.
59. World Bank, *World Development Report 1997* (Washington, DC), 1–6.
60. Jacob Citrin, "The Alienated Voter," *Taxing and Spending* (October/November 1978): 7–11.

CHAPTER THREE

1. The typology employing these concepts draws heavily on Vincent and Elinor Ostrom, "Public Goods and Public Choices," in *Alternatives for Delivering Public Services*, ed. E.S. Savas (Boulder, CO: Westview, 1977), 7–14.
2. Ronald H. Coase, "The Lighthouse in Economics," Journal of Law and Economics, 17, no. 2 (October 1974): 357–76.
3. Jesse Malkin and Aaron Wildavsky, "Why the Traditional Distinction Between Public and Private Goods Should Be Abandoned," *Journal of Theoretical Politics*, 3, no. 4 (1991): 355–78.
4. Charles Wolf, Jr, *Markets or Governments: Choosing Between Imperfect Alternatives* (Cambridge, MA: MIT Press, 1993).
5. Robert W. Poole, Jr., *Unnatural Monopolies: The Case for Deregulating Public Utilities* (Lexington, MA: DC Heath, 1985); Walter J. Primeaux, Jr., "Some Problems with Natural Monopoly," *Antitrust Bulletin* 24, no. 1 (Spring 1979): 63–85.
6. William J. Baumol, J.C. Panzar, and R.D. Willig, *Contestable Markets and the Theory of Industry Structure* (San Diego: Harcourt Brace, 1982).
7. A.A. Alchian and R.A. Kessel, "Competition, Monopoly, and the Pursuit of Money," in *Aspects of Labor Economics*, ed. National Bureau of Economic Research (Princeton: Princeton University Press, 1962); L. DeAlessi, "The Economics of Property Rights: A Review of the Evidence," *Research in Law and Economics* 2 (1980): 1; idem, "Property Rights and Privatization," in *Prospects for Privatization (Proceedings of the Academy of Political Science)* 36, no. 3 (1987): 24–35; Terry F. Anderson and Donald R. Leal, *Free Market Environmentalism* (San Francisco: Pacific Research Institute for Public Policy, 1991).
8. Garrett Hardin, "The Tragedy of the Commons," *Science* 162 (13 December 1968): 1243–48.
9. *Aristotle's Politics*, trans. Benjamin Jowett (London: Oxford University Press, 1931), Book II, 57.
10. S. Fred Singer, "Free-for-All Fishing Depletes Stock," *Wall Street Journal*, 10 October 1985.
11. William Vickrey, "Optimization of Traffic and Facilities," *Journal of Transport Economics and Policy* 1, no. 2 (May 1967): 123–36.

CHAPTER FOUR

1. Vincent Ostrom, Charles Tiebout, and Robert Warren, "The Organization of Metropolitan Areas: A Theoretical Inquiry," *American Political Science Review* 55, no. 4 (1961): 831–42.
2. Oliver E. Williamson, "Transaction-Cost Economics: The Governance of Contractual Relations," *Journal of Law and Economics* 22, no. 2 (1979): 233–61.
3. This taxonomy was first developed in E.S. Savas, "Solid Waste Collection in Metropolitan Areas," in *The Delivery of Urban Services: Outcomes of Change*, ed. Elinor Ostrom (Beverly Hills, CA: Sage, 1976), 201–29.
4. E.S. Savas and J.A. Kaiser, *Moscow's City Government* (New York: Praeger, 1985).
5. "Rent-a-Cop Program: The Best Protection Money Can Buy," *New York Times*, June 29, 1998, B1.

6. Michigan Department of Management and Budget, *Privatization in Michigan,* August 1992.
7. Rowan Miranda and Karlyn Andersen, "Alternative Service Delivery in Local Government, 1982–1992," *Municipal Year Book* (Washington, DC: International City Management Association, 1994), 26–35, table 3/6.
8. Douglas Martin, "Private Group Signs Central Park Deal to Be Its Manager," *New York Times,* 12 February 1998, A1.
9. Peter Young, "Privatization Experience in Britain," in *Privatization for New York: Competing for a Better Future,* Report of the New York State Senate Advisory Commission on Privatization, ed. E.S. Savas (Albany, NY: 1992), 288–304.
10. Robert L. Bish and Robert Warren, "Scale and Monopoly Problems in Urban Government Services," *Urban Affairs Quarterly* 8 (September 1972): 97–120.
11. Elinor Ostrom, Roger B. Parks, and Gordon P. Whitaker, *Patterns of Metropolitan Policing* (Lexington, MA: Lexington Books, 1976).
12. *Privatization in America* (Washington, DC: Touche Ross & Co., 1987), p. 3.
13. Miranda and Andersen, "Alternative Service Delivery in Local Government."
14. Carl F. Valente and Lydia D. Manchester, *Rethinking Local Services: Examining Alternative Delivery Approaches* (Washington, DC: International City Management Association, 1984), xiv, xv.
15. *Service Delivery in the 90s: Alternative Approaches for Local Governments* (Washington, DC: International City Management Association, 1989).
16. "Welfare, Inc.," *The Economist,* 25 January 1997, 55–56; *Social Service Privatization,* Report GAO/HEHS-98-6 (Washington, DC: General Accounting Office, October 1997); Robert Melia, "Public Profits From Private Contracts: A Case Study in Human Services," Pioneer Institute White Paper, Boston, MA, June 1997.
17. Keon S. Chi and Cindy Jasper, *Private Practices: A Review of Privatization in Government* (Lexington, KY: Council of State Governments, 1998), 13.
18. Barbara J. Nelson, "Purchase of Services," in *Productivity Improvement Handbook for State and Local Governments,* ed. George Washnis (New York: Wiley, 1978).
19. *Public-Private Mix: Extent of Contracting Out for Real Property Management Services in GSA,* Report GAO/GGD-94-126BR (Washington, DC: General Accounting Office, May 1994), 2.
20. Subcommittee on Employee Ethics and Utilization, House Committee on Post Office and Civil Service, *Hearings on Contracting Out of Jobs and Services,* Serial No. 95-7 (Washington, DC: Government Printing Office, 1977), 29.
21. Jeffrey D. Greene, "How Much Privatization? A Research Note Examining the Use of Privatization by Cities in 1982 and 1992," *Policy Studies Journal,* 24, no. 4, (1996): 632–40.
22. Jeffrey D. Greene, "Cities and Privatization: Examining the Effect of Fiscal Stress, Location, and Wealth in Medium-Sized Cities," *Policy Studies Journal,* 24, no. 1 (1996): 135–44.
23. *Passing the Bucks: The Contracting Out of Public Services* (Washington, DC: American Federation of State, County and Municipal Employees, AFL-CIO, 1983).
24. Joyce Purnick, "Mayor Warns on Union Rules at Javits Center," *New York Times,* 2 November 1985.
25. William Niskanen, Jr., *Bureaucracy and Representative Government* (Chicago: Aldine/Atherton, 1971); Graham T. Allison, "Public and Private Management: Are They Fundamentally Alike in All Unimportant Respects?" in *Current Issues in Public Administration, 2d ed.,* ed. Frederick Lane (New York: St. Martin's, 1982); Thomas E. Borcherding, "Competition, Exclusion and the Optimal supply of Public Goods," *Journal of Law and Economics* 21 (1978): 111–32; Charles Wolf, Jr., "A Theory of Non-market Failures," *Public Interest,* no. 55 (Spring 1979): 114–33; Lawrence N. Bailis, "Comparative Analysis of the Delivery of Human Services in the

Public and Private Sectors," manuscript, Heller Graduate School, Brandeis University, 1984; Anthony Downs, *Inside Bureaucracy* (Boston: Little, Brown, 1967); Hal Rainey, "Public Agencies and Private Firms: Incentive Structures, Goals and Individual Roles," *Administration and Society*, August 1983, 207–42; Marshall W. Meyer, " 'Bureaucratic' versus 'Profit' Organizations," in *Research in Organizational Behavior*, vol. 4 (Greenwich, CT: JAI Press, 1982), 89–125; Lyle C. Fitch, "Increasing the Role of the Private Sector in Providing Public Services," in *Improving the Quality of Urban Management*, ed. Willis D. Hawley and David Rogers (Beverly Hills, CA: Sage, 1974), 501–59; Peter F. Drucker, "Managing the Public Service Institution," *Public Interest*, no. 33 (Fall 1973): 43–60; and James T. Bennett and Manuel H. Johnson, "Tax Reduction without Sacrifice: Private-sector Production of Public Services," *Public Finance Quarterly* 8, no. 4 (October 1980): 363–96.

26. Steve Steckler and Lavinia Payson, "Infrastructure," in *Privatization for New York: Competing for a Better Future*, Report of the New York State Senate Advisory Commission on Privatization, ed. E.S. Savas, (Albany, NY: 1992), 186–214.

27. C. Eugene Stuerle, "Common Issues for Voucher Programs," *Conference Papers*, Conference on Vouchers and Related Delivery Mechanisms: Consumer Choice in the Provision of Public Services, Brookings Institution, Washington, DC, 2–3 October 1998.

28. "Vouchers Would Lift Federal Job Training," *Wall Street Journal*, 29 June 1998, A1; Burt S. Barnow, "Vouchers for Government Sponsored Targeted Training Programs," *Conference Papers*, Conference on Vouchers and Related Delivery Mechanisms: Consumer Choice in the Provision of Public Services, Brookings Institution, Washington, DC, 2–3 October 1998.

29. Paul N. Posner, et al., "A Survey of Voucher Use," *Conference Papers*, Conference on Vouchers and Related Delivery Mechanisms: Consumer Choice in the Provision of Public Services, Brookings Institution, Washington, DC, 2–3 October 1998.

30. Gary Bridge, "Citizen Choice in Public Services: Voucher Systems," in *Alternatives for Delivering Public Services: Toward Improved Performance*, ed. E.S. Savas (Boulder, CO: Westview, 1977).

31. David T. Ellwood and Lawrence H. Summers, "Is Welfare Really the Problem?" *Public Interest*, no. 83 (Spring 1986): 57–78.

32. For an extended discussion of this concept, see R.Q. Armington and William D. Ellis, *More: The Rediscovery of American Common Sense* (Chicago: Regnery Gateway, 1986).

33. See Donald Fisk, Herbert Kiesling, and Thomas Muller, *Private Provision of Public Services: An Overview* (Washington, DC: Urban Institute, May 1978).

34. *New Millennium Project, Part I: American Youth Attitudes on Politics, Citizenship, Government and Voting* (Lexington, KY: National Association of Secretaries of State, 1999), 16.

35. "$140 Million Private Fund Offers Private School Tuition for Poor," *New York Times*, 30 September 1998.

36. Ann E. Kaplan, ed., *Giving USA: The Annual Report on Philanthropy for the Year 1997* (New York: AAFRC Trust for Philanthropy, 1998).

37. Elizabeth Kolbert, "A Map to Suing the City, or 6,000 Pages on the Sidewalks of New York," *New York Times*, 20 April 1998, B1.

38. Ibid.

39. Sue Shellenbarger, "More Children Start Making Plans Early to Care for Elders," *Wall Street Journal*, 8 July 1998, B1.

40. "Harper's Index," *Harper's*, May 1986, 11.

41. James M. Ferris, "Coprovision: Citizen Time and Money Donations in Public Service Provision," *Public Administration Review* 44, no. 4 (July/August 1984): 324–33.

42. E.S. Savas, "Public Policy, Systems Analysis, and the Privatization of Public Services," in *Operational Research '84*, ed. J.P. Brans (New York: Elsevier, 1984).

43. E.S. Savas, *The Organization and Efficiency of Solid Waste Collection* (Lexington, MA: Lexington Books, 1977), 34.

44. Rowan Miranda and Allan Lerner, "Bureaucracy, Organizational Redundancy, and the Privatization of Public Services," *Public Administration Review 55*, no. 2, (March/April 1995): 193–200.

45. Jacques Steinberg, "Edison Project Reports Measurable Progress in Reading and Math at Its Schools," *New York Times*, 17 December 1997, B8.

46. *Alternative Service Delivery Systems: Implications for Minority Economic Advancement* (Washington, DC: Joint Center for Political Studies, April 1985). No more recent data were found.

47. Ibid.

48. E.S. Savas, Sigurd Grave, and Roy Sparrow, *The Private Sector in Public Transportation in New York City: A Policy Perspective* (New York: Institute for Transportation Systems, City University of New York, 1991), 163–66.

49. Hector Ricketts, "Roadblocks Made Just for Vans," *New York Times*, 22 November 1997, A15.

50. Walter E. Williams, *The State Against Blacks* (New York: McGraw-Hill, 1982), 113–19.

51. E.S. Savas, "On Equity in Providing Public Services," *Management Science 24*, no. 8 (April 1978): 800–808.

52. James Brooke, "Minorities Flock to Cause of Vouchers for Schools," *New York Times*, 27 December 1997, 1.

53. James Q. Wilson and Patricia Rachal, "Can the Government Regulate Itself?" *Public Interest*, no. 46 (Winter 1977): 3–14.

54. Michael Knight, "Boston Housing Authority Placed in Receivership," *New York Times*, 26 July 1979, A12.

55. Peter T. Kilborn, "Knowledge Is Clout," *New York Times*, 10 July 1985, A14.

56. Robert F. Durant, Michael R. Fitzgerald, and Larry W. Thomas, "When Government Regulates Itself: The EPA/TVA Air Pollution Control Experience," *Public Administration Review*, 43 (May/June 1983): 209–19.

57. Ron Winslow, "TVA Misled U.S. Regulators on Severity of Nuclear Plant Mishap, Staff Study Says," *Wall Street Journal*, 24 August 1984.

58. Ronald Kessler, "The Great Mail Bungle," *Washington Post*, 9 June 1974.

59. Perry Davis, ed., *Public-Private Partnerships: Improving Urban Life*, Proceedings of the Academy of Political Science, Volume 36, Number 2 (1986).

CHAPTER FIVE

1. E.S. Savas, "Public vs. Private Refuse Collection: A Critical Review of the Evidence," *Journal of Urban Analysis 6* (1979): 1–13; Barbara J. Stevens, "Comparing Public- and Private Sector Productive Efficiency: An Analysis of Eight Activities," *National Productivity Review*, Autumn 1984, 395–406.

2. Michael Knight, "Boston Housing Authority Is Placed in Receivership," *New York Times*, 26 July 1979, A12.

3. Michael P. McLindon, *Privatization & Capital Market Development: Strategies to Promote Economic Growth* (Westport, CT: Praeger, 1996), 14.

4. Manuel Tanoira, "Will Reality Force the Hands of Argentina's Peronists?" *Wall Street Journal*, 9 June 1989, A11.

5. Ann E. Kaplan, "Off-Track Betting in New York City," in *Privatization for New York: Competing for a Better Future*, ed. E.S. Savas, Report of the New York State Senate Advisory Commission on Privatization, 1992, pp. 266–87.

6. Michael A. Miller, "The Public-Private Wage Debate: What Do the Data Show?" *Monthly Labor Review* 15 (Winter 1994): 73–81.
7. Based on numerous personal interviews in Buenos Aires.
8. Hugh Pope, "Helter-Smelter: Why Tajikistan Has an Aluminum Plant," *Wall Street Journal*, 2 July 1998, A1.
9. Lynette Holloway, "Shelters Improve under Private Groups, Raising New Worry," *New York Times*, 12 November 1997, B1.
10. Anthony DePalma, "On Canada's Prairie, a Farmers' Rebellion Flares," *New York Times*, 3 January 1997, A4.
11. Matthew L. Wald, "Power Authority, Facing New Fines, Dismisses Its President," *New York Times*, 8 June 1993.
12. Ron Winslow, "TVA Misled U.S. Regulators on Severity of Nuclear Plant Mishap, Staff Study Says," *Wall Street Journal*, 24 August 1984.
13. Doug McInnes, "Inquiry to See Whether Officials Helped Sell Protected Horses for Slaughter," *New York Times*, 17 December 1995.
14. Terry L. Anderson and Jane S. Shaw, "Grass Isn't Always Greener in a Public Park," *Wall Street Journal*, 28 May 1985.
15. Aristotle, *Politics*, trans. Benjamin Jowett (Oxford, England: Oxford University Press, 1905), Book II, chap. 3.
16. Rowan Miranda and Karlyn Andersen, "Alternative Service Delivery in Local Government, 1982–1992," in *Municipal Year Book 1994* (Washington, DC: International City Management Association, 1994), 26–35.
17. *Privatization in America* (Washington, DC: Touche Ross, 1987).
18. Irwin T. David, *State Government Privatization 1992* (Bethesda, MD: Apogee Research, Inc., 1992).
19. Keon S. Chi and Cindy Jasper, *Private Practices: A Review of Privatization in State Government* (Lexington, KY: Council of State Governments, 1997).
20. McLindon, *Privatization & Capital Market Development*; Ira W. Lieberman and Christopher D. Kirkness, *Privatization and Emerging Equity Markets* (Washington, DC: World Bank, 1998).
21. Diana Jean Schemo, "Politics or No, Brazil Plans to Sell Telebras," *New York Times*, 20 June 1998, D2.
22. Matthew Bishop, John Kay, and Colin Mayer, *Privatization & Economic Performance* (Oxford, England: Oxford University Press, 1994), 299.
23. Jonathan Friedland, "Bolivia Is Selling Off State Firms to Fund Its Citizens' Future," *Wall Street Journal*, 15 August 1995, 1.
24. Richard M. Hammer, H.H. Hinterhuber, and J. Lorentz, "Privatization—A Cure for All Ills?" *Long Range Planning* 22, no. 6 (1989): 19–28.
25. For further discussion of these ideas, see the various publications of Public Service Options, Minneapolis, MN, and those of the Public Services Redesign Project at the Hubert H. Humphrey Institute, University of Minnesota, Minneapolis.
26. Nan Robertson, "France Divides State TV Network into Rival Units," *New York Times*, 4 July 1974.
27. "En Garde: The Battle of French Television Has Begun," *Business Week*, 24 February 1986, 50.
28. Private communication from David Birch, Harvard Business School, 1973.
29. Nicolas van de Walle, "Privatization in Developing Countries: A Review of the Issues," *World Development*, 17, no. 5 (May 1989): 601–15.
30. E.S. Savas, "A Taxonomy of Privatization Strategies," *Policy Studies Journal* 18, no. 2 (1990): 343–55.
31. Miranda and Andersen, "Alternative Service Delivery in Local Government, table 3/5.
32. The Council of State Governments, *State Trends & Forecasts* 2, no. 2 (November 1993).

33. E.S. Savas, *Privatization: The Key to Better Government* (Chatham, NJ: Chatham House, 1987).
34. Jeffrey D. Greene, "How Much Privatization?" *Policy Studies Journal*, 24, no. 4 (1996): 632–40.
35. Irrigation Management Transfer, *Proceedings of the International Conference on Irrigation Management Transfer*, Wuhan, China, 20–24 September, 1994 (Rome: International Irrigation Management Institute, UN Food and Agriculture Organization), 1995.
36. Cento Veljanovsky, *Selling the State: Privatisation in Britain* (London: Weidenfeld and Nicolson, 1987), 136–39.
37. Ron Lobel and Jay Brown, "Privatization Promises to Build Military Family Houses Better, Faster, Cheaper," *Council Insights*, National Council for Public-Private Partnerships, May 1998.
38. Clyde Haberman, "Sell WNYC? Not So Fast, Critics Say, as Sale of TV Station Still Awaits FCC Approval," *New York Times*, 22 March 1996, B3.
39. Madsen Pirie, *Dismantling the State: The Theory and Practice of Privatization* (Dallas, TX: National Center for Policy Analysis, 1985), 50.
40. E.S. Savas, "Is Air Traffic Out of Control?" *New York Newsday*, 9 June 1995; Robert W. Poole, Jr., "Privatizing Air Traffic Control," (Los Angeles, CA: Reason Foundation) February 1995.
41. T.M. Ohashi and T.P. Roth, *Privatization Theory and Practice* (Vancouver, BC: Fraser Institute, 1980), 3–105.
42. Ira W. Lieberman, et al., *Mass Privatization in Central and Eastern Europe and the Former Soviet Union* (Washington, DC: World Bank, 1995).
43. Fuat Andic, "The Case for Privatization: Some Methodological Issues," in *Privatization and Deregulation in Global Perspective*, ed. Dennis J. Gayle and Jonathan N. Goodrich (New York: Quorum Books, 1990), 35–47.
44. *Private Security and Police in America*, Hallcrest Report II (Washington, DC: National Institute of Justice, 1991).
45. *The Economist*, "Building the New Asia," 25 May 1996, 65.
46. E.S. Savas, *Privatizing the Public Sector: How to Shrink Government* (Chatham, NJ: Chatham House, 1982), 118.
47. Roberto Salinas-Leon, "Between Mercantilism and Markets," in *The Privatization Process*, ed. Terry L. Anderson and Peter J. Hill (Lanham, MD: Rowman & Littlefield, 1996), 192.
48. Van de Walle, "Privatization in Developing Countries."
49. Sarah Lyall, "For Britain's Socialized Health Care, a Grim Prognosis," *New York Times*, 30 January 1997, A1.
50. Marcia Chaiken and Jan Chaiken, *Private Provision of Municipal and County Police Functions*, report prepared for the National Institute of Justice (Cambridge, MA: Abt Associates, 1986), 5–7.
51. Glenn Collins, "Many in Work Force Care for Elderly Kin," *New York Times*, 6 January 1986, B5.
52. *Cities within Cities: Business Improvement Districts and the Emergence of the Micropolis*, Staff Report to the Finance Committee, Council of the City of New York, 8 November 1995.
53. Stephen Barton and Carol Silverman, eds., *Common Interest Communities: Private Governments and the Public Interest* (Berkeley, CA: Institute of Governmental Studies Press, 1994).
54. Heather Mac Donald, "BIDs Really Work," *City Journal* 6, no. 2 (1996): 29–42.
55. *The BID Manual: Establishing and Operating a BID* (New York: NYC BIDs Association, 1995).

56. President's Commission on Privatization, *Privatization: Toward More Effective Government,* (Champaign, IL: University of Illinois Press, 1988.)
57. Carroll Rios de Rodriguez, "Pushing the Envelope: Guatemala's Private Delivery Services," *Regulation,* Winter 1998, 41–48.
58. Robert L. Woodson, "Day Care," in *This Way Up: The Local Official's Handbook for Privatization and Contracting Out,* ed. R.Q. Armington and William D. Ellis (Chicago: Regnery, 1984), 159.
59. Hernando de Soto, *The Other Path* (New York: Harper & Row, 1989).
60. "Let the Vans Roll," *Wall Street Journal,* 14 July 1997, A14.
61. "Growth Beats Poverty," *The Economist,* 26 May 1990, 15.
62. Charles Taylor, "Policy Environments and Privatization," *Proceedings of the AID Conference on Privatization* (Washington, DC: Agency for International Development, February 1986).
63. Daniel A. Potash, "Pay-As-You-Go Privatization," *World Cogeneration 9,* no. 3 (May/June 1997): 17.
64. At this point in the project I had to return to the United States, and my role was assumed brilliantly by a bright, dynamic, indefatigable, and unstoppable colleague, Jeffrey Martin.
65. For another formulation of this prescription, see Stuart M. Butler, *Privatizing Federal Spending: A Strategy to Eliminate the Deficit* (New York: Universe Books, 1985).
66. Based in part on Dennis A. Rondinelli, "Privatization and Economic Transformation: The Management Challenge," in *Management for Privatization,* ed. Joseph Prokopenko (Geneva: International Labour Office, 1995).

CHAPTER SIX
1. E.S. Savas, ed., *Privatization for New York: Competing for a Better Future,* Report of the New York State Senate Advisory Commission on Privatization (Lauder Commission), January 1992, 4–7.
2. P.S. Florestano and S.B. Gordon, "Private Provision of Public Services," *International Journal of Public Administration,* 1 (1979): 307–27; P.S. Florestano and S.B. Gordon, "Public vs. Private: Small Government Contracting with the Private Sector," *Public Administration Review,* 40 (1980): 29–34.
3. *Alternative Methods for Delivering Public Services in New Jersey,* Eagleton Institute of Politics, Rutgers University, New Brunswick, NJ, 1986.
4. I.T. David, "Privatization in America," *Municipal Year Book 1998* (Washington, DC: International City Management Association, 1988) table 5/2.
5. Industry Commission, *Competitive Tendering and Contracting by Public Sector Agencies,* Report no. 48 (Melbourne, Australia: Australian Government Publishing Service, 24 January 1996), 506.
6. Robert J. Dilger, Randolph R. Moffert, and Linda Struyk, "Privatization of Municipal Services in America's Largest Cities," *Public Administration Review,* 57, no. 1 (January/February 1997): 21–26.
7. County of Los Angeles, *Report on Contracting Policy in Los Angeles County Government,* 1987, 40.
8. John C. Goodman, Office of Chief Administrative Officer, County of Los Angeles, paper presented at the Third National Conference, Privatization Council, Washington, DC, 11 June 1990.
9. Office of Federal Procurement Policy, *Enhancing Governmental Productivity Through Competition* (Washington, DC: U.S. Office of Management and Budget, 1984).
10. J.P. Wade, Jr., *Report to Congress: The DOD Commercial Activities Program,* 11 April 1986.

11. *Federal Productivity: DOD Functions with Savings Potential from Private Sector Cost Comparisons* GAO/GGD-88-63FS. (Washington, DC: General Accounting Office, 1988).

12. Sam Kleinman, "DOD Commercial Activities Competition Data," (Alexandra, VA: Center for Naval Analyses, 1996).

13. Paul Beresford, *Good Council Guide: Wandsworth, 1978–1987* (London: Centre for Policy Studies, 1987).

14. *Public-Private Mix: Extent of Contracting Out for Real Property Management Services in GSA*, GAO/GGD-94-126BR (Washington, DC: General Accounting Office, May 1994), derived from table I.5.

15. S. Farago, C. Hall, and S. Domberger, "Contracting of Services in the Western Australian Public Sector," Graduate School of Business, University of Sydney, October 1994.

16. Lawrence L. Martin, "Public-Private Competition in the United Kingdom: Lessons for U.S. Local Government?" *State and Local Government Review* 29, no. 2 (Spring 1997): 81–89.

17. Barbara J. Stevens, "Comparing Public and Private-sector Productivity Efficiency: An Analysis of Eight Activities," *National Productivity Review*, 1984, 395–406.

18. Simon Domberger, C. Hall, and E. Ah Lik Li, "The Determinants of Price and Quality in Competitively Tendered Contracts," *Economic Journal* 105, no. 433 (November 1995): 1454–70.

19. John Hilke, *Competition in Government-Financed Services* (Westport, CT: Greenwood, 1992).

20. National Commission for Employment Policy, *The Long-term Implications of Privatization* (Washington, DC: Government Printing Office, 1989).

21. Robin A. Johnson and Norman Walzer, "Privatization in Illinois Municipalities," Office of the Comptroller, State of Illinois, Springfield, 1997.

22. National Commission for Employment Policy, *Long-term Implications*.

23. Stevens, "Comparing Public and Private-sector Efficiency," 545.

24. Ibid.

25. Director of Engineering, "Report on Street Cleaning," Newark, NJ, 16 March 1994.

26. E.S. Savas, "An Empirical Study of Competition in Municipal Service Delivery," *Public Administration Review* 37 (1977): 717–24; Ronald W. Jensen, "Public/Private Competition: The Phoenix Approach to Privatization," testimony before the House Subcommittee on Small Business, Hearing on the Impact of Deregulation and Privatization, Washington, DC, 3 June 1987.

27. Rowan Miranda, "Privatization and the Budget-Maximizing Bureaucrat," *Public Productivity & Management Review*, 17, no. 4 (Summer 1994), 355–69.

28. Mayor Stephen Goldsmith, *The Twenty-First Century City* (Washington, DC: Regnery Publishing, 1997), 134.

29. Simon Domberger and David Hensher, "On the Performance of Competitively Tendered Public Sector Cleaning Contracts," *Public Administration*, 71 (Autumn 1993): 441–54.

30. Rowan Miranda and Karlyn Anderson, "Alternative Service Delivery in Local Government, 1982–1992," *Municipal Year Book 1994* (Washington, DC: International City Management Association, 1994), 26–35.

31. Dilger, Moffett, and Struyk, "Privatization of Municipal Services."

32. E.S. Savas, "Public versus Private Refuse Collection: A Critical Review of the Evidence," *Journal of Urban Analysis* 6 (1979): 1–13; Peter Kemper and John M. Quigley, *The Economics of Refuse Collection* (Cambridge, MA: Ballinger, 1976); Harry M. Kitchen, "A Statistical Estimation of an Operating Cost Function for Municipal Refuse Collection," *Public Finance Quarterly* 4, no. 1 (January 1976):

56–76; Werner W. Pommerehne and Bruno S. Frey, "Public versus Private Production Efficiency in Switzerland: A Theoretical and Empirical Comparison," in *Comparing Urban Service Delivery Systems*, ed. Vincent Ostrom and Frances P. Bish, Urban Affairs Annual Review, vol. 12 (Beverly Hills, CA: Sage, 1977): 221–41; John N. Collins and Bryan T. Downes, "The Effects of Size on the Provision of Public Services: The Case of Solid Waste Collection in Smaller Cities," *Urban Affairs Quarterly* 12, no. 3 (March 1977): 333–347; William M. Petrovic and Bruce L. Jaffee, "Aspects of the Generation and Collection of Household Refuse in Urban Areas," Institute for Real Estate and Applied Urban Economics, Graduate School of Business, Indiana University, Bloomington, Ind., 1977; K. Hamada and S. Aoki, " 'Spinning Off' in Japan: The Upsurge in Privatization," in *Cutback Management: A Trinational Perspective*, ed. G.G. Wynne (New Brunswick, NJ: Transaction, 1983); James C. McDavid, "The Canadian Experience with Privatizing Residential Solid Waste Collection Services," *Public Administration Review* 45 (1985): 602–8; Stevens, "Comparing Public- and Private-sector Productive Efficiency"; S. Domberger, S.A. Meadowcroft, and D.J. Thompson, "Competitive Tendering and Efficiency: The Case of Refuse Collection," *Fiscal Studies*, 7, no. 4 (November 1986): 69–85. See also John D. Donohue, *The Privatization Decision: Public Ends, Private Means* (New York: Basic Books, 1989) 60–70.

33. Werner Z. Hirsch, "Cost Functions of an Urban Government Service: Refuse Collection," *Review of Economics and Statistics*, 47 (February 1965): 87–92.

34. William J. Pier, Robert B. Vernon, and John H. Wicks, "An Empirical Comparison of Government and Private Production Efficiency," *National Tax Journal* 27, no. 4 (December 1974), 653–56.

35. Savas, "Public versus Private Refuse Collection."

36. E.S. Savas, "Policy Analysis for Local Government: Public vs. Private Refuse Collection," *Policy Analysis* 3, no. 1 (Winter 1977): 49–74; E.S. Savas, Barbara J. Stevens, and Eileen B. Berenyi, "Solid Waste Collection: Organization and Efficiency of Service Delivery," *The Policy Cycle*, ed. Judith V. May and Aaron B. Wildavsky (Beverly Hills, CA: Sage, 1978), 145–65; Stevens, "Comparing Public- and Private-sector Productive Efficiency."

37. Savas, "Policy Analysis for Local Government"; Barbara J. Stevens, "Service Arrangement and the Cost of Refuse Collection," *The Organization and Efficiency of Solid Waste Collection*, ed. E.S. Savas (Lexington, MA: Heath, 1977), 121–38; Barbara J. Stevens, *Delivering Municipal Services Efficiently: A Comparison of Municipal and Private Service Delivery* (Washington, DC: Office of Policy Development and Research, Department of Housing and Urban Development, June 1984).

38. James C. McDavid, "The Canadian Experience with Privatizing Residential Solid Waste Collection Services," *Public Administration Review* 45 (1985): 602–8.

39. John Cubbin, Simon Domberger, and Shirley Meadowcroft, "Competitive Tendering and Refuse Collection," *Fiscal Studies*, 8, no. 3 (August 1987): 49–58.

40. Stevens, *Delivering Municipal Services Efficiently.*

41. Savas, "Policy Analysis for Local Government."

42. "Customers Rate Refuse Service," *Waste Age* 12 (November 1981): 82–88. This article is based on Donald Sexton, "Effectiveness, Equity and Responsiveness of Solid Waste Collection Services," Center for Government Studies, Graduate School of Business, Columbia University, 1979. A study limited to the Tucson metropolitan area found no difference in people's perceptions of the quality of municipal and free-market private service: Julia Marlowe, "Private Versus Public Provision of Refuse Removal Service: Measures of Citizen Satisfaction," *Urban Affairs Quarterly* 20, no. 3 (March 1985): 355–63.

43. Stevens, *Delivering Municipal Services Efficiently*, 182.

44. "Customers Rate Refuse Service."

45. Selwyn Raab, "Cheaper Trash Pickup with New York's Crackdown on Mob Cartel," *New York Times*, 11 May 1998, A17.
46. Savas, "An Empirical Study"; idem, "Intracity Competition between Public and Private Service Delivery," *Public Administration Review* 41 (1981): 46–52.
47. Stevens, "Service Arrangement."
48. "Privatisation," *The Economist*, 21 March 1998, 125.
49. David G. Davies, "The Efficiency of Public versus Private Firms: The Case of Australia's Two Airlines," *Journal of Law and Economics* 14 (April 1971): 149–65.
50. Douglas W. Caves and Laurits R. Christensen, "The Relative Efficiency of Public and Private Firms in a Competitive Environment: The Case of Canadian Railroads," *Journal of Political Economy* 88, no. 5 (1980): 958–76.
51. Anthony E. Boardman and Aidan R. Vining, "Ownership and Performance in Competitive Environments: A Comparison of the Performance of Private, Mixed, and State-Owned Enterprises," *Journal of Law and Economics* 32 (April 1989): 1–33; Robert Millward and David M. Parker, "Public and Private Enterprise: Comparative Behavior and Relative Efficiency," in *Public Sector Economics*, ed. Millward, Parker et al. (New York: Longman, 1983), 199–263; Hilke, *Cost Savings from Privatization*.
52. Boardman and Vining, "Ownership and Performance."
53. Paul W. MacAvoy and George S. McIsaac, "The Performance and Management of United States Federal Government Corporations," in *Privatization and State-Owned Enterprises*, ed. Paul MacAvoy, et al. (Boston: Kluwer, 1989), 77–142.
54. Richard Funkhouser and Paul W. MacAvoy, "A Sample of Observations on Comparative Prices in Public and Private Enterprises," *Journal of Public Economics* 11 (1979): 353.
55. A. Galal, L. Jones, P. Tandon, and Inge Vogelsang, *Welfare Consequences of Selling Public Enterprises* (Washington, DC: World Bank, 1992).
56. Hafeez Shaikh, et al., *Argentina Privatization Program: A Review of Five Cases* (Washington, DC: World Bank: 1996), 155–79.
57. Ibid.
58. William L. Megginson, Robert C. Nash, and Matthias Van Randenborgh, "The Financial and Operating Performance of Newly Privatized Firms: An International Empirical Analysis," *Journal of Finance* 49, no. 2 (June 1994): 403–52.
59. Narjess Boubakri and Jean-Claude Cosset, "Privatization in Developing Countries—An Analysis of the Performance of Newly Privatized Firms," *Public Policy for the Private Sector*, no. 15 (December 1998): 37–40.
60. Gerhard Pohl, Robert E. Anderson, Stijn Claessens, and Simeon Djankov, *Privatization and Restructuring in Central and Eastern Europe* (Washington, DC: World Bank, 1997).
61. Roman Frydman, et al., "Private Ownership and Economic Performance: Evidence from Transition Economies," C.V. Starr Center for Applied Economics, New York University, September 1997.
62. See, for example, Roman Frydman, et al., *The Privatization Process in Russia, Ukraine, and the Baltic States* (London: Central European University Press, 1993); Andreja Bohm and Vladimir G. Kreacic, eds., *Privatization in Eastern Europe* (Ljubljana, Yugoslavia: International Center for Public Enterprises in Developing Countries, 1991); V.V. Ramanadham, *Privatisation in Developing Countries* (London: Routledge, 1989); Geeta Gouri, ed., *Privatisation and Public Enterprise: The Asia-Pacific Experience* (New Delhi: Oxford and IBH Publishing, 1991).
63. Matthew Bishop, John Kay, and Colin Mayer, "Introduction: Privatization in Performance," in *Privatization and Economic Performance*, ed. Matthew Bishop, John Kay, and Colin Mayer (London: Oxford University Press, 1994), 2.
64. Ibid., 348.

65. Keith Boyfield, *Privatisation: A Prize Worth Pursuing?* (London: European Policy Forum, 1997).
66. David M. Newbery and Michael G. Pollitt, "The Restructuring and Privatization of the U.K. Electricity Supply: Was It Worth It?" *Viewpoint,* Research Note 124 (Washington, DC: World Bank, September 1997).
67. Ian A. Crossley, Donald Brailey, and Susan Melamud, "Privatization: What Can the U.S. Utilities Learn from the English Experience? How Can We Apply Those Lessons to the American Environment?" Proceedings of the Third Annual Water Industry Summit, Shoreham Hotel, Washington, DC, May 1996.
68. Rafael La Porta and Florencio Lopez-de-Silanes, "Benefits of Privatization: Evidence From Mexico," *Public Policy for the Private Sector,* No. 10 (June 1997).

CHAPTER SEVEN

1. Jeffrey D. Greene, "How Much Privatization? A Research Note Examining the Use of Privatization by Cities in 1982 and 1992," *Policy Studies Journal,* 24, no. 4, (1996): 632–40.
2. Robert W. Poole, Jr., "Looking Back: How City Hall Withered," in *Cutting Back City Hall* (New York: Universe Books, 1980).
3. "La Mirada: A City with a Different View," *Government Executive,* May 1981, 47–48.
4. Stephen Goldsmith, *The Twenty-First Century City: Resurrecting Urban America* (Washington, DC: Regnery, 1997).
5. See also H. Edward Wesemann, *Contracting For City Services* (Pittsburgh: Innovations Press, 1981); and John T. Marlin, *Contracting Municipal Services: A Guide For Purchase from the Private Sector* (New York: Wiley, 1984); John A. Rehfuss, *Contracting Out in Government: A Guide to Working with Outside Contractors to Supply Public Services* (San Francisco, CA: Jossey-Bass, 1989); Simon Domberger, *The Contracting Organization: A Strategic Guide to Outsourcing* (Melbourne, Australia: Oxford University Press, 1998); John A. O'Looney, *Outsourcing State and Local Government Services* (Westport, CT: Quorum Books, 1998).
6. Ronnie LaCourse Korosec and Timothy D. Mead, "Lessons From Privatization Task Forces: Comparative Case Studies," *Policy Studies Journal,* 24, no. 4, (1996): 641–48.
7. Philip K. Porter and James F. Dewey, "The Political Economy of Privatization," in *Restructuring State and Local Services,* Arnold H. Raphaelson, ed. (Westport, CT: Praeger, 1998), 71–89; Owen E. Hughes, *Public Management and Administration: An Introduction,* 2d ed. (New York: St. Martin's Press, 1998), 12–14.
8. Weseman, *Contracting for City Services,* 31–35; Rehfuss, *Contracting Out in Government,* 67.
9. *Privatization: Lessons Learned by State and Local Governments,* GAO/GGD-97-48 (Washington, DC: General Accounting Office, March 1997).
10. James M. Ferris, "The Decision to Contract Out: An Empirical Analysis," *Urban Affairs Quarterly* 22, no. 2 (December 1986); 289–311.
11. Eileen B. Berenyi, "Privatization of Residential Refuse Collection Services: A Study of Institutional Change," *Urban Interest* 3, no. 1 (Spring 1981): 30–42.
12. Based on examination of various city documents and reports.
13. Adapted from Lawrence L. Martin, "Selecting Services for Public-Private Competition," *MIS Report* 28, no. 3. (1996).
14. Martin Tolchin, "Congress Wary on Plan to Sell Assets," *New York Times,* 6 February 1986, B16.
15. E.S. Savas, "How Much Do Government Services Really Cost?" *Urban Affairs Quarterly* 15, no. 1 (September 1979): 23–42.
16. Ibid.

17. Wesemann, *Contracting for City Services,* 35–47; Marlin, *Contracting Municipal Services,* 19–25.
18. U.S. Office of Management and Budget, Circular A-76 (Washington, DC: Government Printing Office, 29 March 1979).
19. Steven Globerman, "A Framework for Evaluating the Government Contracting-Out Decision with an Application to Information Technology," *Public Administration Review* 56, no. 6 (November/December 1996): 577–86.
20. Oliver E. Williamson, "Transaction-Cost Economies: The Governance of Contractual Relations," *Journal of Law and Economics* 22, no. 2 (1979): 233–61.
21. Franklin R. Edwards and Barbara J. Stevens, "The Provision of Municipal Sanitation Services by Private Firms: An Empirical Analysis of the Efficiency of Alternative Market Structures and Regulatory Arrangements," *Journal of Industrial Economics* 27, no. 2 (December 1978): 133–47.
22. For a related point, see Gregg G. Van Ryzin and E. Wayne Freeman, "Viewing Organizations as Customers of Government Services," *Public Productivity and Management Review,* 20, no. 4, (June 1997): 419–31.
23. Mark Schlesinger, Robert A. Dorwart, and Richard D. Pulice, "Competitive Bidding and States' Purchase of Services," *Journal of Policy Analysis and Management 5* (Winter 1986): 245–63.
24. Charles A. Lave, "The Private Challenge to Public Transportation—An Overview," in *Urban Transit: The Private Challenge to Public Transportation,* ed. Charles A. Lave (San Francisco: Pacific Institute, 1985), 16.
25. John Contney, statement, U.S. House of Representatives, *Hearings on Contracting Out of Jobs and Services, Part II, Subcommittee on Employee Ethics and Utilization, Committee on Post Office and Civil Service,* Serial no. 95–29 (Washington, DC: Government Printing Office, 1977), 74–75.
26. Marlin, *Contracting Municipal Services,* 46–49.
27. James C. Dobbs, "Rebuilding America: Legal Issues Confronting Privatization," *Privatization Review* 1 (Summer 1985): 28–38.
28. Stephen Chapple, "Privatization of Pollution Control Financing: Antitrust Implications," *Privatization Review* 1 (Summer 1985): 48–59.
29. Harvey Goldman and Sandra Mokuvos, "Financing: Privatization from a Banker's Perspective," *Privatization Review* 1 (Summer 1985): 39–47.
30. Lawrence Dlugos and Howard B. Whitmore, "Lessons Learned from Resource Recovery: Insuring Privatization Projects," *Privatization Review* 1 (Summer 1985): 16–23.
31. James L. Mercer and Edwin H. Koester, *Public Management Systems* (New York: AMACOM, 1978), 177–85.
32. Raymond G. Hunt, "Award Fee Contracting as a J-Model Alternative to Revitalize Federal Program Management," *Public Administration Review* 45 (September/October 1985): 586–92.
33. Douglas K. Ault and John B. Handy, *Smarter Contracting for Installation Support Services* (Bethesda, MD: Logistics Management Institute, May 1986.)
34. Stuart M. Butler, *Privatizing Federal Spending: A Strategy to Eliminate the Deficit* (New York: Universe Books, 1985), 57–62, 108–18, 155–65.
35. Ibid., 13.
36. William D. Eggers, "Competitive Neutrality: Ensuring a Level Playing Field in Managed Competition," Reason Public Policy Institute, Los Angeles, CA, October 1997.
37. Ron Jensen deserves the credit for this wonderful phrase.
38. E.S. Savas, "An Empirical Study of Competition in Municipal Service Delivery," *Public Administration Review* 37, no. 6 (November/December 1977): 717–24.
39. Brian E. Cox, *Evaluation of the U.K. System of Incentives for Efficiency in Road Maintenance Organisation and Possible Lessons for Developing Countries,* Report

to the Transportation Department (Washington, DC: World Bank, 31 October 1985).

40. Richard W. Stevenson, "Britain Is Streamlining Its Bureaucracy, Partly Privatizing Some Work," *New York Times,* 16 April 1995.

41. Bennett C. Jaffee, "Contracts for Residential Refuse Collection," in *The Organization and Efficiency of Solid Waste Collection,* ed. E.S. Savas (Lexington, MA: Heath, 1977), 153–68.

42. James M. Pierce, statement to Subcommittee on Employee Ethics and Utilization, House Committee on Post Office and Civil Service, *Hearings on Contracting Out of Jobs and Services,* Serial no. 95-7 (Washington, DC: Government Printing Office, 1977, 41–43.

43. Jonas Prager and Swati Desai, "Privatizing Local Government Operations," *Public Productivity & Management Review,* 20, no. 2 (December 1996): 185–203.

44. Savas, *Organization and Efficiency.*

45. Prager and Desai, "Privatizing Local Government Operations."

46. Rehfuss, *Contracting Out.*

47. Esther B. Fein, "In Columbia Pact, New York City Ties Pay to Hospital Productivity," *New York Times,* 8 January 1997, A1.

48. Wesemann, *Contracting for City Services,* 83.

49. Harry P. Hatry et al., *How Effective Are Your Community Services? Procedures for Monitoring the Effectiveness of Municipal Services* (Washington, DC: Urban Institute, 1977); see also Kenneth Webb and Harry P. Hatry, *Obtaining Citizen Feedback: The Application of Citizen Surveys to Local Governments* (Washington, DC: Urban Institute, 1973).

50. Rehfuss, *Contracting Out in Government;* O'Looney, *Outsourcing State and Local Government Services.*

CHAPTER EIGHT

1. Jeanne K. Laux and Maureen A. Molot, *State Capitalism: Public Enterprise in Canada* (Ithaca, NY: Cornell University Press, 1988), 65.

2. *Privatization/Divestiture Practices in Other Nations,* GAO/AIMD-96-23 (Washington, DC: General Accounting Office, December 1995), 26

3. "From Boots to Electronics," *The Economist,* 21 June 1997, 28–30.

4. "Connie Lee Privatization Yields $184 million for DC Schools; CEO Presents Check to Hillary Clinton," *AOLNewsProfiles,* 4 March 1997.

5. Paul Beckett and Scott Ritter, "Shareholders Oust Sallie Mae's Board; Privatization Is Approved For Student-Loan Firm," *Wall Street Journal,* 1 August 1997, A3.

6. Agis Salpukas, "U.S. Oilfield Will Be Sold to Occidental," *New York Times,* 7 October 1997, D1.

7. Sam Howe Verhovek, "Closing of Helium Reserve Raises New Issues," *New York Times,* 8 October 1997, A12.

8. United States Enrichment Corporation, *Plan for the Privatization of the United States Enrichment Corporation, Submitted to The President and the Congress of the United States,* June 1995; The White House, Statement by the Press Secretary, 25 July 1997; "Privatization Completed; United States Enrichment Corporation Sold in Initial Public Offering," *AOL News,* 28 July 1998.

9. "Privatization of TVA Suggested," Associated Press, 19 November 1997.

10. "Conny Kullman Outlines Vision of INTELSAT Privatization in the Competitive Global Market," *AOL News,* 30 September 1998.

11. "Inmarsat Privatization Progresses Rapidly," *AOL News,* 27 April 1998.

12. Charles V. Bagli, "New York to Sell Mental Facilities," *New York Times,* 26 May 1997, A1; Tracy Rozhon, "A Fight to Preserve Abandoned Asylums," *New York Times,* 18 November 1998, B1.

13. Vivian S. Toy, "Giuliani Details Uses of WNYC-Sale Windfall," *New York Times,* 4 August 1995.
14. Clyde Haberman, "For WNYC Radio, There Is a Price for Independence from an Old Master," *New York Times,* 5 July 1996, B3.
15. David M. Halbfinger, "A Hong Kong–based Chain Will Buy U.N. Plaza Hotel," *New York Times* 7 May 1997, B4.
16. Steven Lee Myers, "On Going Private: Mayor Wants to Sell Canarsie Cemetery," *New York Times,* 8 March 1995.
17. "Marriott Buys Rebuilt Vista Hotel for $141.5M," *New York Post,* 10 November 1995.
18. Matthew Bishop and John Kay, *Does Privatization Work?* (London: London Business School, 1988).
19. Matthew Bishop, John Kay, and Colin Mayer, eds, *Privatization and Economic Performance* (Oxford, England: Oxford University Press, 1994).
20. "Labour Party Considers Privatizing London's Underground," *Wall Street Journal,* 17 June 1997, A14.
21. Warren Hoge, "The London Tube, in the Dumps, Could Be Put Up for Sale," *New York Times,* 26 February 1997, A3.
22. *Privatization/Divestiture Practices in Other Nation,* table 1.
23. Paul Cook and Colin Kirkpatrick, *Privatisation in Less Developed Countries: An Overview* (New York: St. Martin's, 1988), 5.
24. Charles Vuylsteke, *Techniques of Privatization of State-Owned Enterprises,* vol. 1: *Methods and Implementation,* World Bank Technical Paper No. 88 (Washington, DC: 1988).
25. Barbara Lee and John Nellis, *Enterprise Reform and Privatization in Socialist Economies,* Discussion Paper 104 (Washington, DC: World Bank, 1990); Branko Milanovic, "Privatization in Post-Communist Societies," *Communist Economics and Economic Transformation,* 3, no. 1 (1990–91), 5–39; "Perestroika Survey," *The Economist,* 28 April 1990, 11.
26. The government had sold only about a third of the shares in 1985 and announced in 1998 that it would sell another 6 percent.
27. "Homestead and Exemption Laws," *Encyclopaedia Britannica* 11 (1965): 645.
28. E.S. Savas, "Privatization in Post-Socialist Countries," *Public Administration Review* 52, no. 6 (November/December 1992): 573–81.
29. Michael P. McLindon, *Privatization and Capital Market Development* (Westport, CT: Praeger, 1996): 111–31.
30. Ira W. Lieberman, Stilpon S. Nestor, and Raj M. Desai, *Between State and Market: Mass Privatization in Transition Economies* (Washington, DC: World Bank, 1997).
31. McLindon, *Privatization and Capital Market Development.*
32. Savas, "Privatization in Post-Socialist Countries."
33. Interregional Network on Privatisation, *Guidelines on Privatisation* (New York: United Nations Development Programme, 1991), 71–73.
34. Bertrand Jacquillat, *Désétatiser* (Paris: Éditions Robert Laffont, 1985), 138.
35. L. Gray Cowan, *Privatization in the Developing World* (New York: Praeger, 1990); Sunita Kikeri, John Nellis, and Mary Shirley, *Privatization: The Lessons of Experience* (Washington, DC: World Bank, 1992); McLindon, *Privatization and Capital Market Development;* Dennis Rondinelli and Max Iacono, *Policies and Institutions for Managing Privatization* (Geneva: International Labour Office, 1996); Ravi Ramamurti and Raymond Vernon, *Privatization and Control of State-Owned Enterprises* (Washington, DC: World Bank, 1991); Cento Veljanovsky, *Selling the State* (London: Weidenfeld and Nicolson, 1987).
36. *Privatization: Toward More Effective Government,* Report of the President's Commission on Privatization (March 1988).

37. For a partial list of reports of such commissions, see "Privatization," *State Trends & Forecasts* 2, no. 2 (Lexington, KY: Council of State Governments, November 1993), table 1. As an example, see "PERM: Privatize, Eliminate, Retain or Modify: Recommendations to the Governor on Improving Service Delivery and Increasing Efficiency in State Government," Michigan Public-Private Partnership Commission, Final Report, December 1992.
38. *Privatization/Divestiture Practices in Other Nations,* 7.
39. Pierre Guislane, *The Privatization Challenge: A Strategic, Legal, and Institutional Analysis of International Experience* (Washington, DC: World Bank, 1997).
40. Daniel Kaufmann and Paul Siegelbaum, "Privatization and Corruption in Transition Economies," *Journal of International Affairs* 50, no. 2 (Winter, 1996): 419–58.
41. Ibid.
42. Ibid.
43. Leroy P. Jones, Pankaj Tandon, and Ingo Vogelsang, "Selling State Enterprises: A Cost-Benefit Approach," in Ramamurti and Vernon, *Privatization and Control,* 29–53.
44. "As Argentine Economy Booms, Workers Fret They'll Be Left Behind," *Wall Street Journal,* 25 June 1997, A1.
45. Veljanovsky, *Selling the State,* 131.
46. Tissa Jayasinghe, "Publicising Privatization: Sri Lanka's Public Awareness Program," unpublished manuscript.
47. Videotapes by the Center for Financial Engineering in Development, Washington, DC, 1996.
48. Fred Hawrysh, "The Pivotal Role of Communication in the Privatization Process," *Emerging Markets Economic Review,* 1, no. 1 (1995).
49. "Growth Beats Poverty," *The Economist,* 26 May 1990, 15.
50. Veljanovski, *Selling the State,* chaps. 7–9.
51. *From Plan to Market,* World Development Report 1996 (Washington, DC: World Bank, 1996).
52. Ivan Bergeron, "Privatization Through Leasing: The Togo Steel Case," in Ramamurti and Vernon, *Privatization and Control,* 153–75.
53. Jim Waddell, "The Privatization of Monopolies," *Economic Perspectives, an Electronic Journal of the U.S. Information Agency* 2, no. 1, January 1997.
54. Pedro-Pablo Kuczynski, "Marketing Divested State-Owned Enterprises in Developing Countries," in *Privatization and Development,* ed. Steve H. Hanke (San Francisco: Institute for Contemporary Studies, 1987), 111–17.
55. Cowan, *Privatization in the Developing World.*
56. Ibid., p. 56.
57. Interregional Network on Privatization, *Guidelines on Privatisation,* 52–54.
58. Rosendo J. Castillo, "Financing Privatization," in Hanke, *Privatization and Development,* 119–26.
59. Roger Leeds, "Privatization Through Public Offerings: Lessons From Two Jamaica Cases," in Ramamurti and Vernon, *Privatization and Control,* 86–125.
60. Ibid, 64.
61. Kikeri et al., *Privatization,* 67.
62. Private discussion with government and business leaders.
63. Ibid., 66.
64. Castillo, "Financing Privatization," 123–24.
65. Kikeri et al., *Privatization,* 67–69.
66. Interregional Network on Privatisation, *Guidelines on Privatisation,* 81.
67. Peter Grant, "Privatization Offers Up Some Monsters," *Global Finance,* November 1996, 94–97.
68. "Privatisation in Europe: Is the Price Right?" *The Economist,* 23 November 1996, 87–88.

CHAPTER NINE

1. T. Irwin David, *Privatization in America* (Washington, DC: Touche Ross, 1987), fig. 2.
2. T. Irwin David, *State Government Privatization 1992* (Bethesda, MD: Apogee Research, Inc., 1992), fig. 6.
3. Jose Gomez-Ibanez and John R Meyer, *Going Private: The International Experience with Transport Privatization* (Washington, DC: Brookings Institution, 1993.)
4. Steven A. Steckler and Lavinia Payson, "Infrastructure," in *Privatization for New York: Competing for a Better Future,* ed. E.S. Savas, Report of the New York State Senate Advisory Commission on Privatization, 1992.
5. *Legislative Initiatives for Public-Private Partnerships in Transportation Infrastructure: A Guide for Lawmakers* (Washington, DC: Privatization Council, 1991), 6.
6. *UNIDO BOT Guidelines* (Vienna, Austria: United Nations Industrial Development Organization, 1996).
7. Steven A. Steckler, *A Guide to Public-Private Partnerships in Infrastructure: Bridging the Gap Between Infrastructure Needs and Public Resources* (Washington, DC: Price-Waterhouse, 1993).
8. Christine Kessides, "Institutional Options for the Provision of Infrastructure," World Bank Discussion Paper 212, Washington, DC, 1993, 25.
9. "Milwaukee's Sewage Plant Outsourcing Is a Big Deal," *Governing,* June 1998, 84.
10. S.H. Johnson, D.L. Vermillion, and J.A. Sagardoy, eds., *Irrigation Management Transfer,* Proceedings of the International Conference on Irrigation Management Transfer, Wuhan, China, September, 1994 (Rome, Italy: Food and Agriculture Organization of the United Nations, 1995).
11. Kessides, "Institutional Options," 42.
12. Ibid., 33.
13. Pierre Guislane and Michel Kerf, "Concessions—The Way to Privatize Infrastructure Sector Monopolies," *Public Policy for the Private Sector,* October 1995.
14. Ibid.
15. Jae So and Ben Shin, "The Private Infrastructure Industry," in *Public Policy for the Private Sector* (Washington, DC: World Bank, June 1996).
16. Peter Smith, "End of the Line for the Local Loop Monopoly?" *Public Policy for the Private Sector* (Washington, DC: World Bank, June 1996), 61–64.
17. Kessides, "Institutional Options," 39.
18. Bernard Tenenbaum, "The Real World of Power Sector Regulation," *Public Policy for the Private Sector* (Washington, DC: World Bank, June 1996), 25–28.
19. Jeffrey H. Rohlfs, "Regulating Telecommunications: Lessons From U.S. Price Cap Experience," *Public Policy for the Private Sector* (Washington, DC: World Bank, June 1996), 65–68.
20. Ian Alexander and Timothy Irwin, "Price Caps, Rate-of-Return Regulation, and the Cost of Capital," *Public Policy for the Private Sector* (Washington, DC: World Bank, September 1996), 25–28.
21. Craig Torres, "French Water Giant Vivendi Learns Costly Lesson about Privatizations in Latin American Provinces," *Wall Street Journal,* 5 June 1998.
22. Antony W. Dnes, "Testing for Regulatory Capture," *Public Policy for the Private Sector* (Washington, DC: World Bank, June 1996), 69–72.
23. "Infrastructure Privatization," Report of the 3rd Session of the Working Group on Privatization, United Nations Conference on Trade and Development (UNCTAD), November 1993.
24. Steven A. Steckler, "Comparing Public and Private Costs," *Finance Alert* 3, no. 4 (November 1989).

25. Charles Friedlander and Roger B. Wagner, "The Utility Privatization Market: Models for Success," *Transactional Finance* 6, no. 2 (December 1994).
26. City of New York, Office of the Comptroller, "Dilemma in the Millennium: Capital Needs of the World Capital City," August 1998.
27. Steckler, *Guide to Public-Private Partnerships.*

CHAPTER TEN

1. Herbert J. Walberg, "Spending More While Learning Less: U.S. School Productivity in International Perspective," *Fordham Report* 2, no. 6 (July 1998).
2. Myron Lieberman, *The Teacher Unions: How the NEA and AFT Sabotage Reform and Hold Students, Parents, Teachers, and Taxpayers Hostage to Bureaucracy* (New York: Free Press, 1997).
3. Richard E. Wagner, "American Education and the Economics of Caring," in *Parents, Teachers, and Children: Prospects for Choice in American Education* (San Francisco: Institute for Contemporary Studies, 1977).
4. Gabriel Roth, *Private Provision of Public Services in Developing Countries* (New York: Oxford University Press, 1987).
5. *Pierce v Society of Sisters* (1925); see also Murray N. Rothbard, *For a New Liberty* (New York: Macmillan, 1978), 126.
6. Jane Wollman, "Teaching at Home with Help of Computers," *New York Times,* 9 February 1984.
7. Diane Ravitch, "New Schools," in *New Schools for a New Century,* ed. Diane Ravitch and Joseph P. Viteritti (New Haven, CT: Yale University Press, 1997).
8. Milton Friedman, "The Role of Government in Education," in *Economics and the Public Interest,* ed. Robert A. Solo (New Brunswick, NJ: Rutgers University Press, 1955). See also Milton Friedman, *Capitalism and Freedom* (Chicago: University of Chicago Press, 1962), 85–107.
9. John E. Chubb and Terry M. Moe, *Politics, Markets, and America's Schools* (Washington, DC: Brookings Institution, 1990).
10. "Reforming K–12 Education through Savings Incentives," U.S. Congress, Joint Economic Committee, Washington, DC, December 1997.
11. *Charter Schools: New Model for Public Schools Provides Opportunities and Challenges,* GAO/HEHS-95-42 (Washington, DC: General Accounting Office, 1995).
12. "Charter Schools: A Progress Report, Part I: Achievement," Center for Education Reform, Washington, DC, October 1998.
13. Theodore Rebarber, *Charter School Innovations: Keys to Effective Charter Reform,* Policy Study 228 (Los Angeles, CA: Reason Public Policy Institute, July 1997).
14. Amity Shlaes, "The Next Big Free Market Thing," *Wall Street Journal,* 9 July 1998, A18.
15. Myron Lieberman, *Public Education: An Autopsy* (Cambridge, MA: Harvard University Press, 1998).
16. Arthur M. Hauptman, "The Use of Vouchers in American Higher Education," in *Vouchers and Related Delivery Mechanisms: Consumer Choice in the Provision of Public Services,* conference papers, Brookings Institution, Washington, DC, 2–3 October 1998, 112–34.
17. John H. Bishop, "Privatizing Education: Lessons from Canada and Europe," in *Vouchers and Related Delivery Mechanisms: Consumer Choice in the Provision of Public Services,* conference papers, Brookings Institution, Washington, DC, 2–3 October 1998, 169–203.
18. Isabel V. Sawhill with Shannon L. Smith, "Vouchers for Elementary and Secondary Education," in *Vouchers and Related Delivery Mechanisms,* 136–67.

19. Myron Lieberman, *Privatization and Educational Choice* (New York: St. Martin's 1989), 136.
20. Arthur E. Wise and Linda Darling-Hammond, *Education by Voucher: Private Choice and the Public Interest,* paper no. P-6838 (Santa Monica, CA: Rand Corporation, December 1982).
21. Estelle James, "Benefits and Costs of Privatized Public Services: Lessons from the Dutch Educational System," *Comparative Education Review* 8, no. 4 (November 1984): 605–24.
22. Shlaes, "Next Big Free Market Thing."
23. Ibid.
24. Paul E. Peterson, Jay P. Greene, and Chad Noyes, "School Choice in Milwaukee," *Public Interest,* no. 125 (Fall 1996): 38–56.
25. Henry M. Levin, "Educational Vouchers: Effectiveness, Choice, and Costs," *Policy Analysis and Management* 17, no. 3 (Summer 1998): 373–92.
26. Amity Shlaes, "Voucher Program Passes a Test," *Wall Street Journal,* 30 October 1998, A18.
27. James Coleman, Thomas Hoffer, and Sally Kilgore, *High School Achievement* (New York: Basic Books, 1982).
28. Theodore J. Forstmann and Bruce Kovner, "How to Energize Education," *New York Times,* 3 January 1998, A11.
29. Carol Marie Cropper, "Texas Business Foundation to Pay for School Vouchers," *New York Times,* 23 April 1998.
30. Jacques Steinberg, "Voucher Program for Inner-city Children," *New York Times,* 10 June 1998, B11.
31. "Vouchers Work," *Wall Street Journal,* 28 November 1997, A10.
32. "Asides," *Wall Street Journal,* 11 December 1997.
33. James Brooke, "Minorities Flock to Cause of Vouchers for Schools," *New York Times,* 27 December 1997, 1.
34. Seymour Fliegal, "Debbie Meier and the Dawn of Central Park East," *City Journal* 4, no. 1 (Winter 1994): 68–77.
35. June Kronholz, "Wisconsin School-Voucher Plan Is Upheld," *Wall Street Journal,* 10 November 1998, A2.
36. Clint Bolick, "School Choice and the Supreme Court," *Wall Street Journal,* 15 June 1998, A29.
37. *Mueller v Allen,* 77 L. Ed. 2d 721, 728 (1983).
38. Clint Bolick, "Solving the Education Crisis: Market Alternatives and Parental Choice," in *Beyond the Status Quo,* ed. David Boaz and Edward H. Crane (Washington, DC: Cato Institute, 1985), 207–21.
39. Reggie White and Sara White, "School Choice Restores Faith in Education," *Wall Street Journal,* 11 June 1998, A22.
40. Paul E. Peterson, David Myers, Josh Haimson, and William G. Howell, "Initial Findings from the Evaluation of the New York School Choice Scholarship Program," Harvard Program on Education Policy and Governance, Kennedy School of Government, Harvard University, November 1997.
41. Coleman et al., *High School Achievement.*
42. Denis Doyle, "Reforming the Schools to Save the City," Calvert Institute for Policy Research, Baltimore, MD, 1997.
43. John E. Coons and Joseph Kul, "Schools: What's Happening to Local Control?" *Taxing and Spending* 1, no. 1 (October–November 1978): 39.
44. Marsha Levine and Denis P. Doyle, "Private Meets Public: An Examination of Contemporary Education, in *Meeting Human Needs,* ed. Jack A. Meyer (Washington, DC: American Enterprise Institute, 1982), 286–87.
45. Peterson, et al, "Evaluation of the New York School Choice Program."

46. "Trust-busting Education," *Wall Street Journal*, 13 February 1985; see also Thomas A Johnson, "Black-Run Private Schools Lure Growing Numbers in New York," *New York Times*, 5 April 1980, 1.
47. John S. Ambler, "Who Benefits from Educational Choice?: Some Evidence From Europe," *Journal of Policy Analysis and Management*, 13, no. 3 (Summer 1994): 454–476.
48. "Asides."
49. Stuart M. Butler, *Privatizing Federal Spending* (New York: Universe Books, 1985), 109; see also Bolick, "Solving the Education Crisis," 211–12.
50. "Trust-busting Education," *Wall Street Journal*; Johnson, "Black-Run Private Schools."
51. Peterson et al., "Initial Findings."
52. "Reforming K–12 Education," 7.
53. *Charter School Newsletter*, 4, no. 3 (Boston, MA: Pioneer Institute, Fall 1998), 1.
54. "What the Report Card Says," *New York Times*, 6 January 1997, A16.
55. Ibid.
56. "Choice Inspires Consumer Guides to Good Schools," *School Reform News*, 1, no. 10 (Palatine, IL: The Heartland Institute, December 1997), 11.
57. Mark Schneider, et al., "School Choice Builds Community," *Public Interest* 129 (Fall 1997).
58. Ibid.
59. Brooke, "Minorities Flock to Vouchers."
60. Arthur Levine, "Why I'm Reluctantly Backing Vouchers," *Wall Street Journal*, 15 June 1998, A28.
61. This section has benefited from discussions with Myron Lieberman.
62. George Judson, "Private Business, Public Schools: Why the Hartford Experiment Failed," *New York Times*, 11 March 1996, 1.
63. Karen W. Anderson, "Miami Teachers in Edison Project Will Be Offered Stock Options," *New York Times*, 22 October 1998, A16.
64. Peter Applebome, "For-Profit Education Venture to Expand," *New York Times*, 2 June 1997, A12; Jacques Steinberg, "Edison Project Reports Measurable Progress in Reading and Math at Its Schools," *New York Times*, 17 December 1997, B8.
65. Somini Sengupta, "Trying to Cut Special Education Rolls: City Announces Plan to Privatize and Simplify the Referral System," *New York Times*, 10 June 1998, B5.
66. *Competitive Contracting in Ohio Public Schools* (Dayton, OH: Buckeye Institute, 1996); Janet R. Beales, *Doing More With Less: Competitive Contracting for School Support Services* (Midland, MI: Mackinac Center, November 1994).
67. Michel T. Moe and R. Keith Gay, *The Emerging Investment Opportunity in Education* (San Francisco: Montgomery Securities, 1996).
68. Jim Yardley, "Why Johnny's Doing Calculus: The Booming Education Industry," *New York Times*, 2 August 1998, Section 4a, Education Life section, 28.
69. Robert W. Poole Jr., "Toward Free Public Education," *Fiscal Watchdog*, no. 33 (Los Angeles, CA: Reason Foundation, July 1979).
70. Edward B. Fiske, "Schools for Profit," *New York Times*, 26 July 1979, B1; "State Seeks Tighter Control of Vocational Education," *New York Times*, 27 July 1979, B1; "Playing Politics with Public Money" (editorial) *New York Times*, 7 November 1980.
71. Joe Loconte, *Seducing the Samaritan: How Government Contracts are Reshaping Social Services* (Boston, MA: Pioneer Institute, 1997).
72. Charles Murray, *Losing Ground: American Social Policy, 1950–1980* (New York: Basic Books, 1984).
73. Lawrence M. Mead, *Beyond Entitlement: The Social Obligations of Citizenship* (New York: Macmillan, 1986).

74. Esther Iverem, "A Church in Brooklyn Closes Its Men's Shelter," *New York Times,* 18 April 1987, 23. (Supplemented by a telephone interview with Father Joseph A. Nugent, Our Lady of Victory Roman Catholic Church.)

75. John C. Goodman and Michael D. Stroup, *Privatizing the Welfare State,* NCPA Policy Report no. 123 (Dallas: National Center for Policy Analysis, June 1986), 18.

76. Michael L. Probst, "Welfare Reform: A Paradigm Revisited," *Wall Street Journal,* 12 December 1995.

77. Peter L. Berger and Richard John Neuhaus, *To Empower People: The Role of Mediating Structures in Public Policy* (Washington, DC: American Enterprise Institute, 1977). See also Amitai Etzioni, *The Spirit of Community* (New York: Simon & Schuster, 1994).

78. Glenn C. Loury, "The Moral Quandary of the Black Community," *Public Interest,* no. 79 (Spring 1985): 9–22.

79. Kathleen Teltsch, "Teen-age Mothers Get Aid in Study," *New York Times,* 19 May 1985, 27.

80. Jacques Rigaudiat, "Deux Cent Ans d'histoire" (Two Hundred Years of History), *Cahiers Français,* March/April 1984, 10–17.

81. Marvin Olasky, *The Tragedy of American Compassion* (Washington, DC: Regnery, 1995).

82. "Charities as Receivers of Government Subsidies," *New York Times,* 5 February 1996.

83. Richard Nathan, "The Nonprofitization Movement: An Examination of the Effects of Devolution on Nonprofit Organizations," paper presented at a conference of the Program on Public Policy, University of Minnesota, 12 June 1996.

84. Steven R. Smith and Michael Lipsky, *Nonprofits for Hire* (Cambridge, MA: Harvard University Press, 1993).

85. Goodman and Stroup, *Privatizing the Welfare State,* 18.

86. Peter S. Barwick, *A Working Solution to the Welfare Crisis* (Harrisburg, PA: Commonwealth Foundation, 1996).

87. Ann E. Kaplan, ed., *Giving USA 1998: The Annual Report of Philanthropy for the Year 1997* (New York: AAFRC Trust for Philanthropy, 1998).

88. Senator Dan Coats et al., "Can Congress Revive Civil Society?" *Policy Review,* January–February 1996, 25–33.

89. Robert Pear, "More Welfare Recipients Going to Work, Study Finds," *New York Times,* 19 June 1998, A22.

90. Rudolph W. Giuliani, "Why We Will End Welfare by 2000," *New York Post,* 21 July 1998, 27.

91. Helene Cooper, "All of Europe Watches as Britain's Tony Blair Hacks Away at Welfare," *Wall Street Journal,* 25 June 1998, A18.

92. Smith and Lipsky, *Nonprofits for Hire;* Loconte, *Seducing the Samaritan.*

93. "Welfare, Inc.," *The Economist,* 25 January 1997, 55–56.

94. Tamar Lewin, "Private Firms Help Single Parents Get What's Due," *New York Times,* 21 May 1994, A1.

95. Brett Pulley, "New Jersey Considers Privatizing Its Child Welfare," *New York Times,* 2 March 1996, 21.

96. Michael Selz, "Teaching Job-Hunting Basics to Trim Welfare Rolls," *Wall Street Journal,* 14 October 1996, B1.

97. *Social Service Privatization,* GAO/HEHS-98-6 (Washington, DC: General Accounting Office, October 1997).

98. E.S. Savas, "Competition and Choice in New York City Social Services," April 1999, in manuscript.

99. Laurence J. Kotlikoff, "Privatizing Social Security the Right Way," *Jobs & Capital,* 7, no. 3/4 (Summer/Fall 1998): 21–27.

100. Martin Feldstein, "The Case for Privatization," *Foreign Affairs*, July–August 1997, 24–38.
101. Daniel L.Mitchell, "Why Government-Controlled Investment Would Undermine Retirement Security," *Heritage Backgrounder*, no. 1248 (Washington, DC: Heritage Foundation, 5 February 1999).
102. M. Wayne Marr Jr., John R. Nofsinger, and John L. Trimble, *Economically Targeted and Social Investment Management and Pension Fund Performance* (Charlottesville, VA: Research Foundation of the Institute of Chartered Financial Analysts, November 1995).
103. Michael Weinstein, "Economic Scene," *New York Times*, 3 December 1998, C4.
104. Lieberman, *Teacher Unions*.

CHAPTER ELEVEN
  1. Madsen Pirie, Adam Smith Institute, London, private communication.
  2. Irwin T. David, "Privatization in America," in *Municipal Year Book 1988* (Washington, DC: International City Management Association, 1988), 43–55.
  3. *State Government Privatization 1992* (Bethesda, MD: Apogee Research, Inc., 1992), 10.
  4. William D. Eggers and Raymond Ng, *Social and Health Service Privatization: A Survey of County and State Governments* (Los Angeles: Reason Foundation, 1993).
  5. *Status Report on Public-Private Partnerships in Municipal Water and Wastewater* (Washington, DC: U.S. Conference of Mayors, 1997).
  6. Edward K. Morlok et al., "Privatization of Public Transit," Systems Department and Decision Sciences Department, University of Pennsylvania, Report No. PA-11-0032, prepared for the Urban Mass Transportation Administration, May 1988, table 3.4.
  7. Robin A. Johnson, "Mobilizing Political Support for a Partnership Agreement," *Proceedings of the Eleventh Annual Conference of the National Council for Public-Private Partnerships*, St. Louis, MO, 15–17 October 1997, 93–97.
  8. Jerry Ellig, "The $7.7 Billion Mistake: Federal Barriers to State and Local Privatization," testimony before the Joint Economic Committee, U.S. Congress, Washington, DC, February 1996.
  9. Glenn Burkins, "Big Public-Sector Union Backs a Move to Boost Dues to Organize and Lobby," *Wall Street Journal*, 26 August 1998.
 10. Robert Kuttner, *Everything for Sale: The Virtues and Limits of Markets* (New York: Alfred A. Knopf, 1997), 98.
 11. David Sherman, "Indianapolis Advanced Wastewater Treatment Facilities: One Year Summary," report to the Indianapolis City County Council, 20 March 1995.
 12. Jonathan Friedland, "Argentina's Macri Takes on the Post Office," *Wall Street Journal*, 8 September 1997, A15.
 13. F. Jaspersen, "Aguas Argentinas," in *The Private Sector and Development: Five Case Studies* (Washington, DC: World Bank, 1997), 15–27.
 14. International Finance Corporation, *Privatization: Principles and Practice* (Washington, DC: World Bank, 1995), 44.
 15. Ibid., 43.
 16. Ibid.
 17. Jonathan Haskell and Stefan Szymanski, "Privatization and the Labour Market: Facts, Theory, and Evidence," in Matthew Bishop, John Kay, and Colin Mayer, eds., *Privatization and Economic Performance* (Oxford, England: Oxford University Press, 1994), 336–51.
 18. Private communication from Town Manager Don Marquis, October 1998.
 19. H. Edward Wesemann, *Contracting for City Services* (Pittsburgh: Innovations Press, 1981), 87–92.

20. V.V. Ramanadham, ed., *Privatisation in Developing Countries* (New York: Routledge, 1989), 41.

21. James M. Pierce, statement to Subcommittee on Employee Ethics and Utilization, House Committee on Post Office and Civil Service, *Hearings on Contracting Out of Jobs and Services*, Serial no. 95-7 (Washington, DC: Government Printing Office, 1977), 41–43.

22. Shawni Littlehale, "Massachusetts Law Stops Competitive Contracting in Its Tracks," Center for Restructuring Government, Newsletter, 1, no. 3 (Boston, MA: Pioneer Institute for Public Policy Research, August 1997).

23. Jonathan P. Hicks, "Council Votes First Override of Giuliani; Privatization Bill Vote Seen as Show of Strength," *New York Times*, 15 June 1994, B1.

24. Vivian S. Toy, "Veto of 'Prevailing Wage' Bill Is Overridden by City Council," *New York Times*, 12 September 1996, B4.

25. Paul Kengore and Grant Gulibon, " 'Poison Pills' for Privatizations: Legislative Attempts at Regulating Competitive Contracting," Allegheny Institute Report No 96-22, December 1996, Pittsburgh, PA.

26. Dudek & Company, "The Long Term Employment Implications of Privatization," report for the National Commission for Employment Policy, Washington, DC, March 1989.

27. Sunita Kikeri, John Nellis, and Mary Shirley, *Privatization: The Lessons of Experience* (Washington, DC: World Bank, 1992), 59.

28. Ibid., 61.

29. Ismail MD Salleh, "Port Klang, Malaysia: A Privatisation Case Study," in *Privatisation and Public Enterprise: The Asia-Pacific Experience*, ed. Geeta Gouri (New Delhi: Oxford & IBH Publishing Co., 1991), 371–81.

30. Marilyn J. Cohodas, "Outsourcing's Ins and Outs," *Governing*, December 1997, p. 84.

31. International Finance Corporation, *Privatization: Principles and Practice*, 43.

32. Personal conversation with Jacques Rogozinski, who was in charge of privatization for the Mexican government, August 1996.

33. William L. Megginson, Robert C. Nash, and Matthias Van Randenborgh, "The Financial and Operating Performance of Newly Privatized Firms: An International Empirical Analysis," *Journal of Finance* 49, no. 2 (June 1994) 403–52.

34. Kikeri, Nellis, and Shirley, *Privatization*, 59.

35. "Methods to Privatize Appropriate State Government Functions through the Development of Employee-Owned Companies (ESOPs)," *Report of the Secretary of Administration and Commonwealth Competition Council to the Governor and the General Assembly of Virginia*, Richmond, VA 1998.

36. Dennis A. Rondinelli, "Privatization and Economic Transformation: The Management Challenge," in *Management for Privatization: Lessons from Industry and Public Service*, ed. J. Prokopenko (Geneva: International Labour Office, 1995), 3–45.

37. Steven A. Ludsin, "To Privatize Faster, Try a U.S. Yard Sale," *New York Times*, 28 February 1996, A16.

38. Andrew Jones and Richard Seline, "Executive Overview: Federal Privatization Task Force Report," *Proceedings of the Eleventh Annual Conference of the National Council for Public-Private Partnerships*, St. Louis, MO, 15–17 October 1997, 99–109.

39. Scott Peters, "Caveat Emptor: Real Politic of Budgeting, Cultural, and Market Reforms of the Bureaucracy," paper presented at the American Political Science Association meeting, Washington, DC, 28 August 1997.

40. Sergio Aguayo, "Behind the Public Profile of Mexico's Private Sector," *Wall Street Journal*, 18 December 1987, 23.

41. "Car-Bomb Attack in Lima," *New York Times,* 30 December 1997, A3.
42. Reported to the author by Jacques Rogozinski, August 1996.
43. The director of Greece's privatization program, George N. Yannopoulos, was named the number 1 assassination target by a leftist terrorist group; I experienced his safety precautions (three armed guards and a bullet-proof limousine) at first hand, nervously, when I spent a week working with him in Athens in the summer of 1990.
44. E.S. Savas, ed., *Alternatives for Delivering Public Services: Toward Improved Performance* (Boulder, CO: Westview, 1977).
45. Stephen Goldsmith, *The Twenty-First Century City: Resurrecting Urban America* (Washington, DC: Regnery Publishing, 1997), 70.
46. Robert F. Durant, Michael R. Fitzgerald, and Larry W. Thomas, "When Government Regulates Itself: The EPA/TVA Air Pollution Control Experience," *Public Administration Review,* 43 (May–June 1983), 209–19.
47. Ron Winslow, "TVA Misled U.S. Regulators on Severity of Nuclear Plant Mishap, Staff Study Says," *Wall Street Journal,* 24 August 1984.
48. Ronald Kessler, "The Great Mail Bungle," *Washington Post,* 9 June 1974.
49. Raymond Vernon, "Introduction," in *The Promise of Privatization,* ed. R. Vernon (New York: Council on Foreign Relations, 1988), 1–22.
50. William A. Orme Jr., "El Al at a Turning Point," *New York Times,* 5 March 1999, C1.
51. Kathy Megyery and Frank Sader, "Facilitating Foreign Participation in Privatization," Foreign Investment Advisory Service Occasional Paper 8 (Washington, DC: World Bank, 1996).
52. Ismail MD Salleh, "The Privatisation of Public Enterprises: A Case Study of Malaysia," in Gouri, *Privatisation and Public Enterprise,* 595–633.
53. Roger Leeds, "Privatization through Public Offerings: Lessons from Two Jamaica Cases," in *Privatization and Control of State-Owned Enterprises,* ed. Ravi Ramamurti and Raymond Vernon (Washington, DC: World Bank, 1991), 86–125.
54. Michael P. McLindon, *Privatization & Capital Market Development* (Westport, CT: Praeger, 1996).
55. Martin Tolchin, "Congress Wary on Plan to Sell Assets," *New York Times,* 6 February 1986, B16.
56. Rondinelli, "Privatization and Economic Transformation," 33.
57. Ramanadham, *Privatisation in Developing Countries,* 41.
58. Donald F. Kettl, *Sharing Power: Public Governance and Private Markets* (Washington, DC: The Brookings Institution, 1993), 163.
59. Ibid., 200–201.
60. Ibid., 160.
61. E.S. Savas, "Privatization in Post-Socialist Countries," *Public Administration Review,* 52, no. 6 (November–December 1992), 573–81.
62. *Passing the Bucks: The Contracting Out of Public Services* (Washington, DC: American Federation of State, County, and Municipal Employees, AFL-CIO, 1983). For a strongly ideological attack on privatization, see Dexter Whitfield, *Making It Public: Evidence and Action against Privatization* (London: Pluto Press, 1983).
63. E.J. Dionne Jr., "Unions Awaiting Carey's Quid Pro Quo," *New York Times,* 4 December 1978, B6.
64. Myron Lieberman, *The Teacher Unions* (New York: Free Press, 1997).
65. Ibid.
66. Dudley Clendinen, "Problems of Boston Pension System Lead to State and Federal Inquiries," *New York Times,* 21 May 1982, A14.
67. New York City Comptroller Harrison J. Goldin, addressing the Privatization Conference, Baruch College, New York, 27 October 1986.

68. Susan Rose-Ackerman, "The Political Economy of Corruption—Causes and Consequences," *Public Policy for the Private Sector,* Quarterly, no. 6 (March 1996), 45–48.

69. Susan Rose-Ackerman, "Redesigning the State to Fight Corruption—Transparency, Competition, and Privatization," *Public Policy for the Private Sector Quarterly,* no. 6 (March 1996): 49–52.

70. Donald F. Kettl, *Sharing Power: Public Governance and Private Markets* (Washington, DC: The Brookings Institute, 1993), 179–211.

71. Ibid.

72. Dennis A. Rondinelli, "Privatization and Economic Transformation: The Management Challenge," in ed. J. Prokopenko, *Management for Privatization: Lessons from Industry and Public Service* (Geneva: International Labour Office, 1995), 3–45.

73. Bill Eggers, "The Nuts and Bolts: Overcoming the Obstacles to Privatization," speech delivered to the Commonwealth Foundation, Harrisburg, Pennsylvania, April, 1997.

74. Rondinelli, "Privatization and Economic Transformation," 3–45.

75. Mark Schlesinger, Robert A. Dorwart, and Richard T. Pulice, "Competitive Bidding and States' Purchase of Services," *Journal of Policy Analysis and Management,* 5, no. 2 (Winter 1986): 245–63.

76. Kuttner, *Everything for Sale,* 358.

CHAPTER TWELVE

1. Dennis A Rondinelli, "Privatization, Governance, and Public Management: The Challenges Ahead," *Business and the Contemporary World,* 10, no. 2 (1998): 149–70.

2. Dennis Daley, "The Politics and Administration of Privatization," *Policy Studies Journal,* 24, no. 4, (1996): 629–31.

3. Joyce Wadler, "Belying the Legend of the Crusty Old Salt," *New York Times,* 1 July 1998.

4. Orri Vigfusson, "How Markets Save Salmon," *PERC Reports* (Bozeman, MT: Political Economy Research Center, September 1998).

5. James Brooke, "Land Trusts Multiplying, Study Shows," *New York Times,* 1 October 1998, A20.

6. John H. Cushman Jr., "Washington Skirmishes over Treaty on Warming," *New York Times,* 11 November 1998, p. A11.

7. Wade Hudson, "New Hampshire and Georgia Lease State-Owned Resorts," *Privatization Watch,* October 1998.

8. Lisa Snell, "Indianapolis Parks Bloom under Church Management," *Privatization Watch,* October 1998.

9. Tony Walker, "Private Sector Revitalizes New York's Mean Streets," *Financial Times,* 2 July 1998, 8.

10. Charles V. Bagley, "A Deal Is Struck for Coliseum Site," *New York Times,* 28 July 1998, A1.

11. Douglas Feiden, "City's Land Sale: Prime Real Estate Is Up for Grabs," *Daily News,* 26 October 1998, 3.

12. "U.S. to Auction Land Near Las Vegas and Give State the Money," *New York Times,* 25 October 1998, 33.

13. Robert Hanley and Steve Strunsky, "Jersey City Weighs Private Management of Libraries," *New York Times,* 29 June 1998, B1.

14. W. Stanley Jordan, "The Turnkey Approach," *Public Works,* September 1997, p. 93–94.

15. "Central Parking Corporation Awarded Contract to Manage On-Street Parking in Richmond; Contract Highlights Continued Growth in Privatization of Municipal Parking Programs," *AOL News,* 13 July 1998.

16. "24 x 7 Automated Parking Ticket Payment Program Introduced by Nextlink Interactive in NYC," *AOL News,* 1 October 1998.
17. Michael Janofsky, "Midshipmen To Get Milk through Middleman," *New York Times,* 19 July 1998, A16.
18. Judith Miller, "Company Led by Top Admiral Buys Michigan Vaccine Lab," *New York Times,* 8 July 1998, A19.
19. Amy Harmon, "U.S. Expected to Support Shift in Administration of the Internet," *New York Times,* 20 October 1998, D1; Jeri Clausing, "Clinton's Envoy to the Internet Will Resign by Year's End," *New York Times,* 9 November 1998, C2.
20. "The Wackenhut Corporation Wins Contract for Embassy Security," <http:www.prnewswire.com> (15 October 1998).
21. Greg Schneider, "Lockheed Gets NASA Space Pact," *Baltimore Sun,* 26 September 1998, 12C.
22. "Conny Kullman Outlines Vision of INTELSAT Privatization in the Competitive Global Market," *AOL News,* 30 September 1998.
23. Ron Lobel and Jay Brown, "Privatization Promises to Build Military Family Houses Better, Faster, Cheaper," *Council Insights Newsletter* (Washington, DC: National Council for Public-Private Partnerships, May 1998); Ron Lobel and Kim Marchand, "Military Housing Privatization—The Nuts and Bolts," *Council Insights Newsletter* (Washington, DC: National Council for Public-Private Partnerships, June 1998).
24. "Savings Low in Pentagon Homes Plan," *Associated Press,* AP-NY-07-21-98, 1653 EDT.
25. Douglas Borgeson, "The Armament Retooling and Manufacturing Support Team," paper presented at the Annual Conference of the National Council for Public-Private Partnerships, Atlanta, GA, 14–16 October 1998.
26. "Arizona Firm Wins Contract to Sell $8 Billion in Military Surplus," *AOL News,* 23 September 1998.
27. "St. Lawrence Seaway Goes Private," *Associated Press,* AP-NY-09-30-98, 1401 EDT.
28. Erik Eckholm, "A Novelty for China: Owning a Home," *New York Times,* 19 June 1998.
29. Nicholas Bray, "Britain's Labor, Miming Tories, Unveils 3-Year Privatizing Plan," *Wall Street Journal,* 12 June 1998, A9.
30. "Queen's Airline Might Go Private," Associated Press, AP-NY-11-15-98, 1143EST.
31. Linda Kaboolian, "The New Public Management: Challenging the Boundaries of the Management vs Administration Debate," *Public Administration Review 58,* no. 3, May–June 1998, 189–93.
32. The foregoing borrows heavily from Rondinelli.
33. *Government Corporations,* GAO/GGD-96-14 (Washington, DC: General Accounting Office, December 1995), 1.
34. "Postal Workers Rally against Priority Mail Giveaway," *AOL News,* 26 May 1998.
35. Robert W. Poole, Jr., "Good News for Hotlanes and Tollways," *Privatization Watch,* September 1998.
36. Robert W. Poole, Jr., "Sharing Rights of Way a Win-Win Deal for States, Companies," *Privatization Watch,* September 1998.
37. John Urquhart, "Canada's House of Commons to Approve Bill on Privatizing Air-Traffic Control," *Wall Street Journal,* 3 June 1996, C13.
38. Bray, "Britain's Labor."
39. Robert W. Poole, Jr., "Building a Safer and More Effective Air Traffic Control System," *Policy Insight,* no. 126 (Los Angeles: Reason Foundation, February 1991); Al Gore, *Creating a Government That Works Better and Costs Less,* Report of the National Performance Review (Washington, DC: Government Printing Office, 7 September 1993): 149; E.S. Savas, "Is Air Traffic Out of Control?" *New York Newsday,* 9 June 1995, A36.

40. Douglas Franz, "F.A.A. Reorganizes with Eye toward Privatizing Air Control," *New York Times,* 1 December 1994, A16; Jeff Cole and Andy Pasztor, "U.S. Air System Seen as Threat to the Economy; Partial Privatization of FAA, Greater Self Regulation Is Urged in Broad Study," *Wall Street Journal,* 11 December 1997, A4.

41. Keon S. Chi, "Prison Privatization," *State Government News,* March 1998, 38.

42. Charles W. Thomas, "Testimony Regarding Correctional Privatization," given before the Little Hoover Commission, State of California, Sacramento, CA, 21 August 1997.

43. Christopher Swope, "The Inmate Bazaar," *Governing,* October 1998, 18–22.

44. J. Michael Quinlan, "Prison Privatization Moves to the Next Level," *Council Insights Newsletter* (Washington, DC: National Council for Public-Private Partnerships, July 1998).

45. "Social Insurance: Privatising Peace of Mind," *The Economist,* 24 October 1998, special section, 22.

46. Ibid., 3.

47. Ibid., 4.

48. Peter Berger and Richard John Neuhaus, "Peter Berger and Richard John Neuhaus Respond," in *To Empower People: From State to Civil Society, 2nd ed.,* ed. Michael Novak (Washington, DC: AEI Press, 1996), 150.

49. P. Nelson Reid, "Reforming the Social Services Monopoly," *Social Work,* November 1972, 44–54; motivated by E.S. Savas, "Municipal Monopoly," *Harper's,* December 1971, 55–60; Robert Pruger and Leonard Miller, "Competition and Public Social Services," *Public Welfare,* Fall 1973, 16–25.

50. Alexis de Toqueville, *Travels in America* (New York: Washington Square Press, 1964; first published in France in 1835), 181.

51. The term *mediating structures* was used by Peter Berger and Richard John Neuhaus, in *To Empower People: From State to Civil Society;* see also the second edition, ed. Michael Novak, 1996. The concept was introduced earlier by, for example, Richard C. Cornuelle, *Reclaiming the American Dream: The Role of Private Individuals and Voluntary Associations* (New York: Random House, 1965).

52. "Communities That Strengthen Families," *Governing,* October 1997, special section by the National Civic League, 3.

53. Stephen Goldsmith, "Rebuilding Civil Society," in *The Twenty-First Century City: Resurrecting Urban America* (Washington, DC: Regnery Publishing, 1997), 171–92; April Lassiter, *Congress and Civil Society: How Legislators Can Champion Civic Renewal in Their Districts* (Washington, DC: Heritage Foundation, 1998).

54. David Blankenhorn, *Fatherless America: Confronting Our Most Urgent Social Problem* (New York: HarperCollins, 1996).

55. Quoted in Goldsmith, *Twenty-First Century City,* 183.

56. Samuel G. Freedman, *Upon This Rock: The Miracles of a Black Church* (New York: HarperCollins, 1994); George F. Will, "A Man Who Makes His Community Grow," *New York Post,* 15 November 1998, 63; Collin Levy, "Civil Society's Paramedics," *Wall Street Journal,* 20 November 1998, W17.

57. *New Millennium Project, Part 1: American Youth Attitudes on Politics, Citizenship, Government and Voting* (Lexington, KY: National Association of Secretaries of State, 1999), 16–17, 28–31.

58. Everett Carll Ladd, "Why Clinton's Scandals Helped His Party," *Wall Street Journal,* 5 November 1998, A22.

Index